THE
PUERTO RICAN
EXPERIENCE

THE
PUERTO RICAN
EXPERIENCE

See last pages of this volume
for a complete list of titles

THE
PUERTO RICANS

Migration
and
General Bibliography

ARNO PRESS

A New York Times Company

New York — 1975

Reprint Edition 1975 by Arno Press Inc.

"Studies of Puerto Rican Children in
American Schools", reprinted from
The Journal of Human Relations,
Copyright © 1968 by Central State
University was reprinted by permission
of The Journal of Human Relations,
Central State University.

The Impact of Puerto Rican Migration on
Governmental Services in New York City,
edited by Martin B. Dworkis, Copyright © 1957
by New York University Press, Inc. was reprinted
by permission of New York University Press.

A List of Books, With References to Periodicals
on Porto Rico was reprinted from a copy in
The State Historical Society of Wisconsin Library.

The Puerto Rican Experience
ISBN for complete set: 0-405-06210-9
See last pages of this volume for titles.

Manufactured in the United States of America

————◆————

Library of Congress Cataloging in Publication Data

Main entry under title:

The Puerto Ricans : migration and general bibliography.

    (The Puerto Rican experience)
    Reprint of A selected bibliography on Puerto Rico and
the Puerto Ricans, by C. Senior and J. de Roman, first
published 1951; of Bibliography on Puerto Ricans in the
United States, by C. Senior, first published 1959; of
The people of Puerto Rico, a bibliography, by F. Cordasco, first published 1968; of Puerto Rican migrants on
the mainland of the United States, first published 1968;
of Studies of Puerto Rican children in American schools,
a preliminary bibliography, by F. M. Cordasco and
L. Covello, first published 1968; of Doctoral research
on Puerto Rico and Puerto Ricans, by J. J. Dossick, first
published 1967; of Puerto Rican migration, by Puerto
Rican Research and Resources Center, inc., first published 1971; of The impact of Puerto Rican migration on
governmental services in New York City, by the Graduate
School of Public Administration and Social Service, New
York University, M. B. Dworkis, ed., first published
1957; and of A list of books, with references to
periodicals, on Porto Rico, by A. P. C. Griffin, first
published 1901.
    1. Puerto Rico--Bibliography. 2. Puerto Ricans in
the United States--Bibliography. I. Series.
[Z1551.P86]   016.9173'06'687295   74-14245
ISBN 0-405-06232-X

CONTENTS

A Selected Bibliography **on**

puerto rico

and the

puerto ricans

compiled **and annotated by**

CLARENCE SENIOR and JOSEFINA DE ROMAN

TABLE OF CONTENTS

THE PUERTO RICAN MIGRANT

A Program of Education for Puerto Ricans in New York City. A report prepared by a committee of the Association of Assistant Superintendents. New York, Board of Education, 1947. 107 pp. (mimeographed).

    1. Backgrounds; 2. migration to the mainland; 3. problems of assimilation; 4. the education of the Puerto Rican pupil; 5. recommendations.

de Román, Josefina. New York's Latin Quarter. The Inter-American, Washington, D.C. January, 1946. pp 10-12, 36-37. Illus.

    Puerto Ricans in Harlem.

Grieser, Norman. Airborne from San Juan. New Republic. November 3, 1947. pp. 21-24.

    About a group of migrants - their background and how they fared after coming to New York.

Know Your Fellow American Citizen From Puerto Rico. Washington, Office of Puerto Rico, 1948. 64 pp. illus.

    Simple text and many pictures; an introduction to the migrant's background and his role on the continent.

Mayor's Committee on Puerto Rican Affairs. Puerto Rican Pupils in New York City Schools. New York, 1951. (mimeographed).

    A survey of elementary and junior high schools by the Subcommittee on Education, Recreation and Parks of the Mayor's Advisory Committee on Puerto Rican Affairs in New York City.

Mills, C. Wright; Senior, Clarence; and Goldsen, Rose Kohn. The Puerto Rican Journey. New York, Harper's, 1950. 236 pp.

    Prepared by three members of Columbia University's Bureau of Applied Social Research. Well documented study of 5,000 Puerto Ricans living in Harlem and the Morrisania section of the Bronx.

Puerto Rican Children. Some Aspects of Their Needs and Related Services. elfare
    Council, New York, 1949. 7 pp.

    Report of a committee to study the needs of Puerto Rican children in New
    York City.

Puerto Ricans Filling Manpower Gap. Washington, D. C. Office of the Government of
    Puerto Rico, 1951.

    Reprints of newspaper articles on Puerto Rican workers in mainland jobs.

Puerto Ricans in New York City. The report of the Committee on Puerto Ricans in
    New York City of the Welfare Council. New York, elfare Council, 1948. 60 pp.

    1. Size and location of the Puerto Rican population; 2. Problems of neighborhood
    groups of Puerto Rican citizens; 3. Education, employment and health; 4. Use of
    Spanish-speaking personnel in social agencies; 5. Migration and resettlement;
    6. Recommendations.

Robison, Sophia. Can Delinquency be Measured? New York, Columbia University Press,
    1936. pp. 236-49.

    Treatment of an earlier group than that covered by Schepses.

Ruiz, Paquita. Vocational Needs of Puerto Rican Migrants in New York City. Rio
    Piedras, Social Science Research Center, University of Puerto Rico, 1947.
    84 pp. (mimeographed)

Schepses, Edwin. Puerto Rican Delinquent Boys in New York City. Social Service
    Review. March, 1949. pp. 51-56.

Selected References for Teachers of Non-English Speaking Children. New York,
    Board of Education, Division of Instructional Research, Bureau of Reference,
    Research and Statistics. n.d., 5 pp.

Senior, Clarence. The Puerto Rican Migrant in St. Croix. Rio Piedras, Social
    Science Research Center, University of Puerto Rico, 1947.

Senior, Clarence. The Puerto Ricans of New York City. Washington,
Office of Puerto Rico, 1948. 102 pp. (mimeographed).

    1. The island of Puerto Rico; 2. metropolis, panorama of contrasts;
    3. the city of migration; 4. the new world of the Puerto Rican;
    5. App., Welfare Facilities in Puerto Rico, by Carmen Isales.

Speech Problems of Puerto Rican Children. A report of the Committee on Individualization of Speech Improvement. Board of Education of the City
of New York, Department of Speech Improvement. n.d., 15 pp. (mimeographed)

Status of Puerto Ricans in New York Improving. Better Times, December 1, 1950.
(Reprint available from Department of Labor of Puerto Rico, 21 W. 60 St.,
New York 23, N. Y.)

Tentative Report of the Committee on Classification. New York, Bilingual
Committee of the Junior High School Division. Bulletin No. 1, June,
1949. 12 pp.

Contains questionnaires for newly-arrived pupils and a bibliography for
teachers.

The Lorain and Gary Experience with Puerto Rican Workers. Reprint of 6
articles from the Gary Post Tribune. Washington, D. C., Office of
Puerto Rico, 1948.

The Department of Labor of Puerto Rico in 1947 placed several hundred
workers in steel mills in Lorain, Ohio and Gary, Indiana. These articles
report on the experience of the management and the men.

Werner, M. R. The Puerto Ricans: Slum to Slum. The Reporter, New York,
September 12 and September 26, 1950.

II.

BACKGROUND--HISTORICAL AND DESCRIPTIVE

Abbad Lassierra, Fray Iñigo. Carácter y diferentes castas de los habitantes de
la Isla de San Juan de Puerto Rico. (En: Historia Geográfica, Civil y
Natural de San Juan Bautista de Puerto Rico. Anotada por José Julián
Acosta. Imprenta Acosta, San Juan, Puerto Rico, 1866.)

A history by a Spanish churchman of the period. One of the "standard"
historical references.

Blanshard, Paul. Puerto Rico. (In: Democracy and Empire in the Caribbean. New
York, MacMillan, 1947. pp. 209-228.)

Brief general political and economic examination.

Diffie, Bailey W. and Justine W. Diffie. Puerto Rico: a Broken Pledge. New York,
Vanguard Press, 1931.

Documents on the Constitutional History of Puerto Rico. Office of Puerto Rico,
1026 Seventeenth St., N.W., Washington, D. C.

Contains Constitution of 1897; Treaty of Paris; Military Government (1898-
1900); First Organic Act of Puerto Rico (1900); Organic Act of 1917;
Elective Governor Act (1947); Cases on Political Status of United States
Territories.

Enamorado Cuesta, José. Porto Rico, Past and Present. Eureka Printing Co.,
New York, 1929. 170 pp.

The island after thirty years of American rule.

Fernández García, E., ed. The Book of Porto Rico. San Juan, El Libro Azul, 1923.
1188 pp.

An immense illustrated descriptive work, with contributions by many writers
and text in Spanish and English.

Garver, Earl S. and Fincher, E. B. Puerto Rico, Unsolved Problem. Elgin, Ill.
    The Elgin Press, 1945. 110 pp. illus.

    One of the best introductions to the island.

General Information on Puerto Rico.   ashington, D. C. Office of Puerto Rico, 1949.
    4 pp.

    Highly condensed basic information.

Haas, William H. Pre-Spanish Puerto Rico. Proceedings. Second General Assembly,
    Pan American Institute of Geography and History. pp. 142-50.

Hill, Robert. The People of Porto Rico. (In: Cuba and Porto Rico. Century,
    New York, 1898. Chap. XVIII. 429 pp.)

Hill, Robert T. Race Problems in the West Indies. (In: Cuba and Porto Rico.
    Century, NewYork, 1898. 429 pp. Chap. XXXVII)

Introduction to Puerto Rico. United StatesArmy Air Forces. Borinquen Field,
    Puerto Rico, 1945. Unpaged.

    Mostly photographs.

Jones, Joseph M. Let's Begin ith Puerto Rico. Fortune, May, 1944.

    An analysis of current political and economic conditions.

Miller, Paul G. Historia de Puerto Rico. Rand MacNally, New York, 1947.

    A history, also published in English. Used as textbook in the island's schools.

Norte, New York, October, 1949. 9(9), 1-74. Illus. maps.

    The entire number is devoted to Puerto Rico.

Picó, Rafael. The Geographic Regions of Puerto Rico. Rio Piedras, University of Puerto Rico Press, 1950. 256 pp.

By the outstanding geographer who is also chairman of the Puerto Rico Planning Board.

Picó, Rafael, and William H. Haas. Puerto Rico. (In: Haas, William H., ed. The American Empire; a study of the outlying territories of the United States. Chicago, Ill. The University of Chicago Press, 1940. pp. 25-91)

Petrullo, Vincenzo. Puerto Rican Paradox. Philadelphia, University of Pennsylvania Press, 1947. 181 pp.

An anthropologist's "once-over". An over-all picture which is the most recent general book on the island.

Puerto Rico. A guide to the island of Boriquén, compiled and written by the Puerto Rico Reconstruction Administration in cooperation with the Writers' Program of the Works Progress Administration. Sponsored by the Puerto Rico Department of Education. American guide series. New York, The University Society, Inc., 1940. 409 pp. illus. Maps, plates.

Probably the best general introduction to the island for the general reader.

Puerto Rico: a study in courage. The International Review. International Telephone and Telegraph Co., June, 1951. pp. 1-13. ill.

Popular review of current progress.

Reck, Daisy. Puerto Rico and the Virgin Islands. New York, Farrar and Rinehart, 1939.

Richardson, Lewis C. and Rotkin, Charles. Puerto Rico, Caribbean Crossroads. Produced under the sponsorship of the University of Puerto Rico. New York, U. S. Camera Publishing Corp., 1947. 144 pp. illus.

A picture book with text.

Tugwell, Rexford G. The Stricken Land. The story of Puerto Rico. New York, Doubleday and Company, 1947. 704 pp. illus.

Reminiscences of the last non-Puerto Rican governor, shedding important light on recent events, particularly on economic and political relations between the island and the mainland.

White, Trumball. Puerto Rico and its People. New York, Frederick A. Stokes, 1938. 383 pp. illus. maps.

III.

ECONOMIC, SOCIAL AND HEALTH CONDITIONS

Annual Book on Statistics of Puerto Rico. Fiscal Year 1948-1949. Department of Agriculture and Commerce. San Juan, Puerto Rico, 1950. 335 pp. (mimeographed).

The Puerto Rican equivalent of the Statistical Abstract of the United States.

Bartlett, Frederic P. The Population Problem in Puerto Rico. Santurce, Puerto Rico, Puerto Rico Planning, Urbanizing and Zoning Board, 1944.

Bienestar Publico, Revista editada por la División de Bienestar Publico del Departamento de Salud. San Juan.

A monthly of interest to social workers who read Spanish (occasional English articles).

Bonsal, Stephen. The Golden Horseshoe.Extracts from the letters of Lieut. Lawrence Gill. A.D. C. to the Military governor of Puerto Rico. London and New York, MacMillan Company, 1900. 316 pp.

Blanco, Tomás. El Prejuicio Racial en Puerto Rico. San Juan, Puerto Rico, Editorial, Biblioteca de Autores Puertorriqueños, 1942. pp. 82.

Durch, Guy I. U.S.S.R. and Puerto Rico Increasing Fastest. Population Reference Bureau, Population 2(4), 24-26, April, 1946.

Carrol, H. K. Report on the Island ofPorto Rico. U.S. Government Printing Office, Washington, D. C., 1899.

A report by a special commissioner sent by President McKinley to investigate conditions on the island. Extremely valuable for comparing conditions at the time of the American occupation with those of today.

Clark, Elmer T.and Spencer, H. G. Latin America, U.S.A. Methodist Church, New York City, 1942.

Clark, Victor. Porto Rico and Its Problems. Washington, The Brookings Institution, 1930. 707 pp.

A thorough survey by a team of experts. Much of the data is now superseded by that in the Perloff report.

Cohen, Felix S. The Myth of Puerto Rican Overpopulation. News Letter, Institute of Ethnic Affairs, 810 - 18th Street, N. ., Washington 6, D. C., October, 1947. pp. 1-3.

Condensation of an article in Journal of Social Issues, Fall, 1947, in which migration and birth control are attacked as solutions for insular population problems. Cohen's position is attacked by Clarence Senior, "Puerto Rico Is Overpopulated", News Letter, Institute of Ethnic Affairs, March, 1948., pp. 1-3, which carries a rejoinder by Cohen, "Puerto Rico's Problem-- Colonialism", pp. 3-4.

Confay, Katherine R., ed., Socio-Economic Conditions in Puerto Rico Affecting Family Life. San Juan, Puerto Rico, May, 1945. 80 pp.

Deals with: food and nutrition, housing, clothing, child development, health and general social problems.

Cordero Dávila, César. Puerto Rico Housing Authority. Caribbean Commission, Monthly Information Bulletin, November, 1947. pp. 17-18.

Summary of the island's public housing program.

Crawford, Fred L. Operation Bootstrap. A report on the activities of the Government of Puerto Rico in its effort to provide fuller employment for members of its manpower task force. Washington, D. C., House Committee on Interior and Insular Affairs, 1951, 15 pp.

Crawford, Fred L. Report to the Public Lands Committee on Puerto Rico and the Virgin Islands. Washington, Committee on Public Lands, April, 1950. 40 pp.

A congressman's view of the situation during a visit in March, 1950 in connection with pending legislation. Contains Governor Muñoz' 1950 message to the Legislature. pp. 24-27.

Creamer, Daniel and Henrietta L. Gross Product of Puerto Rico, 1944-1946.
    Rio Piedras, University of Puerto Rico, 1949. 14 pp.

Creamer, Daniel. The Net Income of the Puerto Rican Economy, 1940-1944.
    Rio Piedras, University of Puerto Rico, 1947. 96 pp.

Davis, Kingsley. Population and Progress in Puerto Rico. Foreign Affairs,
    New York, July, 1951.

    A discussion on population and probable future developments. Includes
    a general discussion of industrialization and economic changes since 1938.

Davis, Kingsley. Puerto Rico's Population Problem: Research and Policy.
    Milbank Memorial Fund Quarterly, July, 1948. pp. 300-08.

    Outlines alternatives faced by the island and some of the research projects
    undertaken to lay the basis for policy formulation.

Davis, J. Merle. The Church in Puerto Rico's Dilemma. A study of the Economic
    and Social Basis of the Evangelical Church in Puerto Rico. Department of
    Social and Economic Research and Counsel, International Missionary Council,
    New York, 1942. 80 pp.

    Discusses: Problem Child of the Caribbean, The Evangelical Church in
    Puerto Rico; Some self-Supporting Churches; The Puerto Rican Pastor Looks
    at His Church; Constructive Measures; Obstacles; Looking to the Future.

De Alvarado, Carmen R. and Tietze, Christopher. Birth Control in Puerto Rico.
    Human Fertility. March, 1947. 12(1), 15-17, pp. 24-25.

    History of the birth control movement in Puerto Rico.

Descartes, Sol L. Puerto Rico. Basic statistics on Puerto Rico. Washington,
    D.C., Office of Puerto Rico, 1946. 103 pp.

Descartes, Sol L. Financing Economic Development in Puerto Rico, 1941-1949.
    Department of Finance, San Juan, June, 1950. 39 pp. - tables.

Dinwiddie, W. Puerto Rico; its conditions and possibilities. Harper Brothers,
    New York, 1899. (Life among the Peasants, Chap. XIV.)

DiVenuti, Biagio. Money and Banking in Puerto Rico   Rio Piedras, University of Puerto Rico Press. 1950. 307 pp.

Structure and functions of the banking system.

Economic Development of Puerto Rico, 1940-50 and 1951-60. Santurce, Puerto Rico Planning Board. 1951. 179 pp.

A review of the past decade and objectives for the future. Prepared under the direction of Harvey Perloff.

Fox, Arthur J., Jr. Puerto Rico. School for Point Four Engineers. Engineering News-Record, February 15, 1951. pp. 32-35, illus.

Gayer, Arthur D. The Sugar Economy of Puerto Rico. New York, Columbia University Press, 1938. 326 pp. maps; tables.

Includes chapters on population and social function, agriculture in general, external trade and financial relations, distribution of income from sugar, in addition to a thorough study of sugar's economic role on the island.

Half a Century of Progress. The Economic Review, The Chamber of Commerce of Puerto Rico, June 1945. Vol. 6 No. 1. pp. 78.

The indices of Puerto Rico's progress, socially, economically and commercially since the end of the 19th century.

Hanson, Alice C. and Pérez, Manuel A. Incomes and Expenditures of Wage Earners in Puerto Rico. Puerto Rico Department of Labor in Cooperation with the U. S. Bureau of Labor Statistics. Bulletin No. 1, May 1, 1947. 152 pp.

This report presents the major findings of an island-wide survey of incomes and expenditures of families of wage earners in Puerto Rico. Since the field work was carried on in 1941 and the early part of 1942, the survey describes prewar conditions and provides "a basis for judging the effect of wartime and postwar price and employment changes upon Puerto Rican workers' living standards". A summary of the findings is followed by 38 tables presenting the detailed data. Pp. 70-152 contain an "Appendix on procedures," which includes a discussion of the sample covered, description of the schedules and forms used, and detailed instructions to the field agents.

Hanson, Alice. Incomes and Expenditures of Wage Earners in Puerto Rico, 1940-1941. Monthly Labor Review, February, 1943. p. 9

Harris, Marshall. Tenure Reform in Puerto Rico. Land Policy Review, 1946.
Vol. IX No. 1. pp. 22-26

Those interested in satisfactory land tenure and who realize its connection
with the general well-being of citizens will want to know of the progress
of land reform in Puerto Rico, for it has long been recognized that land
problems were one of the causes of the island's poverty.

Janer, José L. Population Growth in Puerto Rico and Its Relation to Time Changes
in Vital Statistics. Human Biology. December, 1945. Vol. 17 No 4.
pp. 267-313.

Johnson, Earl S. A Sociologist Looks at Puerto Rico. Journal of Legal and
Political Sociology, New York, 1945. pp. 41-50.

King, Marguerite N. Cultural Aspects of Birth Control in Puerto Rico. Human
Biology, February, 1948. pp. 21-35.

Outstanding contribution to an understanding of the factors involved.

Lindsay, Samuel McCune. Porto Rico Revisited. Contrasts in twenty five years.
Review of Reviews, New York, May, 1926. Volume 73:511.

Martocci, Frank T. Puerto Rico. Planning,1944. Chicago, American Society of
Planning Officials, 1944. pp. 160-164.

Describes housing conditions at the time and discusses the "land and utility"
projects and zoning regulations.

Mejías, Félix. Condiciones de Vida de las Clases Jornaleras de Puerto Rico.
Rio Piedras, Universidad de Puerto Rico, 1946. 215 pp.

1. Fondo histórico; 2. Los Hechos (jornada, jornales, consumo de alimentos,
la vivienda, la salud, el abrigo, el patrimonio, educación, diversiones);
3. Mirando al porvenir. Bibliografía.

Meléndez Muñoz, M. Estado Social del Campesino Puertorriqueño. Imprenta Cantero,
Fernández y Compañía, San Juan, Puerto Rico, 1916. 124 pp.

Morales Otero, Pablo, et al. Health and Socio-Economic Studies in Puerto Rico. Health and Socio-Economic Conditions in the Tobacco, Coffee and Fruit Regions. Puerto Rico Journal of Public Health and Tropical Medicine, March, 1939. pp. 201-289.

The report on this field survey of 246 rural barrios in 47 municipalities covers health (population, housing, nutrition, and general health conditions), social conditions (families, marital status, education, religion, use of shoes, etc.), and economic conditions (gainful workers, earnings, property and debts). For the first report in these series, see: Ibid. Health and socio-economic studies in Puerto Rico. I. Health and socio-economic conditions on a sugar cane plantation. Ibid. 12(4):405-490. June, 1937.

Morales Otero, Pablo. Nuestros Problemas. San Juan, Biblioteca de Autores Puertorriqueños. 2nd ed., 1945. 220 pp.

16 essays on a wide variety of social and economic topics, including health, food, housing, religion, race relations and "proposed solutions".

Morales Otero, Pablo. Puerto Rico's Nutritional Problem. Boletín de la Oficina Sanitaria Panamericana, Año (Vol.) 25, No. 3, March, 1946. pp. 229-240.

A study by the then Director of the Puerto Rico School of Tropical Medicine.

Muñoz Marín, Luis. Caribbean Dilemma. The Inter-American, June, 1946, pp. 12-15.

Puerto Rico's Popular Party leader and present governor presents his program for the solution of the island's problems of over-population and economic insufficiency.

Pedreira, Antonio S. Insularismo. Madrid, Tipografía Artística, 1934. 237 pp.

Incisive comments on insular life; valuable for Spanish readers.

New York Herald Tribune. Special Puerto Rico section. Dec. 10, 1948; Dec. 5, 1949.

New York Times. Business and Financial Review. Jan. 3, 1949; Jan. 3, 1950.

Pepper, C. M. Spanish Population of Porto Rico and Cuba. Annals of the American Academy of Political Science. Philadelphia, 1901. Vol. 18:163.

Pérez, Manuel A. Living Conditions Among Farmers in Puerto Rico. Research Bulletins on Agriculture and Livestock, Insular Department of Agriculture and Commerce, San Juan, 1942, Bulletin No. 2. 98 pp. - tables, graphs.

The sixth in a series of studies of socio-economic conditions among workers in Puerto Rico begun in 1936. The present study covers 3,069 rural families of small farmers operating tracts of land ranging from 5 to 34 acres. The survey included almost two-thirds of the rural barrios of the island located in 60 of the 77 municipalities. The following are discussed: farms, land utilization, tenure, workers employed, wages, income, mortgages, composition of the family, education, marital conditions, housing, food and nutrition, religion.

Perloff, Harvey S. Puerto Rico's Economic Future. A study in planned development. Chicago, University of Chicago Press, 1950. 435 pp. illus.

1. Historical background; 2. Characteristics and trends of the economy; 3. Population; 4. Principles and programs of planned economic development. Exceptionally important.

Perloff, Harvey S. El Futuro Económico de Puerto Rico. Condensación y revisión de la obra original, "Puerto Rico's Economic Future" del mismo autor por Daisy D. Reck. Traducción, Antonio Colorado. Universidad de Puerto Rico, Río Piedras, 1951.

A condensation and translation of Puerto Rico's Economic Future.

Picó, Rafael. The Agricultural Problems of Puerto Rico. U.S. Puerto Rico Reconstruction Administration, San Juan, 1936. 7 pp. (mimeographed)

Picó, Rafael. Studies in the Economic Geography of Puerto Rico. Río Piedras, Puerto Rico, The University, 1937. 84 p. illus. (maps) tables, diagrs. The University of Puerto Rico, Bulletin. Series VIII No. 1. Sept. 1937.

Picó, Rafael. A Year of Planning in Puerto Rico. Planning, 1944. Chicago, American Society of Planning Officials, 1944. pp. 22-30.

By the President of the Puerto Rico Planning Board.

Picó, Rafael. Puerto Rico Believes in Point IV. United Nations World. New York, February, 1951. pp. 60-61.

Platt, O. H. Spanish Population of Puerto Rico. Our relation to the people of Puerto Rico. Annals of the American Academy of Political Science. New York. (Special annual meeting number) 1901, pt. 4.

Puerto Rico. Health and Slums. Department of Health. San Juan, 1946. 8 pp. bilingual, Spanish title: La Salud y los Arrabales.

Puerto Rico. Information transmitted by the United States to the Secretary-General of the United Nations pursuant to Article 73(e) of the Charter. Washington, Department of the Interior, 1948. 110-xxvi.

1. social conditions; 2. educational conditions; 3. economic conditions; 4. pictorial supplement; 5. statistical appendices.

Puerto Rico's Sugar Problems. Bulletin of the Office of Puerto Rico, Washington, D. C., February, 1950. pp. 1-2.

The 1950 edition of the annual sugar crisis explained.

Reuter, E. B. Culture Contacts. American Journal of Sociology, September, 1946. pp. 91-101

Rigby, William Cattron. The Shipping Situation in Puerto Rico. Washington, D. C., 1940. 28 pp.

Facts about Puerto Rico's water transportation facilities; memorandum submitted to the Inter-American maritime conference, by Col. William C. Rigby and Enrique Ortega.

Rippy, J. Fred. The Caribbean Danger Zone. New York, 1940.

Discusses United States policy.

Rivera Santos, Luis. Puerto Rico Has a New Approach to Low Cost Rural Housing Problems. Journal of Housing, May, 1951. pp. 167-169.

Roberts, Lydia J. and Stefani, Rosa L. Patterns of Living in Puerto Rican Families.
Rio Piedras, University of Puerto Rico, 1949. 411 pp.

A survey of a sample of households on the island; primarily of interest to
domestic science specialists, but there is raw material for social scientists.

Rogler, Charles Cordier. Comerio, A Study of a Puerto Rican Town. Lawrence, Kansas,
University of Kansas, 1940.

A community survey of a tobacco town in the interior. Deals with population
problems, social classes, racial distinctions, economic life, courtship,
marriage, family life, politics, education, etc.

Rogler, Charles C. The Morality of Race Mixing in Puerto Rico. Social Forces,
October, 1946. Vol. 25, No. 1. pp. 77-81.

Rogler, Charles C. The Role of Semantics in the Study of Race Distance in Puerto
Rico. Social Forces. Vol. 22, No. 4, May, 1944. pp. 448-453.

Rosario, José Colombán and Carrión, Justina. El Negro. Haití, Estados Unidos,
Puerto Rico. San Juan, Puerto Rico, Negociado de Materiales, Imprenta y
Transporte, 1940. 174 pp.

A comparative study of Negro social problems.

Rosario, José C. The Puerto Rican Peasant and His Historical Antecedents.
.Porto Rico and Its Problems, Brookings Institution, 1930. pp. 537-81.

1. population elements; 2. the question of color; 3. socio-economic conditions; 4. education; 5. cultural opportunities.

Senior, Clarence. Disequilibrium Between Population and Resources: The Case of
Puerto Rico. Proceedings of the Inter-American Conference on the Conservation
of Renewable Natural Resources. Denver, September 7-20, 1948. Washington,
Department of State, 1950. pp. 143-49.

Senior, Clarence. Population Pressures and the Future of Puerto Rico. Journal of
Heredity, May, 1947. pp. 131-34.

Senior, Clarence. Puerto Rican Emigration. Rio Piedras. Social Science Research Center, University of Puerto Rico. 1947. 166 pp. (mimeographed).

Previous experience and future possibilities.

The Sugar Industry of the Caribbean. Crop Inquiry Series, No. 6. Washington and Port-of-Spain, Caribbean Commission, 1947. 343 pp.

Porto Rico, pp. 107-37.

U. S. Congress. House Committee on Insular Affairs. Investigation of political, economic and social conditions in Puerto Rico. Report of the Committee on Insular Affairs, House of Representatives, Seventy-ninth Congress, First Session, pursuant to H. Res. 159 (Seventy-eighth Congress) and H. Res 99 (Seventy-ninth Congress). Washington, Government Printing Office, 1945. 50 pp.

Chap. IV, "Social Conditions", and Chap. V, "Economic Conditions", present broad resumes of the Spanish heritage, racial statistics, marital status, levels of mortality and fertility and population density in relation to land use. The detailed recommendations include a study of the possibilities for emigration, especially to South and Central America.

U. S. Congress. House. Committee on Insular Affairs. Investigation of political, economic, and social conditions in Puerto Rico. Hearings before the subcommittee of the Committee on Insular Affairs, House of Representatives, Seventy-eighth Congress, first session, pursuant to H. Res. 159. Washington, U. S. Government Printing Office, 1943.

U. S. Congress. Senate. Committee on Territories and Insular Affairs. Economic and social conditions in Puerto Rico. Hearings before a subcommittee of the Committee on Territories and Insular Affairs, United States Senate, Seventy-eighth Congress, first session, pursuant to S. Res. 26, a resolution authorizing an investigation of economic and social conditions in Puerto Rico. Washington, U. S. Government Printing Office, 1943.

U. S. Tariff Commission. The economy of Puerto Rico, with special reference to the economic implications of independence and other proposals to change its political status under the general provisions of section 332, part II, title III, Tariff Act of 1930. Washington, 1946.

United States and Non-Self Governing Territories. Summary of information regarding the United States and non-self governing territories with particular reference to Chapters 11, 12, and 13 of the Charter of the United Nations. Washington, Government Printing Office, 1948. 106 pp. Map.

Williams, Eric. Race Relations in Puerto Rico and the Virgin Islands. Foreign Affairs, January, 1945. pp. 308-17.

Wylie, K. H. Rivers of Puerto Rico. Agriculture in the Americas. February, 1947. 7; pp. 37-40

    Includes agricultural production along the streams.

IV.

RECONSTRUCTION PROGRAM AND LABOR

Alonso Torres, Rafael. Cuarenta Años de Lucha Proletaria. San Juan, Imprenta Baldrich, 1939.

Ames, Azel. Labor Conditions in Porto Rico. United States Bureau of Labor Bulletin, May, 1901. Number 34, Vol. 6. pp. 377-439. Also in House Document 315, part 3, 56th Congress, 2nd session.

Chase, Stuart. "Operation Bootstrap" in Puerto Rico: Report of progress, 1951. Washington, National Planning Association. 1951. 72 pp.

    Stuart Chase, in his usual felicitous style, outlines the principal problems of Puerto Rico and the Government program to solve them, and then interprets the program in the light of "Point Four".

    This pamphlet, which is a report prepared for the business committee of the National Planning Association, provides the best available short introduction to present-day Puerto Rico.

Colon-Torres, Ramon. Programming for the Utilization of Agricultural Resources in Puerto Rico. (In: A. Curtis Wilgus, The Caribbean at Mid-Century. Gainesville, University of Florida Press. 1951. 284 pp.) pp. 111-126.

Extension of Social Security to Puerto Rico and the Virgin Islands. Report to the Committee on Ways and Means. February 6, 1950. Washington, Government Printing Office. 22 pp.

Farm Credit Administration in Puerto Rico. Caribbean Commission, Monthly Information Bulletin. November, 1949. pp. 135-38

Summary of the operations of four farm credit institutions, with some comparisons with continental experience.

Grimble, June A. Puerto Rico Means Business. Americas. Pan American Union, Washington, D. C., June, 1950. pp. 2-5 & 41-42; illus.

The reconstruction program.

Hibben, Thomas and Picó, Rafael. Industrial Development of Puerto Rico and the Virgin Islands. Port-of-Spain, Caribbean Commission. 1949. 268 ⨍ 32 pp.

Encyclopedic.

Iglesias, Santiago. Luchas Emancipadoras. Crónicas de Puerto Rico. Vol. 1. Imprenta Cantero, Fernández & Company, San Juan, Puerto Rico, 1929. 388 pp.

Industrial Opportunities in Puerto Rico. Puerto Rico Industrial Development Company San Juan, 1946. 47pp. illus.

Lewis, W. Arthur. Industrial Development in Puerto Rico. Caribbean Economic Review. December, 1949. pp. 153-176

An indispensable critique of the program and an analysis of the relation between over-population and industrialization.

Man of the People. Time. May 2, 1949. pp. 33-36

Capsule biography of Governor Luis Muñoz Marín against background of island conditions and programs.

Marcus, Joseph. Labor Conditions in Porto Rico. Department of Labor. Government Printing Office, Washington, 1919. 67 pp.

Menéndez Ramos, R. Apuntes Para la Historia del Movimiento Cooperativo en Puerto Rico. Revista del Café 2(7), San Juan, December, 1946; pp. 164-168.

Minimum Wages. Business Week, May 13, 1950.

> Deals with effects of application of continental 75 cent per hour minimum wage rate on insular economy and cites recommended hourly rates.

Nazario, L. A. Las Cooperativas en el Futuro Económico de Puerto Rico. Revist del Café 2(7), Diciembre, 1946. pp. 25-27.

Nicholas, William H. Growing Pains Beset Puerto Rico. National Geographic Magazine, April, 1951. pp. 419-460. illus.

> A general article on contemporary Puerto Rico. Discusses housing, industrialization, etc.

Pérez, Manuel A. Economic Background of Puerto Rico as an essential determinent in social problems. Puerto Rico Health Bulletin, Vol. 6 No. 12. December, 1942. pp. 381-387.

> Malthusian pressure, economic maladjustment, inequalities in distribution and other factors are described as they influence the health problems of Puerto Rico.

Puerto Rican Land Authority Receives Better Bids. Journal of Commerce, New York, May 22, 1950.

> The Land Authority, charged with redressing the maladjustments of the old absentee landowning system, sold $7 million worth of its bonds to provide funds for crop loans at the unusually low rate of 1.8%; the rate four years ago was 2.9%.

Puerto Rico, Marking 50 Years Under U.S. Flag, Looks to New Progress. New York Herald-Tribune, Special Supplement, December 10, 1948. pp. 35-58.

> A special supplement containing articles describing island's industrial, social and economic progress.

Puerto Rico, U.S.A., Moving Forward. San Juan, Puerto Rico, Industrial Development Company, 1949. 16 pp.

> Comparisons of the island's economic situation with that of U.S. states and Latin American countries.

Puerto Rico's Governor Outlines **Island's** Progress. Caribbean **Commission**, Monthly
Information Bulletin. August, 1951. pp. 15-19, 22.

Report to the Legislature on developments between 1940 and 1950.

Reglamentos de Debates para Reuniones Generales. Serie Sobre Educación Obrera.
No. 2. División de Asuntos Sociales y de Trabajo, Unión Panamericana,
Washington, D. C., 1950. 33 pp.

An elementary treatment of parliamentary law, based on a booklet published
by the Amalgamated Clothing Workers of America, "How to Conduct Your Union
Meeting". Useful for all sorts of meetings, but particularly aimed at
labor gatherings. Single copies available on request to the Pan American
Union.

Rottenberg, Simon. The Collective Agreement in Puerto Rico. Caribbean Economic
Review. Dec., 1949. pp. 14-22

Sierra Berdecía, Fernando. Testimonio del Comisionado del Trabajo de Puerto Rico
y del...Candido Oliveras, ante los subcomites de Educación y Trabajo... .
San Juan, Departamento del Trabajo. 1950. 85 pp.

Valuable statistical data on wages on the island and the probable effects
of the extension of the federal minimum wage law to insular industries.

Sierra Berdecía, Fernando. Protecting Puerto Rico's Labor. Washington, D. C.,
Office of Puerto Rico, 1949. 19 pp.

Succinct statement of the island's labor laws and the machinery for their
enforcement.

Social Legislation in Puerto Rico. (Legislación Social de Puerto Rico).
Compilada y anotada por Vicente Géigel Polanco. San Juan, Negociado de
Publicaciones y Educación Obrera, 1944. 928 pp.

The Progress of Puerto Rico, U.S.A. Government Development Bank for Puerto Rico,
San Juan.

Statistics on the economic picture.

Fernós-Isern, A. The Transportation Needs of Puerto Rico.   ashington, Office of
    Puerto Rico, 1949. English and Spanish. 38 pp.

Tugwell, Rexford and Grace. Puerto Rico's Bootstraps. Harper's, February, 1947.
    pp. 160-69.

    Lists new agencies and describes their functions. Discusses Puerto Rican
    temperament.

Weyl, W. E. Labor Conditions in Porto Rico. United States Bureau of Labor Bulletin,
    Washington, November, 1905. Vol. 11: pp. 723-856.

V.

EDUCATION

A Manual for the Teaching of American English to Spanish-speaking Children in
    Puerto Rico. San Juan, Department of Education. Publications and Documents
    Section, 1949. 674 pp.

Benítez, Jaime. Education and Democracy in Puerto Rico. Washington, Office of
    Puerto Rico, 1948. 15 pp.

    The University of Puerto Rico is a vital factor in the island's economic re-
    construction. This pamphlet, written by the Chancellor, describes the role of
    education in the program.

Blauch, L. E. Education in the territories and outlying possessions of the United
    States. Journal of Negro Education. 15, pp. 462-479. Summer, 1946.

    Includes rural schools in Alaska and Puerto Rico.

Cebollero, Pedro A. A School Language Policy for Puerto Rico. Rio Piedras,
    Superior Educational Council, 1945. 133 pp.

    1. historical development; 2. social needs for English in Puerto Rico;
    3. conclusions and recommendations. Also published in Spanish as La Política
    Lingüístico-Escolar de Puerto Rico.

Dolgado, Emilio. El Destino de la Lengua Española en Puerto Rico. Introducción por
    Andrés Iduarte. New York, Hispanic publishers, 1946. 18 pp.

Mellado, Ramón. Culture and Education in Puerto Rico. Hato Rey, Puerto Rico. Teachers' Association, 1948. 140 pp.

Deals with the conflicts between inherited beliefs and modern demands for action: "from traditional individualism to socialization; from religious intolerance to religious liberalism; from idealism to experimentalism" with suggestions for an educational program to take advantage of the conflict. (Available at library of Teachers College, Columbia University)

Osuna Juan José. A History of Education in Puerto Rico. Rio Piedras, Universidad de Puerto Rico, 1949. 657 pp.

1. Spanish education; 2. Education under the government of the U. S. (1898-1920); 3. Education in Puerto Rico, 1920-1945; 4. "The wonder of the century"; 5. Puerto Ricans Take Over.

Public Education and the Future of Puerto Rico. A curriculum survey, 1948-49. New York, Bureau of Publications, Teachers College, Columbia University, 1950. 614 pp.

1. The vision of a people; 2. The socio-economic potential; 3. the power of values; 4. attaining a better life; 5. the school curriculum; 6. special problems and plans for action.

Puerto Rico's Vocational Training Program Highlights Trend Toward Industrialization. Commercial and Financial Chronicle, March 23, 1950.

Rodríguez Bou, Ismael. El Analfabetismo en Puerto Rico. San Juan, Consejo Superior de Enseñanza, 1945. 130 pp. Tables, diagrs.

Sendra, Clara Lugo. Cooperative Education in Puerto Rico. Monthly Information Bulletin, Caribbean Commission, June, 1951. pp. 813-17.

The Problem of Education in Puerto Rico. Washington, Office of Puerto Rico, 1949. 8 pp.

A summary of the situation after 50 years under the American flag.

Williams, E. Education in Dependent Territories in America. Journal of Negro Education. 15; pp. 534-51. Summer, 1946.

VI

POLITICS AND PUBLIC ADMINISTRATION

Allen, Devere. The Caribbean, Laboratory of World Cooperation. New York, League
for Industrial Democracy, 1943. 40 pp.

A general view of the Caribbean as a colonial area with frequent specific
references to Puerto Rico.

Arnold, Edwin G. Self-government in U. S. territories. Foreign Affairs, July, 1947.
pp. 655-666.

Fernós-Isern, A. Relations between Puerto Rico and the United States.
Congressional Record, April 5, 1950. pp. 1-2

Advocacy of H. R. 7674 and its Senate companion bill S. 3336, allowing the
people of Puerto Rico to draft their own constitution.

Fernós-Isern, A. Organization of a Constitutional Government in Puerto Rico.
Congressional Record Index, March 14, 1950. pp. 1-2

Explanation of reasons for H. R. 7674.

Fox, Annette Baker. Freedom and Welfare in the Caribbean. New York, Harcourt,
Brace, 1949. 272 pp.

Comparisons between the policies of the four empires in the region.

Céigel Polanco, Vicente. La Independencia de Puerto Rico, sus bases históricas,
económicas y culturales. Río Piedras, Imprenta Falcón, 1943. 30 pp.

Haas, William Herman, ed. The American Empire. Chicago, University of Chicago
Press, 1940. 408 pp.

Informative essays on the historical, political and economic aspects of
American colonial policy. A useful book that fills a real need.

Hackett, William H. The Nationalist Party. U. S. Government Printing Office, Washington, 1951.

A factual study of the Puerto Rican insurrectionists under Albizu Campos, and the Blair House shooting, prepared at the request of Hon. Fred L. Crawford, Member of the Committee on Interior and Insular Affairs, U. S. House of Representatives.

Holmes, Olive. Puerto Rico. An American Responsibility. Foreign Policy Reports, March 1, 1947. pp. 281-92.

Succinct statement of economic and political problems and programs by the Latin American expert of the Foreign Policy Association.

Labarthe, Pedro Juan. ¿Quién es el Gobernador de Puerto Rico? La Nueva Democracia, New York, Julio, 1949. pp. 64-77.

Biographical sketch.

Manual of Government Agencies in Puerto Rico. Executive Branch. Public Administration Monograph #2, School of Public Administration, College of Social Sciences, University of Puerto Rico, 1950.   . 341pp

Muñoz Marín, Luis. Cultura y Democracia. La Nueva Democracia, Comité de Cooperación de la América Latina, 156 Fifth Ave., New York. Julio, 1949. pp. 26-30.

Revealing essay by the Governor of Puerto Rico on the meaning of democracy.

Muñoz Marín, Luis. Inaugural Address of the First Elected Governor of Puerto Rico. San Juan, Office of the Governor, January 2, 1949. 10 pp.

An impressive statement, with world-wide implications, on liberty for colonial people. (Published in Spanish also)

Muñoz Marín, Luis. Statement by the Governor of Puerto Rico. Hearing before the Committee on Public Lands, House of Representatives. H.R. 7674. A bill to provide for the organization of a constitutional government by the people of Puerto Rico. Washington, Government Printing Office, March 14, 1950. 19 pp.

Padín, José. Consideraciones en torno al régimen colonial. San Juan, Universidad de Puerto Rico, 1945. 33 pp.

A commencement address delivered at the University of Puerto Rico.

Pagán, Bolívar. Puerto Rico. The Next State. Washington, privately printed, 1942. 108 pp. illus.

The position of statehood advocates.

Puerto Rico's Future Political Status. What the Record Shows. Washington, D. C., Office of Puerto Rico, n. d. 32 pp.

Excerpts from various official documents, public hearings and editorial comment on the Muñoz Marín proposal for a plebiscite on the island's status.

Out-of-print, but may be found in many libraries.

Puerto Rico's Referendum. A report on the conduct of the Election on the Question of a Constitutional Convention; Voters Overwhelmingly Approve Public Law 600. Prepared by Hon. Frank T. Bow, Member of the Committee on Interior and Insular Affairs. United States House of Representatives, U. S. Government Printing Office, Washington, 1951.

Reid, Charles F. Puerto Rico, Key to the Caribbean. (In Overseas America, Foreign Policy Association Headline Books No. 35. New York, 1942. pp. 64-76.)

Report on the Reorganization of the Executive Branch of the Government of Puerto Rico. San Juan, Office of the Governor, 1949. 179 pp.

Report of a "little Hoover commission"; important for an understanding of the structure and functions of the various organizations involved in the extensive reconstruction of the economy of the island.

Senior, Clarence. Self-Determination for Puerto Rico. Post War World Council, New York, 1946. 29 pp.

This pamphlet analyzes various proposals about the island's future, points out that it is widely used as a test of our democratic sincerity, and urges that we do not set Puerto Rico adrift, without regard to her economic necessities.

Taussig, Charles W. A four-Power Program in the Caribbean. Foreign Affairs, July, 1946. pp. 699-710.

Comparisons of the situation in the British, Dutch, French and U. S. possessionsand what the metropolitan governments were doing.

The Organization of a Constitutional Government by the People of Puerto Rico. Statement by Oscar Chapman, Secretary of the Interior, Governor Luis Muñoz Marín and Resident Commissioner A. Fernós-Isern. Hearing before the Committee on Interior and Insular Affairs, U. S. Senate, March 13, 1950. Washington, Government Printing Office. 12 pp.

Tugwell, Rexford Guy. Changing the Colonial Climate. San Juan, Bureau of Supplies, Printing and Transportation, 1942. 265 pp.

The story told through his official messages, of Governor Rexford Guy Tugwell's efforts to bring democracy to an island possession which serves the United Nations as a warbase.

Tugwell, Rexford Guy. The Puerto Rican Public Papers of R. G. Tugwell, Governor. San Juan, Service Office of the Government of Puerto Rico, Printing Division, 1945. 378 pp.

University of Puerto Rico. Civil Service Commission. San Juan, 1947. 301 pp.

Puerto Rico and its public administration program.

U. S. Congress. Senate. Committee on Territories and Insular Affairs. Puerto Rico. Hearings before the Committee on Territories and Insular Affairs, United States Senate, Seventy-eighth Congress, first session, on S. 952, a bill to provide for the withdrawal of the sovereignty of the United States over the island of Puerto Rico and for the recognition of its independence and so forth. Washington, U. S. Government Printing Office, 1943. 335 pp; tables, diagr.

VII

FICTION, CHILDREN'S BOOKS, POETRY, FILMS

A Girl from Puerto Rico. 16 mm. Color and Sound. 15 minutes. Available through
the Department of Labor of Puerto Rico, 21 W. 60 St., New York, N. Y. (Free rental)

How a newly arrived girl from Puerto Rico and her fellow students in a
New York City school learn to know and to adjust to each other. All
parts played by teachers and student body of the Joan of Arc Junior
High School, where the picture was shot.

Movies in Spanish for educational and recreational programs. Puerto Rico Department
of Labor, 21 West 60 St., New York 23. 8 pp. (mimeographed).

Lists, with brief descriptions, 16 mm. films covering health, nutrition,
geography, Puerto Rico and other subjects. Available free on request.

Delaney, Eleanor C. Spanish Gold. Illustrated by George M. Richards. NewYork,
The MacMillan Company, 1946. 426 pp. illus.

Kelsey, Alice Greer. Ricardo's White Horse. New York, Longmans, Green, 1948.

The story of a road mender's son and his horse, Blanquita; against a
background of island life and work.

Labarthe, Pedro Juan. Antología de Poetas Contemporáneos de Puerto Rico. Ciudad
de México, Editorial Clásica, 1946. 349 pp.

An anthology of contemporary poetry, with brief biographical sketches of
the poets.

Lee de Muñoz Marín, Muna. Pioneers of Puerto Rico. Illustrated by Katharine
Knight. Boston, D. C. Heath and Company, 1944. 80 pp. illus.

Historical incidents written for children.

Mason, J.A. Puerto Rican Folklore;ed. by A. M. Espinosa. Journal of American
Folklore, Apr. 1921, v. 34, 143-208; Jan. 1922, v. 35, 1-61; July, 1924,
v. 37; 247-344;Oct. 1925, v. 38, 507-618; July, 1926, v. 39, 227-369;
Oct. 1927, v. 40, 313-444;Apr. 1929, v. 42, 85-156.
Fairy tales, riddles, picaresque stories.

Mason, J. A. Porto Rican Folk-lore. Décimas, Christmas Carols, Nursery rhymes, and other popular songs. Edited by Aurelio M. Espinosa. *Journal* of *American Folk-lore*, New York, July-September, 1918. Vol. 31. 289 pp.

Ramírez de Arellano, Rafael W. Folk-lore Puertorriqueño. Cuentos y Adivinanzas recogidos de la tradición oral. Madrid, 1928, Junta para Ampliación de Estudios, Centro de Estudios Históricos, Madrid. 290 pp.

Stories and riddles.

Roberts, Edith. Candle in the Sun. Bobbs-Merrill, 1937. 391 pp.

A novel by the wife of a continental educator who spent many years on the island.

VIII

MUSIC

Records

One cannot understand the island and its people without knowing at least some of its music. Local composers have added to the vast heritage of folk melodies and rythms from Spain. Many of these are available on records. As an introduction, a few suggestions follow.

Danzas. The epitome of the various cultural strains found in Puerto Rico is this form which reached its greatest heights in the work of Juan Morel Campos (1857-1896). Some of the best are available in the two albums mentioned below:

Puerto Rican Danzas, played by the famous Puerto Rican artist, Jesús María Sanromá, soloist for the Boston Symphony Orchestra. Victor Album M-849. Contains 8 examples, with introductory notes on the origin and development of the form.

Danzas Fuertorriqueñas, Orquesta Borinquen. Album put out by the Puerto Rico Recording Co. Also contains 8 danzas, seven of which are not included in the Morel Campos album.

Seis. The seis, one of the characteristic dances of the jíbaro - the peasant of the mountainous interior of Puerto Rico; originally came from southern Spain. We have chosen three of the many recordings available:

1. Seis Zapateao (danced in tap style) - Decca 69104 (#4 on reverse)
2. Mi Terruño - Victor 23-0515
3. Fiesta en Casa de Siño Juancho - Victor 23-1322 (#5 on reverse)

<u>Aguinaldos</u>. Christmas songs which get their name from the eagle on the Spanish coins given the carolers in olden days.

4. Aguinaldos puertorriqueños - Decca 69113 (#1 on reverse)
5." Las Flores de Mi Jardín - Victor 23-1322

<u>Plenas</u>. The plena is a local relative of the Mexican corrido and the Caribbean calypso. It tellsthe story of some event, or more often, gossips about some person or group. It is the quintessence of Puerto Rican rythm.

6. Plena de Sociedad - Seeco SR-1136
7. Juana Peña - Decca 69105
8. Lola, Lola - Columbia 5490-X

<u>Other Folk songs</u>. The Library of Congress folksong collection from Puerto Rico contains selections ranging from childrens' singing games through the plena and seis to funeral and religioussongs. A pamphlet gives both Spanish and English words and the circumstances under which the song was recorded. (Album XVIII, Folk Music of the Americas).

<u>Contemporary music</u>, including popular songs and dance music.

9. Romance del Campesino - Seeco PR 4005
10. Lamento Borincano (Bolero by Rafael Hernández, Puerto Rico's most famous living composer). - Odeon 9687
11. Preciosa (Bolero, Rafael Hernández) - Victor 23-0387
12. Recuerdos Infantiles (Guaracha) - Decca 21216
13. Quiero un Sombrero (Guaracha) - Verne V-0138
14. Cuchifrito (Guaracha, Rafael Hernández) - Decca 69103 (#5 on reverse)
15. Serenata Rítmica (Rumba lenta by Noro Morales, famous composer and orchestra leader) - Seeco SR 1143
16. Cu-Tu-Cu-Ru (A rumba , often called Jack, Jack, Jack, by Armando Castro) - Verne V-0100
17. Jinguili-Jongolo (Rumba-calypso, one of several by Armando based on themes he heard in Trinidad. The others include Cose, Cose, Cose; Mary Ann; Matilda) - Seeco PR 4043.

New recordings, including many from Puerto Rico, are played twice weekly by Pru Devon on "Nights in LatinAmerica", WQXR. The best of these are listed in the "For Your Record Library" section of <u>Americas</u>, monthly magazine of the Pan American Union.

<u>Chorus of the University of Puerto Rico</u>. Rio Piedras, University of Puerto Rico, n.d., 16 pp.

Repertoire, photo of chorus and comments and its successful **tour of the** continent. Out of print but may be found in many libraries.

Henius, Frank. <u>Songs and Games of the Americas</u>. New York, Scribners, 1943. 56 pp.

    Contains Puerto Rican items.

Muñoz, Maria Luisa, ed. <u>Canciones de Navidad</u>. San Juan (no imprint) 1950. unpaged

    Twenty Christmas songs, music and words. (Available from the Department of
    Labor of Puerto Rico, 21 W. 60 St., New York 23, N.Y. Free)

<u>Puerto Rican Singer</u>. NewYork, American Book Company, 1948. 219 pp.

This is Puerto Rico (a recorded documentary). A 6-part radio series, each a
    15 minute program with musical background and occasional full numbers.
    Covers: 1. the island; 2. the contrasts; 3. the people; 4. the customs;
    5. the land; 6. past, present and future.

    Produced by the U. S. Department of the Interior, with a manual for
    teachers prepared by Joyce Bartell of the Wisconsin School of the Air in 1946.
    It is out of date on political matters, but otherwise still valuable for
    either radio or classroom reproduction on a 33 rpm play-back.

IX

COOKERY

Dooley, Eliza Bellows (King). <u>Puerto Rican Cookbook</u>. Illustrated by the author.
    Richmond, Dietz Press, 1948. 175 pp.

Food the World Over - Puerto Rican. Brooklyn, Nutrition Service, Visiting Nurse
    Association, 138 S. Oxford St., n.d. 22 pp. (mimeographed)

    Recipes and suggestionsfor improved diets.

X

BIBLIOGRAPHIES

Bird, Augusto. Bibliografía Puertorriqueña de Fuentes para Investigaciones
    Sociales, 1930-1945. Edición Provisional. Río Piedras, Universidad de
    Puerto Rico, 1946. Tomo I. 180 pp. Tomo II pp. 181-547.

    1. Fuentes bibliográficas; 2. información general; 3. historia natural.
    4. la salud; 5. economía social; 6. historia política y administrativa;
    7. organización cultural; 8. historia de Puerto Rico.

    Useful, although poorly organized in this preliminary edition. Supple-
    ments the outstanding Bibliografía Puertorriqueña, 1493-1930, compiled
    by Antonio S. Pedreira.

Brown, Ann Duncan. Puerto Rico. A Selected List of References. Washington,
    Library of Congress, 1939. 50 pp (mimeographed)

Handbook of Latin American Studies, prepared by the Hispanic Foundation of the
    Library of Congress and published by the Harvard University Press. Appears
    annually, since 1938.

    This is an invaluable source for both official and private reports, studies,
    articles, etc. dealing with both republics and colonies of Latin America.

Pedreira, Antonio S. Bibliografía Puertorriqueña, 1493-1930. Madrid, 1932. 707 pp.

Puerto Rico. A bibliography. Library of Congress, Washington, D. C. 1943. 44 pp.
    (mimeographed)

Tapia y Rivera, Alejandro, ed. Biblioteca Histórica de Puerto Rico que contiene
    varios documentos de los siglos XV, XVI, XVII y XVIII, coordinados y anotados.
    2a. ed. San Juan, Puerto Rico, Instituto de Literatura Puertorriqueña, 1945.
    612 pp.

XI

SOURCES OF FURTHER INFORMATION

Division of Territories, U. S. Department of the Interior, Washington, D. C.

Office of the Government of Puerto Rico, 1026-17th St. N.W., Washington, D. C.

Puerto Rico Sugar-Producers Association, Shoreham Bldg., Washington, D. C.

The Migration Division, P. R. Department of Labor, 17 W. 60 St., New York, N.Y., and 750 S. Wabash Ave., Chicago, Ill

Economic Development Administration, 600 Fifth Ave., New York, N. Y;
120 S. LaSalle St., Room 1761, Chicago, Ill.
530 W. Sixth St., Los Angeles, Calif.

Puerto Rico Visitors Bureau, 600 Fifth Ave., New York, N.Y.

Publishes maps, folders and a periodical review of current happenings, "This Week in Puerto Rico" ("Que Pasa en Puerto Rico").

University of Puerto Rico, Rio Piedras, Puerto Rico.

Issues a monthly, Universidad, and lists of books published by its Press.

<u>Bibliography on</u>

P U E R T O   R I C A N S

in the

U N I T E D   S T A T E S

April 1959

Annotated by

CLARENCE SENIOR
Chief
Migration Division

INTRODUCTION

In 1951, the Migration Division published a bibliography on Puerto Rico and the Puerto Rican migration to the continental United States (A Selected Bibliography on Puerto Rico and the Puerto Ricans, compiled and annotated by Clarence Senior and Josefina de Roman). The section on the migration took three pages. Today, eight years later, this 37-page bibliography devoted solely to the migration attests to the increased interest in this topic.

The present bibliography includes only those works which contain some significant or fairly extensive references to Puerto Ricans. The Puerto Rican migration, however, is not an isolated phenomenon. Some five million Americans move across county lines every year and another five million move from one state to another; migration from Puerto Rico has averaged less than one percent of total interstate migration each year. For anyone studying migration as a whole, these works should be supplemented by others presenting an over-all view or other aspects of the subject and its role in the national economy; studies of the immigrations of the past may also be found of value.

This bibliography has been annotated by Dr. Clarence Senior, Chief of the Migration Division. His annotations, however, do not necessarily reflect any official viewpoint of the government of the Commonwealth of Puerto Rico.

An attempt has been made to include all publications of importance relating to Puerto Rican migration issued prior to the end of 1958, and addenda covering the period January 1 - April 30, 1959. The Migration Division plans to publish supplementary lists from time to time, and users of this bibliography are urged to submit additions and corrections to the Information Section of the Migration Division, 322 West 45th Street, New York 36, N.Y.

INFORMATION SECTION

CONTENTS

Abrams, Charles. Forbidden Neighbors. New York: Harper, 1955.
See esp. Chap. 6, "The Puerto Rican Airlift," pp. 56-69.

An excellent book by one of the country's outstanding
authorities on housing, with the exception of the chapter
on Puerto Ricans which is superficial and, in several
respects, misleading.

Abrams, Charles. "How to Remedy Our 'Puerto Rican Problem':
Whence it Arose; What do Do." Commentary, Feb. 1955,
vol. 19, no. 12, pp. 120-127.

Covers the same material as the chapter in Forbidden
Neighbors.

Anastasi, Anne, and Jesús, Cruz de. "Language Development and
Non-verbal IQ of Puerto Rican Preschool Children in
New York City." Journal of Abnormal and Social Psychology,
July 1953, vol. 48, no. 3, pp. 357-366.

Comparisons with white and Negro preschool groups previously tested. The Puerto Rican children equaled the
American white norms despite their low socio-economic
status. On the basis of this preliminary study, it is
tentatively concluded that "inferior performance of older
Puerto Rican children tested in other studies may result
from cumulative effects of very low socio-economic level,
as well as from intellectual and emotional effects of
bilingualism. Prior to school entrance, when bilingualism
has not become a serious problem for such a group, test
performance and language development appear to be normal."

Around the World in New York: A Guide to the City's Nationality
Groups. New York: Caroline Zachry Institute of Human
Development and the Common Council for American Unity,
1950. 112 pp.

Arter, Rhetta M. Between Two Bridges: A Study of Human Relations
in the Lower East Side of Manhattan, the Area Served by
the Educational Alliance. Human Relations Monograph No. 5.
Interpretation by Dan W. Dodson. New York: New York
University, Center for Human Relations Studies, 1953. 32 pp.

Arter, Rhetta M. Living in Chelsea. Human Relations Monograph No. 4.
New York: New York University, Center for Human Relations
Studies, and the Hudson Guild, 1954. 43 pp.

Arter, Rhetta M. Mid-City. Human Relations Monograph No. 3.
New York: New York University, Center for Human Relations
Studies, 1953. 32 pp.

A study of human relations in the area of Manhattan served
by the Christ Church House. Contains helpful suggestions on
securing participation from Spanish-speaking families who
will take part "if they become convinced that their
participation is desired" (p. 29).

Audio-Visual Resources for Use in Classes with Puerto Rican
    Children in Junior High Schools. New York: New York
    City Board of Education, Bureau of Audio-Visual
    Instruction, Dec. 1956. 53 pp.

Babín, María Teresa. "Un Nuevo Plan Educativo en la New York
    University." La Torre (Universidad de Puerto Rico),
    abril-junio de 1955, año 3, núm. 10, págs. 141-146.

Back to School for a Thousand Farmers: They Learn the ABC's of
    the Puerto Rican Labor Program. Trenton: New Jersey
    Farm Bureau, 1957. 4 pp.

Banítez, Jaime. "El Problema Humano de la Emigración."
    La Torre (Universidad de Puerto Rico), enero-marzo
    de 1956, año 4, núm. 13, págs. 13-21.

Berger, S. "Puerto Rican Migrants Create Housing Problems."
    Real Estate News, Aug. 1942, vol. 33, no. 8, pp. 265-267.

    A defense of the landlord on slum conditions in Puerto
    Rican neighborhoods.

Berle, A. A., Jr. "How Long Will New York Wait?" The Reporter,
    Sept. 8, 1955, vol. 13, no. 2, pp. 14-18.

Berle, Beatrice Bishop. 80 Puerto Rican Families in New York
    City: Health and Disease Studied in Context. New York:
    Columbia University Press, 1958. 331 pp.

    An intensive study of health and related problems of 80
    Puerto Rican families living in a New York City slum.
    See also the anthropological study, covering some of the
    same families and others, Up From Puerto Rico by
    Elena Padilla.

Berle, Beatrice Bishop. "Sterilization and Birth-Control Practices
    in a Selected Sample of Puerto Ricans Living in a Manhattan
    Slum." Fertility and Sterility, May-June 1957, vol. 8, no. 3,
    pp. 267-281.

Blair, William C. "Spanish-Speaking Minorities in a Utah Mining Town."
    Journal of Social Issues, 1st Quarter 1952, vol. 8, no. 1,
    pp. 4-9.

"Boricuas No Viven en Arrabales." El Diario de Nueva York,
    12 de enero de 1956, págs. 2, 10.

    Points out that no Puerto Ricans ever lived in the slums
    which former New Jersey Judge Lloyd blamed them for
    creating.

Boroff, David. "Jews and Puerto Ricans." Congress Weekly
(American Jewish Congress), April 15, 1957, vol. 24,
no. 15, pp. 10-13.

Braestrup, Peter. "Life Among the Garment Workers." New York
Herald Tribune. Sept. 29-Oct. 10, 1958 (Series of ten
articles)

"Life Among Today's Garment Workers," Sept. 29; "Life Among
the Garment Workers," Sept. 30; "Life Among N.Y. City's
Garment Workers," Oct. 1; "Life Among City's Garment Workers,"
Oct. 2; "Union Helping Puerto Ricans," Oct. 3; "Color Still
Bar to Skills, Union Office," Oct. 6; "Life Among the Garment
Workers: I.L.G.W.U. Sets pace for Labor," Oct. 7; "Puerto
Rican Workers Rebel Against Boss -- And Union," Oct. 8;
"They Get Union Cake at Outings, But No Copies of Union
Contracts," Oct. 9; "How the Unions Fail the Exploited,"
Oct. 10.

Braestrup, Peter. "New York's Puerto Ricans." New York Herald
Tribune, Oct. 16-18, 20, 21, 1957. (Series of five
articles.)

"A Cold New World," Oct. 16, pp. 1, 19; "A Search for a
Job, A Place of My Own," Oct. 17, p. 21; "They Live in
Squalor at Park Avenue Rent," Oct. 18, p. 10; "Ebb and Flow
of Their Migration Held Barometer of U.S. Economy," Oct. 20,
p. 40; "Their Position Is Improving," Oct. 21, p. 14.

Brown, Stuart. "Philadelphia's Puerto Ricans: Language Barrier
Is Chief Source of Problems Faced by Migrants."
Philadelphia Sunday Bulletin, March 16, 1958, section 2,
pp. 1, 2.

Burma, John Harmon. Spanish-Speaking Groups in the United States.
Durham, N. C.: Duke University Press, 1954. 214 pp.

Includes a thumbnail sketch of the Puerto Ricans,
undertaking to link them with other Spanish-speaking groups
that have been in this country for a longer period of time.
See critical reviews by Lyle Saunders, Ciencias Sociales,
marzo de 1956, vol. 3, núm. 37, págs. 64-66, and Clarence
Senior, Rural Sociology, Sept. 1954, pp. 309-310.

Capodiferro, Clelia. Developmental Reading Project. New York:
The Puerto Rican Study of the New York City Board of
Education, 1957. 18 pp.

Castaño, Carlos. "The First 10 Years . . . The Puerto Rican
    Migratory Program." Employment Security Review,
    March 1958, vol. 25, no. 3, pp. 31-33.

    A brief review of the Commonwealth of Puerto Rico's
    program for seasonal agricultural workers in the United
    States.

Characteristics of Passengers Who Travelled by Air Between Puerto
    Rico and the United States. San Juan: Commonwealth of
    Puerto Rico, Dept. of Labor, Bureau of Labor Statistics,
    1956-.

    A continuing series of quarterly and annual reports of
    statistical data.

Chenault, Lawrence R. The Puerto Rican Migrant in New York City.
    New York: Columbia University Press, 1938. 190 pp.

    Deals with earlier movements to New York City and their
    effects upon the established community and the migrant.

Chesterton-Mangle, Maenna. "By Opposing, End Them," pp. 33-41.
    In: Mabel M. Sheibley (ed.). Accent on Liberty.
    New York: Friendship Press, 1952. 149 pp.

Clark, Blake. "New York's Puerto Rican Problem." Reader's
    Digest, Feb. 1953, vol. 62, no. 370, pp. 61-65.

Collazo, Francisco. The Education of Puerto Rican Children in
    the Schools of New York City. San Juan: Commonwealth of
    Puerto Rico, Department of Education, 1954. 14 pp.

Colón, Jesús de. The Pilot Guidance Project for Tenth-Grade
    Puerto Rican Pupils at the High School of Commerce. The
    Puerto Rican Study of the New York City Board of Education,
    1955. 18 pp.

Colón, Jesús M., and Miranda, Belmira. Helping Transitional-Stage
    Pupils in the Subject Class. New York: The Puerto Rican
    Study of the New York City Board of Education, 1956. 4 pp.

Colón, Jesús M., and Miranda, Belmira. Project for Transitional-
    Stage Puerto Rican Pupils in the High School: Pupil
    Descriptive Data. New York: The Puerto Rican Study of
    the New York City Board of Education, 1956. 27 pp.

Colón, Petroamérica Pagán de. Emotional Adjustment Problems of
    the Puerto Rican Migrant. New York: Commonwealth of
    Puerto Rico, Department of Labor, Migration Division,
    n.d. 11 pp.

Colón, Petroamérica Pagán de. Northeastern Ohio and the Puerto
    Rican Migration. New York: Commonwealth of Puerto Rico,
    Department of Labor, Migration Division, 1955. 11 pp.

Colón, Petroamérica Pagán de. Programa de Colocaciones de
    Trabajadores Agrícolas Puertorriqueños en Estados Unidos.
    San Juan: Estado Libre Asociado de Puerto Rico,
    Departamento del Trabajo, n.d. 50 pp.

Commission on Race and Housing. Where Shall We Live? Berkeley and
    Los Angeles, Univ. of California Press, 1958. 77 pp.

    First of a series of reports growing out of a three-year
    study of racial discrimination in housing. Contains many
    references to Puerto Ricans and provides a valuable over-all
    picture of housing discrimination in the United States.

Complaints Alleging Discrimination Because of Puerto Rican National
    Origin: July 1, 1945 -- September 1, 1958. New York:
    New York State Commission Against Discrimination, 1958. 13 pp.

Conclusion of Migration Conference, Held in San Juan, Puerto Rico,
    March 1-7, 1953, Under the Auspices of the Commonwealth of
    Puerto Rico, Department of Labor. New York: Commonwealth
    of Puerto Rico, Department of Labor, Migration Division,
    1953. 15 pp.

Consumer Analysis of the New York Spanish Market. New York:
    El Diario de Nueva York, circa 1953. 24 pp.

Costa, Richard H. "Latest Migration: Puerto Rico Moves Upstate."
    Utica (N.Y.) Observer-Dispatch. May 27-29, 1957. (Series
    of three articles.)

    "Spanish Accent Comes to East Utica: Here's First of a
    Series on Newcomers," May 27, p. 1A; "Mercy Mission Told
    George He 'Belonged,'" May 28, p. 2A; "Utican is 'Mother'
    to Many Confused by Strange, New Land," May 29, p. 2A.

Cotto-Thorner, Guillermo. Trópico en Manhattan. San Juan:
    Editorial Occidente, 1951. 242 págs.

    An engaging human account of a Puerto Rican family in New
    York City. A rich source for the study of the hispanization
    of common English words.

Covello, Leonard, with D'Agostino, Guido. The Heart is the Teacher.
    New York: McGraw-Hill, 1958. 275 pp.

    Moving autobiography of a teacher who has devoted most of his
    life to helping underprivileged children, mostly in East
    Harlem. Dr. Covello is now Educational Consultant to the
    Migration Division.

¿Cuáles son sus Derechos Civiles en Connecticut? Bridgeport, Conn.: Bridgeport Inter-Group Council, Inc., n.d. 10 pp.

Cunningham, John T. "Migrants Pose Problems for N.J. Farmers Who Need Them." Reprinted from Newark News Magazine, Sept. 1, 1957, by the Commonwealth of Puerto Rico, Department of Labor, Migration Division. 4 pp. (Out of print.)

Current Population Estimates. New York: New York City Department of City Planning, March 1, 1955.

> City-wide and borough figures and trends, projected to 1970. Suffers from lack of consideration of employment trends.

Cursos Gratis de Educación Vocacional en Nueva York 1955- 1956. Nueva York: Estado Libre Asociado de Puerto Rico, Departamento del Trabajo, División de Migración, 1955. 29 págs.

Datos Sobre Empleo: Protección de Seguro Contra el Desempleo para Empleados de Pequeños Negocios. Nueva York: Departamento del Trabajo del Estado de Nueva York, División de Empleo, n.d. 5 págs.

Derechos y Deberes del Inquilino y el Casero. Introducción por José Monserrat. Nueva York: Estado Libre Asociado de Puerto Rico, Departamento del Trabajo, División de Migración, en colaboración con el Consejo de Organizaciones Hispano-Americanas de Nueva York, oct. de 1957 (3a edición). 16 págs.

> Spanish translation of the booklet "What Every Landlord and Tenant Should Know" published by the Citizens' Housing and Planning Council of New York.

La División de Migración . . . Sirviendo a los Puertorriqueños en los Estados Unidos. Nueva York: Estado Libre Asociado de Puerto Rico, Departamento del Trabajo, División de Migración, 1957. 8 págs.

Dodson, Dan W. Between Hell's Kitchen and San Juan Hill: A Survey. Human Relations Monograph No. 1. New York: New York University, Center for Human Relations Studies, 1952. 32 pp.

> A neighborhood study sponsored by the Broadway Tabernacle Church as a basis for its neighborhood program.

Donahue, Frances M. "A Study of the Original Puerto Rican Colony in Brooklyn, 1938-1943." (Unpublished master's thesis.) New York: Fordham School of Social Work, 1945. 87 pp.

"Don Eduardo," The New Yorker, July 3, 1954, vol. 30, no. 20, pp. 14-15.

    An interview with Edward G. Miller, chairman of the now
    defunct Committee on Puerto Rican Affairs.

Donovan, Robert J. "Annals of Crime: A Demonstration at Blair
    House." The New Yorker, July 19, 1952, vol. 28, no. 22,
    pp. 32-55.

Dossick, Jesse J. "Workshop Field Study in Puerto Rican Education
    and Culture." Journal of Educational Sociology, Dec. 1954,
    vol. 28, no. 4, pp. 174-180.

    Report on the New York University - University of Puerto
    Rico annual summer workshop.

Dworkis, Martin B. (ed.). The Impact of Puerto Rican Migration on
    Governmental Services in New York City. New York: New
    York University Press, 1957. 74 pp.

    Includes brief chapters on housing, employment, welfare,
    education, health and hospital services, and crime and
    delinquency.

"Effect of Labor Costs and Migration on Puerto Rican Economy."
    Monthly Labor Review, June 1953, vol. 76, no. 6, pp. 625-627.

    A summary of articles by Simon Rottenberg and Clarence Senior
    in the Annals of the American Academy of Political and Social
    Science, Jan. 1953.

"La Educación y el Emigrante." Temas, nov. de 1957, vol. 14, núm. 85,
    págs. 124-127.

English-Speech Language Arts for Senior High Schools. New York:
    New York City Board of Education, 1956. 100 pp.

Estire Sus Dólares. Nueva York: Estado Libre Asociado de Puerto Rico,
    Departamento del Trabajo, División de Migración, 1957. 6 págs.

    A consumer-education folder.

Estudio Sobre La Emigración en Puerto Rico: Encuesta en la Semana
    del 21 al 27 de Abril de 1952. San Juan: Oficina del
    Gobernador, Negociado del Presupuesto, División de Estadís-
    ticas, dic. de 1952. 47 págs.

Expanded Plan of Operations Pertaining to Puerto Rico Agricultural
    Workers. New York: Commonwealth of Puerto Rico, Department
    of Labor, Migration Division, circa 1953, 9 pp.

Fact Book on Children in New York City. New York: Community Council
    of Greater New York, Research Department, April 1957. 145 pp.

    A valuable collection of data, including various statistics
    on Puerto Rican children. One of a series of three reports
    on dependent age groups which also includes a Fact Book on
    the Aged and a Fact Book on Youth.

Fernández Méndez, Eugenio. "¿Asimilación o Enquistamiento? Dos Polos
    del Problema de la Emigración Transcultural Puertorriqueña."
    La Torre (Universidad de Puerto Rico), enero-marzo de 1956,
    año 4, núm. 13, págs. 137-145.

"Fiesta." Time, July 2, 1956, vol. 68, no. 1, p. 58.

    How San Juan Day was celebrated in New York and Chicago.

Finocchiaro, Mary, and Huebener, Theodore. Our School, Home, and City.
    New York: Noble and Noble, 1955. 64 pp.

Finocchiaro, Mary. "Puerto Rican Newcomers in Our Schools." Journal
    of Educational Sociology, Dec. 1954, vol. 28, no. 4, pp. 157-166.

Fitzpatrick, Joseph P. "The Integration of Puerto Ricans." Thought
    (Fordham University Quarterly), Fall 1955, vol. 30, no. 118,
    pp. 402-420.

Fitzpatrick, Joseph P. "Mexicans and Puerto Ricans Build a Bridge."
    America, Dec. 31, 1955, vol. 44, no. 14, pp. 373-375.

    The importance of the role played by these two groups in
    explaining our country to the 170,000,000 Latin Americans
    "south of the border."

Galíndez, Jesús de. Puerto Rico en Nueva York. México: Cuadernos
    Americanos, circa 1952. 63 págs.

García, Alonso. "Discrimination Against Puerto Ricans," pp. 79-80. In:
    (Report of the) Governor's Advisory Commission on Civil Rights.
    Springfield, O: Governor's Advisory Commission on Civil Rights,
    Dec. 1958. 118 pp.

    A report by Rev. García discussing employment attitudes and
    discrimination in Lorain, Ohio is inserted verbatim in the
    Commission's report.

Gernes, Arthur C. "Implicaciones de la Emigración Puertorriqueña al Continente Fuera de la Ciudad de Nueva York." La Torre (Universidad de Puerto Rico), enero-marzo de 1956, año 4, núm. 13, págs. 97-111.

Gernes, Arthur C. Implications of Puerto Rican Migration to the Continent Outside New York City. Address before the Ninth Annual Convention on Social Orientation, University of Puerto Rico, Dec. 10, 1955. New York: Commonwealth of Puerto Rico, Department of Labor, Migration Division, 1956. 15 pp.

The role of the United States Employment Service in helping the dispersion process, and the value of Puerto Rico as a source of manpower. English version of preceding entry.

Gittler, Joseph B. (ed.). Understanding Minority Groups. New York: John Wiley, 1956. 139 pp.

Glazer, Nathan. "New York's Puerto Ricans," Commentary. Dec. 1958, vol. 26, no. 6, pp. 469-478.

A critical review of the recent books The Puerto Ricans by Christopher Rand, Up From Puerto Rico by Elena Padilla, and 80 Puerto Rican Families in New York City by Beatrice Bishop Berle. Suffers from the misconception that Puerto Rican children are not interested in higher education.

Golden, Harry. Only in America. Cleveland and New York: World Publishing Co., 1958. 317 pp.

In "A Short Story of America" (pp. 127-129), the author sees the whole history of the United States recapitulated in boys and girls waiting for books on a Sunday afternoon in the New York Public Library -- many of them Puerto Rican boys and girls, just as in the past it was Irish, Jewish, Italian, and Negro boys and girls. "The immigrant needed to accelerate the process of integration, of proving his individual worth, of achieving his self-esteem as quickly as possible."

Golub, Fred T. The Puerto Rican Worker in Perth Amboy, New Jersey. Occasional Studies No. 2. New Brunswick, N. J.: Rutgers University, Institute of Management and Labor Relations, March 1956. 18 pp.

Goodman, Samuel M. Who Were the Teachers in the Puerto Rican Study Experimental Schools in 1953-54? - A Survey of Teacher Background, Attitudes and Practices. New York: The Puerto Rican Study of the New York City Board of Education, 1955. 27 pp.

Goodman, Samuel M.; Diamond, Lorraine K.; and Fox, David J.
    Who Are the Puerto Rican Pupils in the New York City Public
    Schools? New York: The Puerto Rican Study of the New York
    City Board of Education, 1956. 88 pp.

Greiser, Norman. "Airborne from San Juan." New Republic, Nov. 3,
    1947, vol. 108, no 2, pp. 21-24.

    About a group of migrants --- their background and how they
    fared after coming to New York.

Gruber, Ruth. "E. 110th St. Isn't the Universe: The Puerto Rican
    in New York." New York Herald Tribune. Dec. 6, 1958.

    Governor Luis Muñoz Marín, his wife Doña Inés, and Joseph
    Monserrat discuss the problems of the Puerto Rican in
    New York.

Halper, Albert. "The Wallet." The New Yorker, Feb. 3, 1951,
    vol. 26, pp. 60-65.

    A Brooklyn family returns a Puerto Rican girl's lost wallet,
    and their son receives a birthday gift from her.

Hanson, Earl Parker. Transformation: The Story of Modern Puerto Rico
    New York: Simon and Schuster, 1955. 416 pp.

    The most recent over-all account of political, economic, and
    social development in Puerto Rico. Includes a chapter (21)
    on the migration.

Helfgott, Roy B. Puerto Rican Integration in the Skirt Industry in
    New York City New York: New York State Commission Against
    Discrimination, 1958. 34 pp.

Helping Puerto Ricans Help Themselves. New York: Commonwealth of
    Puerto Rico, Department of Labor, Migration Division,
    Sept. 1958. 16 pp.

    Brief account of the Division's first ten years of service.

Hickey, Edna C. "Adjusting the Curriculum for Bilingual Children."
    National Elementary Principal, Sept. 1956, vol. 36, no. 1,
    pp. 53-57.

Hochhauser, Aidalina. A Pilot Study of "Problem Children" of Puerto
    Rican Background. New York: The Puerto Rican Study of the
    New York City Board of Education, 1956. 16 pp.

How to Hire Agricultural Workers from Puerto Rico. New York:
     Commonwealth of Puerto Rico, Department of Labor, Migration
     Division, in cooperation with the U. S. Department of Labor,
     Bureau of Employment Security, U. S. Employment Service,
     Farm Placement Service, 1953, 1954, 1955, 1957, 1958. 16 pp.

     A brief explanation of the Puerto Rican farm labor program
     and a copy of the work agreement.

Illich, Ivan. "Puerto Ricans in New York." Commonweal, June 22, 1956,
     vol. 64, no. 12, pp. 294-297.

     Discussion: August 3, 1956, p. 442; Sept. 14, 1956, pp. 589-590.

An Insight into Social Problems Facing Spanish-speaking American
     Residents of Bridgeport. Proceedings of the Conference on
     Spanish-speaking American Services, held in Bridgeport on
     September 16, 1957. Bridgeport: Bridgeport Inter-Group
     Council, Inc., 1957. 30 pp.

Interim Report. New York: Labor Advisory Committee on Puerto Rican
     Affairs, AFL-CIO, New York, 1955. 6 pp.

Interviewing Puerto Rican Parents and Children in Spanish: A Guide
     for School Personnel. New York: New York City Board of
     Education, n.d. 10 pp.

Jaffe, A. J. "Demographic and Labor Force Characteristics of New York
     City Puerto Rican Population," pp. 3-29. In: A. J. Jaffe (ed.).
     Puerto Rican Population of New York City. New York: Columbia
     University, Bureau of Applied Social Research, Jan. 1954. 61 pp.

     An examination of the close relation between the movement of
     Puerto Ricans to New York City and the needs of the local
     labor market, by an outstanding authority on labor market
     analysis.

The Jobs We Do. New York: Commonwealth of Puerto Rico, Department of
     Labor, Migration Division, 1956. 16 pp.

Johnson, J. T. "Teaching the English Language to Non-English Speaking
     Children." National Elementary Principal, Sept. 1956, vol. 36,
     no. 1, pp. 58-61.

Jones, Isham B. The Puerto Rican in New Jersey: His Present Status,
     July 1955. Newark: N. J. State Department of Education,
     Division Against Discrimination, July 1955. 48 pp.

     Includes a discussion of where Puerto Ricans are located and
     some community reactions, both helpful and antagonistic.

Katz, Irwin. Conflict and Harmony in an Adolescent Interracial Group. New York: New York University Press, 1956. 47 pp.

Kavetzky, Joseph. A Survey of Practice in the Teaching of English to Puerto Rican Pupils -- School Year 1954-1955. New York: The Puerto Rican Study of the New York City Board of Education, 1956. 27 pp.

Kihss, Peter. "Puerto Rico and Us." Three articles from The New York Times. Reprinted by the Commonwealth of Puerto Rico, Department of Labor, Migration Division, 1953. 8 pp. (Out of print.)

The series includes the following articles: "Flow of Puerto Ricans Here Fills Jobs, Poses Problems," Feb. 23, 1953; "Puerto Rico Combats Exodus by a Drive to Raise Income," Feb. 24, 1953; "Puerto Rico Will to Work Stressed," Feb. 25, 1953.

Kihss, Peter. "Gains Made by Puerto Ricans Here" and "City Relief Roll Held Down Despite Job-Hunter Influx." Two articles from The New York Times, May 31 and June 2, 1957. Reprinted by the Commonwealth of Puerto Rico, Department of Labor. Migration Division, 1957. 4 pp.

Knox, Maryel. "Ray of Sunshine in Harlem." Wellesley Alumnae Magazine, May 1953, pp. 73-75, 96.

Know Your Fellow American Citizen from Puerto Rico. Washington, D.C.: Office of the Government of Puerto Rico, n.d. 64 pp. (Out of print.)

Simple text and many pictures. An introduction to the migrant's background and his role on the continent.

"Labor Comunal de la División de Migración." Temas, nov. de 1957, vol. 14, núm. 85, págs. 113-115.

Langdale, A. Barnett. Teaching Reading to the Pupils of Puerto Rican Background. New York: The Puerto Rican Study of the New York City Board of Education, 1957. 61 pp.

The Leisure Time Problems of Puerto Rican Youth in N.Y.C.: A Study of the Problems of Selected Group Work Programs. New York: Archdiocese of New York, Catholic Youth Organization, Jan. 1953. 81 pp.

Levitas, Mitchel. "New York's Labor Scandal: The Puerto Rican Workers." New York Post, July 15-19 and 21, 1957.

Six articles reporting on the exploitation of Puerto Rican workers through such devices as "phantom unions" and "sweetheart contracts."

Leviton, Bertha. Census of Puerto Rican and Foreign-Born Pupils:
Provisional Report. New York: New York City Board of
Education, Bureau of Administrative and Budgetary Research,
Feb. 1956. 29 pp. (Census of October 31, 1955.)

Lind, Andrew W. Hawaii's People. Honolulu: University of Hawaii,
1955. 107 pp.

Includes numerous references to Puerto Ricans in Hawaii.

La Llave del Exito. Nueva York: Estado Libre Asociado de Puerto
Rico, Departamento del Trabajo, División de Migración,
circa 1952. 7 págs.

Leaflet in the annual "Learn English" campaign of the Migration
Division.

The Lorain and Gary Experience with Puerto Rican Workers. Six articles
reprinted from the Gary Post Tribune. Washington, D. C.:
Office of the Government of Puerto Rico, 1948. (Out of print.)

In 1947, the Department of Labor of Puerto Rico placed several
hundred workers in steel mills in Lorain, Ohio, and Gary,
Indiana. These articles report on the experience of the
management, the men, and the communities.

Lorge, Irving, and Mayans, Frank, Jr. "Vestibule vs. Regular Classes
for Puerto Rican Migrant Children." Teachers College Record
(Columbia University), Feb. 1954, vol. 55, no. 5, pp. 231-237.

Discussion of a study appraising English mastery and attitudes
of Puerto Rican migrants in New York City schools. "Despite
its possible limitations, the study does suggest that
'stretching' children to understand in the real setting has
marked advantages."

Low, Frances. School - Puerto Rican Parent Relations, 1955-56.
New York: The Puerto Rican Study of the New York City Board
of Education, 1957. 61 pp.

Main, Willett S. Memorandum on "In-Migration of Puerto Rican Workers,"
Milwaukee: Wisconsin State Employment Service, Sept. 3, 1952.

Ways in which local offices of the Employment Service are helpful in speeding up the adjustment process. (Followed by
"In-Migration of Puerto Rican Workers: Progress Report,"
Dec. 16, 1952, and a collection of English and Spanish materials
utilized in the program.)

Marja, Fern, with McElroy, Peter J., and Dufty, William. "Incident
in Central Park." New York Post, Feb. 10-11, 13-17, 1955.
(Series of seven award-winning articles on the Santos-Cabán
case, in which two boys, falsely accused of rape, found
justice.)

"How Delayed Justice Cost Two Boys 159 Days," Feb. 10, p. 4;
"A Judge Sounds Off While Justice Stalls," Feb. 11, p. 4;
"How the Fake Script Was Written," Feb. 13, p. 4; "A Woman
Lies, Justice Stalls," Feb. 14, p. 4; "Justice and Two Puerto
Rican Boys: A Cop's 'Eyewitness' Hoax," Feb. 15, p. 4; "Two
Puerto Rican Boys in Trouble: A Grand Jury Indicts, A Hoax
Goes On," Feb. 16, p. 4; "The Case of the Puerto Rican Boys:
Justice -- After 159 Days in Jail," Feb. 17, p. 4.

Martin, Joseph, and Santora, Phil. "A Search for the Truth." (Series
of six articles.) New York Daily News, July 7-12, 1958.

Articles about "the pursuit of the elusive truth concerning
the alleged beating" of a New York Correction Officer of
Puerto Rican background by New York Police.

Massimine, Virginia E. Challenges of a Changing Population. New York:
New York University, Center for Human Relations Studies, 1954.
35 pp.

McCready, Fred. "Prejudice, Language Barrier Add to Puerto Rican
Problem" and "Community Council Seeks Way to Ease Lot of Puerto Ricans." Allentown (Pa.) Call, May 2-3, 1958. (Series of
two articles.)

McKeon, John. "The Ortiz Family." Jubilee, June 1953, vol. 1, no. 2,
pp. 22-23.

Sketch of a Puerto Rican family which migrated into the new
community: ". . . it is doubtful whether any immigrant group,
Catholic in culture, tradition and practice, has at any time
in our national history faced the contempt and opprobrium
that has been the average potion meted the Puerto Rican in
his efforts to integrate himself into our society. And far
from welcoming the increase to the Faith. . . the reaction of
the American Catholic laity has to date ranged from one of
stolid indifference to one of outspoken contempt."

Mid-Century Pioneers and Protestants. New York: Protestant Council
of the City of New York, Department of Church Planning and
Research, March 1954 (2nd edition). 29 pp.

A report on the activities of New York City Protestant churches
among Spanish-speaking people.

The Migration Division: Policy, Functions, Objectives. New York:
Commonwealth of Puerto Rico, Department of Labor, Migration
Division, 1957. 6 pp.

A folder briefly describing the work of the Division.

Mills, C. Wright; Senior, Clarence; and Goldsen, Rose Kohn. The
Puerto Rican Journey. New York: Harper, 1950. 238 pp.

A documented study of Puerto Ricans in New York City based
on a scientific survey of 5,000 Puerto Ricans living in
Harlem and in the Morrisania section of the Bronx.

Mirkin, Sidney. Series of six articles on Puerto Ricans in New York.
New York Daily News, Jan. 3-7, 1955.

"The Fact of Puerto Ricans," Jan. 3, pp. 3, 18; "The Puerto
Rican Problem: They Change Here Island Feels," Jan. 4,
pp. 3, 24; "The Puerto Rican Problem: Island Fights for
Better Living," Jan. 5, pp. 3, 30; "Faked Puerto Rican Records
Let in Cons," Jan. 6, pp. 3, 30; "Islanders' Work, Confidence
Help Allay New York Doubt," Jan. 6, p. 30; "Some Puerto Ricans
Feel Political Oats," Jan. 7, pp. 3, 34.

Monserrat, José. "La Emigración: Realidad y Problema en la Ciudad
de Nueva York." La Torre (Universidad de Puerto Rico), enero-
marzo de 1956, año 4, núm. 13, págs. 73-96.

Monserrat, Joseph. Background and General Information on Puerto Rico
and the Puerto Rican Migrant. New York: Commonwealth of
Puerto Rico, Department of Labor, Migration Division, n.d.
9 pp.

Monserrat, Joseph. Migration Division, Department of Labor of
Puerto Rico: Philosophy and Function. New York: Commonwealth of Puerto Rico, Department of Labor, Migration Division,
n.d. 4 pp.

Montag, Jenny, and Finocchiaro, Mary. "Guidance and Curriculum for
Puerto Rican Children." High Points (New York City Board
of Education), Jan. 1951, pp. 34-42.

Montross, Harold K. "Meeting the Needs of the Puerto Rican Migrant,"
Employment Security Review, Jan. 1959, vol. 26, no. 1,
pp. 31-33.

Morrison, J. Cayce. A Letter to Friends of Puerto Rican Children.
New York: The Puerto Rican Study of the New York City Board
of Education, 1955. 8 pp.

Morrison, J. Cayce. "The Puerto Rican Study: What It Is, Where It
Is Going." Journal of Educational Sociology, Dec. 1954,
vol. 28, no. 4, pp. 167-173.

A preliminary account of the Ford Foundation study in the
New York City public schools.

Muñoz Marín, Luis. Un Mensaje a las Comunidades Puertorriqueñas
del Continente. Nueva York: Estado Libre Asociado de
Puerto Rico, Departamento del Trabajo, División de Migración,
25 de julio de 1953. 8 págs.

Murra, Elizabeth. "Learning a Second Language." Journal of Educational Sociology, Dec. 1954, vol. 28, no. 4, pp. 181-192.

Differences between age-groups in approach to learning a
new language, reported by a perceptive preschool teacher.

No Tiene que Ser Mago para Asegurar Su Futuro. Nueva York: Estado
Libre Asociado de Puerto Rico, Departamento del Trabajo,
División de Migración, 1957. Edición de Nueva York, 8 págs.
Fuera de Nueva York, 4 págs.

Educational campaign folder.

Novak, Robert T. "Distribution of Puerto Ricans on Manhattan Island."
Geographical Review, April 1956, vol. 46, no. 2, pp. 182-186.

Nueva York y Usted. Nueva York: Estado Libre Asociado de Puerto Rico,
Departamento del Trabajo, División de Migración, 1957. 64 págs.
(Out of print.)

A guide to living in New York -- including transportation,
legal aid, climate, clothing, employment, churches, public
libraries, education, taxes, veterans' rights, etc. Subway
map attached.

O'Brien, Robert W. Cleveland Puerto Rican Survey Tabulations.
Cleveland: Nationalities Services Center of Cleveland and
Ohio Wesleyan University, Sociology Department, 1954.

Preliminary data from a survey similar to the author's Lorain
study (below).

O'Brien, Robert W. A Survey of the Puerto Ricans in Lorain, Ohio.
Lorain: Neighborhood House Association of Lorain, 1954.
85 pp.

Number, distribution, origin in Puerto Rico, time of arrival,
attitudes, etc.

Occupations of Puerto Ricans in New York City. Special Labor News
Memo No. 50. New York: New York State Department of Labor,
Division of Research and Statistics, June 17, 1954. 10 pp.

First- and second-generation Puerto Ricans in New York City
compared with the general population in corresponding age groups.

O'Gara, James. "Strangers in the City." Commonweal, Oct. 10, 1952,
        vol. 57, no. 1, pp. 7-9.

    Discusses the problems of Puerto Ricans in general terms

One in Twenty: The Facts About the Puerto Ricans Among Us and What
        the Boys Athletic League is Doing About It. New York:
        Boys Athletic League, circa 1956. 15 pp.

"Operation Breadbasket." Great Silver Fleet News (Eastern Airlines),
        Sept.-Oct. 1955, vol. 19, no. 5, pp. 6-10.

    About the world's largest labor airlift which has harvested
    crops worth over $120,000,000 annually in New Jersey and other
    Eastern States in recent years.

Opler, Marvin K. "The Influence of Ethnic and Class Subcultures on
        Child Care." Social Problems, July 1955, vol. 3, no. 1,
        pp. 12-21.

    Includes a very brief discussion on Puerto Ricans in New York
    City.

Our Changing Community. New York: Community Council of Greater New
        York, 1957, 45 pp.

    Report on a forum dealing with important changes in New York
    City's population and their significance for health and
    welfare organizations. Harry L. Shapiro, Stanley P. Davies,
    Lawrence M. Orton, Clarence Senior, Buel G. Gallagher,
    Frank S. Horne, Roscoe P. Kandle, Ralph W. Whelan, and
    J. Donald Kingsley participating.

Padilla, Elena. Up From Puerto Rico. New York: Columbia University
        Press, 1958. 317 pp.

    An anthropological survey of Puerto Ricans living in a section
    of East Harlem. Care must be taken not to generalize about
    all persons of Puerto Rican origin on the basis of the
    experiences reported for those living in this particular
    slum subculture.

Paul, Irven. "Migrants and Culture Change." Hartford Seminary Founda-
        tion Bulletin, Winter 1955-56, no. 21, pp. 24-27.

    Based on experiences with farm workers near Erie, Penna.

Phrases with Spanish Equivalents for Use in Schools: An Aid for
        Teachers of Children of Puerto Rican Background. New York:
        New York City Board of Education, June 28, 1954. 13 pp.

¿Piensa Vivir en los Estados Unidos? Nueva York: Estado Libre
Asociado de Puerto Rico, Departamento del Trabajo, División de Migración, 1955.

A continuing series of orientation folders for migrants,
distributed in Puerto Rico and the U.S. The series includes
such topics as preparing for a good job, where to look for
work, drivers' licenses, documents, etc.

Population Changes in New York City. New York: New York City Department of City Planning, Nov. 22, 1954. 6 pp.

Probabilities concerning age, sex, ethnic, religious, and
racial backgrounds -- for the purpose of planning government
services.

Population of Puerto Rican Birth or Parentage, New York City, 1950.
New York: Welfare and Health Council of New York City,
Research Bureau, Sept. 1952. 57 pp.

Special tabulations of the 1950 Census, reporting Puerto Rican
population of New York City by census tracts and health areas.

Probst, Nathan and Olmsted, Sophia A. "The Rising Puerto Rican Problem."
Bar Bulletin (New York County Lawyers Association), March 1952,
pp. 5-12.

A Program of Education for Puerto Ricans in New York City. A report
prepared by a committee of the Association of Assistant
Superintendents. New York: New York City Board of Education,
1947. 107 pp.

(1) Backgrounds; (2) Migration to the mainland; (3) Problems
of assimilation; (4) The education of the Puerto Rican
pupil; (5) Recommendations.

Puerto Rican Children: Some Aspects of Their Needs and Related
Services. New York: New York City Welfare Council, 1949.
7 pp.

Report of a committee to study the needs of Puerto Rican
children in New York City.

Puerto Rican Employment in New York City Hotels. New York: New York
State Commission Against Discrimination, Oct. 1958, 9 pp.

Puerto Rican Farm Workers in Florida. Washington, D. C.: U.S. Department of Labor, Bureau of Employment S curity, Feb. 1955. 7 pp.

Puerto Rican Farm Workers in the Middle Atlantic States. Washington,
     D. C.: U.S. Department of Labor, Bureau of Employment
     Security, Nov. 1954. 11 pp.

"Puerto Ricans Key Source of Labor." Highlights (New York City
     Department of Commerce and Public Events), Oct. 1956, vol. 1,
     no. 8, pp. 1, 3

"Puerto Rican Migrants Jam New York." Life, Aug. 25, 1947, pp. 25-29.

Puerto Rican Migration to New York City. New York: New York City
     Department of City Planning, Feb. 1957. 9 pp.

Puerto Rican Neighbors. New York: National Council of the Episcopal
     Church, 1958. 24 pp.

Puerto Ricans Filling Manpower Gap. Washington, D. C.: Office of
     the Government of Puerto Rico, 1951. 14 pp. (Out of print.)

     Reprint of a series of six articles by Erwin Crewe Rosenau
     in the Gary Post Tribune, June 7-12, 1948, on a group of
     Puerto Rican workers who were recruited on the island to
     fill a vital manpower shortage in Gary, Ind. Also contains
     reprints from other newspapers which reflect the views of
     the established community on their Puerto Rican neighbors.

Puerto Rican Pupils in New York City Schools. New York: Mayor's
     Committee on Puerto Rican Affairs, 1951.

     A survey of elementary and junior high schools by the Sub-
     committee on Education, Recreation and Parks of the Mayor's
     Advisory Committee on Puerto Rican Affairs in New York City.

"Puerto Ricans in New York City." Geographical Review, Jan. 1954,
     vol. 44, pp. 143-144.

Puerto Ricans in New York City. Report of the Committee on Puerto
     Ricans in New York City of the Welfare Council of New York
     City. New York: Welfare Council, 1948. 60 pp.

     (1) Size and location of the Puerto Rican population;
     (2) problems of neighborhood groups of Puerto Rican citizens;
     (3) education, employment, and health; (4) use of Spanish-
     speaking personnel in social agencies; (5) migration and
     resettlement; (6) recommendations.

Puerto Ricans in New York City. New York: Welfare and Health Council
     of New York City, April 1953. 4 pp.

"Puerto Ricans in the New York State Labor Market." Industrial
        Bulletin. (New York State Department of Labor), August 1957,
        vol. 36, no. 8, pp. 17-19.

        (Reprints available from the Commonwealth of Puerto Rico,
        Department of Labor, Migration Division.)

The Puerto Ricans of New York City. Washington, D. C.: Office of
        the Government of Puerto Rico, 1948. 102 pp. (Out of print.)

THE PUERTO RICAN STUDY

(Studies made by the Puerto Rican Study of the New York City Board
of Education under a special research grant from the Fund for the
Advancement of Education of the Ford Foundation.)

PRINTED REPORTS

Goodman, Samuel M.; Diamond, Lorraine K.; Fox, David J. Who Are the
        Puerto Rican Pupils in the New York City Public Schools?
        1956. 88 pp.

A Guide to the Teaching of English to Puerto Rican Pupils (Inter-
        mediate Grades). 1956. 153 pp.

A Guide to the Teaching of English to Puerto Rican Pupils in the
        Junior High Schools. 1955. 134 pp.

A Guide to the Teaching of Science to Puerto Rican Pupils in
        Junior High Schools -- Experimental Edition. 1956. 95 pp.

Morrison, J. Cayce. A Letter to Friends of Puerto Rican Children.
        1955. 8 pp.

Resource Units for Classes with Puerto Rican Pupils in the First
        Grade. 1955. 145 pp.

Resource Units for Classes with Puerto Rican Pupils in the Second
        Grade. 1956. 119 pp.

Resource Units for Classes with Puerto Rican Pupils in the Fourth
        Grade. 1955. 143 pp.

Resource Units for Classes with Puerto Rican Pupils in the Fifth
     Grade. 1956. 175 pp.

Resource Units Suggested for Use in Seventh Grade Classes with
     Puerto Rican Pupils. 1955. 95 pp.

Resource Units in the Teaching of Occupations -- An Experiment in
     Guidance of Puerto Rican Teen Agers. 1956. 149 pp.

Resource Units for Classes with Puerto Rican Pupils: Secondary
     Schools -- Orientation Stage. 1957. 117 pp.

Sample Lessons for Teaching Science to Puerto Rican Pupils in the
     Junior High School -- Experimental Edition. 1956. 79 pp.

Teaching English to Puerto Rican Pupils in Grades 1 and 2. 1956.
     183 pp.

MIMEOGRAPHED OR HECTOGRAPHED REPORTS

Capodiferro, Clelia. Developmental Reading Project. 1957. 18 pp.

Colón, Jesús de. The Pilot Guidance Project for Tenth-Grade Puerto
     Rican Pupils at the High School of Commerce. 1955. 18 pp.

Colón, Jesús M., and Miranda, Belmira. Helping Transitional-Stage
     Pupils in the Subject Class. 1956. 4 pp.

Colón, Jesús M., and Miranda, Belmira. Project for Transitional-
     Stage Puerto Rican Pupils in the High School: Pupil
     Descriptive Data. 1956. 27 pp.

Goodman, Samuel M. Who Were the Teachers in the Puerto Rican Study
     Experimental Schools in 1953-54? -- A Survey of Teacher Back-
     ground, Attitudes and Practices. 1955. 27 pp.

Hochhauser, Aidalina. A Pilot Study of "Problem Children" of Puerto
     Rican Background. 1956. 16 pp.

Kavetsky, Joseph. A Survey of Practice in the Teaching of English
     to Puerto Rican Pupils -- School Year 1954-55. 1956. 27 pp.

Langdale, A. Barnett. Teaching Reading to the Pupils of Puerto Rican
     Background. 1957. 61 pp.

Low, Frances. School - Puerto Rican Parent Relations, 1955-56.
     1957. 61 pp.

Rigney, Margaret C. Practices and Procedures Used by Teachers in Furthering Second Language Learning in the Primary Grades. 1956. 13 pp.

Rigney, Margaret C. Puerto Rican Children as Second Language Learners. 1956. 98 pp.

Rodríguez, María Luisa. Follow-up Study of the Graduating Classes of Two Junior High Schools. 1955. 34 pp.

Theobald, Jacob. The Orientation and Adjustment of New Pupils. 1955. 45 pp.

Wacher, Sara A. Home and School Relations in New York City as Seen by Puerto Rican Children and Parents. 1955. 27 pp.

THE FOLLOWING PUBLICATIONS WERE IN PRESS AT THE TIME THIS BIBLIOGRAPHY WAS COMPILED. THE PAGE NUMBERS GIVEN ARE APPROXIMATE.

A Doorway to Science. 1958. 90 pp.

Resource Units for Pupils of Puerto Rican Background in the "Extended Orientation Stage" in Junior High Schools. 1958. 40 pp.

Resource Units for Classes with Puerto Rican Pupils : Secondary Schools -- Transition Stage. 1958. 123 pp.

Resource Units for Classes with Puerto Rican Pupils in the Third Grade. 1958. 150 pp.

Resource Units for Classes with Puerto Rican Pupils in the Sixth Grade. 1958. 150 pp.

Teaching English to Puerto Rican Pupils in Grades 3 and 4. 1958. 196 pp.

Tests and Testing. 1958.

Rand, Christopher. The Puerto Ricans, New York: Oxford University Press, 1958. 178 pp.

An expanded account of the material covered in the author's New Yorker series (see following entry).

Rand, Christopher. "A Reporter at Large: The Puerto Ricans."
The New Yorker, Nov. 30 - Dec. 21, 1957. (Series of four
articles.)

Includes: "El Barrio de Nueva York," Nov. 30, pp. 57-93;
"Down on the Island," Dec. 7, pp. 105-137; "Among the
Cold People," Dec. 14, pp. 93-131; and "Joining the Stream,"
Dec. 21, pp. 56-78. An informative and often insightful
account of Puerto Ricans in New York, somewhat weakened by
a tendency to cite the exception rather than the rule and
to emphasize "picturesqueness" at the expense of deeper
understanding. The article on the island is excellent.

Raushenbush, Carl. "A Comparison of the Occupations of First and
Second Generation Puerto Ricans in the Mainland Labor Market
and How the Work of the New York State Department of Labor
Affects Puerto Ricans," pp. 56-61. In: A. J. Jaffe (ed.).
Puerto Rican Population of New York City. New York: Columbia
University, Bureau of Applied Social Research, Jan. 1954.
61 pp.

Raushensbush, Winifred. "New York and the Puerto Ricans." Harper's,
May 1953, vol. 206, no. 1236, pp. 78-83.

Report on Survey of Brooklyn Agencies Rendering Services to Puerto
Ricans. New York: Brooklyn Council for Social Planning,
June 1953. 23 pp.

Report of the Third Migration Conference Between New York City and
Puerto Rican Officials: 1958. New York: Commonwealth of
Puerto Rico, Department of Labor, Migration Division, 1958.
12 pp

Rigau, Angel. "Un Estudio Puertorriqueño." La Prensa de Nueva York,
April 3-10, 1956.

Eight articles reporting on the Puerto Rican Study of the
New York City Board of Education.

Rigney, Margaret G. Practices and Procedures Used by Teachers in
Furthering Second Language Learning in the Primary Grades.
New York: The Puerto Rican Study of the New York City
Board of Education, 1956. 13 pp.

Rigney, Margaret G. Puerto Rican Children as Second Language Learners.
New York: The Puerto Rican Study of the New York City Board
of Education, 1956. 98 pp.

Rizzo Costa, Clara, and Robinett, Betty Wallace. La Familia Vázquez en los Estados Unidos. San Juan: Estado Libre Asociado de Puerto Rico, Departamento de Instrucción Pública, 1955.

Forty lessons in practical English for people who are thinking of moving to the U.S. English expressions are translated into "the Spanish currently used in conversation in Puerto Rico."

Robison, Sophia. Can Delinquency Be Measured? New York: Columbia University Press, 1936. See esp. pp. 236-249.

Treatment of an earlier group of Puerto Rican children than that covered by Schepses (listed below). Illustrative of fundamental considerations in this field of research and social action.

Robison, Sophia M. "Social and Welfare Statistics on the New York Puerto Rican Population," pp. 45-55. In: A. J. Jaffe (ed.). Puerto Rican Population of New York City. New York: Columbia University, Bureau of Applied Social Research, Jan. 1954. 61 pp.

Data on dependency, housing, school attendance, juvenile delinquency, and attitudes toward living in New York City.

Rodríguez, María Luisa. Follow-up Study of the Graduating Classes of Two Junior High Schools. New York: The Puerto Rican Study of the New York City Board of Education, 1955. 34 pp.

Román, Josefina de. "New York's Latin Quarter." The Inter-American, Jan. 1946, vol. 1, no. 1, pp. 9-13, 36-37.

Puerto Ricans in Harlem as seen by a Puerto Rican Journalist.

Rosario, Charles. "La Emigración Como Experiencia Vital." La Torre (Universidad de Puerto Rico), enero-marzo de 1956, año 4, núm. 13, págs. 23-31.

Ruiz, Paquita. Vocational Needs of Puerto Rican Migrants in New York City. Río Piedras: University of Puerto Rico, Social Science Research Center, 1947. 84 pp.

Ruiz, Ruperto, and Present, H. L. Puerto Ricans in the United States. New York: Spanish-American Youth Bureau, June 1946. 13 pp.

Rusk, Howard A. "The Facts Don't Rhyme: An Analysis of Irony in Lyrics Linking Puerto Rico's Breezes to Tropic Diseases." New York Times, Sept. 29, 1957. (Reprints available from the Migration Division.)

The Times' medical editor examines the health situation in Puerto Rico and concludes that the lyrics "island of tropical breezes . . . island of tropic diseases" in the Broadway musical "West Side Story" are not based on fact.

Salisbury, Harrison. The Shook-Up Generation. New York: Harper, 1958. 256 pp.

An expanded version of an excellent series of articles that appeared in the New York Times, March 24-30, 1958, by a Pulitzer Prize-winning journalist. The author discusses inadequate housing, civic neglect, the failures of education, and parental indifference as causal factors in juvenile delinquency of all ethnic groups. The Puerto Ricans are viewed as presenting no unique problems.

Samuels, Gertrude. "Plans to Salvage the 'Problem Family.'" New York Times Magazine, May 12, 1957.

Samuels, Gertrude. "Puerto Rico: Land of Paradox; Thousands Leave for Lack of Opportunities, Yet It Is Potentially an 'Island of Hope.'" New York Times Magazine, Oct. 30, 1955, pp. 18, 62, 64, 67.

Samuels, Gertrude. "Rebirth of a Community." New York Times Magazine, Sept. 25, 1955, pp. 26, 37-39, 42, 44.

·How Morningside Heights went about rebuilding a blighted area without causing undue hardship to those being uprooted. An example of humane slum relocation.

Samuels, Gertrude. "Two Case Histories out of Puerto Rico." New York Times Magazine, Jan. 22, 1956.

"San Juan Day: Mainland Puerto Ricans Honor Their Patron Saint." Jubilee, Sept. 1946, pp. 48-51.

Illustrated report on the celebration of the feast of San Juan Bautista in New York City, Chicago, and Philadelphia, June 24, 1956.

Sanua, Victor D.; Diller, Leonard; Loomer, Alice; and McCavitt, Martin E. The Vocational Rehabilitation Problems of Disabled Puerto Ricans in New York City. New York: New York University - Bellevue Medical Center, Institute of Physical Medicine and Rehabilitation, 1957. 69 pp.

A valuable examination of popular conceptions (and misconceptions) about reactions to pain, educability, ambition, etc.

Sayers, Raymond S. "New York Teachers in Puerto Rican Schools."
High Points (New York City Board of Education), Nov. 1957,
vol. 39, no. 8, pp. 5-16.

An account of the author's experiences in Puerto Rico as a
participant in the Puerto Rico Department of Education's
teacher-exchange program. (Reprints available from the
Migration Division.)

Schepses, Edwin. "Puerto Rican Delinquent Boys in New York City."
Social Service Review (University of Chicago), March 1949,
vol. 23, no. 1, pp. 51-56.

An examination of statistics and a comparison with other
groups, showing Puerto Ricans little "out of line."

Scotfield, John R. Within These Borders: Spanish-speaking Peoples
in the U.S.A. New York: Friendship Press, 1953. 151 pp.

Selected References on Migratory Workers and Their Families: Problems
and Programs, 1950-56. Washington, D. C.: U.S. Department
of Labor, Bureau of Labor Standards, April 1956. 16 pp.

Selected References for Teachers of Non-English Speaking Children.
New York: New York City Board of Education, Division of
Instructional Research, Bureau of Reference, Research and
Statistics, n.d. 5 pp.

Senior, Clarence. Background Data for Discussion on the Changing
City Scene. New York: Commonwealth of Puerto Rico,
Department of Labor, Migration Division, 1957. 10 pp.

Senior, Clarence. Dispersion of Puerto Rican Migration. Speech
Delivered at Annual Conference of Welfare and Health Council
of New York City, May 7, 1953. New York: Commonwealth of
Puerto Rico, Department of Labor, Migration Division, 1953.
6 pp.

Senior, Clarence. Implications of Population Redistribution. New
York: National Association of Intergroup Relations Officials,
1957. 19 pp.

Senior, Clarence. "Migrants: People, Not Problems," pp. 371-375.
In: Transactions of the Fiftieth Anniversary Meeting of the
National Tuberculosis Association, 1954.

Senior, Clarence. "Migration and Economic Development in Puerto Rico."
Journal of Educational Sociology, Dec. 1954, vol. 28, no. 4,
pp. 151-156.

Senior, Clarence. "Migration and Puerto Rico's Population Problem."
Annals of the American Academy of Political and Social Science,
Jan. 1953, vol. 285, pp. 130-136.

Contains a table of annual migration as a percentage of
natural increase, 1942-1951.

Senior, Clarence. "Puerto Rican Dispersion in the United States."
Social Problems, Oct. 1954, vol. 2, no. 2, pp. 93-99.

Senior, Clarence. Puerto Rican Emigration. Río Piedras: University
of Puerto Rico, Social Science Research Center, 1947. 166 pp.

Previous experience and future possibilities.

Senior, Clarence. The Puerto Rican Migrant in St. Croix. Río Piedras:
University of Puerto Rico, Social Science Research Center,
1947.

Senior, Clarence. Puerto Rican Migration: Spontaneous and Organized.
Commonwealth of Puerto Rico, Department of Labor, Migration
Division, 1957. 14 pp.

Senior, Clarence. "The Puerto Ricans in the United States." pp. 109-125.
In: Joseph B. Gittler (ed.). Understanding Minority Groups.
New York: John Wiley. 1956. 139 pp.

Senior, Clarence. The Puerto Ricans of New York City. Washington, D. C.:
Office of the Government of Puerto Rico, 1948. 102 pp.

(1) The island of Puerto Rico; (2) metropolis, panorama
of contrasts; (3) the city of migration; (4) the new world
of the Puerto Rican; (5) Appendix, "Welfare Facilities in
Puerto Rico," by Carmen Isales.

Senior, Clarence. "Puerto Rico: Migration to the Mainland." Monthly
Labor Review, Dec. 1955, vol. 78, no. 12, pp. 1354-1358.

Senior, Clarence. "Research on the Puerto Rican Family in the United
States." Marriage and Family Living, Feb. 1, 1957, vol. 19,
no. 1, pp. 32-38.

Senior, Clarence. "The Sociological Approach to Assimilation."
(Excerpts from a Speech at the Fiftieth Anniversary Meeting
of the National Tuberculosis Association, 1954.) Population
Bulletin, vol. 23, no. 2, pp. 30-31.

Senior, Clarence. Speech Problems of Puerto Rican Children. (Report
of the Committee on Individualization of Speech Improvement.)
New York: New York City Board of Education, Department of
Speech Improvement, n.d. 15 pp.

Senior, Clarence. Strangers -- and Neighbors: The Story of Our
    Puerto Rican Citizens. New York: Anti-Defamation League
    of B'nai B'rith, 1952. 53 pp.

Shotwell, Louisa Rossiter. "Puerto Rican Migrant Workers Plunge
    Eagerly into Study of English." Reprint from Christian Science
    Monitor, New York, 1952. 2 pp.

Shotwell, Louisa Rossiter. "Puerto Rican Neighbors." Presbyterian
    Tribune, Sept. 1953, vol. 68, no. 11, pp. 1-3.

Shotwell, Louisa Rossiter. This is the Migrant. New York: Friendship
    Press, 1958. 24 pp.

Siegel, Arthur; Orlans, Harold; and Greer, Loyal. Puerto Ricans
    in Philadelphia: A Study of Their Demographic Characteristics,
    Problems, and Attitudes. Philadelphia: Philadelphia
    Commission on Human Relations, April 1954. 135 pp.

    One of the few scientific surveys made concerning the Puerto
    Rican migrant living outside New York City.

Sierra Berdecía, Fernando. A la Tierra que Fueres Haz Lo Que Vieres.
    San Juan: Estado Libre Asociado de Puerto Rico, Departamento
    del Trabajo, mayo de 1955. 4 págs.

Sierra Berdecía, Fernando. La Emigración Puertorriqueña: Realidad y
    Política Pública. San Juan: Estado Libre Asociado de Puerto
    Rico, Editorial del Departamento de Instrucción Pública, 1956.
    23 págs. Also published in La Torre (Universidad de Puerto Rico),
    enero-marzo de 1956, año 4, núm. 13, págs. 33-54.

Sierra Berdecía, Fernando. Puerto Rican Migration: Reality and Public
    Policy. San Juan: Commonwealth of Puerto Rico, Department of
    Labor, Office of Industrial, Labor and Public Relations, 1956.
    23 pp.

    Paper read on December 10, 1955, at the Ninth Convention on
    Social Orientation, University of Puerto Rico. English version
    of preceding entry.

Sierra Berdecía, Fernando. Un Mensaje del Secretario del Trabajo a
    los Obréros que Desean Ir a Trabajar en Fincas de los Estados
    Unidos. Nueva York: Estado Libre Asociado de Puerto Rico,
    Departamento del Trabajo, División de Migración, 1957. 21 págs.

    Orientation booklet for Puerto Rican seasonal farm workers in
    the U.S.

Siga Estos Pasos . . . . Nueva York: Estado Libre Asociado de Puerto
   Rico, Departamento del Trabajo, División de Migración, 1958.
   10 págs.

   One of a series of leaflets for the Division's annual "Learn
   English and a Trade" campaign.

"Sounds of English Difficult for Spanish-Speaking Children." (Phono-
   graph record.) New York: New York City Board of Education,
   Bureau for Speech Improvement, Recording Committee. No. XTV 21389.

Speech Problems of Puerto Rican Children. Report of the Committee on
   Individualization of Speech Improvement. New York: New York
   City Board of Education, Department of Speech Improvement,
   n.d. 15 pp.

Spiritual Care of Puerto Rican Migrants: Report on a Conference.
   New York: Archdiocese of New York, Office of the Coordinator
   of Spanish-American Catholic Action, 1955. 228 pp.

   The conference was held in Puerto Rico with an attendance of
   priests from most of the major centers of Puerto Rican
   population in the continental United States.

The Status of the Public School Education of Negro and Puerto Rican
   Children in New York City. New York: Public Education
   Association, assisted by Research Center for Human Relations,
   New York University, Oct. 1955. 24 pp.

· Sternau, Herbert. Puerto Rico and the Puerto Ricans. New York:
   Council of Spanish-American Organizations and American Jewish
   Committee, Feb. 1958. 36 pp.

   An outline of basic facts for speakers, educators, civic and
   religious leaders.

A Summary in Facts and Figures: 1. Progress in Puerto Rico.
   2. Puerto Rican Migration. New York: Commonwealth of
   Puerto Rico, Department of Labor, Migration Division,
   Jan. 1959. 21 pp.

   Basic statistics on Puerto Rico and the migration. New
   editions issued at least once a year.

Talese, Gay. "Hottest Fighter in Town." The New York Times Magazine,
Nov. 30, 1958, pp. 80, 82, 84.

The story of José Torres, middleweight prize-fighter who wants
to be the first Puerto Rican to hold a world's championship
since Sixto Escobar.

Tannenbaum, Dora; McCaulley, Sara; and Carpenter, H. Daniel.
The Puerto Rican Migration: A Report. New York: Hudson
Guild Neighborhood House, Colony House, and Grand Street
Settlement, 1955. 13 pp.

See criticism in Citizens' Housing News (Citizens' Housing
and Planning Council of New York), Feb. 1956, vol. 14, no. 6,
p. 3, "Another Point of View: The Puerto Rican Migration"
by Clarence Senior.

Teaching Children of Puerto Rican Background in New York City Schools:
Suggested Plans and Procedures. New York: New York City
Board of Education, Division of Elementary Schools, Junior
High Schools and Curriculum Development, 1954. 76 pp.

Tentative Report of the Committee on Classification. Bulletin No. 1.
New York: New York City Board of Education, Bilingual
Committee of the Junior High School Division, June 1949. 12 pp.

Contains questionnaires for newly-arrived pupils and a
bibliography for teachers.

"Thank Heaven for Puerto Rico." (An Editorial.) Life, March 15, 1954.

The shooting in Congress by four members of the Nationalist
Party prompted this editorial which looks closely at Puerto
Rico's progress and relations with the U.S.

Theobald, Jacob. The Orientation and Adjustment of New Pupils.
New York: The Puerto Rican Study of the New York City Board
of Education, 1955. 45 pp.

Tió, Salvador. "La Emigración: Cambios Sugeridos en la Política
Pública." La Torre (Universidad de Puerto Rico), enero-
marzo de 1956, año 4, núm. 13, págs. 113-136.

Torruellas, Luz M. "La Emigración: Impacto Sobre la Estructura
Económica y Social de Puerto Rico." La Torre (Universidad
de Puerto Rico), enero-marzo de 1956, año 4, núm. 13,
págs. 55-72.

Tough, Rosalind, and MacDonald, Gordon D. "Manhattan's Real Property Values and the Migrant Puerto Ricans." Land Economics: A Quarterly Journal of Planning, Housing and Public Utilities (University of Wisconsin), Feb. 1958, vol. 34, no. 1, pp. 1-18.

Trabajadores Agrícolas de Puerto Rico: Bienvenidos a Pennsylvania, U.S.A. (Puerto Rican Farm Workers: Welcome to Pennsylvania, U.S.A.) Harrisburg: Pennsylvania Bureau of Employment Security, 1957, 45 pp.

An orientation booklet, in Spanish and English, for seasonal farm workers

Trade Unions and Puerto Rican Workers: Report on a Conference Held May 17, 1952. New York: Commonwealth of Puerto Rico, Department of Labor, Migration Division, 1952. ?? pp.

A discussion of Puerto Ricans and organized labor with various labor leaders and Puerto Rican government officials participating.

"Unit on Puerto Rico." World Week, Scholastic Magazine, April 28, 1954, vol. 24, no. 12, pp. 9-11.

U.S. Bureau of Census. "Puerto Ricans in Continental United States." U.S. Census of Population: 1950, vol. 4, Special Reports, Part 3. Chapter D. Washington, D. C.: Government Printing Office, 1953. 18 pp.

Data on population, age, sex, occupations, etc. Also available as a separate booklet (Special Report P-E No. 3D) from the G.P.O. and Field Offices of the Department of Commerce.

Use Su Derecho a Votar. Introducción por José Monserrat. Nueva York: Estado Libre Asociado de Puerto Rico, Departamento del Trabajo, División de Migración, 1953. 8 pp.

How and where to register in primaries and general elections. Advantages of being well informed on public issues. One of a series of register-and-vote folders published by the Migration Division.

Villaronga, Mariano. "Program of Education for Puerto Rican Migrants." Journal of Educational Sociology, Dec. 1954, vol. 28, no. 4, pp. 146-150.

Sketch of what is done by the school system in Puerto Rico to help the adjustment process of those who might migrate.

Wacher, Sara A. Home and School Relations in New York City as Seen by Puerto Rican Children and Parents. New York: The Puerto Rican Study of the New York City Board of Education, 1955. 27 pp.

Wakefield, Dan. "The Gang That Went Good." Harper's, June 1958, vol. 216, no. 1297, pp. 36-43.

The material included in this article and in the two following entries will also appear, in somewhat different form and with additional material, in the author's forthcoming book Island in the City: The World of Spanish Harlem, (Boston: Houghton Mifflin, 1959. 278 pp.), scheduled for publication February 12.

Wakefield, Dan. "Politics and the Puerto Ricans." Commentary, March 1958, vol. 25, no. 3, pp. 226-236.

A Puerto Rican journalist makes an unsuccessful bid for a seat on the New York City Council during the elections of 1957.

Wakefield, Dan. "The Vulnerable Stranger." The Nation, April 13, 1957, vol. 184, no. 15, pp. 315-317, 321-322.

Walker, R. C. "I Like Puerto Ricans." Rural New Yorker, August 4, 1956, vol. 106, no. 5865, p. 504.

A Pennsylvania farmer discusses his Puerto Rican workers.

Weiner, Louis. "Vital Statistics in New York City's Puerto Rican Population," pp. 30-44. In: A. J. Jaffe (ed.). Puerto Rican Population of New York City. New York: Columbia University, Bureau of Applied Social Research, Jan. 1954. 61 pp.

Birth and death rates, etc., with some comparisons. Also see pp. 10-13.

Wells, Robert W. "Our Latin Newcomers." The Milwaukee Journal, April 6-9, 1958. (Series of four articles.)

"Housing, Work Woes Plague Migrants Here," April 6, pp. 1, 6; "Puerto Ricans Among First to Be Laid Off," April 7, pp. 1, 3; "Vincentians Increase Aid to Puerto Ricans," April 8, p. 12; "Young Puerto Ricans Able to Adapt Easily," April 9, p. 26.

Werner, M. R. "The Puerto Ricans: Slum to Slum." The Reporter, Sept. 12, 1950, vol. 3, no. 6, pp. 20-22. (First of two articles.)

Werner, M. R. "The Puerto Ricans in New York." The Reporter, Sept. 26, 1950, vol. 3, no. 7, pp. 20-23. (Second of two articles.)

Wertham, Fredric. The Circle of Guilt. New York: Rinehart, 1956. 211 pp.

Psychiatric exploration of a teenage gang killing by a Puerto Rican youth, concluding that the victim was far from being the "model boy" portrayed by the press.

Willoughby, Wes. "Puerto Rican Story." Bethlehem (Penn.) Globe-Times, July 7-12, 1958. (Series of six articles.)

"Labor Rates Make City Major Center of Influx," July 7, pp. 1, 3; "Religion, Male Superiority, Baseball Dominate Living," July 8, pp. 1, 10; "Area Islanders Encounter Less and Less Prejudice," July 9, pp. 1, 13; "Auto Troubles Biggest of All: Betting, Narcotics No Problem," July 10, pp. 1, 8; "Islanders Solidly Democrat, But Clubs Hard to Organize," July 11, pp. 1, 3; "Spanish-Speaking Services Ease Assimilation Problems," July 12, pp. 1, 2.

Woodbury, Clarence. '"Our Worst Slum." The American, Sept. 1949, vol. 148, no. 3, pp. 3, 31, 128, 132.

An exaggerated account of living conditions, crime, and vice in East Harlem, calling the neighborhood a potential breeding ground for communism.

Workshop Conference on Puerto Ricans. New York: Brooklyn Council for Social Planning, Oct. 1953, 24 pp.

Yezierska, Anzia. "The Lower Depths of Upper Broadway." The Reporter, Jan. 19, 1954, vol. 10, no. 2, pp. 26-29.

The author writes of her experiences in a rent-decontrolled building catering to Puerto Ricans and other minority groups.

Your American Pupil From Puerto Rico. New York: Bronx Districts 17 and 18, New York City Board of Education, Sept. 1956. 15 pp.

ADDENDA[*]

Aines, Ronald O. Puerto Rican Farm Workers in New Jersey. New
    Brunswick, N. J.: Rutgers University, Dept. of Agricultural
    Economics, New Jersey Agricultural Experiment Station, Feb.
    1959. A.E. 232. 5 pp.

Barry, David W. "The Puerto Rican Adapts Remarkably." Washington
    Post and Times Herald, March 8, 1959.

"Behind New York's Facade: Slums and Segregation." Look, Feb. 18,
    1958, vol. 22, p. 71.

Bender, Lauretta, and Nichtern, Sol. "Two Puerto Rican Boys in New
    York City," pp. 245-264. In: Georgene Seward (ed.). Clinical
    Studies in Culture Conflict. New York: Ronald Press, 1958.
    598 pp.

¡Bienvenidos a Paterson, Amigos! Paterson, N. J.: Paterson Inter-
    Group Council, 1958. 33 págs.

Bone, Bob. Series of eight articles on Puerto Ricans in Middletown,
    New York. Middletown Daily Record, March 9-13, 16-18.

Breisky, Bill. "Looking for the Promised Land." Saturday Evening
    Post, April 11, 1959, pp. 18-19, 40-41, 44.

Clark, Rosemarie. "New York and the Puerto Rican 'Problem.'" Unesco
    Features, Jan. 12, 1959, no. 322, pp. 4-6.

Clark, Rosemarie. "Nueva York y el 'Problema' Portorriqueño." Pers-
    pectivas de la Unesco, 12 de enero de 1959, núm. 322, págs. 2-4.

    Spanish version of preceding entry.

Directorio de Chicago para Nuevos Vecinos. Chicago: Comisión de Re-
    laciones Humanas y Comité del Alcalde pro Nuevos Residentes, 1959.
    15 págs.

Ecclesine, Margy. "A Puerto Rican Steps Forward." Catholic Digest,
    vol. 23, no. 6, April 1959, pp. 43-46.

"La Escuela Pública Orienta al Emigrante." Educación (Depto. de
    Instrucción de Puerto Rico), año 6, núm. 50, marzo de 1957,
    págs. 2, 8.

    How public schools in Puerto Rico orient the migrant.

---

[*] Covering the period January 1 - April 30, 1959, and earlier publications
just received or noted.

A Guide to the Teaching of Science: For Use with Puerto Rican Pupils
in the Secondary School. New York: The Puerto Rican Study of the
New York City Board of Education, 1957. 173 pp.

Hartford y Usted: Un Guía. Hartford, Conn.: Greater Hartford Council
of Churches, n.d. 17 pp.

A Spanish-language orientation guide to Hartford.

"In-Migrants: Number, Location, and Selected Characteristics." Statistics (Welfare Council of Metropolitan Chicago, Research Dept.),
vol. 23, no. 11-12, Nov.-Dec. 1956, pp. 1-7.

Lee, Robert, and Orr, Clara. Upper Manhattan: A Community Study of
Washington Heights. New York: Protestant Council of the City of
New York, Dept. of Church Planning and Research, June 9, 1954. 20 pp.

Llave a Lorain. Lorain, Ohio: Community Welfare Council, 1953. 20 pp.

An orientation "key" to Lorain.

Malzberg, Benjamin. "Mental Disease Among Puerto Ricans in New York City."
Journal of Nervous and Mental Diseases, March 1956, vol. 123, pp. 263-269.

Malzberg, Benjamin. "Mental Disease Among Puerto Ricans in New York State."
Psychiatric Quarterly, 1948, vol. 22, part 2, pp. 300-308.

Manhattan Communities: Summary Statements of Population Characteristics.
New York: Community Council of Greater New York, Research Dept.,
1955. Ca. 75 pp.

Mannes, Marya. "School Trouble in Harlem." The Reporter, Feb. 5, 1959,
pp. 13-19.

Massolo, Arthur. "Puerto Rico's Muñoz Marín." New York Post, March 10,
1959, p. 10. (Second of a series of six articles.)

In this article, Governor Muñoz comments on Puerto Ricans in New York.

"Migrant Farm Labor in New York." Industrial Bulletin (New York State
Dept. of Labor), vol. 37, no. 6, June 1958, pp. 7-11.

Brief mention of Puerto Ricans.

Monserrat, Joseph. "Some Data on Population Trends in New York City, 'Must'
Information for Its Citizens." Journal of Educational Sociology,
Nov. 1952, vol. 28, no. 3, pp. 108-114.

Morrison, J. Cayce. The Puerto Rican Study, 1953-1957: A Report on
the Education and Adjustment of Puerto Rican Pupils in the Public
Schools of the City of New York. New York: The Puerto Rican
Study of the New York City Board of Education, 1958. 265 pp.

The final report of this four-year study sponsored by the Board of
Education under a grant-in-aid from the Fund for the Advancement of
Education. (For additional publications of this Study, see listing
on pp. 20-22 of this Bibliography.)

The Movement of Population and Public Welfare in New York State: A Report on America's Mobile Labor Force and Its Economic Contributions
and Public Welfare Costs to New York State. Albany: New York State
Dept. of Social Welfare, Dec. 1958. 35 pp.

New York City, 1955-1965: A Report to the Community. New York: Welfare
and Health Council of New York City, 1955. 37 pp.

Notes on Migration and Workers' Attitudes Toward It. (Preliminary Release,
Manpower Resources Project.) Río Piedras: Univ. of Puerto Rico,
Social Science Research Center, n.d. 10 pp.

Opler, Marvin K. "Dilemmas of Two Puerto Rican Men," pp. 223-244. In:
Georgene Seward (ed.) Clinical Studies in Culture Conflict. New
York: Ronald Press, 1958. 598 pp.

Opotowsky, Stan. "Harlem." New York-Post, March 7, 1958, p. M2. (Fifth
of a series of articles.)

Includes some comments on Puerto Ricans living in Harlem.

Orientación al Recién Llegado. Chicago: Chicago Commission on Human Relations, Mayor's Committee on New Residents, n.d. 8 pp.

A folder for newcomers.

Our Children from Puerto Rico: A Report on Their Island Home by the Visiting
Puerto Rican Workshop of 1955. New York: New York City Board of Education, 1957. 72 pp.

Owens, James M. "These Are Puerto Ricans." Hartford Courant, March 15-22,
1959. (Series of eight articles.)

"Newcomers to Hartford Face Many Problems," March 15; "Average Migrant
Found Law-Abiding Citizen," March 16; "Family Ties Strong with Island
Natives," March 17; "Religion Plays a Major Role in Daily Life of
Island People," March 18; "Puerto Ricans Aided Here by Own Dept.,"
March 19; "Friendly Puerto Ricans Welcome U.S. Visitors," March 20;
"450 Children Like School, Learn Quickly," March 21; "Hard Working
Family Asks Only Fair Share," March 22.

"Puerto Rican Number." The Bible in New York (New York Bible Society),
vol. 49, Feb. 1958, pp. 1-8.

Snyder, Eleanor M. Public Assistance Recipients in New York State,
January-February 1957: A Study of the Causes of Dependency During
a Period of High-Level Employment. New York: New York State Inter-
departmental Committee on Low Incomes, October 1958. 159 pp.

Stein, William W. Preliminary Report on Proceedings of the Dade County
Council on Community Relations with Regard to Problems of Latin
American Residents of Greater Miami. Univ. of Miami, July 5, 1958,
7 pp.

Su Guía a New Haven. New Haven, Conn.: New Haven Human Relations Council,
1959. 88 pp.

Urban Renewal. New York: New York City Planning Commission, 1958. 96 pp.

    A report on the West Side Urban Renewal Study, including some data
    on Puerto Rican population.

Wakefield, Dan. Island in the City: The World of Spanish Harlem. Boston:
Houghton Mifflin, 1959. 278 pp.

THE PEOPLE OF PUERTO RICO

A BIBLIOGRAPHY

[Francesco Cordasco]

Abrams, Charles. Forbidden Neighbors. New York:
    Harper, 1955.

Abrams, Charles. "How to Remedy Our 'Puerto Rican
    Problem': Whence it Arose; What to Do." Commentary,
    Feb. 1955, vol. 19, no. 12, pp. 120-127.

Action on the Lower East Side: Progress Report and
    Proposal, July 1962-June 1964. New York:
    Mobilization for Youth, Inc.

Aines, Ronald O. Puerto Rican Farm Workers in New Jersey,
    New Brunswick, N.J.: Rutgers University, Dept. of
    Agricultural Economics, New Jersey Agricultural Experiment
    Station, Feb. 1959. A.E. 232, 5 pp.

Alers-Montalvo, Manuel, The Puerto Rican Migrants of New
    York City: A Study of Anomie, Unpublished Masters'
    thesis, Columbia University. 1951.

Alexander, Robert J. "Stanley Ross and the Battle for New
    York Puerto Ricans." The New Leader, April 14, 1958.

Anastasi, Anne; and Cordova, Fernando A. "Some Effects of
    Bilingualism Upon the Intelligence Test Performance of
    Puerto Rican Children in New York City." Journal of
    Educational Psychology, Jan. 1953, pp. 1-19.

Anastasi, Anne; and Jesús, Cruz de. "Language Development
    and Non-verbal I Q of Puerto Rican Preschool Children
    in New York City." Journal of Abnormal and Social
    Psychology, July 1953, vol. 48, no. 3, pp. 357-366.

Antonovsky, Aaron; and Lewis L. Lorwin, (eds.)Discrimination
    and Low Incomes, New York: State of New York Inter-
    department Committee on Low Income, 1959.

Arán Gasnell, Patria, The Puerto Ricans in New York City.
    Unpublished Master's thesis, New York University,
    1945.

Armstrong, O.K. "When They Shot the Congressmen." Reader's Digest. Nov. 1960, vol. 77, p. 215.

Arter, Rhetta M. Between Two Bridges: A Study of Human Relations in the Lower East Side of Manhattan, the Area Served by the Educational Alliance. Human Relations Monograph No. 5. Interpretation by Dan W. Dodson. New York: New York University, Center for Human Relations Studies, 1953. 32 pp.

Arter, Rhetta M. Living in Chelsea. Human Relations Monograph No. 4, New York: New York University, Center for Human Relations Studies, and the Hudson Guild, 1954. 43 pp.

Arter, Rhetta M. Mid-City. Human Relations Monograph No. 3 New York: New York University, Center for Human Relations Studies, 1953. 32 pp.

Audio-Visual Resources for Use in Classes with Puerto Rican Children in Junior High Schools. New York: New York City Board of Education, Bureau of Audio-Visual Instruction, Dec. 1956. 53 pp.

Babín, María Teresa. "Un Nuevo Plan Educativo en la New York University." La Torre (Universidad de Puerto Rico), abril-junio de 1955, año 3, núm. 10, págs. 141-146.

Back to School for a Thousand Farmers: They Learn the ABC's of the Puerto Rican Labor Program. Trenton: New Jersey Farm Bureau, 1957. 4 pp.

Barry, David W. "Opportunity for Protestant Churches Among Puerto Ricans." National Council Outlook, May 1959, vol. 9, pp. 9-10.

Barry, David W. "The Puerto Rican Adapts Remarkably." Washington Post and Times Herald, March 8, 1959.

Bates, B. "New York and its Puerto Ricans." Survey, Sept. 1949, vol. 85, p. 857.

"Behind New York's Facade: Slums and Segregation." Look, Feb. 18, 1958, vol. 22, p. 71.

Bender, Lauretta, and Nichtern, Sol. "Two Puerto Rican Boys in New York City," pp. 245-264. In: Georgene Seward (ed.). Clinical Studies in Culture Conflict. New York: Ronald Press, 1958, 1958. 598 pp.

Benítez, Jaime. "El Problema Humano de la Emigración." La Torre (Universidad de Puerto Rico), enero-marzo de 1956, año 4, núm. 13, págs. 13-21.

Berger, Josef. Poppo, New York: Simon and Schuster,1962.

Berger, S. "Puerto Rican Migrants Create Housing Problems." Real Estate News, Aug. 1942, vol. 33, no. 8, pp. 265-267.

Berkowitz, Elaine. "Family Attitudes and Practices of Puerto Rican and Non-Puerto Rican Pupils." High Points, March 1961, vol. 43, pp. 25-344.

Berle, A.A., Jr. "How Long Will New York Wait?" The Reporter Sept. 8, 1955, vol. 13, no. 2, pp. 14-18.

Berle, Beatrice Bishop. 80 Puerto Rican Families in New York City: Health and Disease Studied in Context. New York: Columbia University Press, 1958. 331 pp.

Berle, Beatrice Bishop. "Sterilization and Birth Control Practices in a Selected Sample of Puerto Ricans Living in a Manhattan Slum." Fertility and Sterility, May-June 1957, vol. 8, no. 3, pp. 267-281.

¡Bienvenidos a Paterson, Amigos!:Paterson, N.J.: Paterson Inter-group Council, 1958. 33 págs.

Blair, William C. "Spanish-Speaking Minorities in a Utah Mining Town." Journal of Social Issues, 1st Quarter 1952, vol. 8, no. 1, pp. 4-9.

"Bloody Session." Newsweek, March 8, 1954, vol. 43.

Bone, Bob. Series of eight articles on Puerto Ricans in
    Middletown, New York. Middletown Daily Record,
    March 9-13, 16-18, 1959.

"Boricuas No Viven en Arrabales." El Diario de Nueva York,
    12 de enero de 1956, págs. 2, 10.

Boroff, David. "Jews and Puerto Ricans." Congress Weekly
    (American Jewish Congress), April 15, 1957, vol. 24,
    no. 15, pp. 10-13.

Bouquet, Susana. Acculturation of Puerto Rican Children in
    New York and Their Social Attitudes Towards Negroes and
    Whites. Doctoral dissertation, Columbia Univ., 1962.

Braestrup, Peter. "Life Among the Garment Workers." New
    York Herald Tribune. Sept. 29 - Oct. 10, 1958 (Series
    of ten articles).

Braestrup, Peter. "New York's Puerto Ricans." New York
    Herald Tribune, Oct. 16-18, 20, 21, 1957. (Series
    of five articles).

Brameld, T.B.H. The Remaking of a Culture. New York:
    Harper & Brothers, 1959. 478 pp.

Breisky, Bill. "Looking for the Promised Land." Saturday
    Evening Post, April 11, 1959. pp. 18-19, 40-41, 44.

Brown, Myrtle Irene. Changing Maternity Care Patterns in
    Migrant Puerto Ricans, Unpublished Doctoral dissertation,
    New York University, 1961.

Brown, Stuart. "Philadelphia's Puerto Ricans: Language
    Barrier is Chief Source of Problems Faced by Migrants."
    Philadelphia Sunday Bulletin, March 16, 1958, section 2,
    pp. 1, 2.

Bucchioni, Eugene. A Sociological Analysis of the Functioning
    of Elementary Education for Puerto Rican Children in the
    New York City Public Schools. Doctoral dissertation,
    New School for Social Research, 1965.

Bureau of Labor Statistics. Income, Education and Un-
    employment in Neighborhood: New York City. Washington:
    United States Department of Labor, 1963. (Available
    for 35 cities).

Burma, John Harmon. Spanish-Speaking Groups in the United
    States. Durham, N.C.: Duke University Press, 1954.
    214 pp.

Capodiferro, Clelia. Developmental Reading Project. New
    York: The Puerto Rican Study of the New York City
    Board of Education, 1957. 18 pp.

Carleton, R.O. "New Aspects of Puerto Rican Migration."
    New York City Monthly Labor Review, Feb. 1960, vol.
    83, pp. 133-35.

Castan, S. "Victims of Welfare." Look, March 26, 1963, vol.
    27, pp. 68-71.

Castaño, Carlos. "The First 10 Years . . . The Puerto Rican
    Migratory Program." Employment Security Review, March
    1958, vol. 25, no. 3, pp. 31-33.

Cebollero, Pedro Angel. Reactions of Puerto Rican Children
    in New York City to Psychological Tests. San Juan:
    The Puerto Rico School Review, 1936.

"Channel Puerto Rican Migration." Commonweal, Feb. 27, 1948,
    vol. 47, p. 484.

Characteristics of Passengers Who Travelled by Air Between
    Puerto Rico and the United States. San Juan, Puerto
    Rico: Commonwealth of Puerto Rico, Department of Labor,
    Bureau of Labor Statistics, 1956-

Chartock, Sarah K. A Descriptive Study of the Programs
    Undertaken by the Riverside Neighborhood Assembly to
    Further Democratic Integration on the West Side of
    Manhattan. Doctoral dissertation, New York Univ.,
    1957.

Chenault, Lawrence R. The Puerto Rican Migrant in New York
    City. New York: Columbia University Press, 1938. 190
    pp.

Chesterton-Mangle, Maenna. "By Opposing, End Them," pp. 33-41. In: Mabel M. Sheibley (ed.). Accent on Liberty. New York: Friendship Press, 1952. 149 pp.

"Chicago Riot: Venganza." Newsweek, June 1966, vol. 67, p. 23.

"Chicago's Puerto Ricans." New Republic, Feb. 22, 1954, vol. 130, pp. 3-4.

Child, Irvin L., Italian or American - The Second Generation in Conflict. Yale University Press, 1943.

Clark, Blake. "New York's Puerto Rican Problem." Reader's Digest, Feb. 1953, vol. 62, no. 370, pp. 61-65.

Clark, Rosemarie. "Nueva York y el 'Problema' Puertorriqueño." Perspectivas de la UNESCO, 12 de enero de 1959, núm. 322, págs. 2-4.

Clark, Rosemarie. "New York and the Puerto Rican 'Problem'." UNESCO Features, Jan. 12, 1959, no. 322, pp. 4-6.

Collazo, Francisco. The Education of Puerto Rican Children in the Schools of New York City. San Juan: Commonwealth of Puerto Rico, Department of Education, 1954. 14 pp.

Coleman, James S. Community Conflict, Glencoe, Ill., Free Press, 1957.

Colón, Jesús de. A Puerto Rican in New York and Other Sketches. New York: Mainstream Publishers, 1961.

Colón, Jesús de. The Pilot Guidance Project for Tenth-Grade Puerto Rican Pupils at the High School of Commerce. The Puerto Rican Study of the New York City Board of Education, 1955. 18 pp.

Colón, Jesšu M. and Miranda, Belmira. Helping Transitional-Stage Pupils in the Subject Class. New York: The Puerto Rican Study of the New York City Board of Education, 1956. 4 pp.

Colón, Jesús M. and Miranda, Belmira. Project for Transitional-Stage Puerto Rican Pupils in the High School: Pupil Descriptive Data. New York: The Puerto Rican Study of the New York City Board of Education, 1956. 27 pp.

Colón, Petroamérica Pagán de. Emotional Adjustment Problems of the Puerto Rican Migrant. New York: Commonwealth of Puerto Rico, Department of Labor, Migration Division, n.d. 11 pp.

Colón, Petroamérica Pagán de. Migration Trends. New York: Migration Division, Department of Labor, Commonwealth of Puerto Rico, 1959. 15 pp.

Colón, Petroamérica Pagán de. Northeastern Ohio and the Puerto Rican Migration. New York: Commonwealth of Puerto Rico, Department of Labor, Migration Division, 1955. 11 pp.

Colón, Petroamérica Pagán de. Programa de Colocaciones de Trabajadores Agrícolas Puertorriqueños en Estados Unidos. San Juan: Estado Libre Asociado de Puerto Rico, Departamento del Trabajo, n.d. 50 pp.

Commission on Race and Housing. Where Shall We Live? Berkeley and Los Angeles: Univ. of California Press, 1958. 77 pp.

Complaints Alleging Discrimination Because of Puerto Rican National Origin: July 1, 1945--September 1, 1958. New York: New York State Commission Against Discrimination, 1958. 13 pp.

Conclusion of Migration Conference, Held in San Juan, Puerto Rico, March 1-7, 1953, Under the Auspices of the Commonwealth of Puerto Rico, Department of Labor. New York: Commonwealth of Puerto Rico, Department of Labor, Migration Division, 1953. 15 pp.

Consumer Analysis of the New York Spanish Market. New York: El Diario de Nueva York, 1953. 24 pp.

Cooke, W. Henry. Peoples of the Southwest: Patterns of Freedom and Prejudice. New York: ADL, 1951, 36 pp.

Cordasco, Frank. "Florence Nightingale in the Ghetto: Patricia Sexton's East Harlem." Journal of Human Relations, 4th Quarter, 1965, pp. 572-74.

Cordasco, Frank. "Helping the Language Barrier Student." The Instructor, May, 1963, vol. 72, p. 20.

Cordasco, Frank. "Hudson County (New Jersey) Schools Serve Spanish Speaking Students." New Jersey Education Review, Nov. 1962, pp. 63-64.

Cordasco, Frank. "Nights in the Gardens of East Harlem: Patricia Sexton's East Harlem." Journal of Negro Education, Fall, 1965, vol. 34, pp. 450-51.

Cordasco, Frank. "The Puerto Rican Child." New Jersey Education Review, Dec. 1965, pp. 245-46.

Cordasco, Frank. "The Puerto Rican Child in the American School." American Sociological Association Abstract of Papers, 61st Annual Meeting, pp. 23-24.

Cordasco, Frank. "The Puerto Rican Child in the American School." Congressional Record, October 19, 1965, vol. 111, pp. 26424-26.

Cordasco, Frank. "The Puerto Rican Child in the American School." Kansas Journal of Sociology, Spring 1966, vol. 2, pp. 59-65.

Cordasco, Frank. "Puerto Rican Children in the American School." Journal of Negro Education, Spring 1967.

Cordasco, Frank. "The Puerto Rican Family and the Anthropologist: 'Oscar Lewis' La Vida and the Culture of Poverty'." Teachers College (Columbia Univ-) Record, May 1967.

Cordasco, Frank. "Puerto Rican Pupils and American Education." School and Society, Feb. 18, 1967, vol. 95, pp. 116-19.

Cordasco, Frank. "Schools and the Spanish Speaking Community." Congressional Record, June 12, 1962, vol. 108, pp. A4322-A4323.

Cordasco, Frank. "Spanish Harlem: The Anatomy of Poverty." Phylon: The Atlanta University Review of Race & Culture, Summer, 1965, vol. 26, pp. 195-96.

Cordasco, Frank. "Studies in the Disenfranchised: The Puerto Rican Child." Psychiatric Spectator, Nov. 1966, vol. 3, pp. 3-4.

Costa, Richard H. "Latest Migration: Puerto Rico Moves Upstate." Utica (N.Y.) Observer Dispatch. May 27-29, 1957. (Series of three articles.)

Cotto-Thorner, Guillermo. Trópico en Manhattan. San Juan:
     Editorial Occidente. 1951. 242 págs.

Covello, Leonard, with D'Agostino, Guido. The Heart is the
     Teacher. New York: McGraw-Hill, 1958. 275 pp.

Crespo, Patria Cintrón de. Puerto Rican Women Teachers in
     New York: Self Perception and Work Adjustment as Perceived
     by Themselves and Others. Doctoral dissertation, Columbia
     Univ., 1965.

¿Cuáles son sus Derechos Civiles en Connecticut? Bridgeport,
     Conn.: Bridgeport Inter-Group Council, Inc., 10 pp.

Cunningham, John T. "Migrants Pose Problems for N.J. Farmers
     Who Need Them." Reprinted from Newark News Magazine,
     Sept. 1, 1957, by the Commonwealth of Puerto Rico,
     Department of Labor, Migration Division. 4 pp. (Out of
     print.)

Current Population Estimates. New York: New York City
     Department of City Planning, March 1, 1955.

Cursos Gratis de Educación Vocacional en Nueva York 1955-1956.
     Nueva York: Estado Libre Asociado de Puerto Rico,
     Departamento del Trabajo, División de Migración, 1955.
     29 págs.

Datos Sobre Empleo: Protección de Seguro Contra el Desempleo
     para Empleados de Pequeños Negocios. Nueva York:
     Departamento del Trabajo del Estado de Nueva York,
     División de Empleo, n.d. 5 págs.

Davis, K. and Senior, C. "Immigration from the Western Hemisphere."
     Annals of the American Academy of Political and Social Science,
     March 1949, vol. 262, pp. 77-79.

"De Puerto Rico al Universo." Life (Spanish Ed.), Dec. 9, 1963,
     vol. 22, pp. 66-67.

Dereches y Deberes del Inquilino y del Casero. Introducción por
     Joseph Monserrat. Nueva York: Estado Libre Asociado de
     Puerto Rico, Departamento del Trabajo, División de Migración,
     en Colaboración con el Consejo de Organizaciones Hispano-
     Americanas de Nueva York, oct. de 1957, 16 págs.

Developing a Program for Testing Puerto Rican Pupils in the
New York City Public Schools. New York: The Puerto Rican
Study of the New York City Board of Education, 1959. 143
pp.

Díaz, Eileen. "A Puerto Rican in New York." Dissent, Summer
1961, vol. 8, pp. 383-85.

Díaz, Manuel; and Cintrón, Roland. School Integration and
Quality Education. New York: Puerto Rican Forum, Inc.,
1964.

Díaz, Manuel; Earl Fich and Gangware, et al., The Attitudes
of Puerto Ricans in New York City to Various Aspects
of Their Environment (Projects No. 4317, New York School
of Social Work, June 1953).

Directorio de Chicago para Nuevos Vecinos. Chicago: Comisión
de Relaciones Humanas y Comité del Alcalde pro Nuevos
Residentes, 1959. 15 págs.

"Division Lesson: Problems of Chicago's Puerto Rican Community."
Il. Time, June 24, 1966, vol. 87, pp. 30-31.

La División de Migración . . . Sirviendo a los Puertorriqueños
en los Estados Unidos. Nueva York: Estado Libre Asociado
de Puerto Rico, Departamento del Trabajo, División de
Migración, 1957. 8 págs.

Dodson, Dan W. Between Hell's Kitchen and San Juan Hill: A
Survey. Human Relations Monograph No. 1 New York: New York
University, Center for Human Relations Studies, 1952. 32 pp.

"Don Eduardo," The New Yorker, July 3, 1954, vol. 30, no. 20,
pp. 14-15.

Donahue, Frances M. A Study of the Original Puerto Rican Colony
in Brooklyn, 1938-1943. Unpublished master's thesis.
New York: Fordham School of Social Work, 1945. 87 pp.

Donchian, Daniel. A Survey of New Haven's Newcomers: The Puerto
Ricans. New Haven, Conn.: Human Relations Council of
Greater New Haven, May 1959. 36 pp.

Donovan, Robert J. "Annals of Crime: A Demonstration at Blair House." The New Yorker, July 19, 1952, vol. 28. no. 22, pp. 32-55.

A Doorway to Science. New York: The Puerto Rican Study of the New York City Board of Education, 1958. 58 pp.

Dossick, Jesse J. "Workshop Field Study in Puerto Rican Education and Culture." Journal of Educational Sociology, Dec. 1954, vol. 28, no. 4, pp. 174-180.

Drusine, Leon. Some Factors in Anti-Negro Prejudice Among Puerto Rican Boys in New York City. Doctoral dissertation, New York Univ., 1955.

Dworkis, Martin B. (ed.). The Impact of Puerto Rican Migration on Governmental Services in New York City. New York: New York University Press, 1957.

Eagle, Morris. "The Puerto Ricans in New York." In: Nathan Glazer and Davis McEntire (eds.). Studies in Housing and Minority Groups. Berkely, Calif.: Univ. of California Press, 1960.

"Easternmost Outpost of the U.S.A." Rotarian, Dec. 1945, vol. 67, pp. 28-31.

Ecclesine, Margy. "A Puerto Rican Steps Forward." Catholic Digest, April 1959, vol. 23, no. 6, pp. 43-46.

Eels, Kenneth, et. al. Intelligence and Cultural Differences, Chicago: University of Chicago Press, 1951.

"La Educación y el Emigrante." Temas, nov. de 1957, vol. 14, núm. 85, págs. 124-127.

"Effect of Labor Costs and Migration on Puerto Rican Economy." Monthly Labor Review, June 1953, vol. 76, no. 6, pp. 625-627.

Elam, Sophie E. "Acculturation and Learning Problems of Puerto Rican Children." Teachers College Record, Feb. 1960, vol. 61, pp. 258-64.

Elman, R. M. "Puerto Ricans." Commonweal, Jan. 7, 1966, vol. 83, pp. 405-08.

"Emigrating Puerto Ricans." Commonweal, Aug. 15, 1947, vol. 46, p. 420.

The Emerging Puerto Rican Community of New York. New York: New York Chapter of the Public Relations Society of America, Inc. October 22, 1963. 10 pp.

English-Speech Language Arts for Senior High Schools. New York: New York City Board of Education, 1956. 100 pp.

"La Escuela Pública Orienta al Emigrante." Educación (Depto. de Instrucción de Puerto Rico), año 6, núm. 50, marzo de 1957, págs. 2,8.

Estire Sus Dólares. Nueva York: Estado Libre Asociado de Puerto Rico, Departamento del Trabajo, División de Migración, 1957. 6 págs.

Estudio Sobre La Emigración en Puerto Rico: Encuesta en la Semana del 21 al 27 de Abril de 1952. San Juan: Oficina del Gobernador Negociado del Presupuesto, División de Estadísticas, dic. de 1952. 47 págs.

The Ethnic Survey. A Report on the Number and Distribution of Negroes, Puerto Ricans and Others Employed by the City of New York. New York: City Commission on Human Rights, 1964.

Events in the History of Puerto Rico, vol. I. New York: Research for Urban Education, Inc., 1967. 56 pp.

Expanded Plan of Operations Pertaining to Puerto Rico Agricultural Workers. New York: Commonwealth of Puerto Rico, Department of Labor, Migration Division, 1953, 9 pp.

Fact Book on Children in New York City. New York: Community Council of Greater New York, Research Department, April 1957. 145 pp.

The Facts of Poverty in New York City. U.S. Department of Labor. Bureau of Labor Statistics, 1965, 21 pp.

Fantino, E. "Children of Poverty." Commonweal, June 17, 1955, vol. 62, pp. 271-4; Discussion, July 8, 1955, vol. 62, pp. 267, 354-5.

La Farge, J. "Ashmore on the Negro Ghetto." America, June 4, 1960, vol. 103, p. 328.

Fernández Méndez, Eugenio. "¿Asimilación o Enquistamiento? Dos Polos del Problema de la Emigración Transcultural Puertorriqueña." La Torre (Universidad de Puerto Rico). enero-marzo de 1956, año 4, núm. 13, págs. 137-145.

"Fiesta." Time, July 2, 1956, vol. 68, no. 1, p. 58.

Finocchiaro, Mary. "Puerto Rican Newcomers in Our Schools." Journal of Educational Sociology, Dec. 1954, vol. 28, no. 4, pp. 157-166.

Fitzpatrick, Joseph P. "The Adjustment of Puerto Ricans to New York City," In: Milton L. Barron (ed.). Minorities in a Changing World. New York: Alfred A. Knopf, 1967. Also In: Journal of Intergroup Relations, Winter 1959-1960, vol. 1, pp. 43-51.

Fitzpatrick, Joseph P. "Helping the Mainland." Time, Oct. 26, 1956, vol. 74, p. 34.

Fitzpatrick, Joseph P. "The Integration of Puerto Ricans." Thought, Autumn 1955, vol. 30, pp. 402-20.

Fitzpatrick, Joseph P. "Intermarriage of Puerto Ricans in New York City." American Journal of Sociology, Jan., 1966, vol. 71, no. 4, pp. 395-406.

Fitzpatrick, Joseph P. "Mexicans and Puerto Ricans Build a Bridge." America, Dec. 31, 1955, vol. 44, no. 14, pp. 373-375.

Fitzpatrick, Joseph P. "Oscar Lewis and the Puerto Rican Family." America, Dec. 10, 1966, vol. 115, pp. 778-9.

Fleisher, Belton M. Some Economic Aspects of Puerto Rican Migration to the United States. Doctoral dissertation, Stanford Univ., 1962.

"Foster parents Transcend Racial Differences." America, April 2, 1955, vol. 93, p. 1.

14

Galíndez, Jesús de. _Puerto Rico en Nueva York_. Mexico:
    Cuadernos Americanos, 1952. 63 págs.

García, Alonso. "Discrimination Against Puerto Ricans,"
    pp. 79-80. In: (Report of the) _Governor's Advisory_
    Commission on Civil Rights. Springfield, O: Governor's
    Advisory Commission on Civil Rights, Dec. 1958. 118 pp.

Gernes, Arthur, C. "Implicaciones de la Emigración
    Puertorriqueña al Continente Fuera de la Ciudad de
    Nueva York. " _La Torre_ (Universidad de Puerto Rico),
    enero-marzo de 1956, año 4, núm. 13, págs. 97-111.

Gernes, Arthur C. _Implications of Puerto Rican Migration to_
    the Continent Outside New York City. Address before the
    Ninth Annual Convention on Social Orientation, University
    of Puerto Rico, Dec. 10, 1955. New York: Commonwealth
    of Puerto Rico, Department of Labor, Migration Division,
    1956, 15 pp.

Gillotti, W.P. "Ethnic Clichés." _Commentary_, Jan., 1954,
    vol. 37, p. 6.

Ginzberg, Eli. _The Negro Potential_. New York: Columbia
    University Press, 1956.

Ginzberg, Eli. and Douglas W. Bray. _The Uneducated_, New York:
    Columbia University Press, 1953.

Gittler, Joseph B. (ed.). _Understanding Minority Groups_.
    New York: John Wiley, 1956. 139 pp.

Glazer, Nathan. "New York's Puerto Ricans," _Commentary_, Dec.
    1958, vol. 26, no. 6, pp. 469-478.

Glazer, Nathan. "Puerto Ricans." _Commentary_, July 1963, vol.
    36, pp. 1-9.

Glazer, Nathan; and Moynihan, Daniel P. _Beyond the Melting Pot_:
    The Negroes, Puerto Ricans, Jews, Italians, and Irish of
    New York City. Cambridge, Mass.: M.I.T. Press and Harvard
    Univ. Press, 1964. 360 pp.

Golden, Harry. _Only in America_. Cleveland and New York: World
    Publishing Co., 1958. 317 pp.

Goldsen, Rose K. Puerto Rican Migration to New York City.
Doctoral dissertation, New York Univ., 1945.

Golub, Fred T. The Puerto Rican Worker in Perth Amboy,
New Jersey. Occasional Studies No. 2. New Brunswick,
N.J.: Rutgers University, Institute of Management and
Labor Relations, March 1956. 18 pp.

González, Agustín. Problems of Adjustment of Puerto Rican
Boys. (Project No. 4593, New York School of Social
Work, 1956.)

Goodman, Samuel M.; Diamond, Lorraine K.; Fox, David J. Who
Are The Puerto Rican Pupils in the New York City Public
Schools" 1956. 88 pp.

Goodman, Samuel M. Who Were the Teachers in the Puerto Rican
Study Experimental Schools in 1953-54? - A Survey of
Teacher Background, Attitudes and Practices. New York:
The Puerto Rican Study of the New York City Board of
Education, 1955. 27 pp.

Gosnell, Patria Arán. The Puerto Ricans in New York City.
Doctoral dissertation, New York Univ., 1945.

Greenstein, Marvin N. "Puerto Rican Children." In: Pathways
in Child Guidance, June 1960, vol. 2, no. 4.

Greiser, Norman. "Airborne from San Juan." New Republic,
Nov. 3, 1947, vol. 108, no. 2, pp. 21-24.

Groty, Dorothy R. Puerto Rican Families in the Navy Yard
District of Brooklyn, New York: Unpublished Manuscript,
1931.

Gruber, Ruth. "E. 110th St. Isn't the Universe: The Puerto Rican
in New York," New York Herald Tribune. Dec. 6, 1958.

A Guide to the Teaching of English to Puerto Rican Pupils
(Intermediate Grades) New York: The Puerto Rican Study
of the New York City Board of Education, 1956. 153 pp.

A Guide to the Teaching of English to Puerto Rican Pupils in
the Junior High Schools. New York: The Puerto Rican Study
of the New York City Board of Education, 1955. 134 pp.

A Guide to the Teaching of Science: For Use with Puerto Rican
    Pupils in the Secondary School. New York: The Puerto Rican
    Study of the New York City Board of Education, 1957. 173
    pp.

A Guide to the Teaching of Science to Puerto Rican Pupils in
    Junior High Schools-Experimental Edition. New York: The
    Puerto Rican Study of the New York City Board of Education,
    1956. 95 pp.

Halper, Albert. "The Wallet." The New Yorker, Feb. 3, 1951,
    vol. 26, pp. 60-65.

Hamill, P. "Flavor of Spanish Harlem." Holiday, Feb., 1967,
    vol. 41, pp. 118b=.

Handlin, Oscar. "La Vida." Atlantic, Dec. 1966, vol. 218,
    p. 138.

Handlin, Oscar. The Newcomers. Cambridge: Harvard University
    Press, 1959.

Handlin, Oscar. The Uprooted. Boston: Little, Brown, 1951,
    310 pp.

Hanson, Earl Parker. Transformation: The Story of Modern Puerto
    Rico. New York: Simon and Schuster, 1955. 416 pp.

Harlem Youth Opportunities Unlimited, Inc. Youth in the Getto.
    New York: Unlimited, Inc., 1964.

Harrington, Janette T. "Puerto Rico: Bridge Between The Americas."
    Prebysterian Life, Feb. 1964, vol. 17, pp. 14-21.

Hartford y Usted: Un Guía.   Hartford, Conn.: Greater Hartford
    Council of Churches, n.d. 17 pp.

Hasting, W.F. "Our Puerto Rican Friends." Christian Century,
    Dec. 20, 1950, vol. 67, p. 1525.

Helfgott, Roy B. Puerto Rican Integration in the Skirt Industry
    in New York City. New York: New York State Commission
    Against Discrimination, 1958. 16 pp.

Helping Puerto Ricans Help Themselves. New York: Commonwealth
    of Puerto Rico, Department of Labor, Migration Division,
    Sept. 1958. 16 pp.

Hernández, J. "El Centro en Jersey City." America, Nov. 14, 1959, vol. 102, p. 199.

Hernández, Joseph W. The Sociological Implications of Return Migration in Puerto Rico: An Exploratory Study. Doctoral dissertation, Univ. of Minesota, 1964.

Hickey, Edna C. "Adjusting the Curriculum for Bilingual Children." National Elementary Principal, Sept. 1956, vol. 36, no. 1, pp. 53-57.

Hill, Reuben; Stycos, J.M.; and Back, Kurt, W. The Family and Population Control: A Puerto Rican Experiment in Social Change. Chapel Hill: University of North Carolina Press, 1959. 481 pp.

Hochhäuser, Aidalina. A Pilot Study of "Problem Children" of Puerto Rican Background. New York: The Puerto Rican Study of the New York City Board of Education, 1956. 16 pp.

How to Hire Agricultural Workers from Puerto Rico. New York: Commonwealth of Puerto Rico, Department of Labor, Migration Division, in Employment Security, U.S. Employment Service, Farm Placement Service, 1953, 1954, 1955, 1957, 1958. 16 pp.

The I. Q. and other Testing Procedures. New York: Commonwealth of Puerto Rico, Department of Labor, Migration Division, 1956.

Illich, Ivan, "Puerto Ricans in New York." Commonweal, June 22, 1956, vol. 64, no. 12, pp. 294-297.

"In-Migrants: Number, Location, and Selected Characteristics." Statistics (Welfare Council of Metropolitan Chicago, Research Dept.), vol. 23, no. 11-12, Nov.-Dec. 1956, pp. 1-7.

An Insight into Social Problems Facing Spanish-Speaking American Residents of Bridgeport. Proceedings of the Conference on Spanish-Speaking American Services, held in Bridgeport on September 16, 1957. Bridgeport: Bridgeport Inter-Group Council, Inc., 1957. 30 pp.

Interim Report. New York: Labor Advisory Committee on Puerto Rican Affairs, AFL-CIO, New York, 1955. 6 pp.

Interviewing Puerto Rican Parents and Children in Spanish: A Guide for School Personnel. New York: New York City Board of Education n.d. 10 pp.

Jaffe, A.J. "Demographic and Labor Force Characteristics of New York City Puerto Rican Population," pp. 3-29. In: A.J. Jaffe (ed.) Puerto Rican Population of New York City. New York: Columbia University, Bureau of Applied and Social Research, 1954. 61 pp.

Jaffe, A.J. (ed.) Puerto Rican Population of New York City. New York: Columbia University, Bureau of Applied Social Research, 1954. 61 pp.

Jahr, A.V. "Spanish Harlem." Today's Health, Feb. 1953, vol. 31, pp. 30-4.

Jenkins, Shirley. Reciprocal Empathy in Intergroup Relations: An Exploratory Study of Puerto Rican and Negro Groups in New York City. Doctoral dissertation, New York Univ. 1957.

Jiménez - Malaret, R. "Puerto Ricans Look Ahead." Asia, April 1945, vol. 45, p. 216.

The Jobs We Do. New York: Commonwealth of Puerto Rico, Department of Labor, Migration Division, 1956. 16 pp.

Johnson, J.T. "Teaching the English Language to Non-English Speaking Children." National Elementary Principal, Sept. 1956, vol. 36, no. 1, pp. 58-61.

Jones, Isham B. The Puerto Rican in New Jersey: His Present Status, July 1955. Newark: N.J. State Department of Education, Division Against Discrimination, July 1955. 48 pp.

Jones, Wyatt, "Uncommon Commonwealth," Town & Country, Aug., 1958.

Kaplan, Mordecai M., The Future of the American Jew. New York: McMillan Co., 1948.

Katz, Irwin. Conflict and Harmony in an Adolescent Interracial Group. New York: New York University Press, 1956. 47 pp.

Kavetzky, Joseph. A Survey of Practice in the Teaching of English to Puerto Rican Pupils -- School Year 1954-1955. New York: The Puerto Rican Study of the New York City Board of Education, 1956. 27 pp.

Kerth-Lucas, Alan. Decisions About People in Need. Chapel Hill: University of North Carolina Press, 1957.

Kihss, Peter. "Gains Made by Puerto Ricans Here and City Relief Roll Held Down Despite Job-Hunter Influx." Two articles from The New York Times, May 31 and June 2, 1957. Reprinted by the Commonwealth of Puerto Rico, Department of Labor, Migration Division, 1957, 4 pp.

Kihss, Peter. "Puerto Rico and Us." Three articles from The New York Times. Reprinted by the Commonwealth of Puerto Rico, Department of Labor, Migration Division, 1953. 8 pp. (out of print.)

Knox, Maryel. "Ray of Sunshine in Harlem." Wellesley Alumnae Magazine, May 1953, pp. 73-75, 96.

Know Your Fellow American Citizen from Puerto Rico. Washington, D.C.: Office of the Government of Puerto Rico, n.d. 64 pp. (out of print.)

Koch, J.E. "Puerto Ricans Come to Youngstown." Commonweal, Oct. 9, 1953, vol. 59, pp. 9-11.

Komarousky, Mirra. The Unemployed Man and His Family, New York: Dryden Press, Inc. 1940.

Koss, Joan D. Puerto Ricans in Philadelphia: Migration and Accomodative Processes. Doctoral dissertation, Pennsylvania Univ. 1965.

Kramer, Judith; and Leventman, Seymour. Children of the Gilded Ghetto. Yale University Press, 1961.

Kriedler, Charles. A Study of the Influence of English on the Spanish of Puerto Ricans in Jersey City, New Jersey. Doctoral dissertation, Michigan State Univ., 1958.

"Labor Comunal de la División de Migración." Temas, nov. de 1957, vol. 14, núm. 85, págs. 113-15.

Langdale, A. Barnett. Teaching Reading to the Pupils of Puerto Rican Background. New York: The Puerto Rican Study of the New York City Board of Education, 1957. 61 pp.

Lee, Robert; and Orr, Clara. Upper Manhattan: A Community Study of Washington Heights. New York: Protestant Council of the City of New York, Dept. of Church Planning and Research, June 9, 1954. 20 pp.

The Leisure Time Problems of Puerto Rican Youth In N.Y.C.: A Study of the Problems of Selected Group Work Programs. New York: Archdiocese of New York, Catholic Youth Organization, Jan. 1953. 81 pp.

Lelyveld, J. "¿Se Habla Español?" il. N.Y. Times Mags. June 14, 1964. pp. 65-6+

Lennon, John J. A comparative Study of the Patterns of Acculturation of Selected Puerto Rican Protestant and Roman Catholic Families in an Urban Metropolitan Area (Chicago), Univ. of Notre Dame, 1963.

Levitas, Mitchel. "New York's Labor Scandal: The Puerto Rican Workers." New York Post, July 15-19 and 21, 1957.

Leviton, Bertha. Census of Puerto Rican and Foreign-Born Pupils: Provisional Report. New York: New York City Board of Education, Bureau of Administrative and Budgetary Research, Feb. 1956. 29 pp. (Census of October 31, 1955.)

Lewis, Oscar. "Culture of Poverty." Scientific American, Oct., 1966, vol. 215, pp. 19-25.

Lewis, Oscar. "In New York You get Swallowed by a Horse." Commentary, Nov. 1964, vol. 38, pp. 69-73.

Lewis, Oscar. "Portrait of Gabriel: Puerto Rican family in San Juan and New York." Harper, Jan. 1966, vol. 232, pp. 54-9.

Lewis, Oscar. La Vida. New York: Random House, 1966. 669 pp.

Lewis, Oscar. "La Vida," Excerpt. Commentary, Aug. 1966, vol. 42, pp. 44-47.

Lind, Andrew W. Hawaii's People. Honolulu: University of Hawii, 1955. 107 pp.

La Llave del Exito. Nueva York: Estado Libre Asociado de Puerto Rico, Departamento del Trabajo, División de Migración, 1952, 7 págs.

Llave a Lorain. Lorain, Ohio: Community Welfare Council, 1953. 20 pp.

The Lorain and Gary Experience with Puerto Rican Workers. Six articles reprinted from the Gary Post Tribune. Washington, D.C. Office of the Government of Puerto Rico, 1948. (Out of print.)

Lorge, Irving, and Mayans, Frank, Jr. "Vestibule vs. Regular Classes for Puerto Rican Migrant Children." Teachers College Record (Columbia University), Feb. 1954, vol. 55, no. 5, pp. 231-237.

Low, Frances. School - Puerto Rican Parent Relations, 1955-56. New York: The Puerto Rican Study of the New York City Board of Education, 1957. 61 pp.

MacLeod, Hope. "The Poughkeepsie Case." New York Post, May 4-5, 1959.

"Maid Problem." New Republic, April 28, 1947, vol. 116, p. 7.

Main, Willett S. Memorandum on "In-Migration of Puerto Rican Workers." Milwaukee: Wisconsin State Employment Service, Sept. 3, 1952.

Maldonado, A. W. "Puerto Rican Tide Begins to Turn: Migrants Returning to Their Island Now Match the Numbers Moving to the Island of Manhattan." il. N.Y. Times Mag. Sept. 20, 1964 pp.84.

Maldonado, A. W. "Puerto Rico: The Migration Reverses." il. Nation, March 16, 1964, vol. 198, pp. 255-57.

McKeon, John. "The Ortiz Family." _Jubilee_, June 1953, vol. 1, no. 2, pp. 22-23.

Mencher, Joan P. _Child Rearing and Family Organization Among Puerto Ricans in Eastville, El Barrio de Nueva York_. Doctoral dissertation, Columbia Univ., 1958.

Mid-Century Pioneers and Protestants. New York: Protestant Council of the City of New York, Department of Church Planning and Research, March 1954 (2nd Edition). 29 pp.

"Migrant Farm Labor in New York." Industrial Bulletin (New York State Dept. of Labor), June 1958, vol. 37, no. 6, pp. 7-11.

"Migrants:The Puerto Ricans." _Newsweek_, March 24, 1947, vol. 29, p. 2718.

The Migration Division: Policy, Functions, Objectives. New York: Commonwealth of Puerto Rico, Department of Labor, Migration Division, 1957. 6 pp.

Miller, H. "New York City's Puerto Rican Pupils: A Problem of Acculturation." _School and Sociology_, Aug. 30, 1952, vol. 76, pp. 129-32.

Mills, C. Wright; Senior, Clarence; and Goldsen, Rose Kohn. _The Puerto Rican Journey_. New York: Harper, 1950. 238 pp.

Mirkin, Sidney. Series of six articles on Puerto Ricans In New York. _New York Daily News_, Jan. 3-7, 1955.

"Mixed Schools, Problem in New York City, Too." _U.S. News_, March 30, 1956, vol. 40, pp. 53-6.

Monserrat, Joseph. _Background and General Information on Puerto Rico and the Puerto Rican Migrant_. New York: Commonwealth of Puerto Rico, Department of Labor, Migration Division, n.d. 9 pp.

Monserrat, Joseph. "Education of Puerto Rican Children in New York City." _Journal of Educational Sociology_, Dec. 1954, vol. 28, no. 4, pp. 146-192.

Malzberg, Benjamin. "Mental Disease Among Puerto Ricans in New York City." Journal of Nervous and Mental Diseases, March 1956, vol. 123, pp. 263-269.

Malzberg, Benjamin. "Mental Disease Among Puerto Ricans in New York State." Psychiatric Quarterly, 1948, vol. 22, part 2, pp. 300-308.

Manhattan Communities: Summary Statements of Population Characteristics. New York: Community Council of Greater New York, Research Dept., 1955. 75 pp.

Mannes, Marya. "School Trouble in Harlem." The Reporter, Feb. 5, 1959, pp. 13-19.

Marja, Fern. with McElroy, Peter J.; and Dufty, William. "Incident in Central Park." New York Post, Feb. 10-11-, 13-17, 1955. (Series of seven award-winning articles on the Santos-Cabán case, in which two boys, falsely accused of rape, found justice.)

Martin, J.B. "Crime Without Reason." Saturday Evening Post, Nov. 5, 1960, vol. 233, pp. 19-21.

Martin, Joseph; and Santora, Phil. "A Search for the Truth." (Series of six articles.) New York Daily News, July 7-12, 1958.

Massimine, Virginia E. Challenges of a Changing Population. New York: New York University, Center for Human Relations Studies, 1954. 35 pp.

Massolo, Arthur. "Puerto Rico's Muñoz Marín." New York Post, March 10, 1959, p. 10 (Second of a series of Six articles.)

"Matter of Integration." Commonweal, Jan. 27, 1956, vol. 63, p. 418.

Myans, Frank Jr. Puerto Rican Migrant Pupils in New York City Schools; A Comparison of the Effects of Two Methods of Instructional Grouping on English Mastery and Attitudes. Doctoral dissertation, Columbia Univ., 1953.

McCready, Fred. "Prejudice, Language Barrier Add to Puerto Rican Problem" and "Community Council Seeks Way to Ease Lot of Puerto Ricans." Allentown (Pa.) Call, May 2-3, 1958. (Series of two articles.)

Monserrat, Joseph. "La Emigración: Realidad y Problema en la Ciudad de Nueva York." La Torre (Universidad de Puerto Rico), enero-marzo de 1956, año 4, núm. 13, págs. 73-96.

Monserrat, Joseph. "Industry and Community-A Profitable Partnership." Journal of Educational Sociology, Dec. 1953, vol. 27, no. 4, pp. 171-181.

Monserrat, Joseph. "Integración Escolar." Temas, April 1964, vol. 24, pp. 24-29.

Monserrat, Joseph. "Literacy Tests: Puerto Rican Perspective." Sunday Herald Tribune Magazine, Oct. 13, 1963, pp. 9-10.

Monserrat, Joseph. Migration Division, Department of Labor of Puerto Rico: Philosophy and Function. New York: Commonwealth of Puerto Rico, Department of Labor, Migration Division, n.d. 4 pp.

Monserrat, Joseph. School Integration: A Puerto Rican View. New York: Commonwealth of Puerto Rico, Department of Labor, Migration Division, 1963, 16 pp.

Monserrat, Joseph. "Some Data on Population Trends in New York, 'Must' Information for Its Citizens." Journal of Educational Sociology, Nov. 1952, Vol. 28, no. 3, pp. 108-114.

Monserrat, Joseph. "La Vida," Review. Natural History, April 1967, vol. 76, no. 4, pp. 70, 72.

Montag, Jenny; and Finocchiaro, Mary. "Guidance and Curriculum for Puerto Rican Children." High Points (New York City Board of Education), Jan. 1951, pp. 34-42.

Montross, Harold K. "Meeting the Needs of the Puerto Rican Migrant," Employment Security Review, Jan. 1959, vol. 26, no. 1, pp. 31-33.

Morgan, T. B. "Real West Side Story; Life of Jose Rivera." Look, Feb. 16, 1960, vol. 24, pp. 22-7.

Morrison, J. Cayce. A Letter to Friends of Puerto Rican Children. New York: The Puerto Rican Study of the New York City Board of Education, 1955. 8 pp.

Morrison, J. Cayce. The Puerto Rican Study, 1953-1957:
A Report on the Education and Adjustment of Puerto
Rican Pupils in the Public Schools of the City of New
York. New York: The Puerto Rican Study of the New York
City Board of Education, 1958. 265 pp.

Morrison, J. Cayce. "The Puerto Rican Study: What It Is,
Where It Is Going." Journal of Educational Sociology,
Dec. 1954, vol. 28, no. 4, pp. 167-73.

Moskin, J. Robert. "Puerto Rico: Island at a Crossroads."
Look, March 24, 1964, vol. 28, pp. 26, 42.

Moskin, J. Robert. "Surprising Puerto Rico." Look, Jan. 17,
1961, vol. 25, pp. 21-36, 38-39, 43-44.

Moskin, J. Robert. "Million on the Mainland." Look, Jan. 17,
1961, vol. 25, p. 44.

The Movement of Population and Public Welfare in New York State:
A Report on America's Mobile Labor Force and Its Economic
Contributions and Public Welfare Costs to New York State.
Albany: New York State Dept. of Social Welfare, Dec. 1958.
35 pp.

Mozer, R.J. "Victims of Exploitation: New York's Puerto Ricans."
Catholic World, Sept., 1959, vol. 189, pp. 441-6.

Muñoz Marin, Luis. Un Mensaje a las Comunidades Puertorriqueñas
del Continente. Nueva York: Estado Libre Asociado de
Puerto Rico, Departamento del Trabajo, División de Migración,
25 de julio de 1953. 8 pp.

Murra, Elizabeth. "Learning a Second Language." Journal of
Educational Sociology, Dec. 1954, vol. 28, no. 4, pp.
181-192.

Murra, J.V. "Up to the Slums." Nation, May 2, 1959, vol. 188,
pp. 411-12.

Muste, A.J. "Communists' Gain." Christian Century, Dec. 15,
1954, vol. 71, pp. 1521-2.

Narita, Ruth. The Puerto Rican Delinquent Girl in New York City.
Unpublished Master's Thesis, Fordham University, 1954.

The Needs of Children of Puerto Rico. Washington, D.C.:
    Federal Security agency, 1950. 22 pp.

Newfield, J. "Harlem Sí, Tammany No." Commonweal, Sept. 29,
    1961, vol. 75, pp. 10-12.

New York City, 1955-1965: A Report to the Community. New York:
    Welfare and Health Council of New York City, 1955. 37 pp.

"New York's Puerto Ricans." America, May 11, 1957, vol. 97, p.
    185.

"900,000 Puerto Ricans in the United States: Their Problems
    and Progress." U.S. News, Dec. 7, 1959, vol. 47, pp. 91-5.

1964 Study of Poverty Conditions in the New York Puerto Rican
    Community. New York: Puerto Rican Forum, Inc., 1964.
    145 pp.

"No Hablo Inglés: Police Blamed for Puerto Rican Riots." New
    Republic, June 25, 1966, vol. 154, p. 7.

Notes on Migration and Workers' Attitudes Toward It. (Preliminary
    Release, Manpower Resources Project.) Rio Piedras: Univ. of
    Puerto Rico, Social Science Research Center, n.d. 10 pp.

Novak, Robert T. "Distribution of Puerto Ricans on Manhattan
    Island." Geographical Review, April 1956, vol. 46, no. 2,
    pp. 182-186.

Nueva York y Usted. Nueva York: Estado Libre Asociado de Puerto
    Rico, Departamento del Trabajo, División de Migración, 1951.
    64 págs. (out of print.)

O'Brien, Robert W. Clevland Puerto Rican Survey Tabulations.
    Cleveland: Nationalities Services Center of Cleveland and
    Ohio Wesleyan University, Sociology Department, 1954.

O'Brien, Robert W. A Survey of the Puerto Ricans in Lorain,
    Ohio. Lorain: Neighborhood House Association of Lorain,
    1954. 85 pp.

Occupations of Puerto Ricans in New York City. Memo. No.50
    New York: New York State Department of Labor, Division of
    Research and Statistics, June 17, 1954. 10 pp.

O'Dea, Thomas F.; and Poblete, Renato. "Anomie and the Quest
    for Community; the Development of Sects Among Puerto Ricans
    in New York City." American Catholic Sociological Review,
    1959, vol. 21, pp. 18-36.

O'Gara, James. "Strangers in the City." Commonweal, Oct. 10,
    1952. vol. 57, no. 1, pp. 7-9.

"One Step Forward: Grievances of Puerto Rican Workers in New
    York City." Nation, May 11, 1957, vol. 184, p. 402.

One in Twenty: The Facts About the Puerto Ricans Among Us and
    What the Boys Athletic League is Doing About It. New York:
    Boys Athletic League, 1956. 15 pp.

Opler, Marvin K. "Dilemmas of Two Puerto Rican Men." pp. 223-224.
    In: Georgene Seward (ed.) Clinical Studies in Culture
    Conflict. New York: Ronald Press, 1958. 598 pp.

Opler, Marvin K. "The Influence of Ethnic and Class Subcultures
    on Child Care." Social Problems, July 1955, vol. 3, no. 1,
    pp. 12-21.

Opotowsky, Stan. "Harlem." New York Post, March 7, 1958, p. M2.
    (Fifth of a Series of articles.)

Orientación al Recién Llegado. Chicago: Chicago Commission on
    Human Relations, Mayor's Committee on New Residents, n.d.
    8 pp.

Our Changing Community. New York: Community Council of Greater
    New York, 1957, 45 pp.

Our Children from Puerto Rico: A Report on Their Island Home
    by the Visiting Puerto Rican Workshop of 1955. New York:
    New York City Board of Education, 1957. 72 pp.

"Our Puerto Rican Catholics." America, June 30, 1956, vol. 95,
    p. 314.

Our Puerto Rican Fellow Citizens. New York: National Conference
    Sponsored by AFL-CIO Community Service Activities, Jan. 15,
    1960.

28

Owens, James M. "These Are Puerto Ricans." Hartford Courant, March 15-22, 1959. (Series of eight articles.)

Padilla, Elena. Up From Puerto Rico, New York: Columbia University Press, 1958. 317 pp.

Pagán de Colón, P. "Status of the Migrant." Vital Speeches, May 1, 1962, vol. 28, pp. 445-8.

Parker, E.C. "Spanish-speaking Churches." Christian Century, April 12, 1961, vol. 466, p. 8. Reply: Cotto-Thorner, A., June 28, 1961, p. 28.

Passow, A. Harry. (ed.). Education in Depressed Areas. New York: Bureau of Publications, Teachers College, Columbia University, 1963.

Paul, Irven. "Migrants and Culture Change." Hartford Seminary Foundation Bulletin, Winter 1955-56, no. 21, pp. 24-27.

Pérez Jusino, David. A Suggested Human Relations Program for Puerto Ricans in Spanish Harlem. Doctoral dissertation, Teachers College, Columbia Univ., 1952.

Perlman, Ruth. Our Mobile Population and the Schools: Some Problems of Teaching Immigrant Children in Metropolitan School Districts. Doctoral dissertation, Teachers College, Columbia Univ., 1953.

Perutti, L. "Have Your Puerto Rican Pupils Help Themselves." English Journal, Dec. 1966, vol. 55, pp. 1201-06.

Phrases with Spanish Equivalents for use in School: An Aid for Teachers of Children of Puerto Rican Background. New York: New York City Board of Education, June 28, 1954. 13 pp.

¿Piensa Vivir en los Estados Unidos? Nueva York: Estado Libre Asociado de Puerto Rico, Departamento del Trabajo, División de Migración, 1955.

Poblete, Renato, and Thomas F. O'Dea. "Anomie and the 'Quest for Community' Among the Puerto Ricans of New York." American Catholic Sociological Review, Spring, 1960, vol. 21, no. 1, pp. 18-36.

Population Changes in New York City. New York: New York City
    Department of City Planning, Nov. 22, 1954. 6 pp.

Population of Puerto Rican Birth or Parentage, New York City,
    1950. New York: Welfare and Health Council of New York
    City, Research Bureau, Sept. 1952, 57 pp.

"Power of Words: Exploitation of Puerto Rican Workers in New
    York City." Nation, Aug. 17, 1957, vol. 185, p. 62.

Practical Techniques for the Enrollment and Orientation of the
    Puerto Rican Child. New York: Commonwealth of Puerto Rico,
    Department of Labor, Migration Division, 1963.

Probst, Nathan, and Olmsted, Sophia A. "The Rising Puerto
    Rican Problem." Bar Bulletin (New York County Lawyers
    Association), IX March-1952, vol. 9, pp. 5-12.

A Program of Education for Puerto Ricans in New York City.
    A report prepared by a committee of the Association of
    Assistant Superintendents. New York: New York City Board
    of Education, 1947. 107 pp.

Project to Preserve the Integration of the Puerto Rican Migrant
    Family. New York: Puerto Rican Family Institute, 1965.
    19 pp.

Puerto Rican Children. New York. New York City Board of Education,
    Annual Report 1955-56. 27 pp.

Puerto Rican Children: Some Aspects of Their Needs and Related
    Services. New York: City Welfare Council, 1949. 7 pp.

Puerto Rican Employment in New York City Hotels. New York:
    New York State Commission Against Discrimination, Oct.
    1958, 9 págs.

Puerto Rican Farm Workers in Florida. Washington, D.C.: U.S.
    Department of Labor, Bureau of Employment Security, Feb.
    1955, 7 pp.

Puerto Rican Farm Workers in the Middle Atlantic States. Bureau
    of Employment Security, Nov. 1954. 11 pp.

"Puerto Rican Migrants Jam New York." Life, Aug. 25, 1947, pp.
    25-29.

Puerto Rican Migration to New York City. New York: New York
    City Department of City Planning, Feb. 1957. 9 pp.

Puerto Rican Neighbors. New York: National Council of the
    Episcopal Church, 1958. 24 pp.

"Puerto Rican Number." The Bible in New York. (New York Bible
    Society), vol. 49, Feb. 1958, pp. 1-8.

"Puerto Rican Pupils." Senior Scholastic, May 1, 1959, vol. 74,
    pp. 4T-5T.

Puerto Rican Pupils in New York City Schools. New York: Mayor's
    Committee on Puerto Rican Affairs, 1951.

"Puerto Rican Study." Newsweek, July 19, 1948, vol. 32, pp. 78-9.

Puerto Ricans Filling Manpower Gap. Washington, D.C. : Office of
    the Government of Puerto Rico, 1951. 14 pp. (Out of print.)

"Puerto Ricans Find Church Homes." Christian Century, March 26,
    1958, vol. 75, p. 365.

"Puerto Ricans Key Source of Labor." Highlights (New York City
    Department of Commerce and Public Events), Oct. 1956, vol.
    1, no. 8, pp. 1, 3.

"Puerto Ricans in New York City." Geographical Review, Jan. 1954,
    vol. 44, pp. 143-144.

Puerto Ricans In New York City. New York: Commonwealth of Puerto
    Rico, Department of Labor, Migration Division, 1965. 8 pp.

Puerto Ricans in New York City. New York: Welfare Council of
    New York City, Feb. 1948. 60 pp.

Puerto Ricans in New York City. New York: Welfare and Health
    Council of New York City, April 1953. 4 pp.

The Puerto Ricans of New York City. Washington, D.C.: Office
    of the Government of Puerto Rico, 1948. 102 pp. (Out of
    print).

Puerto Ricans in New York City. Report of the Committee on Puerto
    Ricans in New York City of the Welfare Council of New York City.
    New York: Welfare Council, 1948. 60 pp.

"Puerto Ricans in the New York State Labor Market." Industrial
    Bulletin. (New York State Department of Labor) August
    1957, vol. 36, no. 8, pp. 17-19.

"Puerto Ricans Start Up Labor Ladder." Business Week, May 2,
    1953, p. 150-2.

Rand, Christopher. "Puerto Ricans." Saturday Review, Sept. 13,
    1958, vol. 41, p. 36.

Rand, Christopher. The Puerto Ricans. New York: Oxford University
    Press, 1958. 178 pp.

Rand, Christopher. "A Reporter at Large: The Puerto Ricans."
    The New Yorker, Nov. 30-Dec. 21, 1957. (Series of four
    articles.)

Raushenbush, Carl. "A Comparison of the Occupations of First
    and Second Generation Puerto Ricans in the Mainland Labor
    Market and How the Work of the New York State Department
    of Labor Affects Puerto Ricans" pp. 56-61. In: A.J. Jaffe
    (ed.) Puerto Rican Population of New York City. New York:
    Columbia University Bureau of Applied Social Research, Jan.
    1954. 61 pp.

Raushenbush, Winifred. "New York and the Puerto Ricans." Harper's
    May 1953, vol. 206, no. 1236, pp. 13-15, 78-83.

"Really Fantastic: Bronx Puerto Rican Theater." Time, March 28,
    1949, vol. 53, p. 83.

Reiss, Paul J., Backgrounds of Puerto Rican Delinquency in New
    York City, Unpublished Master's thesis, Fordham University,
    1954.

Renek, Morris. "Community Hospital in the Ghetto." New Republic,
    Dec. 10, 1966, vol. 155, no. 24, p. 9.

Report on the Protestant Spanish Community in New York City.
    New York: Protestant Council of the City of New York, 1960.

Report on Survey of Brooklyn Agencies Rendering Services to
    Puerto Ricans. New York: Brooklyn Council for Social
    Planning, June 1953. 23 pp.

Report of the Third Migration Conference Between New York
City and Puerto Rican Officials: 1958. New York:
Commonwealth of Puerto Rico, Department of Labor,
Migration Division, 1958. 12 pp.

Resource Units for Classes with Puerto Rican Pupils: Secondary
School-Orientation Stage. New York: The Puerto Rican
Study of the New York City Board of Education, 1957.
117 pp.

Resource Units for Classes with Puerto Rican Pupils: Secondary
Schools-Transition Stage. New York: The Puerto Rican Study
of the New York City Board of Education, 1958. 123 pp.

Resource Units for Classes with Puerto Rican Pupils in the First
Grade. New York: The Puerto Rican Study of the New York
City Board of Education, 1956. 145 pp.

Resource Units for Classes with Puerto Rican Pupils in the Fifth
Grade. New York: The Puerto Rican Study of the New York
City Board of Education, 1956. 175 pp.

Resource Units for Classes with Puerto Rican Pupils in the Fourth
Grade. New York: The Puerto Rican Study of the New York
City Board of Education, 1955. 143 pp.

Resource Units for Classes with Puerto Rican Pupils in the Second
Grade. New York: The Puerto Rican Study of the New York
City Board of Education, 1956. 119 pp.

Resource Units for Classes with Puerto Rican Pupils in the Sixth
Grade. New York: The Puerto Rican Study of the New York City
Board of Education, 1958. 150 pp.

Resource Units for Classes with Puerto Rican Pupils in the Third
Grade. New York: The Puerto Rican Study of the New York
City Board of Education, 1958. 150 pp.

Resource Units for Pupils of Puerto Rican Background in the
"Extended Orientation Stage" in Junior High Schools.
New York: The Puerto Rican Study of the New York City
Board of Education, 1958. 40 pp.

Resource Units Suggested for Use in Seventh Grade Classes with
Puerto Rican Pupils. New York: The Puerto Rican Study of
the New York City Board of Education, 1955. 95 pp.

Resource Units in the Teaching of Occupations-An Experiment
in Guidance of Puerto Rican Teen Agers. New York: The
Puerto Rican Study of the New York City Board of
Education, 1956. 149 pp.

Reville, Janet N., and Rivera, Alfonso. The Psychological
Adjustment of Puerto Rican Boys. (Project No. 4623.)
New York: New York School of Social Work, 1956.

Reynolds, Lloyd G., and Shister, Joseph, Job Horizons-A Study
of Job Satisfaction and Labor Mobility. New York:
Harper and Brothers, 1949.

Riessman, Frank. The Culturally Deprived Child. New York:
Harper Brothers, 1962.

Rigau, Angel. "Un Estudio Puertorriqueño." La Prensa de
Nueva York, April 3-10, 1956.

Rigney, Margaret G. Practices and Procedures Used by Teachers
in Furthering Second Language Learning in the Primary Grades.
New York: The Puerto Rican Study of the New York City Board
of Education, 1956. 13 pp.

Rigney, Margaret G. Puerto Rican Children as Second Language
Learners. New York: The Puerto Rican Study of the New York
City Board of Education, 1956. 98 pp.

Rizzo Costa, Clara; and Robinett, Betty Wallace. La Familia
Vázquez en los Estados Unidos. San Juan: Estado Libre
Asociado de Puerto Rico, Departamento de Instrucción
Publica, 1955.

Robinson, Gertrude A. A Case Study of Puerto Rican Children in
Junior High School 65, Manhattan, New York City, New York.
Doctoral dissertation, New York Univ., 1956.

Robinson, Sophia M. Can Delinquency Be Measured?" New York:
Columbia University Press, 1936. See esp. pp. 236-249.

Robinson, Sophia M. "Social and Welfare Statistics on the New
York Puerto Rican Population," pp. 45-55. In: A.J. Jaffe
(ed.) Puerto Rican Population of New York City. New York:
Columbia University Bureau of Applied Social Research, Jan.
1954. 61 pp.

Rodriguez, María Luisa. Follow-Up Study of the Graduating Classes
of Two Junior High Schools. New York: The Puerto Rican Study
of the New York City Board of Education, 1955. 34 pp.

Román, Josefina de. "New York's Latin Quarter." The Inter-
American, Jan. 1946, vol. 1, no. 1, pp. 9-13, 36-37.

Rosado E. "New York's Latin Quarter." Reply. Inter American,
Feb. 1946, vol. 5, p. 47.

Rosario, Charles. "La Emigración Como Experiencia Vital."
La Torre (Universidad de Puerto Rico), enero-marzo de
1956, año 4, núm. 13, págs. 23-31.

Rosenthal, Alan G. Pre-School Experience and Adjustment of
Puerto Rican Children. Doctoral dissertation, New York
Univ., 1955.

Rosner, Milton S. A Study of Contemporary Patterns of
Aspirations and Achievements of the Puerto Ricans of Hells
Kitchen. Doctoral dissertation, New York Univ., 1957.

Rosten, N. "Puerto Ricans in New York." Holiday, Feb. 1961,
vol. 29, pp. 48-9.

Ruíz, Ruperto. Understanding Civil Liberties and Human Relations
as they Affect Puerto Ricans and Negroes. New York, 1966.
15 pp.

Ruíz, Ruperto. What Can a Puerto Rican or a Person of Hispanic
Descent Do To Become an Effective American Citizen? New
York, 1966. 4 pp.

Ruiz, Ruperto, and Present, H.L. Puerto Ricans in the United
States. New York: Spanish American Youth Bureau, June
1966. 13 pp.

Ruíz, Arreche, Paquita. Vocational Needs of the Puerto Rican
Migrant in New York City. Doctoral dissertation, Fordham
Univ., 1946.

Ruoss, M. "What About New York's Puerto Ricans?" National
Council Outlook, May 1954, vol. 4, p. 12.

Rusk, Howard A. "The Facts Don't Rhyme: An Analysis of Irony
in Lyrics Linking Puerto Rico's Breezes to Tropic Diseases."
New York Times, Sept. 29, 1957.

Ryan, Louise T. Common Errors in English Language Usage Made by Spanish speaking Pupils. Doctoral dissertation, New York Univ., 1950.

Salisbury, Harrison. The Shook-Up Generation. New York: Harper, 1958. 256 pp.

Samuels, Gertrude. "I don't think the Cop is my Friend." il. N.Y. Times Mag. March 29, 1964. pp. 28.

Samuels, Gertrude. The People vs. Baby. Garden City, New York: Doubleday and Company, 1967. 292 pp.

Samuels, Gertrude. "Plan to Salvage the 'Problem Family'." New York Times Magazine, May 12, 1957.

Samuels, Gertrude. "Puerto Rico: Land of Paradox; Thousands Leave for Lack of Opportunities, Yet it is Potentially an Island of Hope." New York Times Magazine, Oct. 30, 1955, pp. 18, 62, 64, 67.

Samuels, Gertrude. "Rebirth of a Community." New York Times Magazine, Sept. 25, 1955, pp. 26, 37-39, 42, 44.

Samuels, Gertrude. "Two Case Histories out of Puerto Rico." New York Times Magazine, Jan. 22, 1956.

Samuels, Gertrude. "Walk Along the Worst Block; East 100th Street." New York Times Magazine, p. 18-19, Sept. 30, 1962.

San Juan Day: Mainland Puerto Ricans Honor Their Patron Saint." Jubilee, Sept. 1946, pp. 48-51.

Sanguinetti, Carmen. Adapting Science Instruction in New York City Junior High Schools to the Needs of Puerto Rican Background Pupils. Doctoral dissertation, Teaching College, Columbia Univ., 1956.

Sanua, Victor D.; Diller, Leonard; Loomer, Alice; and McCavitt, Martin E. The Vocational Rehabilitation Problems of Disabled Puerto Ricans in New York City. New York: New York University-Bellevue Medical Center, Institute of Physical Medicine and Rehabilitation, 1957. 69 pp.

Sayers, Raymond S. "New York Teachers in Puerto Rican Schools." High Points (New York City Board of Education), Nov. 1957, vol. 39, no. 8, pp. 5-16.

Schaefer, Dorothy F. Prejudice in Mentally Retarded, Average and Bright Negro and Puerto Rican Adolescents. Doctoral dissertation, Columbia Univ., 1965.

Schepses, Edwin, "Puerto Rican Delinquent Boys in New York City." Social Service Review (University of Chicago), March 1949, vol. 23, no. 1, pp. 51-56.

Scotfied, John R. Within These Borders: Spanish-speaking Peoples in the U.S.A. New York: Friendship Press, 1953. 151 pp.

Seda, Angel Luis. Implications for Puerto Rico in a Study of the Hospital Chaplaincy in the United States. Doctoral dissertation, Teachers College, Columbia Univ., 1958.

Seda-Bonilla, Edwin. "Social Structure and Race Relations." Social Forces, Dec., 61, vol. 40, pp. 141-48.

Selected References on Migratory Workers and Their Families: Problems and Programs, 1950-56. Washington, D.C.: U.S. Department of Labor, Bureau of Labor Standards, April 1956. 16 pp.

Selected References for Teachers of Non-English Speaking Children. New York: New York City Board of Education, Division of Instructional Research, Bureau of Reference Research and Statistics, n.d. 5 pp.

Senior, Clarence. Background Data for Discussion on the Changing City Scene. New York: Commonwealth of Puerto Rico, Department of Labor, Migration Division, 1957. 10 pp.

Senior, Clarence. Dispersion of Puerto Rican Migration. Speech Delivered at Annual Conference of Welfare and Health Council of New York City, May 7, 1953. New York: Commonwealth of Puerto Rico, Department of Labor, Migration Division, 1953. 6 pp.

Senior, Clarence. Implications of Population Redistribution. New York: National Association of Intergroup Relations Officials, 1957. 19 pp.

Senior, Clarence. "Migrants: People, Not Problems," pp. 371-375. In: Transactions of the Fiftieth Anniversary Meeting of the National Tuberculosis Association, 1954.

Senior, Clarence. "Migration and Economic Development in Puerto Rico." Journal of Educational Sociology, Dec. 1954, vol. 28, no. 4, pp. 151-156.

Senior, Clarence. "Migration to the Mainland." Monthly Labor Review, Dec. 1955, vol. 78, pp. 1354-8.

Senior, Clarence. "Migration and Puerto Rico's Population Problem." Annals of the American Academy of Political and Social Science, Jan. 1953, vol. 285, pp. 130-136.

Senior, Clarence. "Puerto Rican Dispersion in the United States." Social Problems, Oct. 1954, vol. 2, pp. 93-99. no. 2.

Senior, Clarence. Puerto Rican Emigration. Rio Piedras: University of Puerto Rico. Social Science Research Center, 1947. 166 pp.

Senior, Clarence. The Puerto Rican Migrant in St. Croix. Rio Piedras: University of Puerto Rico, Social Science Research Center, 1947.

Senior, Clarence. Puerto Rican Migration: Spontaneous and Organized. Commonwealth of Puerto Rico, Department of Labor, Migration Division 1957. 14 pp.

Senior, Clarence. The Puerto Ricans: Strangers-Then Neighbors. Chicago, Quadrangle Books, 1965, 128 pp.

Senior, Clarence. "Puerto Ricans on the Mainland." Americas, Aug. 1961, vol. 13, pp. 36-43.

Senior, Clarence. The Puerto Ricans of New York City. Washington, D.C.: Office of the Government of Puerto Rico, 1948. 102 pp.

Senior, Clarence. "The Puerto Ricans in the United States." pp. 109-125. In: Joseph B. Gittler (ed.) Understanding Minority Groups. New York: John Wiley, 1956. 139 pp.

Senior, Clarence. "Puerto Rico: Migration to the Mainland." Monthly Labor Review, Dec. 1955, vol. 78, no. 12, 1354-1358.

Senior, Clarence. "Research on the Puerto Rican Family in the United States." Marriage and Family Living. Feb. 1957, vol. 19, pp. 32-38.

Senior, Clarence. "The Sociological Approach to Assimilation." (Excerpts from a Speech at the Fiftieth Anniversary Meeting of the National Tuberculosis Association, 1954.) Population Bulletin, vol. 23, no. 2, pp. 30-31.

Senior, Clarence. Speech Problems of Puerto Rican Children. (Report of the Committee on Individualization of Speech Improvement.) New York: New York City Board of Education, Department of Speech Improvement, n.d. 15 pp.

Senior, Clarence. Strangers--and Neighbors: The Story of our Puerto Rican Citizens. New York: Anti-Defamation League of B'nai B'rith, 1952. 53 pp.

Sexton, Patricia Cayo. Spanish Harlem. New York: Harper & Row, 1965. 208 pp.

Shotwell, Louisa Rossiter. "Puerto Rican Migrant Workers Plunge Eagerly into Study of English." Reprint from Christian Science Monitor, New York, 1952. 2 pp.

Shotwell, Louisa Rossiter. "Puerto Rican Neighbors." Presbyterian Tribune, Sept. 1953, vol. 68, no. 11, pp. 1-3.

Shotwell, Louisa Rossiter. This is the Migrant. New York: Friendship Press, 1958. 24 pp.

Siegel, Arthur L. "The Social Adjustments of Puerto Ricans in Philadelphia." Journal of Sociology, Aug. 1957, vol. 46, pp. 99-110.

Siegel, Arthur L.; Orland, Harold; and Greer, Loyal. Puerto Ricans in Philadelphia: A Study of Their Demographic Characteristics, Problems, and Attitudes. Philadelphia: Philadelphia Commission on Human Relations, April 1954. 135. pp.

Sierra Berdecía, Fernando. La Emigración Puertorriqueña: Realidad y Política Pública. San Juan: Estado Libre Asociado de Puerto Rico, Editorial del Departamento de Instrucción Pública. 1956. 23 págs. Also published in La Torre (Universidad de Puerto Rico), enero-marzo de 1956, año 4, núm. 13, págs. 33-54.

Sierra Berdecía, Fernando. Un Mensaje del Secretario del Trabajo a los Obreros que Desean Ir a Trabajar en Fincas de los Estados Unidos. Nueva York: Estado Libre Asociado de Puerto Rico, Departamento del Trabajo, División de Migración, 1957. 21 págs.

Siga Estos Pasos . . . Nueva York: Estado Libre Asociado de Puerto Rico, Departamento del Trabajo, Division de Migración, 1958. 10 págs.

Skardon, J.A. "On The Fringe of Trouble: Peché Sánchez." Coronet, Aug. 1956, vol. 40, pp. 120-30.

Smart, P. "Experiment in Boston: Services to Puerto Rican Newcomers." Wilson Library Bulletin, Feb. 1960, vol. 34, p. 415.

Snyder, Eleanor, M. Public Assistance Recipients in New York State, January-February 1957: A Study of the Causes of Dependency During a Period of High-Level Employment. New York: New York State Inter-Departmental Committee on Low Incomes, Oct. 1958. 159 pp.

"So Heinous, So Infamous." Time, July 19, 1954, vol. 64, p. 19.

Sobrino, James F. Group Identification and Adjustment in Puerto Rican Adolescents. Unpublished Doctoral dissertation, Yeshiva University, 1965.

"Solution for Puerto Rico: Emigration." Scholastic, April 22, 1946, vol. 48, p. 11.

"Spanish-speaking Americans." National Council Outlook, May 1954, vol. 4, p. 12.

Speech Problems of Puerto Rican Children. Report of the Committee on Individualization of Speech Improvement. New York: New York City Board of Education, Department of Speech Improvement, n.d. 15 pp.

Spiritual Care of Puerto Rican Migrants: Report on a Conference. New York: Archdiocese of New York, Office of the Coordinator of Spanish-American Catholic Action, 1955. 228. pp.

Stambler, Ada. A Study of Eighth Grade Puerto Rican Students at Junior High School 65 Manhattan, with Implications for Their Placement, Grouping and Orientation. Doctoral dissertation, Teachers College, Columbia Univ., 1958.

Statistical Guide for New York City. New York, New York City Department of Commerce and Industrial Development, 1957.

The Status of the Public School Education of Negro and Puerto Rican Children in New York City. New York: Public Education Association, assisted by Research Center for Human Relations, New York University, Oct. 1955. 24 pp.

Stein, William W. Preliminary Report on Proceedings of the Dade County Council on Community Relations with Regard To Problems of Latin American Residents of Greater Miami. Univ. of Miami, July 5, 1958, 7 pp.

Sternau, Herbert. Puerto Rico and the Puerto Ricans. New York: Council of Spanish-American Organizations and American Jewish Committee, Feb. 1958. 36 pp.

Steward, Julian (ed.) The People of Puerto Rico: A Study in Social Anthropology. Urbana, Ill.: University of Illinois Press, 1956; 540 pp. (A Social Science Research Center Study, College of Social Sciences, University of Puerto Rico.)

Stout, W.W. "Do We Want the West Indies?" Saturday Evening Post, April 21, 1945, vol. 217, pp. 9-11.

Suchman, Edward A.; and Alksne, Lois. "Communication Across Cultural Barriers." American Catholic Review, Winter 1961, vol. 22, pp. 306-313.

"Sugar-Bowl Migrants, New York Spanish Harlem." Time, Aug. 11, 1947, vol. 50, p. 20.

Su Guía a New Haven. New Haven, Conn.: New Haven Human Relations Council, 1959. 88 pp.

A Summary in Facts and Figures: 1. Progress in Puerto Rico. 2. Puerto Rican Migration. New York: Commonwealth of Puerto Rico, Department of Labor, Migration Division 1964-1965. 21 pp.

Suraci, Anthony. Reactions of Puerto Rican and Non-Puerto
    Rican Parents to Their Mentally Retarded Boys. Doctoral
    dissertation, New York Univ., 1966.

Talase, Gay. "Hottest Fighter in Town." The New York Times
    Magazine, Nov. 30, 1958, pp. 80, 82, 84.

Tannenbaum, Dora; McCaulley, Sara; and Carpenter, H. Daniel.
    The Puerto Rican Migration: A Report. New York: Hudson
    Guild Neighborhood House, Colony House, and Grand Street
    Settlement, 1955. 13 pp.

Teaching Children of Puerto Rican Background in New York City
    Schools. New York: The Puerto Rican Study of the New York
    City Board of Education, 1954. 76 pp.

Teaching English to Puerto Rican Pupils in Grades 1 and 2.
    New York: The Puerto Rican Study of the New York City
    Board of Education, 1956. 183 pp.

Teaching English to Puerto Rican Pupils in the Secondary School.
    The Puerto Rican Study of the New York City Board of
    Education, 1957. 156 pp.

Tendler, Diana. Social Service Needs in a Changing Community:
    A Study of the Use of Voluntary Social Agencies by Puerto
    Rican Clients. Doctoral dissertation, New York Univ.,
    1965.

Tentative Report of the Committee on Classification Bulletin
    No. 1 New York: New York City Board of Education, Bilingual
    Committee of the Junior High School Division, June 1949.
    12 pp.

"Thank Heaven for Puerto Rico." (An Editorial.) Life, March 15,
    1954.

Theobald, Jacob. The Orientation and Adjustment of New Pupils.
    New York: The Puerto Rican Study of the New York City;
    Board of Education, 1955. 45 pp.

Thomas, Piri. Down These Mean Streets. New York: Alfred A.
    Knopf, 1967. 333 pp.

Tió, Salvador. "La Emigración: Cambios Sugeridos en la
Política Pública." La Torre (Universidad de Puerto
Rico), enero-marzo de 1956, año 4, número 13, págs.
113-136.

Torruellas, Luz M. "La Emigración: Impacto Sobre La Estructura
Económica y Social de Puerto Rico." La Torre (Universidad
de Puerto Rico), enero-marzo de 1956, año 4, núm. 13, págs.
55-72.

Toth, C.W. "Strangers in the City." Commonweal, Nov. 28, 1952,
vol. 57, pp. 200-1.

Tough, Rosalind, and MacDonald, Gordon D. "Manhattan's Real
Property Values and the Migrant Puerto Ricans." Land
Economics: A Quarterly Journal of Planning, Housing and
Public Utilities (University of Wisconsin), Feb. 1958,
vol. 34, no. 1, pp. 1-18.

Trabajadores Agrícolas de Puerto Rico: Bienvenidos a Pennsylvania,
U.S.A. (Puerto Rican Farm Workers: Welcome to Pennsylvania,
U.S.A.) Harrisburg: Pennsylvania Bureau of Employment
Security, 1957. 45 pp.

Trade Unions and Puerto Rican Workers: Report on Conference Held
May 17, 1952. New York: Commonwealth of Puerto Rico,
Department of Labor, Migration Division, 1952. 22 pp.

"Tropics in New York." Americas, June 1952, vol. 4, pp. 32-3.

"Unit on Puerto Rico." World Week, Scholastic Magazine, April 28,
1954, vol. 24, no. 12, pp. 9-11.

Units for the Teaching of Practical English to Puerto Rican Adults.
San Juan, Puerto Rico: Commonwealth of Puerto Rico, Department
of Education, Adult Education Program, 1957. 112 pp.

Urban Renewal. New York: New York City Planning Commission,
1958. 96 pp.

Use su Derecho a Votar. Introducción por José Monserrat. Nueva
York: Estado Libre Asociado de Puerto Rico, Departamento
del Trabajo, División de Migración, 1953. 8 pp.

Villaronga, Mariano. "Program of Education for Puerto Rican Migrants." Journal of Educational Sociology, 1954, vol. 28, no. 4, pp. 146-150.

Vivas, G.E. "Our Spanish-speaking U.S. Catholics." Americas, May 15, 1954, vol. 91, pp. 187-8.

Vivas, Julio. The Puerto Ricans of Cleveland: A Challenge to Community Organization, Cleveland: Western Reserve University, 1951.

Wacher, Sara A. Home and School Relations in New York City as Seen by Puerto Rican Children and Parents. New York: The Puerto Rican Study of the New York City Board of Education, 1955. 27 pp.

Wachs, William. A Study of the Extent to Which Textbooks Teaching English to Foreign-born Hispanic Adults in New York City Help Them Comprehend the Daily English Newspapers They Read. Doctoral dissertation, New York Univ., 1946.

Wagner, G.P. "Puerto Rico in Harlem" New Republic, August 23, 1954, vol. 131, pp. 16-18.

Wakefield, Dan. "The Gang That Went Good." Harper's, June 1958, vol. 216, no. 1297, pp. 36-43.

Wakefield, Dan. Island in the City: The World of Spanish Harlem. Boston: Houghton Mifflin, 1959. 278 pp.

Wakefield, Dan. "Other Puerto Ricans." New York Times Magazine, Oct. 11, 1959, pp. 24-54.

Wakefield, Dan. "Politics and the Puerto Ricans." Commentary, March 1958, vol. 25, no. 3, pp. 226-236.

Wakefield, Dan. "200,000 New Yorkers Can't Vote." Nation, Feb. 28, 1959, vol. 188, pp. 183-85.

Walker, R.C. "I Like Puerto Ricans." Rural New Yorkers, Aug. 4, 1956, vol. 106, no. 5865, p. 504.

De Weaver, N.C. ACTU Labor Schools for Spanish-speaking."
     <u>America</u>, Aug. 6, 1955, vol. 93, pp. 451-3.

Weiner, Louis. "Vital Statistics in New York City's Puerto
     Rican Population." pp. 30-44. In: A.J. Jaffe (ed.)
     <u>Puerto Rican Population of New York City</u>. New York:
     Columbia University, Bureau of Applied Social Research
     Jan. 1954. 61 pp.

Weissman, Julius. <u>An Exploratory Study of Communication
     Patterns of Lower Class Negro and Puerto Rican Mothers
     and Pre-School Children</u>. Doctoral dissertation, Teachers
     College, Columbia Univ., 1966.

Wells, Robert W. "Our Latin Newcomers." <u>The Milwaukee Journal,</u>
     April 6-9, 1958. (Series of four articles.)

Werner, M.R. "The Puerto Ricans: Slum to Slum." <u>The Reporter,</u>
     Sept. 12, 1950, vol. 3, no. 6, pp. 20-22. (First of two
     articles.)

Werner, M.R. "The Puerto Ricans in New York." <u>The Reporter,</u>
     Sept. 26, 1950, vol. 3, no. 7, pp. 20-23. (Second of
     two articles.)

Wertham, Fredric. <u>The Circle of Guilt</u>. New York: Rinehart,
     1956. 211 pp.

Whitman, F.L. "New York's Spanish Protestants." <u>Christian
     Century</u>, Feb. 7, 1962, vol. 79, pp. 160-4. Reply:
     Mercado, Juan E., March 28, 1962, vol. 79, p. 388.

Willis, Robert. <u>An Analysis of the Adjustment and Scholastic
     Achievement of Forty Puerto Rican Boys Who Attended Transition
     Classes in New York City</u>. Doctoral dissertation, New York
     Univ., 1961.

Willoughby, Wes. "Puerto Rican Story." Bethlehem (Penn.)
     <u>Globe-Times</u>, July 7-12, 1958. (Series of six articles.)

Wirth, Louis. <u>The Ghetto</u>. University of Chicago Press, Chicago
     Illinois, 1929.

Woodbury, Clarence. "Our Worst Slum." <u>The American</u>, Sept. 1949,
     vol. 148, no. 3, 31, 128, 132.

Workshop Conference on Puerto Ricans. New York: Brooklyn
    Council for Social Planning, Oct. 1953, 24 pp.

"World They Never Made: New York Puerto Ricans." Time,
    June 12, 1950, vol. 55, pp. 24-6.

Yezierska, Anzia. "The Lower Depths of Upper Broadway."
    The Reporter, Jan. 19, 1954, vol. 10, no. 2,
    pp. 26-29.

Yinger, J.M., and Simpson, G.E. "Integration of Americans
    of Mexican, Puerto Rican and Oriental Descent."
    Annals of the American Academy of Political and
    Social Science, March 1956, vol. 304, pp. 124-31.

Your American Pupil From Puerto Rico. New York: Bronx
    Districts 17 and 18, New York City Board of Education,
    Sept. 1956. 15 pp.

PUERTO RICAN MIGRANTS
ON THE MAINLAND
OF THE UNITED STATES

IRCD BULLETIN

PUBLICATION OF THE ERIC INFORMATION
RETRIEVAL CENTER ON THE DISADVANTAGED

PROJECT BEACON - FERKAUF GRADUATE SCHOOL OF HUMANITIES AND SOCIAL SCIENCES - 55 FIFTH AVENUE, N.Y., N.Y. 10003
YESHIVA UNIVERSITY

Volume IV, No. 1   January 1968

Puerto Rican Migrants on the Mainland of the United States

A REVIEW OF THE LITERATURE

Gertrude S. Goldberg, M.S.

In attempting to increase our knowledge of Puerto Ricans on the mainland of the United States, we are confronted with several types of potentially relevant materials. As is the case with all newcomers, there is the culture of the former home, as well as the way of life that develops in the new world. And, in view of the wealth of the American experience with migration, there is also the literature of the European immigrations to consider. This discussion of potential sources of knowledge concerning mainland Puerto Ricans will be confined to materials available in English.

In reviewing these materials, it should be noted that we are dealing with a population group larger than the nearly 900,000 persons of Puerto Rican birth and parentage on the continent according to the 1960 census,[1] for there has been considerable return migration. For example, the New York City schools received 54,750 Puerto Rican pupils from Puerto Rico between 1956 and 1961 and discharged 32,210 to Puerto Rico during the same period.[2] It has been estimated by a member of the Puerto Rico Planning Board that there were over 100,000 return migrants between 1955 and 1963.[3] Finally, although New York City is the home of about 72 percent of the migrants on the continent,[4] dispersion to other areas has begun, and only about 60 percent of the net migration since 1957 has been to New York City.[5]

The Island Background

The relevance of materials dealing with the former home depends, to a considerable extent, upon the demographic characteristics of the migrant group, particularly upon their socioeconomic status and their place of residence at the time when they migrate. For even if a society were more

(Continued on Page 2)

GERTRUDE S. GOLDBERG is a Research Associate of ERIC-IRCD.
[1]Puerto Rico Department of Labor, Migration Division, A Summary in Facts and Figures, 1964-1965: Progress in Puerto Rico—Puerto Rican Migration, New York: The Commonwealth, p. 16.
[2]Madeline M. Morrissey and Gary Zouzoulas, Pupil Migration in the New York City Public Schools, 1956–1957 to 1965–1966, New York: Board of Education, 1967, pp. 8 and 15.
[3]Jose Hernandez Alvarez, Return Migration in Puerto Rico, Rio Piedras: Social Science Research Center, University of Puerto Rico, 1964, p. 6. Cited in Clarence Senior and Donald O. Watkins, "Toward a Balance Sheet of Puerto Rican Migration," Status of Puerto Rico: Selected Background Studies Prepared for the United States–Puerto Rico Commission on the Status of Puerto Rico, Washington D.C.: U.S. Government Printing Office, 1966, p. 721.
[4]This estimate is based on figures given for New York City and total mainland Puerto Rican population in 1960 in Puerto Rico Department of Labor, Migration Division, A Summary in Facts and Figures, pp. 16-17.
[5]Puerto Rico Department of Labor, Migration Division, A Summary in Facts and Figures, p. 16.

LA VIDA: WHOSE LIFE?

Gertrude S. Goldberg, M.S.
Edmund W. Gordon, Ed.D.

In her study of Italians in Greenwich Village during the 1920's, Caroline Ware observed the disinterest of the schools in the culture of the immigrants:

> ... the local schools were indifferent to the loyalties and customs of the Italian group and did not consider it necessary to be familiar with the ethnic background of the children in order to prepare them for their role in American life.[1]

Today, educators are likely to maintain a very different attitude toward the "loyalties and customs" of disadvantaged groups. It is, however, by no means certain that the contemporary ethos of cultural pluralism, as it is translated into practice, is any more conducive to educating today's disadvantaged groups than the ethnocentric approach described by Ware. One finds a tendency either to assume prima facie that all of the poor are culturally different from the rest of us or to develop stereotyped and over-generalized notions about the culture of those who do have styles of life which deviate from the American middle class. An education which scarcely emphasizes careful study of disadvantaged population groups and a professional life which rarely permits time to offset this deficiency are some reasons why educators' mere interest in the cultures of today's poor is not in itself an advance over yesterday's disinterest.

Knowledge of the Puerto Ricans, the most recent group to migrate in large numbers to the mainland of the United States, is particularly limited. Their relatively recent arrival, insufficient emphasis on the history of Caribbean peoples throughout our educational system, and a paucity of social science materials directly relevant to the migrant population are factors which compound the barriers to understanding all disadvantaged groups.

Given these sets of conditions, it is likely that a study of Puerto Ricans by Oscar Lewis, the noted anthropologist, would be heavily consulted by practitioners. Such usage is particularly probable because his works read more like literature than most social science—an attribute by no means undesirable per se. Thus, it is the popularity of Lewis' most recent book, La Vida: A Puerto Rican Family in the Culture of Poverty—San Juan and New York, rather than its merits

(Continued on page 6)

EDMUND W. GORDON is Professor and Chairman of the Department of Educational Psychology and Guidance, Yeshiva University.

[1]Caroline F. Ware, Greenwich Village, 1920-1930: A Comment on American Civilization in the Post-War Years, Boston: Houghton Mifflin Co., 1935, p. 167.

THE LITERATURE

(Continued from page 1)

static than Puerto Rico, which all observers regard as a very rapidly changing society, and if it displayed less than the considerable cultural heterogeneity of that small island, it would still be necessary to match migrants' backgrounds with available social science studies. For example, 90 percent of early postwar migrant Puerto Ricans departed from urban areas.[6] Thus, materials describing rural subcultures would be of scant applicability. And now, when nearly two-thirds[7] of the newcomers are coming directly from the rural areas, the studies of rural subcultures, several of them first-rate ethnography, lack blanket relevance, even for rural migrants. Some, like Steward's *The People of Puerto Rico*, are based on field data collected nearly 20 years ago. The life portrayed in the four lower-class subcultures studied by Steward and his associates may be comparable to that experienced by migrants from similar rural subcultures who came during the early 1950's, a time of heavy migration. (Net out-migration from Puerto Rico was over 45,000 every year between 1951 and 1956.[8]) Such materials may also describe life styles that these migrants would attempt to hold onto in their new home, but they would not by the admission of one of Steward's associates, Professor Sydney Mintz, reflect contemporary Puerto Rican subcultures. They would thus not be relevant to the way of life of rural residents who left in the late 1950's although these anthropological studies might describe cultures to which present migrants were exposed earlier in their lives.

The migrants' particular island background is especially important to know in view of the variety of subcultures on the island itself. Steward, for example, found an absence of a common culture, even among lower-class rural Puerto Ricans. Depending largely upon the economic or productive system in a particular rural or lower-class subculture, he found varying cultural patterns. Such cultural features as child rearing, male–female authority in the family, rates of consensual, civil, and religious marriages, and habits of spending and saving differed according to the productive arrangements. Thus, workers on one government owned sugar plantation displayed matrifocal patterns; those working on a privately owned sugar plantation, more equal relations between spouses; and those in one tobacco subculture, a strict patriarchal dominance. It has been maintained by Theodore Brameld, who studied islanders later but far less thoroughly, that "the growth of the welfare state tends to diminish dissimilarities and to encourage common structures, programs, and goals."[9] Mintz, on the other hand, who bases his conclusions on extensive reviews of the literature and on an admittedly brief revisit to his area of study, finds a lack of homogeneity on the island and even fewer shared values than earlier within his subculture, Cánamelar. Of the continuing absence of a common culture, Mintz writes:

... any summary statement of Puerto Rican character or identity and any attempt to describe Puerto Ricans as if their culture were homogeneous, means treading on risky grounds....[10]

---

[6]C. Wright Mills, Clarence Senior, and Rose Goldsen, *The Puerto Rican Journey: New York's Newest Migrants*, New York: Harper and Row, 1950, pp. 32-33. The study found that only about one-fifth of the migrants could be considered from a rural background.

[7]Senior and Watkins, "Toward a Balance Sheet," pp. 710 and 713.

[8]Puerto Rico Department of Labor, Migration Division, *A Summary in Facts and Figures*, p. 15.

[9]Theodore Brameld, *The Remaking of a Culture: Life and Education in Puerto Rico*, New York: Harper and Row, 1959, p. 359.

[10]Sidney Mintz, "Puerto Rico: An Essay in the Definition of a National Character," *Status of Puerto Rico*, p. 371.

What goes by the label of "Puerto Rican National character"—for instance, the speaking of Spanish or a sexual double standard—may not only fail to hold for everyone, but in all likelihood has very different symbolic connotations in different social segments of the national society.[11]

The important sociological work of Tumin, *Social Class and Social Change in Puerto Rico*, emphasizes the importance of knowing the educational attainments of migrants, for this variable was found by him to be the most important predictor of attitudes and behaviors for an island-wide sample. Although Tumin was probably incorrect in the extent to which he de-emphasized the rural–urban variable, since his consideration of rural respondents as a group tended to blur the heterogeneity among the rural subcultures, his stress on the educational variable should be noted.

Despite the importance of such demographic characteristics of migrants as educational levels, former place of residence, and the time at which they migrated, these data are neither complete for the entire postwar period, nor are those available well circulated. For the early postwar years, the Columbia study, reported by Mills, Senior, and Goldsen in *The Puerto Rican Journey*, is an important source of demographic and attitudinal data, as well. Based upon field work in two core areas of Puerto Rican settlement in New York during the spring of 1948, it reflects one of the two heaviest years of net in-migration before 1950—1946 with 39,911.[12] Because it attempted to analyze motivation for migration by means of a "push" from the island and a "pull" toward the continent, its findings help to establish the extent to which the variable of migration affects the cultural allegiance of the newcomers. The findings of Mills and his associates and the more qualified inferences from later data, that the economic promise of the mainland is the main motivation for the journey, would suggest that the cultural allegiance of the migrants is not necessarily affected by the decision to migrate—although their way of life is greatly affected by the migration and the exposure to mainland subcultures.

For the years subsequent to 1948, when the vast majority of migration occurred, there are two island surveys which together provide data for the period 1957–1964, but data dealing with characteristics of migrants during the first half of the 1950's, the period with highest postwar migration, have not appeared in the works reviewed by this writer. And the data on the later arrivals are reported only in a recent article by Clarence Senior and Donald Watkins, itself poorly circulated.

In addition to the caveats concerning the matching of migrants' background and materials depicting island life, there are important problems presented by the literature itself. Related but in some ways distinct from the issues of cultural heterogeneity and societal change is a lack of consensus concerning such crucial areas of study as race relations, the meaning and motivation of consensual marriage, and the nature of the family structure. Perhaps one reason for the apparent disagreement among various observers is a failure on the part of some to specify the region, class, and subculture to which data apply or to generalize findings that apply to one segment of the island population to the Puerto Rican people as a whole.

In-Migration and Immigration

The usefulness of the extensive literature on past immigration depends upon the extent to which the characteristics and experiences of the Puerto Rican in-migrants

---

[11]Mintz, "Puerto Rico: An Essay," p. 381.

[12]Puerto Rico Department of Labor, Migration Division, *A Summary in Facts and Figures*, p. 15.

resemble those of European immigrants of the pre-World War I period. Despite the obvious differences of citizenship status for Puerto Ricans, the relative ease of their journey, and the existence of a non-white group among them, comparisons between them and earlier newcomers are made.[13] Although this discussion concentrates on the differences between Puerto Ricans and the European immigrants as a group, we do not mean to imply that there were not many dissimilarities among the various European nationalities.

Oscar Handlin, a foremost historian of European immigration to America, has studied the migration of Puerto Ricans and Negroes to New York City since the war and has observed both similarities and dissimilarities between earlier and later newcomers. On the one hand, Handlin points out that the increase of Negroes and Puerto Ricans in the metropolitan region, almost 250 percent in little more than a quarter of a century, "is ... a migration comparable in scope to that of the Irish and Germans between 1850 and 1860 and of the Jews and Italians, 1890–1915."[14] Handlin, more than some other scholars, appears sanguine about the Puerto Ricans' ultimate adjustment and the nature of the effort that it will take:

... the experience of the past offers a solid foundation for the belief that the newest immigrants to a great cosmopolitan city will come to play as useful a role in it as any of their predecessors. They themselves need only to show the will and energy, and their neighbors the tolerance to make it possible.[15]

In contrast to the immigrants who relied heavily on independent small businesses for mobility, the present newcomers must find an alternative to the entrepreneurial route—despite what many view as substantial shopkeeping acumen among the Puerto Ricans. The Puerto Ricans must depend much more upon the school system for upward mobility than their predecessors, for they will need the formal education to "break into the developing complex of positions as professional, managerial, or clerical employees and fee receivers."[16] The Puerto Rican Study: 1953–1957 of New York City schools concluded that:

... judging from the gains made by the second generation of Puerto Ricans in New York City schools, it would appear that the third generation should be able to compete on equal terms with their peers of like socioeconomic backgrounds.[17]

Yet, it would seem that this period of grace available to others may need to be foreshortened for our latest arrivals.

Some observers stress the present marginality of jobs for persons with education and skill comparable to that of the majority of Puerto Rican migrants or doubt that the second generation is making sufficient progress to warrant optimism. The latter is, of course, related to one's estimate of the rapidity with which progress must be made. Handlin seems to emphasize the current availability of jobs for the undereducated and relatively unskilled despite the long-term reduction of such opportunities. Others have tended to stress their present scarcity. The longer such employment holds out, so to speak, the longer the newcomers have to prepare themselves or their children for jobs requiring higher education, but the conditions to which current earnings subject them are not conducive to educational betterment.

A report of the Puerto Rican Forum, led by young Puerto Rican professionals in New York City, commented on progress in the Puerto Rican community from the perspective of a proposal to upgrade their people. But they were also influenced in the development of these goals by what they considered to be the poverty of Puerto Rican prospects. Pointing out, first of all, that too small a percentage of the second generation had reached labor force age to make reliable predictions, they concluded:

... it is necessary to know that Puerto Ricans are not making it once they learn English; that the children born in the city of Puerto Rican parents are not becoming successful New Yorkers once they go through the city's school system; that the story of the Puerto Rican will not be the same as the story of groups of immigrants who came before—unless some lessons learned in the past immigrations are applied and the significant differences of the situation are recognized and worked out.[18]

If upward mobility is to occur, however, it will most likely take place after the first generation, and one careful examination of the changing status of a group of second generation Puerto Ricans offers some grounds for optimism. Nathan Kantrowitz of the Columbia University School of Social Work examined U.S. census data for the New York Standard Metropolitan Statistical Area to determine the occupation, education, and income of persons of Puerto Rican parentage who were between 15 and 24 years of age in 1950 and between 25 and 34 years of age in 1960. Even allowing for the stringent test of comparing their achievement over the decade with that of non-Puerto Rican whites, he found that second generation Puerto Ricans were quite mobile:

... the children of Puerto Rican migrants, New York's newest and poorest people ... in this decade have moved more rapidly than expected into the (albeit lower) white collar and High School ranks. If this decade is a prologue for improvement in their remaining lifetime and in their children's another generation may find the ethnic Puerto Rican distributed much as the general population.[19]

The data on Puerto Ricans as a group, who are overwhelmingly first generation, reveal current poverty and undereducation. In 1959, according to the U.S. census, 34 percent of the Puerto Rican families, in contrast to 27 percent of the non-whites and 15 percent of all families in New York City, had incomes under $3,000 a year, a frequently accepted poverty level.[20] Figures for 1963 incomes, based on a random sample of 2,118 adults in New York City of which 192 were Puerto Ricans, suggest such an extraordinary decline in the percentage of Puerto Rican families with incomes under $3,000 that one is led to question the reliability of the Puerto Rican sample. The percentage of all families and of Negro families living below that level declined by 16 percent and 12 percent, respectively, which are figures that are consistent with inflation and a rise in the standard of living. But the percentage of such Puerto Rican families declined precipitously—from 34 percent to 16

[18]The 1960 U.S. census reported that only 26,368 or 3.9 percent of the Puerto Ricans in New York-Northeastern New Jersey area were non-white. Nathan Kantrowitz and Donnell Pappenfort, 1960 Fact Book for the New York-Northeastern New Jersey Standard Consolidated Area: The Nonwhite, Puerto Rican, and White Non-Puerto Rican Populations: Selected Characteristics for Cities of 50,000 or More, New York: Columbia University School of Social Work, 1966, p. 19.

Demographers consider these census figures unreliable. Senior and Watkins state that censuses since 1940 have shown a declining proportion of non-white Puerto Ricans on the mainland of the United States: 11.7 percent in 1940, 9.6 percent in 1950, and 4.7 percent in 1960. It is not known whether the migration is more heavily non-white than the population of the Island (20.3 percent) or whether non-whites return in disproportionate numbers. See Senior and Watkins, "Toward a Balance Sheet," p. 709.

According to Mills, Senior, and Goldsen, The Puerto Rican Journey, p. 90, two-thirds of the migrants would be considered non-white by mainland standards.

[14]Oscar Handlin, The Newcomers—Negroes and Puerto Ricans in a Changing Metropolis, Cambridge: Harvard University Press, 1959, p. 53.

[15]Handlin, The Newcomers, p. 121.

[16]Handlin, The Newcomers, p. 76.

[17]J. Cayce Morrison, The Puerto Rican Study: 1953-1957. New York: Board of Education, 1958, p. 181.

[18]Puerto Rican Forum, Inc., Puerto Rican Community Development Project: A Proposal for a Self-Help Project to Develop the Community by Strengthening the Family, Opening Opportunities for Youth, and Making Full Use of Education, New York: The Puerto Rican Forum, Inc., 1964, p. 9.

[19]Nathan Kantrowitz, "Social Mobility of Puerto Ricans in New York, 1950-1960," 1967, p. 2 (unpublished).

[20]Kantrowitz and Pappenfort, 1960 Fact Book, p. 31.

percent or a 52 percent decrease in four years![21] In the area of educational achievement, Frank Cordasco has pointed out that Puerto Ricans have the lowest level of formal education of any identifiable ethnic or color group in New York City.[22] Yet, these figures are not in themselves conclusive, for considerable poverty and undereducation probably characterized earlier groups at a comparable stage of contact with the new world.

To a certain extent the assessment of progress in relation to other groups may depend upon the variables observed. Father Joseph Fitzpatrick compared intermarriage of first and second generation Puerto Ricans with the comparable practices by immigrants during the period 1908–1912. He concluded that "on the basis of evidence of marriage practice, the process of assimilation to the culture of the U.S. mainland is increasing rapidly."[23] When the variable is language acquisition, organizational strength, or self-help efforts, conclusions may be different, but seldom have comparable data for earlier and later groups, as in the case of Fitzpatrick's work, been gathered. On the other hand, one wonders how a variable like intermarriage is related to economic mobility and whether it has the same meaning for all sets of newcomers.

Despite the differences in the Puerto Rican migration and the European immigrations—of which the economic opportunities appear to be paramount—there is reason to believe that some of the feelings of "the uprooted" may apply to the Puerto Rican strangers, providing that the necessary qualifications are made. These works can sensitize us to the plight of the newcomer who is alien though American and stranded, even though it is possible to return. Similarly, the stages of acculturation of the Italian immigrant—initial contact, conflict, and accommodation[24]—may have different durations and different forms, but Campisi's work, and that of others, reminds us that the time which the migrant has spent on the mainland is crucial to an understanding of his integration of old and new ways of life.

The Literature on Mainland Puerto Ricans

In view of the many limitations of materials indirectly related to mainland Puerto Ricans, one looks nearly exclusively to studies of the migrants themselves. Recommendation for such a course comes from the Puerto Rican anthropologist Elena Padilla, who has studied island subcultures and New York migrants during the 1950's: "It is not possible to speak of a Puerto Rican culture in New York, nor even to pretend to understand the culture of Puerto Ricans in New York in the light of the culture of Puerto Rico."[25] It is, thus, particularly limiting that there are a lack of careful psychological, sociological, and anthropological studies of mainland Puerto Ricans.

We have already discussed data from the two major works on patterns of migration—the early work of Mills, et al., and the recent essay of Senior and Watkins which is the only up-to-date, comprehensive statement on the migration. Despite the sophistication of its approach to the subject of migration, its excellent critical bibliography, and its reference to major surveys which appear not to have been reported elsewhere in English, it has been very poorly circulated.

Elena Padilla's Up From Puerto Rico is "the only cultural anthropological treatment of Puerto Rican migrants in New York City."[26] Field work, which was done during the mid-1950's, involved 18 months of participant observation and a long questionnaire interview of 48 Puerto Rican heads of households. Senior and Watkins warn that "in the light of the limited sample and the lack of quantified conclusions, care should be taken not to use the experience reported in this book as a basis for generalizations about all persons of Puerto Rican origin who were living in New York City in the mid-1950's."[27] Nonetheless, Padilla's work treats carefully such issues as child rearing practices, educational achievement and interaction with school authorities, the functioning of the extended family and the ritual kinship system—both of which are diluted in the American slum setting, and patterns of courtship and marriage.

A recent book by the sociologist, Patricia Cayo Sexton, treats the Puerto Rican community from a very different perspective than that of Padilla. Based upon two years of observation by the author in New York's major Puerto Rican colony, it is most useful for its description of the organizational structure of the community, its social problems, and the proclivity to social action of various ethnic groups (it is a mixed neighborhood) in the community. Problems in the area of housing and urban renewal and education are treated at some length.

Two works, Senior's The Puerto Ricans: Strangers—then Neighbors and the chapter on Puerto Ricans in Glazer and Moynihan's Beyond the Melting Pot, are useful general treatments of the migration and the migrants. Written for the Anti-Defamation League, the Senior book attempts to place the migration within the perspective of the coming of earlier strangers but at the same time presents a variety of information, particularly upon the integration and adjustment of the Puerto Ricans, including the treatment of them by the receiving community. Moynihan and Glazer summarize data collected by others and attempt to characterize the adaptation of the Puerto Ricans "to a city very different from the one to which earlier immigrant groups adapted."[28] The authors conclude that "they are being modified by the new process of adaptation in new and hardly predictable ways . . . and, one can barely imagine what kind of human community will emerge from the process of adaptation."[29]

Father Joseph Fitzpatrick, Edward Seda Bonilla, and Beatrice Berle have done useful studies of particular issues such as race relations, delinquency, intermarriage, and health and medical practices. Berle's companion study to that of Padilla, Eighty Puerto Rican Families in New York City, deals with health, attitudes toward illness and medical care, and use of medical resources, as well as the more general issues of adjustment. Her sample, as Senior and Watkins note, is not of the general Puerto Rican population of New York City but "of some families with problems of sickness."[30] Fitzpatrick observed the frequency of marriage between Puerto Ricans of different race—white, mulatto, and Negro—in six selected parishes in New York City. On the basis of these and Berle's data on racial intermarriage, he concluded that "the widespread acceptance of marriage of people of noticeably different color is continuing in the New York situation and there is no reason, as of the present moment, to expect it to stop."[31] Seda gathered data by means of participant observation in three New York City Puerto Rican neighbor-

---

[21]Jack Elinson, Paul W. Haberman, and Cyrille Gell, Ethnic and Educational Data on Adults in New York City, 1963–1964, New York: Columbia University, School of Public Health and Administrative Medicine, 1967, p. 63. Data were given for Negroes in this survey but for non-whites in the census. Approximately 95 percent of non-whites in the census are American Negroes.
[22]Frank Cordasco, "The Puerto Rican Child in the American School," Journal of Negro Education, 36 (September 1967), p. 182.
[23]Joseph P. Fitzpatrick, "Intermarriage of Puerto Ricans in New York City," American Journal of Sociology, 71 (January 1966), p. 406.
[24]Paul J. Campisi, "Ethnic Family Patterns: The Italian Family in the United States," American Journal of Sociology, 53 (May 1948), pp. 443–49.
[25]Elena Padilla, Up From Puerto Rico, New York: Columbia University Press, 1958, p. 49.

[26]Senior and Watkins, "Toward a Balance Sheet," p. 793.
[27]Senior and Watkins, "Toward a Balance Sheet," p. 794.
[28]Nathan Glazer and Daniel P. Moynihan, Beyond the Melting Pot: The Negroes, Puerto Ricans, Jews, Italians, and Irish of New York City, Cambridge: The M.I.T. and Harvard University Press, 1963, p. 136.
[29]Glazer and Moynihan, Beyond the Melting Pot, p. 136.
[30]Senior and Watkins, "Toward a Balance Sheet," p 791.
[31]Joseph P. Fitzpatrick, Reprint of "Attitudes of Puerto Ricans Toward Color," The American Catholic Sociological Review, 20 (Fall 1959), p. 13.

hoods to study problems of racial and ethnic identity of white, mulatto, and Negro Puerto Ricans during the period 1953–1956. He recognized the "latent functions of conflicting racial identities which the impact of American culture creates among Puerto Ricans."[32]

The research of Nathan Kantrowitz, whose study of second generation mobility we have already noted, will provide considerable amounts of data, largely demographic, on New York Puerto Ricans. A demographic study, which focuses on Negro and Puerto Rican segregation in the New York metropolis and has important implications for social policy, consists of three major parts: 1, a geographical study of the differential migration which has resulted in minority communities; 2, a geographical study of their land use; and, 3, an ecological study of neighborhood segregation and change by census tract. One by-product of the project has been the publication of reference books, the *Social Statistics for Metropolitan New York* series. Volume 2 of the series culls all 1960 census data for which comparisons could be made for Puerto Ricans, non-whites and white non-Puerto Ricans in New York and northeastern New Jersey cities and counties of 50,000 or more.

The combined research of Mobilization for Youth and the Columbia University School of Social Work, directed by Richard A. Cloward, has resulted in some studies with considerable data on Puerto Ricans mostly in one New York City neighborhood, although Puerto Ricans are not the focus of these works. Four of these studies have drawn on data from adult and adolescent surveys of a section of the Lower East Side in 1961. Puerto Ricans comprised 26 percent of the adults and approximately one-third of the youngsters between 10 and 19 years of age in a random sample of 988 households from which one adult and all the youngsters in that age range were interviewed. In all of these studies, there are at least some sections in which data are presented by ethnic group. There are John Michael's work on socialization and school dropout and dissertations by Abraham Alcabes' on *Community Perception and the Use of Neighborhood Centers*, by Frank F. Furstenberg, Jr. on *Transmission of Attitudes in the Family*, and by Paul Lerman on *Issues in Subcultural Delinquency*.[33] Two other research efforts of Columbia University and Mobilization for Youth involve different sets of data from the adult and adolescent surveys. William Martin's study concerns social attitudes, housing conditions, and political orientations and activities of Puerto Rican residents of East Harlem and the Lower East Side who participated in rent strike activities during 1964 and 1965. Research conducted by John Grundy and Judith Baxter under the direction of Leonard Granick deals with work programs for out-of-school, unemployed youth. They will issue a separate report concerning the use of these services by Puerto Rican youth who comprise more than two-thirds of a sample of 1,600 youth.

There are at least two studies of Puerto Ricans outside of New York City—Donchian's of New Haven newcomers and Seigel's of Puerto Ricans in Philadelphia. The Philadelphia study, conducted in the 1950's, provides data on language and medical and religious "adjustment," as well as on leadership and occupational status and aspirations. Donchian's study reports migration patterns, housing conditions, occupation and income, etc. (It is cited in the bibliography that follows Senior and Watkins' article, "Toward a Balance Sheet of Puerto Rican Migration," but is out of print and virtually unavailable.)

In the field of education, up-to-date, methodologically sound, and substantial research is, on the whole, lacking. A very recent bibliography compiled by Frank Cordasco and Leonard Covello on Puerto Rican children in mainland schools has nearly 350 entries, approximately 50 of which are unpublished. Among the latter are a collection of papers of Covello (for nearly 30 years Principal of Benjamin Franklin High School in Spanish Harlem) which is in the process of being edited. One looks in vain among the listings of this bibliography, many· of which are short reports of unevaluated projects and newspaper accounts, for recent "studies."

The Puerto Rican Study: 1953–1957 of the New York City Board of Education, conducted mainly in 32 schools of high Puerto Rican concentration, has already been noted in another context. It contains data on socioeducational adjustment and relations between parents and the school system, as well as information more specifically related to scholastic achievement and English language acquisition. Responsible for numerous curricular innovations and procedures for recording data on Puerto Rican and other migrant and immigrant pupils, it covers the period 1953–1957 and has never been followed up with a report of the efficacy of the practices it instituted or a later assessment of the achievement and adjustment of Puerto Rican pupils.

There have been a few studies of specialized aspects of the learning behavior of Puerto Rican children. For example, there is the well-known article published in 1950 by Anastasi and de Jesús on "Language Development and Nonverbal IQ of Puerto Rican Preschool Children in New York City." Very recently, James Fennessey analyzed data on New York City Puerto Rican pupils from the national survey, *Equality of Educational Opportunity*, conducted by Coleman, et. al. The purpose of his work was to determine the relationship between language spoken in the home and other aspects of ethnic background and what differences are present at several grade levels in vocabulary test scores of Puerto Rican children from contrasting home language backgrounds.

A recent paper by Stella Chess, et al., "Social Class and Child-Rearing Practices," reports some initial findings of a longitudinal study (conducted in the Department of Psychiatry of the New York University Medical Center) on *Retardation in Intellectual Development of Lower-Class Puerto Rican Children in New York City*.[34] There were two samples of three-year-olds, both from stable families, one with highly educated native-born middle- and upper middle-class parents and the other with Puerto Rican unskilled or semiskilled working class parents. The children were tested in order to determine whether there were differential responses to demands for cognitive performance and, if so, their relationship to child rearing practices of the two groups.

The work of the New York University Medical Center research team is characterized by an important recognition that differential functioning in disadvantaged children does not necessarily derive from parental rejection or indicate deficiency in the children, although such acquired patterns of behavior may be a disadvantage in a task-oriented society. The goals of the ongoing research project are to identify: 1, those experimentally determined patterns of behavior and intellectual functioning of a population of lower-class Puerto Rican children in New York City which, given current educational practice, are inconsistent with optimal learning; 2, the specific child care practices which produce such patterns in the children; and, 3, the favorable factors in the children's environment which can be utilized in

[32]E. Seda Bonilla, "Social Structure and Race Relations," *Social Forces*, 40 (December 1961), p. 147.
[33]Furstenberg's dissertation is on file at the Department of Graduate Faculties, Columbia University. Both Lerman's and Alcabes' dissertations are on file at the School of Social Work, Columbia University.

[34]Stella Chess, et al., "Social Class and Child-Rearing Practices, "1967 (unpublished). Findings discussed in this paper are reported in detail in a monograph now in press. M. E. Hertzig, *Class and Ethnic Differences in the Response of Preschool Children to Cognitive Demands*, Chicago: Child Development Monograph.

programs to prevent or remedy impairments in learning efficiency.[35]

Two other studies, both underway at the Ferkauf Graduate School of Humanities and Social Sciences, Yeshiva University, will provide data relevant to the education and language behavior of Puerto Ricans. Vera John and Vivian Horner head an interdisciplinary team which will survey the current status of bilingual education of young children in order to develop new models for bilingual early learning programs. New York Puerto Ricans are one of the three groups upon which the research is focused. A study directed by Joshua A. Fishman seeks to measure and describe relatively stable and widespread intragroup bilingualism. Data, which have been gathered and are in the process of analysis and interpretation, pertain to the linguistic behavior and attitudinal repertoires of a sample of geographically dispersed and geographically focused (living on the same city block) middle-class Puerto Ricans in New York City.

Conclusions

An examination of the various types of social science materials potentially relevant to Puerto Ricans on the mainland of the United States reveals that our knowledge of this group of recent newcomers is somewhat limited. Demographic data on postwar migration, itself poorly circulated and for some years unavailable, indicate the scrutiny with which island studies must be used. Some of the sociological and anthropological materials may be applicable to the pre-migration experiences of *some* of the migrants. *All* of these materials should be used with recognition of the rapid socioeconomic and cultural changes in Puerto Rico, the persisting cultural heterogeneity of the Puerto Rican people, and the lack of consensus among serious students of the island on important social issues. Furthermore, limited knowledge of the motivations for migration of various groups of the Puerto Rican newcomers calls attention to the need to ascertain the cultural allegiance of the migrant before assuming that studies which match his background actually approximate his values and behavior.

Lacking data that would establish definite similarities between the characteristics and experiences of European immigrants and Puerto Rican migrants, we must be wary of making sweeping use of the historical, anthropological, and sociological literature describing earlier groups. Particularly insufficient are data dealing with comparable stages of contact with American society for Puerto Ricans and their antecedents. What information we do have, particularly regarding the different economic conditions under which they have struggled, would suggest that findings from studies of former immigrants must be carefully qualified, if they are used at all.

While a reasonable amount of attention has been given to the study of the migrant group itself, both in New York and in the other cities to which they are going, our knowledge is limited by the relative newness of the migration, by the fluidity of the community itself (largely as a result of the substantial return migration), by the lack of studies which have dealt with a representative sample of the entire Puerto Rican mainland group, and probably by an overriding interest in the Negro among socially disadvantaged groups. One anticipates that the studies in process to which we have alluded will help to fill some of the gaps in our knowledge and offer some guidelines upon which more comprehensive and current research can be based.

---

[35]Alexander Thomas, *Retardation in Intellectual Development of Lower-Class Puerto Rican Children in New York City*, New York: Department of Psychiatry, New York University Medical Center, December 1967.

Six

LA VIDA

(Continued from page 1)

as a piece of research, that prompt us to review it here. It is also hoped that a discussion of its methodology will emphasize the scrutiny with which all background materials must be read and interpreted.

La Vida, published late in 1966, is not only the first full-length portrait of a Puerto Rican urban slum family but also the only intensive study of persons both on the island and after their move to the mainland—and, in some instances, after their return to Puerto Rico. All of the five major subjects in *La Vida* (Fernanda Fuentes and her four children by Cristóbal Ríos) either migrated to or visited the mainland. Thus, *La Vida* would appear to fulfill some criteria of relevance to contemporary Puerto Rican migrants.

> . . . *La Vida* is one more brilliant demonstration of the validity and profundity of the method Lewis has pioneered: the meticulous description, and tape-recorded self-depiction, of the daily life of a single yet archetypical family of the poor. (Michael Harrington, *The New York Times Book Review*, November 20, 1966.)

There is no question that *La Vida* tells us much about the life of one Puerto Rican lower income family in New York and San Juan. Not only has Lewis refined his technique of the tape-recorded biography, which provided us with his vivid Mexican lives,[2] but he has also given us many perspectives other than that of the members of a nuclear family. In *La Vida*, we hear from several of the spouses of Fernanda and her children, Fernanda's aunt, her children's stepmother, a grandchild, and a step grandchild (an hija de crianza or foster child of Felicita Ríos), and close family friends—sixteen persons in all. In addition, Lewis has combined these multiple biographies with "observed typical days."

The biographies provide a subjective view of each of the characters, whereas the days give us a more objective account of their actual behavior. The two types of data supplement each other and set up a counterpoint which makes for a more balanced picture.[3]

The major question, then, is not whether Lewis provides us with much information about the life of the Ríos family but whether the Ríos family members are typical of other San Juan slum dwellers or of San Juan slum dwellers who come to the mainland of the United States. They cannot be typical of the present migrant group, nearly two-thirds of whom come from rural areas. (In *La Vida*, only Fernanda's aunt and three of her spouses came from rural areas before moving on to San Juan and, subsequently, to New York.)

On the one hand, Lewis tells us that the Ríos are only representative of persons whom he characterizes as living in the culture or, more correctly, subculture of poverty. Further, he maintains that *La Vida* deals with only one segment of the Puerto Rican population and that the data should not be generalized to Puerto Rican society as a whole. On the other hand, he appears to make more elaborate claims:

The intensive study of the life of even a single extended family by the methods used in this volume tells us some-

---

[2]See Oscar Lewis, *Five Families: Mexican Case Studies in the Culture of Poverty*, New York: Basic Books, 1959; *The Children of Sanchez*, New York: Random House, 1961; and *Pedro Martinez*, New York: Random House, 1964.
[3]Oscar Lewis, *La Vida: A Puerto Rican Family in the Culture of Poverty—San Juan and New York*, New York: Random House, 1966, p. XXV.

thing about individuals, about family life, about lower-class life as a whole, and about the history and culture of the larger society in which these people live. It may also reflect something of national character, although this would be difficult to prove.[4]

As Nathan Glazer has observed in his review of La Vida, it is Lewis' "ambiguity" on the "crucial question" of the Ríos' representativeness that is "the most serious flaw of this book."[5]

The difficulty in determining the relationship of the Ríos to other low income Puerto Rican families is that Lewis compares them to other families in his sample and in the fictionalized slum La Esmeralda but fails to establish the relationship of his sample to San Juan and New York Puerto Ricans. The comparisons are frequently between the Ríos and "other households we studied," whom they are said to approximate in important characteristics. Yet, he tells us that they deviate even from his sample in several respects. The mean number of years of schooling completed by persons in the New York sample[6] was 6.5 years, whereas that of the Ríos family members in New York was 3.4. On the other hand, the educational level of the Ríos family in San Juan was slightly higher than the island sample group—4.2 vis-à-vis 3.6. The greater schooling of New York than of island sample families is consistent with the pattern of migrants' educational attainments which have consistently exceeded island levels. And the Ríos, whose migrant members were less well educated than the family as a whole, are atypical in this respect.

Another respect in which the Ríos deviate from the sample is in their involvement in prostitution. Lewis minimizes the extent to which the practice of prostitution among three of the four principal female subjects differs from its occurrence in 33 percent of the sample families in La Esmeralda. The latter figure is a sizable minority but still a minority. More important, "an unusually large number of women in La Esmeralda, compared to other San Juan slums, worked as prostitutes in San Juan, catering to the longshoremen and to visiting sailors and soldiers."[7] One is led, therefore, to question whether the Ríos family is typical of families in the sample and in the slum where they lived, which, in regard to prostitution, is unlike the three other San Juan slums studied by Lewis.

Of his San Juan sample, Lewis states that he and his associates collected data on "one-hundred families in Greater San Juan selected from slums which represented significant ecological, racial, socio-economic, and religious variables."[8] But he does not further elaborate this description, except in pointing out that "the principle criteria in the selection of families were low income, relatives in New York, and a willingness to cooperate in the study."[9] Of their selection, he states only that "we located the poorest families with the help of social workers who introduced us to their local barrio comisarios," a liaison officer between the city administration, the local political leaders, and the people of the barrio.[10]

In describing the 32 families in La Esmeralda which were selected for study, Lewis does not specify the criteria for

selecting that particular slum, whose atypicality has been noted above, or the 32 families in it. In La Esmeralda, he agreed to study 10 low income, multi-problem families which had been carefully selected from the rolls of social agencies by Dr. Rosa C. Marín of the School of Social Work, University of Puerto Rico, for her Family-Centered Treatment, Research and Demonstration Project. By coincidence, Cruz Ríos, Fernanda's youngest daughter, and her children were in both the Marín sample, consisting by definition of multi-problem families, and in Lewis' La Esmeralda sample. One is inclined to assume that if the Ríos are representative of the sample, the sample is of multi-problem families.

The relationship between multi-problem families and those who live in the subculture of poverty is not clear. Lewis does, however, concede that "the frequency distribution of this style of life cannot be determined until we have many comparable studies from other slums in Puerto Rico and elsewhere."[11] While Lewis in his attitudes toward families whom social workers would classify as multi-problem is free of a judgmental approach—"I am impressed by the strength in this family . . . by their fortitude, vitality, resilience and ability to cope with problems which would paralyze many middle-class individuals . . ."—he, nonetheless, admits the "presence of considerable pathology."[12] How typical the extent of their pathology is of the sample or of other slum dwellers is not known.

> Casting loose from the data, he (Lewis) expounds an unconvincing theory of the subculture of poverty . . . The definition is . . . circular. The kinds of poor people who act as the Ríos do belong to the subculture of poverty which explains why the Ríos act as they do . . . Why do the other 80 per cent of the American poor not fall within the same pattern? (Oscar Handlin, Atlantic Monthly, December 1966.)

It is particularly unfortunate that Lewis failed to clarify the representativeness of the sample from which the Ríos family was drawn (itself more disadvantaged and problematic, in certain respects, than parts of the sample), in view of the extent to which their behavior appears to deviate from nearly all descriptions of lower-class Puerto Rican family life. Lewis notes "the failure of the women in the Ríos family to accept the traditionally submissive role of women in Puerto Rican society."[13] While one would question an allusion to "the" role of women in view of the heterogeneity of cultural patterns in Puerto Rico, the behavior of the Ríos–Fuentes women appears to deviate even from the matrifocal patterns in some subcultures of Puerto Rican society. It is only among the schizophrenic wives in the Hollingshead and Rogler study (Trapped Families and Schizophrenia, 1965) of 20 well (neither spouse psychotic) and 20 schizophrenic (one or both partners schizophrenic) couples in San Juan slums that one finds comparable ambivalence about their roles as wives and mothers.

The prevailing pattern of authority among well families in the Hollingshead and Rogler study was that of male dominance, while in husband-schizophrenic families, it was the wife who controlled. In the families where a schizophrenic wife was married to either a well or schizophrenic husband, neither was clearly dominant. It is not so much

[4]Lewis, La Vida, p. XV.
[5]Nathan Glazer, "One Kind of Life," Commentary, 93 (February 1967), p. 84.
[6]Of the New York sample, Lewis states, "On the New York side, we located and studied fifty families related to families in our Puerto Rican sample." Lewis, La Vida, p. XXXVII.
[7]Lewis, La Vida, pp. XXXIV–XXXV.
[8]Lewis, La Vida, p. XVIII.
[9]Lewis, La Vida, p. XIX.
[10]Lewis, La Vida, p. XIX.

[11]Lewis, La Vida, p. XXV.
[12]Lewis, La Vida, p. XXIX.
[13]Lewis, La Vida, p. XXVII.

the matrifocality of the Ríos—although it is atypical—which appears deviant but the instability of these women, their vacillating acceptance of maternal and child rearing responsibilities. The practice of serial monogamy (18 husbands for four Ríos women) is not inconsistent with matrifocality, but the frequency of the latter pattern in Puerto Rican slums is not clear. The 40 study families of Hollingshead and Rogler were comparable to a probability sample of 104 low income San Juan slum families, and the study group, incidentally, had educational levels similar to those of the Ríos and their spouses. However, neither serial monogamy nor matrifocality prevailed among these families. None of the women in the study groups in which spouses were between 20 and 39 years of age (Fernanda and her children ranged in age from 17 to 40) had more than two marriages. Lewis states that matrifocality is a common occurrence in the culture of poverty, but, once again, the frequency of that style among urban slum dwellers in Puerto Rico and elsewhere is not known, although other data suggest that it is the pattern of the minority.

> . . . is he indeed describing Puerto Ricans, in San Juan and New York, or is he describing exceptional people, leading exceptional lives, who resemble their fellow Puerto Ricans only in limited ways? (Nathan Glazer, Commentary, February 1967.)

The portrait of life in La Vida, which may tell us more about "the life" than "'life," does not appear to have significance for an understanding of the majority of Puerto Rican slum dwellers—much less all Puerto Rican families—or for most Puerto Rican migrants to the mainland. That it deals with the urban slum dweller at a time when nearly two-thirds of the migrants come from rural areas makes it inapplicable to the majority of mainland Puerto Ricans. Whether it applies to the one-third from urban areas is hard to ascertain from what Lewis tells us. We do know that the Ríos fail to conform to Lewis' New York sample in regard to education and rural residence prior to residence in San Juan. But Lewis never mentions the comparability of his New York sample, the 50 families who are relatives of families in the San Juan sample, to New York Puerto Ricans as a group.

It would be unfair to criticize Lewis for not dealing with rural migrants or for not selecting families representative of mainland Puerto Ricans. His interests lie with urban poverty and the subculture of poverty—not primarily with migration. And it is important, particularly for clinical personnel, to have knowledge of the behavior of multi-problem families providing that we do not misconstrue their representativeness. What does seem unfortunate is his ambiguity, his lack of unequivocal disclaimers in regard to the culture of impoverished Puerto Ricans in San Juan or New York. Also unfortunate is his choice of a title for this book—it tends to make rather universal claims for the work. This lack of modesty is particularly regrettable because the behavior of the Ríos family, regardless of whether Lewis views it within the context of the culture of poverty, appears prurient, immoral, and notorious to many middle-class American readers who have made La Vida a best seller. Moreover, professional educators, social workers, and physicians are neither immune to judgmental attitudes toward the Ríos family itself nor resistant to generalizations based upon what is probably their atypical behavior. Thus, the Puerto Rican community, burdened with its heavy toll of poverty, must also bear the load of Lewis' heavy tome.

Eight

A Review

Down These Mean Streets

Down These Mean Streets is a significant human document. It tells it "like it is" in the experience of one colored Puerto Rican boy growing up in Spanish Harlem. In the vivid and rough but colorful language of the streets, with remarkable descriptive power and the ability to convey emotion and sentiment, with a detailed account of experiences more realistic than anything in La Vida, Piri Thomas opens a window through which the outside world can get a glimpse of the tortured life of a teenage subculture which is rarely visible any other way.

Thomas was born in New York City in 1928. The book is the account of his life in a strong, stable, upwardly mobile Puerto Rican family; his involvement in a teenage street culture which led him through violence, sex, thievery, and drugs; his terrible struggle with the problem of identity based upon the problem of his dark color; his effort to find decent work despite discrimination; his term in jail for attempted armed robbery; his growing awareness of himself and of the value of his life; and his return to a more creative, healthy existence. Apart from the remarkable human testament which it represents, what makes this book significant?

It locates the problem where the problem really is—not in the Puerto Rican people, the Puerto Rican background, or the Puerto Rican family, but in the streets of New York City. Thomas was not raised in a "culture of poverty" family. Even according to middle-class norms it was a good family. But when Thomas hit the streets, the family lost almost all power to cope with the impact of the peer group. This alienation of youth from adults—their creation of a world of their own with its own values, norms, expectations, rewards, and prestige symbols—is a central factor in problems of education, employment, and delinquency. Much more should be known about it. Piri Thomas tells us plenty. The irrelevance of the school to the whole process and its inability to deal with it are distressing.

The book also eloquently documents the problem of color as it affects a colored Puerto Rican. Thomas was tormented in the hope that, because he was a Puerto Rican, his experience would be different from that of American Negroes in a white man's world. It was not. Through personal anguish, he fought his way back to a self-awareness and a self-acceptance that led to a life dedicated to serving others.

A careful reading of Down These Mean Streets will certainly bring understanding about the often strange behavior of teenagers in the city streets. Most of all, it should excite compassion and lead to enlightened efforts to correct the conditions in which potentially rich lives like Piri Thomas' almost destroy themselves.

Joseph P. Fitzpatrick, Ph.D.

PIRI THOMAS, Down These Mean Streets, New York: Knopf, 1967.
JOSEPH P. FITZPATRICK is Professor of Sociology at Fordham University.

A Bibliography on the Puerto Rican Population
and Selected Background Studies

The bibliography that follows is presented in four sections. Section I consists of Island background materials; Section II deals with Puerto Rican migrants on the mainland of the United States; Section III includes four bibliographies with extensive references on the general Puerto Rican population; and Section IV contains a list of reviews of *La Vida*. LEWIS, OSCAR. **La vida: a Puerto Rican family in the culture of poverty—San Juan and New York.** New York: Random House, 1966. 669p.

ERIC–IRCD utilizes the following coding system to assist the reader in gaining access to documents cited in bibliographies. No special notation will be made for articles appearing in regularly published journals, which are readily available to most subscribers in university and other libraries. The relevant code letters which will be placed at the end of each of the remaining appropriate citations are as follows:

C the document is in the ERIC–IRCD collection;

D doctoral dissertation for which microfilm copy is available through University Microfilm;

E the document is available on microfiche cards produced by ERIC, which may be secured through the ERIC Document Reproduction Service (EDRS) and may be found in repositories throughout the country, including ERIC clearinghouses; and

X the unpublished document is in the ERIC–IRCD collection and will be xeroxed upon request at a cost of 10¢ per page.

The numbers following some of the references are accessions numbers. ED indicates the ERIC accession number; UD indicates the ERIC–IRCD accession number. Documents marked **E** should be ordered by their ED numbers and those marked **E** (In Process.) by their UD numbers from the ERIC Document Reproduction Service (EDRS), The National Cash Register Company, Box 2206, Rockville, Maryland 20852.

Island Background

BOURNE, DOROTHY D.; and BOURNE, JAMES R. **Thirty years of change in Puerto Rico: a case study of ten selected rural areas.** New York: Praeger, 1966. 411p. **C** UD 05026
Assesses the changes that have taken place in 10 rural communities as a result of programs planned and executed by the Puerto Rican government. The areas were first studied in 1932. Data were gathered by means of extensive interviewing in the community, and some observation was done by people involved in the earlier study.

BRAMELD, THEODORE. **The remaking of a culture: life and education in Puerto Rico.** New York: Harper, 1959. **C**
Attempts to describe, interpret, and understand the relationship between Puerto Rican culture and education in order to provide ways of improving and clarifying the educational philosophy and program in Puerto Rico. Brameld believes, in contrast to some other observers, that there is a unified Puerto Rican culture. The sample used consisted of people from two rural subcultures, one urban subculture, and national leaders.

GORDON, MAXINE W. **Cultural aspects of Puerto Rico's race problem.** American Sociological Review, 15:382-92, June 1950.
A study of the way in which the Puerto Rican cultural heritage has affected racial prejudice. It looks at the history of race relations, attitudes toward intermarriage, Puerto Rican folklore, and other cultural patterns.

LANDY, DAVID. **Tropical childhood: cultural transmission and learning in a rural Puerto Rican village.** Chapel Hill: University of North Carolina Press, 1959. 291p. **C**
Selected for intensive study were 18 families considered repre-

sentative of the lower-class, cane-dependent population, and living in the village of Valle Caña. The author discusses family composition, living conditions, health, religion, income, education, traditional attitudes toward sex, courtship, and child bearing, and compares child rearing practices and child behavior in the Valle Caña sample with a New England upper–lower and upper–middle class sample.

LEWIS, OSCAR. **La vida: a Puerto Rican family in the culture of poverty—San Juan and New York.** New York: Random House, 1966. 669p. **C** UD 02948
This anthropological study begins with a long introduction which describes Lewis' methods, the setting, and the family involved in the study. A discussion of the theory of the "culture of poverty" is included. The rest of the book is the story of a Puerto Rican family, as told by the members of the nuclear family and some of their relatives and friends.

MINTZ, SIDNEY W. **Puerto Rico: an essay in the definition of a national culture.** In: Status of Puerto Rico: selected background studies, for the United States—Puerto Rico Commission on the Status of Puerto Rico. Washington, D.C.: U.S. Government Printing Office, 1966. p. 339-34. **C** (In process.)
An essay attempting to clarify and bring unity to the writings of sociologists and anthropologists on the nature of Puerto Rican culture. Part I discusses "culture as a term of reference"; Part II, "Puerto Rico in the Caribbean setting"; and Part III, "some views of Puerto Rican culture." Some of the topics included in the appendices are community studies, race relations studies, Puerto Rican family structure and attitudes, national culture, and studies of change.

MINTZ, SIDNEY W. **Worker in the cane: a Puerto Rican life history.** New Haven: Yale University Press, 1960. 288p.
The life story of a cane worker in a small Puerto Rican village, Santa Isabel. The book consists of reports of tape-recorded interviews with the cane worker and background and interpretative materials presented by the author.

PUERTO RICO. DEPARTMENT OF LABOR. MIGRATION DIVISION. NEW YORK CITY OFFICE. **A summary in facts and figures, 1964–1965: progress in Puerto Rico—Puerto Rican migration** 1966. 22p. **X** UD 05023
Contains statistics from a variety of sources on the island of Puerto Rico and the migration of Puerto Ricans to the mainland of the United States. The latter includes net migration figures for all postwar years, Puerto Rican populations by states and selected cities, and data specifically related to the size of the Puerto Rican population in New York City.

ROBERTS, LYDIA J.; and STEFANI, ROSA L. **Patterns of living in Puerto Rican families.** Río Piedras: University of Puerto Rico, 1949. 411p.
An attempt to study Puerto Rican family living at all socioeconomic levels and "formulate the basic needs of Puerto Rican families." The sample consisted of 1,000 families which represented all geographic sections. Data were gathered on housing, health, and diet and presented by income and area of residence.

ROGLER, LLOYD H.; and HOLLINGSHEAD, AUGUST B. **Trapped: families and schizophrenia.** New York: John Wiley, 1965. 436p. **C**
A report on an exploratory study of the effect of schizophrenia on the performance of social roles. The sample consisted of 40 couples, 20 in which either or both spouses were schizophrenic and 20 in which neither was psychotic. Important data on family patterns in urban slums of San Juan are included.

SEDA BONILLA, E. **Social structure and race relations.** Social Forces, 40:141-48, December 1961.
A report on the findings of a study conducted under the auspices of the Social Science Research Center of the University of Puerto Rico which attempts to look at the importance of race in the social structures of Latin America and the United States. Participant observation was done in three Puerto Rican neighborhoods in New York City between 1953–1956.

STEWARD, JULIAN; AND OTHERS. **The people of Puerto Rico.** Urbana: University of Illinois Press, 1956. 540p. **C** UD 00417
The first section of this cultural–historical study attempts to analyze and explain contemporary Puerto Rican culture in terms of the historical changes that have occurred. A major portion is devoted to the study of lower-class rural subcultures by Steward's assistants. The subcultures are: "Tabara—subcultures of a tobacco and mixed crops municipality," by Robert A. Manners; "San Jose—subcultures of a 'traditional' coffee municipality," by Eric R. Wolf; "Nocora—the subculture of workers on a government owned sugar plantation," by Elena Padilla Seda; and "Cánamelar—the subculture of a rural sugar plantation proletariat," by Sidney W. Mintz. Also included is a section on "The Prominent Families of Puerto Rico," by Raymond L. Scheele.

STYCOS, J. MAYONE. **Family and fertility in Puerto Rico: a study of the lower income group.** New York: Columbia University Press, 1955, 332p.
Data were gathered from 72 families; 24 from three rural areas, 24 from an urban area, and 24 from three small towns. The topics discussed are: differential status ideologies of the sexes, child rearing practices, courtship, early marriage and consensual union, marital relations, attitudes toward fertility, and birth control practices.

TUMIN, MELVIN; and FELDMAN, ARNOLD S. **Social class and social change in Puerto Rico.** Princeton: Princeton University Press, 1961. 549p. **C** UD 02853
The class structure of Puerto Rico is analyzed to determine relationships between class characteristics, class relationships, and social change. Data were gathered by means of a field study utilizing an island-wide sample of 1,000 "heads-of-households" from all class groups.

WOLF, KATHLEEN L. **Growing up and its price in three Puerto Rican subcultures.** Psychiatry, 15:401-33, November 1953.
A detailed description of the contrasting patterns of child rearing in three different Puerto Rican subcultures on the island of Puerto Rico: 1, lower-class sugar cane workers; 2, lower-class tobacco workers, and, 3, middle-class urbanites. The author attempts to show that the uniform cultural tradition of Puerto Rico does not produce a uniform Puerto Rican personality type.

Puerto Rican Migrants on the Mainland

ANASTASI, ANNE; and DEJESÚS, CRUZ. **Language development and nonverbal I.Q. of Puerto Rican preschool children in New York City.** The Journal of Social Psychology, 45:357-66, July 1953.
A study in which the performance of 50 five-year-old Puerto Rican children, on tests to measure language development and nonverbal I.Q., is compared with the performance of 50 white and 50 Negro five-year-old children tested by the same procedure.

BERLE, BEATRICE B. **80 Puerto Rican families in New York City.** New York: Columbia University Press, 1958. 331p. **C**
A study of health and related problems of 80 Puerto Rican families living in a New York City slum. The 80 families were chosen from a group of families with sickness. A few of the topics are migration, family organization, housing, language and communication, and welfare.

CHESS, STELLA; AND OTHERS. **Social class and child-rearing practices.** 1967, unpublished. 12p. (Paper prepared for the American Psychological Association Divisional Meeting, November 17, 1967.) (Detailed findings available in Child Development Monographs, No. 1, 1968 series.) **E** (In process.) UD 05028
A study of the effect of child rearing practices on the perform-

ance of the child in a task-oriented society. The sample consisted of 136 children of native born middle- and upper middle-class parents and 95 children of Puerto Rican unskilled and semi-skilled working class parents.

ELINSON, JACK; HABERMAN, PAUL W.; and GELL, CYRILLE. **Ethnic and educational data on adults in New York City: 1963–1964.** New York: School of Public Health and Administrative Medicine, Columbia University, 1967. 226p.
Reports on a sample survey of 2,118 adults interviewed in 1963-1964 to determine social categories of New York City adults by ethnicity. The characteristics studied are educational and occupational mobility, family income, political preference, voting frequency, minority group feeling, and cultural participation. Puerto Ricans are one of the eight ethnic groups to whom data are given.

FENNESSEY, JAMES. **An exploratory study of non-English speaking homes and academic performance.** Baltimore: Research and Development Center for the Study of Social Organization of Schools and the Learning Process, Johns Hopkins University, 1967. 41p. **E** (In process.) UD 03788
*A report that uses data gathered in a national survey, **Equality of Educational Opportunity** (the Coleman Report). It discusses Puerto Rican public school pupils in New York City in terms of the relationship between language spoken in the home and other aspects of ethnic background and the differences present at several grade levels in vocabulary test scores of Puerto Rican children from contrasting home language backgrounds.*

FITZPATRICK, JOSEPH P. **Attitudes of Puerto Ricans toward color.** The American Catholic Sociological Review, 20:219-33, Fall 1959. **X** UD 04283
Probes the question of the extent to which traditional racial intermingling and intermarriage among Puerto Ricans will affect racial intermingling in New York or the extent to which the negative attitudes of New Yorkers will racially split the Puerto Rican migrants. Conclusions were based upon the frequencies of racial intermarriage of Puerto Ricans in six parishes in New York City and among the 80 families studied by Berle.

FITZPATRICK, JOSEPH P. **Intermarriage of Puerto Ricans in New York City.** American Journal of Sociology, 71:395-406, January 1966.
This study seeks to determine the rate of assimilation among Puerto Ricans in New York City by comparing their rate of out-group marriage with that of immigrants between 1908 and 1912.

GLAZER, NATHAN; and MOYNIHAN, DANIEL P. **The Puerto Ricans.** In: Beyond the melting pot: the Negroes, Puerto Ricans, Jews, Italians, and Irish of New York City, by Nathan Glazer and Daniel Moynihan. Cambridge: M.I.T. and Harvard University Press, 1963. p.86-136. **C** UD 01465
Puerto Ricans in New York City are discussed in terms of who migrates to the United States; their relationship to the island of Puerto Rico; business, professional, labor opportunities, and average earnings in New York; and the effect of migration on the culture of the migrants. The Puerto Ricans are compared and contrasted with immigrant groups.

HANDLIN, OSCAR. **The newcomers—Negroes and Puerto Ricans in a changing metropolis.** Cambridge: Harvard University Press, 1959. 171p. **C** UD 00134
A short, but detailed, history of the entrance of different immigrant groups into New York City is presented. The focus of the work is on the migration to the city in the last quarter century of Negroes and Puerto Ricans, about whom data were gathered through census reports and interviews.

KANTROWITZ, NATHAN. **Social mobility of Puerto Ricans in New York, 1950–1960.** 1967, unpublished. 33p. (Author's affiliation: Columbia University School of Social Work.) **X** UD 05029
An examination of the U.S. census data for the New York Standard Metropolitan Statistical Area to determine the mobility of a group of second generation Puerto Ricans by looking at their occupational, educational, and income shifts. The subjects were between the ages of 15 to 24 in 1950 and 25 to 34 in 1960.

KANTROWITZ, NATHAN; and PAPPENFORT, DONNELL M. **1960 fact book for the New York–Northeastern New Jersey standard consolidated area; the nonwhite, Puerto Rican, and white non-Puerto Rican populations: selected characteristics for counties and cities of 50,000 or more.** New York: Columbia University, 1966. 201p. (Social Statistics for Metropolitan New York, Monograph No. 2.)
Contains all 1960 U.S. Bureau of the Census statistics, which can be presented by the following categories: non-white, Puerto Rican, and white non-Puerto Rican, in the New York–North-eastern New Jersey Standard Consolidated Area. The data for social characteristics are tabulated separately for every Standard Metropolitan Statistical Area (SMSA) and for every county and city of 50,000 or more, whether or not it is the central city for the SMSA.

LEWIS, OSCAR. **La vida: a Puerto Rican family in the culture of poverty—San Juan and New York.** New York: Random House, 1966. 669p. **C** UD 02948
See annotation in Section I, Island Background.

MILLS, C. WRIGHT; SENIOR, CLARENCE; and GOLDSEN, ROSE. **The Puerto Rican journey: New York's newest migrants.** New York: Harper, 1950. 238p.
A report of a 1948 Columbia University study of migration of Puerto Ricans to New York City. The statistics pertain only to an early group of Puerto Rican migrants, but there are important concepts particularly concerning the motivation of Puerto Ricans to migrate and their occupational and educational aspirations. The Puerto Ricans' problems and adjustments are compared with those of immigrant groups.

MORRISON, J. CAYCE. **The Puerto Rican study: 1953–1957.** New York: Board of Education, 1958. 265p. **C** UD 01334
Reports on a four year study of the impact of Puerto Rican migration on the public schools of New York City and the effect of the schools on the Puerto Rican children and their parents. It addresses itself to the problems of teaching English as a second language to the Puerto Rican pupils, the "socioeconomic" adjustment of Puerto Rican children and their parents to the community, and discerning who the Puerto Rican pupils are in the New York City schools. The principal sample consisted of 32 schools in New York City with large Puerto Rican concentrations.

PADILLA, ELENA. **Up from Puerto Rico.** New York: Columbia University Press, 1958. 316p. **C**
A cultural anthropological study of Puerto Rican migrants in New York City conducted in a small section of Manhattan in the mid-1950's. It is based upon observations of the community and intensive interviews with 48 Puerto Rican family heads. A few of the topics included are family and kinship, Hispaños and the larger society, and migrants—transients and settlers.

PUERTO RICAN FORUM, INC., NEW YORK CITY. **The Puerto Rican community development project: a proposal for a self-help project to develop the community by strengthening the family, opening opportunities for youth and making full use of education.** 1964. 145p. **C** UD 04007
Contains "supporting data for an outline of program, a design for needed studies, and an estimate of the cost of instituting a self-help project." Statistics on occupation, income, housing, health, and education are presented. The statistics were obtained from several sources.

Puerto Rican population of New York City. New York: Bureau of Applied Social Research, Columbia University, 1954. 61p. (A series of papers delivered before the New York Area Chapter of the American Statistical Association, October 21, 1953.)
Consists of three papers and a discussion: "Demographic and Labor Force Characteristics of the New York City Puerto Rican Population," by A. J. Jaffe, p. 3-29; "Vital Statistics in New York City Puerto Rican Population," by Lewis Weiner, p. 30-44; "Social and Welfare Statistics on the New York Puerto Rican Population," by Sophia M. Robinson, p. 45-55; and "Discussion: A Comparison of the Occupations of 1st and 2nd Generation Puerto Ricans in the Mainland Labor Market," by Earl Raushenbush, p. 56-61.

PUERTO RICO. DEPARTMENT OF LABOR. MIGRATION DIVISION. NEW YORK CITY OFFICE. **A summary in facts and figures,**

1964–1965: progress in Puerto Rico—Puerto Rican migration. 1966. 22p. **X** UD 05023
See annotation in Section I, Island Background.

SENIOR, CLARENCE. **The Puerto Ricans: strangers—then neighbors.** Chicago: Quadrangle Books, 1965. 123p. **C** UD 01078
A brief history of the building and settling of the United States is presented to give emphasis to the fact that we have always been a nation of immigrants. A variety of data on problems that confront Puerto Ricans in trying to settle in the United States is discussed. (Most of the data pertain to Puerto Ricans in New York City.).

SENIOR, CLARENCE; and WATKINS, DONALD O. **Toward a balance sheet of Puerto Rican migration.** In: Status of Puerto Rico: selected background studies, for the United States—Puerto Rico Commission on the Status of Puerto Rico. Washington, D.C.: U.S. Government Printing Office, 1966. p.689-795. **C** (In process.) UD 04887
The balance sheet is drawn in terms of the advantages of migration to the migrants, to the society from which they came, and to the receiving society. It includes considerable data on early and later Puerto Rican migration.

SIEGEL, ARTHUR L. **The social adjustment of Puerto Ricans in Philadelphia.** Journal of Social Psychology, 46:99-110, August 1957.
A paper summarizing the principal findings of a study of the social adjustment of Puerto Ricans in Philadelphia. Some of the topics discussed are language, medical, religious adjustment, and occupations and occupational aspirations. The sample consisted of Puerto Ricans living in major core areas of Puerto Rican settlements and non-Puerto Rican neighbors.

SEXTON, PATRICIA C. **Spanish Harlem: anatomy of poverty.** New York: Harper, 1965. 208p. **C** UD 04134
A book by a sociologist who spent almost two years observing in East Harlem. She discusses poverty, community, power structure, urban renewal, schools, religion, initiative of the community, etc.

Bibliographies

BOURNE, DOROTHY D.; and BOURNE, JAMES R. **Bibliography.** In: Thirty years of change in Puerto Rico, by Dorothy D. Bourne and James R. Bourne. New York: Praeger, 1966. p.403-10. **E** (In process.) UD 05027
A short annotated bibliography on the island of Puerto Rico. Included are items on social change, patterns of living, education, government, etc.

CORDASCO, FRANK M.; and COVELLO, LEONARD. **Studies of Puerto Rican children in American schools: a preliminary bibliography.** New York: Migration Division, Commonwealth of Puerto Rico, Department of Labor, 1967. 24p. **E** (In process.) UD 04886 (This bibliography may also be ordered from the Migration Division.)
A lengthy compilation of items that relate to the education and adjustment of Puerto Rican children in American mainland schools. (Not annotated.)

DOSSICK, JESSE J. **Doctoral research on Puerto Rico and Puerto Ricans.** New York: New York University, 1967. 34p. **X** UD 05049
A list of approximately 350 doctoral dissertations dealing with Puerto Rico and Puerto Ricans. Fifty percent of the research was done by Puerto Ricans. The schools contributing the largest number of dissertations are Columbia University and New York University.

SENIOR, CLARENCE; and WATKINS, DONALD O. **Toward a balance sheet of Puerto Rican migration: bibliography.** In: Status of Puerto Rico: selected background studies, for the United States—Puerto Rico Commission on the Status of Puerto Rico. Washington, D.C.: U.S. Government Printing Office, 1966. p.765-95. **E** (In process.) UD 04887
A critically annotated bibliography of selected items that have significant or extensive references to Puerto Ricans. It is divided into two parts: the first section includes articles, essays, reports, speeches, and surveys; and the second contains only references to books.

Reviews of La Vida

BENDINER, ELMER. **Outside the kingdom of the middle class.** The Nation, 204:22-23, January 2, 1967.

BURGUM, BERRY. **The sociology of Oscar Lewis.** Science and Society, 31:323-37, Summer 1967.

CORDASCO, FRANK M. **The Puerto Rican family and the anthropologist: Oscar Lewis, La vida, and the culture of poverty.** Urban Education, 3 (No. 3):32-38, 1967.

The culture of poverty. Time Magazine, 88:133, November 25, 1966.

DIAMONDSTEIN, BARBARALEE D. **Hopes and fears of all the years.** Saturday Review, 49:58-59, December 10, 1966.

FITZPATRICK, JOSEPH P. **Oscar Lewis and the Puerto Rican family.** America, 115:778-79, December 10, 1966.

GLAZER, NATHAN. **One kind of life.** Commentary, 43:83-85, February 1967.

HANDLIN, OSCAR. **The subculture of poverty.** Atlantic Monthly, 218:138-44, December 1966.

HARRINGTON, MICHAEL, **Everyday hell.** The New York Times Book Review, 7:1-3, November 20, 1966.

HENRIQUES, FERNANDO. **Review of La Vida.** London Magazine, 7:85-88, October 1967.

HENTOFF, NAT. **Life near the bone.** The New Yorker, 43:154-60, March 4, 1967.

HOROWITZ, IRVING L. **Muerte en vida.** Trans-action, 4:50-52, March 1967.

KENISTON, KENNETH. **The drabness of poverty.** The American Scholar, 36:505-09, Summer 1967.

LARNER, SUSAN. **The new poor and the old.** Dissent, 14:235-39, March-April, 1967.

MALOFF, SAUL. **Man's fate?** Newsweek, 68:131-32, November 21, 1966.

MONSERRAT, JOSEPH. **A Puerto Rican family.** Natural History, 76:70-72, April 1967.

MOORE, BARRINGTON. **In the life.** The New York Review of Books, 8:3-4, June 15, 1967.

PRITCHETT, V. S. **Spilling the beans.** New Statesman, 74:404, September 29, 1967.

RENEK, MORRIS. **New windows on poverty.** New Republic, 155:23, December 3, 1966.

The **IRCD BULLETIN** is a bi-monthly publication of the ERIC Information Retrieval Center on the Disadvantaged. It is published five times a year and usually includes status or interpretive statements, book reviews, and a selected bibliography on some aspect of the center's special areas. Subject areas covered by IRCD include the effects of disadvantaged environments; the academic, intellectual, and social performance of disadvantaged children and youth; programs and practices which provide learning experiences designed to compensate for the special problems and build on the characteristics of the disadvantaged; and programs and practices related to economic and ethnic discrimination, segregation, desegregation, and integration in education.

The center is operated under a contract with the Educational Resources Information Center (ERIC) of the U. S. Office of Education and receives additional funds from the College Entrance Examination Board, Yeshiva University, and other agencies for special services.

STUDIES OF PUERTO RICAN CHILDREN IN AMERICAN SCHOOLS

A Preliminary Bibliography

Frank M. Cordasco
and
Leonard Covello

STUDIES OF PUERTO RICAN CHILDREN IN AMERICAN SCHOOLS

A Preliminary Bibliography

FRANK M. CORDASCO AND LEONARD COVELLO

A clear need exists for a convenient handlist of studies on Puerto Rican children and their experiences in American mainland schools. The compilers of the present bibliography intend it as a preliminary list and contemplate its continuing up-dating. It is not intended as a complete list of studies, and inevitably some significant studies will have unfortunately been overlooked. We invite suggestions and additions.

We have not attempted a general bibliography on Puerto Ricans in the United States, although we have included a short bibliographical note on those titles which constitute a working list for the over-all study of the migration and experience of Puerto Ricans on the American mainland. Since the bibliography is essentially limited to the Puerto Rican experience in mainland schools, neither annotation (the individual titles are generally a clear indication of concern) nor subject captioning appeared to be practicable or necessary.

Since the Puerto Rican child is usually found in a context of severe socioeconomic deprivation, many of the titles on the "disadvantaged child" deal (although very briefly) with Puerto Rican children in the context of poverty. These titles (in a burgeoning literature) we have not attempted to list, but we call attention to the *Catalog of Selected Documents on the Disadvantaged: A Number and Author Index* (OE 37001) and a *Subject Index* (OE 37002), Washington: U.S. Government Printing Office, 1966, which the Education Research Information Center (U.S. Office of Education) assembled as "a collection of 1740 documents on the special education needs of the disad-

Reprinted from the *Journal of Human Relations*, Vol. XVI, No. 2, Second Quarter 1968. Copyright 1968 by Central State University.

vantaged) in support of the Elementary and Secondary Education Act of 1965 (P.L. 89-10)." An excellent review of the literature in the field is Harry Miller's *Education for the Disadvantaged* (New York: Free Press, 1967), and good guides to programs for disadvantaged children are: Doxey A. Wilkerson, "Programs and Practices for Compensatory Education for Disadvantaged Children," *Review of Educational Research*, Vol. 35 (December, 1965), pp. 426-40; and Edmond W. Gordon and Doxey A. Wilkerson, *Compensatory Education for the Disadvantaged: Programs and Practices: Pre-School through College* (New York: College Entrance Examination Board, 1966).

The *Covello Papers*, which contain a vast amount of material reflecting the experience of the near quarter-century tenure as principal at Benjamin Franklin School in East Harlem of Leonard Covello, constitute an invaluable repository of source material on the Puerto Rican experience both in the community and the school and are presently being catalogued.

The problems of Puerto Rican children in American schools are in many ways analogous to those faced by non-English speaking children in other eras, and in this connection, Leonard Covello's recently published study of the Italo-American child presents a broadly analogous tableau of the social deprivation, ethnicity, language handicap and different cultural identity which the child brought to the American school.[1] Nor should the literature on the Mexican-American child and his educational needs be neglected. (In five states of the American Southwest there are some 1.75 million school children with Spanish surnames.)[2]

A General Bibliographical Note

The best source on Puerto Rican migration is the Migration Division of the Department of Labor, Commonwealth of Puerto Rico, which maintains a central mainland office in New York City and offices in other United States cities. It also maintains an office in Puerto Rico to carry out a program of orientation for persons who

---

[1]Leonard Covello, *The Social Background of the Italo-American School Child: A Study of the Southern Italian Mores and Their Effect on the School Situation in Italy and America*, edited and with an Introduction by F. Cordasco (Leiden, The Netherlands: E. J. Brill, 1967), xxxii, 488 pp.

[2]See Herschel T. Manuel, *Spanish Speaking Children of the Southwest: Their Education and the Public Welfare* (Austin: University of Texas Press, 1958); and "Bilingualism and the Bilingual Child: A Symposium," *Modern Language Journal*, Vol. 49 (March-April, 1965), pp. 143-239.

intend to migrate to the states. (See Joseph Monserrat, *Puerto Ricans in New York City* [Migration Division, Commonwealth of Puerto Rico, 1967]; and *Bibliography on Puerto Ricans in the United States* [*Ibid.*, April, 1959].) In 1964, the New York City Department of Health placed the Puerto Rican population in New York City at 701,500, representing a 9.3 per cent of the city's population. A projection of this study by the Migration Division of the Puerto Rican Department of Labor estimates the 1966 Puerto Rican population at 762,000.

A vast literature exists on Puerto Rico. Generally, good sociological and anthropological studies are easily available. Among these are Theodore Brameld, *The Remaking of Culture: Life and Education in Puerto Rico* (New York: Harper, 1959); Melvin M. Tumin and Arnold Feldman, *Social Class and Social Change in Puerto Rico* (Princeton, 1961); Julian H. Steward, ed., *The People of Puerto Rico* (University of Illinois, 1956); 2nd pr., 1966; Kurt W. Back, *Slums, Projects and People: Social, Psychological Problems of Relocation in Puerto Rico* (Duke University, 1962); Gordon K. Lewis, *Puerto Rico: Freedom and Power in the Caribbean* (New York: Monthly Press Review, 1963); James R. Bourne and Dorothy P. Bourne, *Thirty Years of Change in Puerto Rico: A Case Study of Ten Selected Rural Areas* (New York: Praeger, 1966); and E. J. Berbusse, *The United States in Puerto Rico, 1898-1900* (University of North Carolina, 1966).

For Puerto Ricans in the United States, see Dan Wakefield, *Island in the City: Puerto Ricans in New York* (Boston: Houghton Mifflin, 1959); Patricia Sexton, *Spanish Harlem: Anatomy of Poverty* (New York: Harper, 1965); Clarence Senior, *The Puerto Ricans: Strangers— Then Neighbors* (Chicago: Quadrangle, 1965); Elena Padilla, *Up From Puerto Rico* (Columbia University, 1958); Nathan Glazer and Daniel P. Moynihan, *Beyond the Melting Pot* (M.I.T.-Harvard, 1963); and Oscar Lewis, *La Vida* (New York: Random House, 1966).

An invaluable source of research studies is Jesse J. Dossick, *Doctoral Research on Puerto Rico and Puerto Ricans* (New York University, School of Education, 1967).

I. *Uupublished Materials**

*Most of these materials are in the *Covello Papers*. See "Introduction," *supra*.

Baldwin, Clare C. "Education of the Non-English Speaking and Bi-Lingual (Spanish) Pupils in the Junior High Schools of Districts 10 and 11, Manhattan." June, 1952, 131 pp.

"Basic Education Facts of the Puerto Rican Educational System."
N.d., 10 pp.

Bureau of Applied Social Research of Columbia University. "Letter
to Governor Jesus T. Pinero Summarizing the Principal Findings
of the Study of Puerto Rican Migrants in New York City which
the Bureau Has Been Conducting since November, 1947." June 15,
1948, 15 pp. In the *Covello Papers—Personal Files.*

Committee of the Association of Assistant Superintendents. "A Program of Education for Puerto Ricans in New York City." 1947,
107 pp.

Commonwealth of Puerto Rico, Department of Labor, Migration Division. "Puerto Rican Migration to the United States." 1 p.

———. "Puerto Rican Population by States (according to the 1960
Census)." May 20, 1964, 1 p.

———. "Puerto Rican Population by States and Cities." (Based on
1960 U.S. Census.) 8 pp.

Community Council of Greater New York. Research Department.
Bureau of Community Statistical Services. "Population of Puerto
Rican Birth or Parentage for New York City, by Borough: 1960."
April 13, 1962, 1 p.

Covello, Leonard. "Recommendations Concerning Puerto Rican Pupils in Our Public Schools." May 1, 1953, 9 pp.

Covello Papers. Files on Puerto Rican Program at Benjamin Franklin
High School. (See "Introduction," *supra.*)

Covello Papers. Personal Files.

Covian, Sherrill "The Effect of Unemployment and Underemployment
on the Puerto Rican Male in New York City." October 27, 1965,
23 pp.

"Demographic Tables" (for East Harlem). X Appendix. September,
1964. Unpaged.

East Harlem Neighborhood Study Club. "Report of Operation, 1965
Summer Session." 11 pp.

"Educational Background in Puerto Rico." N.d., 28 pp.

"Factors Affecting Pupil Registration: Day Schools—Migration Balance in the Movement of Pupil Population to and from Places Outside New York City—School Years 1953-1954 to 1962-1963 (and)
Day Schools—Migration Balance in the Movement of Pupil Population to and from Places Outside New York City, by School Group
and Borough—School Year 1962-1963." 1 p. (Statistical)

Fitzpatrick, Reverend Joseph P., S.J. "Delinquency and the Puerto
Ricans." Address given to Fordham University School of Business,
October 8, 1959. 18 pp.

Kouletsis, Greg. "Guidance Follow-Up Study, Spring, 1964 (Comparative Study—JHS 13 M & JHS 117 M)," Spring, 1964. Unpaged.

Mayar, Frank. "Puerto Rican Pupils in New York City Public Schools: A Comparison of the Effects of Two Methods of Instructional Grouping on English Mastery and Attitudes." A Ph.D. dissertation for Teachers College, Columbia University. 1954, 73 pp.

Mayor's Committee on Puerto Rican Affairs in New York City, Sub-Committee on Education, Recreation and Parks. "Study on Puerto Rican Pupils in Senior and Vocational High Schools." May 1, 1953. Unpaged. (L. Covello, Chairman)

————. "Questionnaire on Puerto Rican Pupils in Our Schools." May 1, 1953, 6 pp.

"Memorandum Re: Day Care Centers." November 30, 1950, 1 p.

"Migration Balance: Day Schools—Migration Balance in the Movement of Pupil Population to and from Places Outside New York City, by Borough and Geographic Area—School Year 1962-1963 (and) Day Schools—Migration Balance in the Movement of Pupil Population to and from Places Outside New York City, by Geographic Area—School Years 1953-1954 to 1962-1963." 1 p. (Statistical)

Morris High School and the Commonwealth of Puerto Rico, Department of Labor, Migration Division. "Study of Puerto Rican Students Who Were Graduated from Morris High School—June 1961." June 21, 1963, 23 pp.

New York City, Department of Welfare, Press and Public Relations. "Statement by the Honorable Raymond M. Hilliard, Welfare Commissioner of the City of New York Upon His Arrival in Puerto Rico, August 21, 1950." 3 pp.

New York University, School of Education. "Proceedings of the Annual Conferences for Puerto Rican Citizens of New York: 1961, 1962, 1963, 1964." Unpaged.

Oliveras, Candido (Secretary of Education of Puerto Rico). "What Are the Educational Needs of Puerto Ricans Who Come to New York?" An address given at the New York University Puerto Rican Conference, January 14, 1961. 11 pp.

Pennisi, Guy V. "Some Suggestions for Helping Non-English Speaking Children, Manual for P.S. 33 Manhattan." Prepared by Guy V. Pennisi (Graduate Student, New York University) under the direction of Principal Morris C. Finkel, P.S. 33. November 23, 1949. Unpaged.

Puerto Rico, Department of Labor, Employment and Migration Bureau. "Progress Report on the Puerto Rican Migrants." April 11, 1950, 10 pp.

————. "Report on Visits to New York City Schools Submitted to Mr. Manual Cabranes, Director, by Dr. J. J. Osuna, Educational Consultant." 1948, 9 pp.

Rausehenbush, Winifred. "New York and the Puerto Ricans." (Manuscript of Article for *Harper's*) 23 pp.

Sanguinetti, Carmen "Adapting Science Instruction in New York City Schools to the Needs of Puerto Rican Background Pupils." A Ph.D. dissertation for Teachers College, Columbia University. 1956, 163 pp. (See Dossick, *infra,* generally.)

Senior, Clarence. "The Newcomer Speaks Out: What Puerto Ricans Want and Need from Voluntary Agencies and the Public." A paper delivered at the National Conference on Social Welfare, Atlantic City, June, 1960. 17 pp.

Shields, Osceola, *et al.* Teachers College Course S 200 FA. "Los Boricuas—Our Newest Neighbors." (Excerpts fro a Group Report), 26 pp.

Three hundred eighty-one cumulative record sheets of the Graduates of Benjamin Franklin High School, June, 1963.

Welfare Council of New York City. "Educational Background in Puerto Rico." 1947, 28 pp.

————. Letter to Dr. Leonard Covello from Adrian P. Burke, Chairman. Committee on Puerto Ricans, January 8, 1951, 1 p.

————. Letter to Dr Leonard Covello from Coverly Fischer, President, C.P.R., September 25, 1950, 1 p.

————. Letter to Dr. Leonard Cavello from James R. Dumpson, Consultant, C.P.R., May 21, 1951, 2 pp.

Welfare Council of New York City, Committee on Puerto Ricans in New York City. "Changes to be Made in Draft of Report." December 17, 1947, 1 p.

————. Letter to Dr. Leonard Covello from James R. Dumpson, Consultant and Secretary, November 2, 1950. 1 p.

————. "Puerto Rican Children: Some Aspects of Their Needs and Related Services." June 30, 1949, 12 pp.

————. "Report." Submitted January, 1948, 69 pp.

————. Sub Committee on Education. "Agenda: May 2, 1947," and "Summary of Minutes," 2 pp. and 4 pp.

————. Sub-Committee to Evaluate Reports. "Summary of Minutes: November 10, 1950." 4 pp.

————. Sub-Committee to Implement Recommendations. "Summary of Minutes: November 17, 1950." 2 pp.

————. Sub-Committee on Questionnaire. "Summary of Minutes: March 20, 1951," 2 pp.

————. Sub-Committee to Survey Progress on Puerto Rican Report. "Agenda: March 20, 1951." 13 pp.

————. "Summary of Minutes: Tuesday, November 18, 1947." 5 pp.

————. "Summary of Minutes: Wednesday, December 3, 1947." 2 pp.

————. "Summary of Minutes: November 1, 1950." 3 pp.

II. *Published Materials*

Abrams, Charles. "How to Remedy Our 'Puerto Rician Problem'," *Commentary*, Vol. XIX, No. 2 (February, 1955), pp. 120-127.

"Activarán La Enseñanza Del Inglés Básico en las communidades Borícuas," *La Prensa*, February 23, 1952.

Alcala, Roberto de. "Nueva York-Ciudad Hispana," *Temos* (February, 1953), pp. 7-8.

Anastasi, Anne and Fernando A. Cordova. "Some Effects of Bilingualism upon the Intelligence Test Performance of Puerto Rican Children in New York City," *The Journal of Educational Psychology*, Vol. XLIV, No. 1 (January, 1953), pp. 1-17.

Anderson, Virginia. "Teaching English to Puerto Rican Pupils," *High Points* (March, 1964), pp. 51-54.

"Antonio Gonzalez es Nombrado Miembro de La Junta Escolar No. 18," *El Diario de Nueva York*, May 7, 1952.

"Aumentan Los Fondos Para Comedores De Escuelas Publicas de Puerto Rico," *El Diario de Nueva York*, August 1, 1952, p. 3.

Baldwin, Claire C. "Program Outlined for Puerto Ricans," *The New York Times*, December 5, 1947.

Bell, John. "Puerto Rican Influx Jams Crowded Schools," *New York World Telegram*, May 3, 1947.

Berkowitz, Blaine. "Family Attitudes and Practices of Puerto Rican and Non-Puerto Rican Pupils," *High Points* (March, 1961), pp. 25-34.

Berle, Beatrice B. *Eighty Puerto Rican Families in New York City*. New York: Columbia University Press, 1958.

Biddick, Mildred L. and Esther A. Harrison. "Spanish-American Children Receive Help in Achieving Status," *School Management* (August, 1947).

"Bi-Lingual Problems in Puerto Rican Study," *Curriculum and Materials*, Vol. XI, No. 2 (February, 1948), pp. 1-2.

Blourock, Barbara. "Aspira in the Junior High School," *High Points* (February, 1966), pp. 53-55.

Briggs, Frances M. "As Five Teachers See Themselves," *Educational*

Forum, Vol. XXVIII, No. 4 (May, 1964), pp. 389-397. (Reprinted by Migration Division, Commonwealth of Puerto Rico, 1965.)

Brameld, Theodore. *The Remaking of a Culture*. New York, 1959, 478 pp.

Bruma, John. *Spanish Speaking Groups in the United States*. Durham, North Carolina: Duke University Press, 1954.

Calitri, Charles J. "A Puerto Rican Story," *American Unity*, Vol. XV, No. 1 (September-October, 1956), pp. 19-24.

"Campana De Saneamiento En Harlem," *El Diario de Nueva York*, June 20, 1949, p. 3.

Cannon, Antoinette. "The Puerto Ricans," *Interpreter Releases*, Vol. XXIV, No. 37 (August 28, 1947), pp. 296-304.

Cebollero, Pedro. *A School Language Policy for Puerto Rico*. San Juan, 1945, 133 pp.

"The Challenge in Working with Puerto Rican Families," *Pathways in Child Guidance*, Vol. II, No. 3 (April, 1960), pp. 3-6.

Chenault, Lawrence R. *The Puerto Rican Migrant in New York City*. New York, 1938, 190 pp.

"Children from Puerto Rico," *Curriculum and Materials* (May-June, 1954, 16 pp.

"City College Da Satisfacción a Maestra Borícua," *El Diario de Nueva York*, July 30, 1952, pp. 1, 17.

Citizens' Committee for Children of New York. *Do You Understand? N-E Program in the New York City Schools*. New York: Citizens' Committee, 1961, 23 pp.

"Cívicas Y Culturales: Asociación de Padres," *El Diario de Nueva York*, June 13, 1952, p. 8.

"Civicas Y Culturales: Centro Cultural Chilena, Inc.," *El Diario de Nueva York*, June 13, 1952, p. 8.

"Civicas Y Culturales: Conferencia Sobre Educacion Escolar," *El Diario de Nueva York*, May 21, 1952, p. 13.

"Civicas Y Culturales: Reunion Civica," *El Diario de Nueva York*, June 2, 1952, p. 5.

"Civicas Y Culturales: Escuela Publica De Calle 109 (Oeste) Abre su Matricula Para Kindergarten," *El Diario de Nueva York*, May 7, 1952.

Collazo, Francisco. *The Education of Puerto Rican Children in the Schools of New York City*. San Juan, Department of Education Press, 1954, 14 pp.

"Columbia Plans Study of Puerto Rican Migration to N.Y.C.," *PM*, October 14, 1947.

"Comprehension Por Conocimiento." (Editorial), *El Diario de Nueva York*, May 27, 1952, p. 9.

Cordasco, F., and Leonard Covello. "Schools and the Spanish Speaking Community," *Congressional Record*, June 12, 1962, pp. A4322-A4323.

Cordasco, F. "Helping the Language Barrier Student," *Instructor*, Vol. 72 (May, 1963), p. 20.

———. "Spanish Harlem: The Anatomy of Poverty," *Phylon*: The Atlanta University Review of Race and Culture,Vol. 23 (Summer, 1965), pp. 195-196.

———. "The Puerto Rican Child in the American School," *Congressional Record*, Vol. CXI, No. 195 (October 19, 1965), pp. 26, 425-26.

———. "Florence Nightingale in the Ghetto: Patricia Sexton's *Spanish Harlem*," *Journal of Human Relations*, Vol. 13 (Fourth Quarter, 1965, pp. 572-574.

———. "Nights in the Gardens of East Harlem: Patricia Sexton's *East Harlem*," *Journal of Negro Education*, Vol. 34 (Fall, 1965), pp. 450-451.

———. "The Puerto Rican Child in the American School," American Sociological Association. *Abstracts of Papers* (61st Annual Meeting), 1966, pp. 23-24.

———. "The Puerto Rican Child in the American School," *Kansas Journal of Sociology*, Vol. II (Spring, 1966), pp. 59-65.

———. "Studies in the Disenfranchised: The Puerto Rican Child," *Psychiatric Spectator*, Vol. III (November, 1966), pp. 3-4.

———. "The Puerto Rican Family and the Anthropologist: Oscar Lewis, *La Vida*, and The Culture of Poverty," *Urban Education*, Vol. III, No. 1 (1967), pp. 32-38.

———. "Puerto Rican Pupils and American Education," *School and Society*, Vol. 95 (February 18, 1967), pp. 116-119.

———. "The Puerto Rican Child in the American School," *Journal of Negro Education*, Vol. 36 (Spring, 1967), pp. 181-186.

———. "The Puerto Rican Family and the Anthropologist," *Teachers College Record*, Vol. 68 (May, 1967), pp. 672-675.

———. "Educational Programs for Puerto Rican Pupils," *The New York Times*, May 30, 1967.

———. "The Non-English Speaking Child in the American School: Continuing Challenge to Education in a Democratic Society." Statement and testimony before the General Education Sub-Committee of the U.S. House of Representatives, June 29, 1967. Washington, 11 pp. (H.R. Bill 9840)

———. "The Puerto Rican Family and the Anthropologist: Oscar Lewis, *La Vida*, and the Culture of Poverty," *Congressional Record*, July 18, 1967, pp. H 8914-H 8915.

———. "The Non-English Speaking Child in the American School: Continuing Challenge to Education in a Democratic Society." Testimony before the Senate Sub-Committee on Bilingual Education, July 21, 1967. Washington, 11 pp. (Senate Bill 428)

———, and Louis Roderer, "Modern Languages and Modern Living," in Joseph S. Roucek, ed., *Changing Aspects of the Foreign Language Teaching in the United States*. New York: Philosophical Library, 1967.

Covello, Leonard, with Guido D'Agostino. *The Heart Is the Teacher*. New York, 1958, 275 pp.

"Crearán un Fondo de Becas para los Borícuas Residentes to N.Y.," *El Diario de Neuva York*, December 9, 1951, p. 14.

"Cree Jansen Que El GBno. Federal y El Estatal Deben Ayudar A Borícuas," *La Presna*, February 1, 1954.

Crozier, Emmet. "Puerto Rico: Frontier of Enterprise," *New York Herald Tribune*, June 10, 1948.

Darcy, Natalie T. "The Performance of Bilingual Puerto Rican Children on Verbal and on Non-Language Tests of Intelligence," *Journal of Educational Research* (March, 1952), pp. 499-506.

"Las Declaraciones de Osuan," *El Diario de Nueva York*, October 29, 1948.

Denny, M. C. "Chicago Meets San Juan," *Instructor*, Vol. 76 (February, 1967), pp 38-39.

Diaz, Eileen. "A Puerto Rican in New York," *Dissent*, Vol. VIII, No. 3 (Summer, 1961), pp. 383-385).

Dossick, Jesse J. *Doctoral Research on Puerto Rico and Puerto Ricans*. New York: New York University, School of Education, 1967 ("Education," pp. 12-19).

Dworkis, Martin B. (ed.) *The Impact of Puerto Rican Migration on Governmental Services in New York City.* New York, 1957, 74 pp.

"Educadora Boricua Llevara a las Cortes Al City College de N.Y. Alega es Victima de Discrimen," *El Diario de Neuva York*, April 24, 1932.

Educatoin-in-the-News. A monthly clip sheet for the use of U.S. editors and radio commentators. New York: Puerto Rican Public Relations Committee, Inc., April 1, 1949, 3 pp.

"Education in Puerto Rico." *San Juan Review*. Special Education Issue, Vol. II, No. 5 (June, 1965), 88 pp.

"Education Is Sparking Puerto Rico's Industrial Growth," *The New York Times* (Special Section on Puerto Rico), November 7, 1965, p. 18.

"Education of Puerto Rican Children in New York City," *The Journal of Educational Sociology*, Vol. XXVIII, No. 4, (December, 1954), pp. 145-192.

"Educación y Orientación en el Plan de Beneficencia Aquí," *La Prensa*, November 28, 1947, pp. 1, 5.

Elam, Sophie E. "Acculturation and Learning Problems of Puerto Rican Children," *Teachers College Record*, Vol. 61 (February, 1960), pp. 258-264.

Emery, Helen T. "How the City's Schools Greet Puerto Ricans," *New York World Telegram and Sun*, November 4, 1953.

———. "Schools Here Aid Progress of Migrants," *New York World Telegraph and Sun*, June 28, 1956, p. 34.

———. "Schools Weigh Problems of Puerto Ricans," *New York World Telegram and Sun*, February 11, 1953.

———. "Seward HS Makes Americans," *New York World Telegram and Sun*, May 11, 1956, p. 34.

Entman, Frederick. "Our Puerto Rican Children: One School's Approach," *Strengthening Democracy*, May, 1955, pp. 3, 5.

"Un Esfurerzo Encomiable." (Editorial), *El Diario de Nueva York*, February 18, 1954, p. 13.

"El Español en Clínicas de la Ciudad," *El Diario de Nueva York*, February 17, 1954.

"Existe el Propósito de Contratar 500 Maestros Hispanos Más para N.Y.," *El Diario de Nueva York*, February 16, 1954, p. 6.

Feigenbaum, Lawrence. "Teaching English to Puerto Rican Youth," *High Points* (January, 1952), pp. 45-48.

Fernis Isern, Antonio. "The Role of Puerto Rico and Its People in the Americas," *The Journal of Educational Sociology*, Vol. 35 (May, 1962), pp. 397-401.

Finocchiaro, Mary. "Puerto Rican Newcomers in Our Schools," *American Unity*, Vol. XIV, No. 3 (January-February, 1956), pp. 12-17.

———. "Our Schools Must Meet the Challenge of a New Migration," *High Points* (March, 1953), pp. 29-33.

———. "A Suggested Procedure in the Teaching of English to Puerto Ricans," *High Points* (May, 1949), pp. 60-66.

———. *Teaching English as a Second Language*. New York, 1958, 335 pp.

Fitzpatrick, J. P. "Oscar Lewis and the Puerto Rican Family," *America*, Vol. 115 (December 10, 1966), pp. 778-779.

Flicker, Jeanette. "Classes for Spanish-Speaking Children," *High Points* (November, 1947),pp. 58-62.

Fox, Rosa Rudami. "Puerto Ricans in Your Town," *American Unity* (a monthly educational guide), Vol. XI, No 5 (May-June, 1952), pp. 3-8.

Galindez, Jesus de. "Crónicas desde Nueva York: Hispano-América en las Universidades Norteamericanas," *El Diario de Nueva York*, August 28, 1951, p. 8.

"$160,000 Gift Here Aids Puerto Ricans," *The New York Times*, August 28, 1953, p. 18.

Glazer, Nathan, and Daniel Moynihan. *Beyond the Melting Pot.* Cambridge: M.I.T. Press, 1964, 360 pp.

Greenberg, Benjamin B. "1955 Puerto Rican Workshop," *Puerto Rico Es Su Casa*, Vol. I, No. 1 (June, 1955), p. 1.

Greenstein, Marvin N. "Puerto Rican Children," *Pathways in Child Guidance*, Vol. II, No. 4 (June, 1960), pp. 1, 3.

Guerra, Emilio L. "Orientación de los Estudiantes de Puerto Rico en la Ciudad de Nueva York," *El Diario de Nueva York,* March 28, 1949, p. 6.

———. "The Orientation of Puerto Rican Students in New York City," *Modern Language Journal* (October, 1948), pp. 415-420.

———. "The Role of the Teacher of Spanish in the Orientation of Non-English Speaking Pupils," *Hispania*, Vol XXXII, No. 1 (February, 1949), pp. 59-63.

"Guidance Is Asked for Puerto Ricans," *The New York Times*, October 28. 1947.

Gurren, Louise. "A Special Class for Puerto Rican Students," *High Points* (February, 1948), pp. 77-80.

Handlin, Oscar. *The Newcomers, Negroes and Puerto Ricans in a Changing Metropolis.* New York: Doubleday, 1962, 177 pp.

"Hay 46, 85: Niños de P. R. en Escuelas de New York," *El Diario de Nueva York,* February 19, 1953, p. 4.

"Hay Tres Nuevas Divisiones en Instrucción," *El Mundo* (San Juan, P.R.), July 16, 1947.

"Helping Puerto Rican Pupils to Achieve Status," *Strengthening Democracy*, Vol. V, No. 6, (May, 1953), pp. 4-5.

"El Hogar Y La Escuela" (Editorial), *El Diario de Nueva York,* November 14, 1951, p. 9.

"Home-School Project Drawn," *New York Sun*, August 6, 1948.

"How to Teach Puerto Ricans," *New York Herald Tribune*, February 13, 1951.

"Incidente Lamentable" (Editorial), *El Diario de Nueva York*, February 24, 1954.

Ingraham, Leonard W. "Our Puerto Rican Students Must Become a Part of All the Children," *High Points* (February, 1951), pp. 11-17.

El Instituto Professional de 1948, November, 1948, 2 pp.

"The Integration Movement in Education," *Curriculum and Materials*, Vol. XVIII, No. 3 (Spring, 1964), p. 1

"Irán a Puerto Rico 20 Trabajadoras Soci Lespor Invitación del Rector, *El Diario de Nueva York*, May 23, 1952, p. 2.

Jaffe, Abraham J. (ed.). *Puerto Rican Population of New York City: A Series of Papers Delivered Before the New York Area Chapter of the American Statistical Association*, October 21, 1963. Bureau of Applied Social Research, January, 1954, 61 pp.

"Joven Damita Hace Honor a Los Borícuas en el Bronx," *El Diario de Nueva York*, March 5, 1952, p. 7.

Juncal, Herman Poza. "La Escuela Norteamaricana y Nuestros Ninos," *Plus Ultra*, October 10, 1948.

Jusino, Gonzalo. "La Organización Cívica Puertoriqueña," *El Diario de Nueva York*, April 17, 1952, p. 11.

Kahnheimer, Leah W. "A Program in Social Living for Puerto Rican Pupils," *High Points* (June, 1954), pp. 58-68.

Kaufman, Maurice. *The Effect of Instruction in Reading Spanish on Reading Ability in English of Spanish-Speaking Retarded Readers*. Unpublished Ph.D. Dissertation. New York University, 1966.

Kelly, Mary. "English in U.S. as 2nd Language," *Christian Science Monitor* (Reprint), October 21, 1963, 3 pp.

Kihas, Peter. "Gains Made by Puerto Ricans Here"; and "City Relief Roll Held Down Despite Job-Hunter Influx." Two Articles from *The New York Times*, May 31, 1957 and June 2, 1957. Reprinted by Commonwealth of Puerto Rico, Migration Division, Department of Labor, 3 pp.

―――. "Puerto Rico and Us." Three articles from *The New York Times*, February 23-25, 1953. Reprinted by Department of Labor of Puerto Rico, Migration Division, 8 pp.

Kleban, Evelyn. "Thanksgiving: An Orientation Project for Newcomers." *Strengthening Democracy*, January, 1963, pp. 3, 6.

Klein, Woody. *Let in the Sun*. New York, 1963, 297 pp.

Kosinski, Leonard U. "A New Look at the Bilingual Student," *Senior Scholastic*, Vol. 82 (October 4, 1963), p. 14.

Landy, David. *Tropical Childhood: Cultural Transmission and Learning in a Rural Puerto Rican Village*. New York, Harper, 1965.

"Lawyers Association Exposes Untruths about Puerto Ricans," *The Daily Compass*, March 31, 1952, pp. 2, 13.

Lewis, C. "Some Puerto Rican Viewpoints," *Childhood Education*, Vol. 43 (October, 1966), pp. 82-84.

Loretan, Joseph O. "Problems in Improving Educational Opportunities for Puerto Ricans in New York," *High Points* (May, 1963), pp. 23-31.

Lorge, Irving and Frank Mayans, Jr. "Vestibule vs. Regular Classes for Puerto Rican Migrant Pupils," *Teachers College Record*, Vol. LV, No. 5 (February, 1954), pp. 231-237.

"Maestra Boricua Hace Llamamiento a Los Padres Hispanos Del Bronx," *El Diario de Nueva York*, April 16, 1952, pp. 6-7.

Massimine, E. Virginia. "The Puerto Rican: Citizen of New York," *The Journal of Pi-Lamda Theta* (New York University), April, 1950, p. 2.

Mataresi, Felicia. "No Debe Segregarse a Los Estudiantes de Puerto Rico," *El Diario de Nueva York*, January 19, 1954.

Mayor's Advisory Committee on Puerto Rican Affairs in New York City, Sub-Committee on Education, Recreation and Parks. *The Puerto Rican Pupils in the Public Schools of New York City: A Survey of Elementary and Junior High Schools*. New York, 1951, 102 pp.

McCuen, John J. "Puerto Rican Survey Seeks Best Methods," *New York World Telegram and Sun*, April 7, 1954, p. 42.

"Meeting the Needs of Puerto Rican Pupils in New York City Public Schools (Facts and Figures)," *Staff Bulletin* (Special Supplement), March 23, 1964, 4 pp.

"Melting Pot Boils in This High School," *The New York Times*, December 14, 1952, p. 45.

Menton, Seymour. "Teaching English to Puerto Rican Students," *High Points*, November, 1952, pp. 67-70.

Messer, Helaine R. *The Puerto Rican Student in the New York City Publis Schools: 1945-1965*. Unpublished M.A. Thesis. Columbia University, 1966.

Miller, Henry. "New York City's Puerto Rican Pupils: A Problem of Accultration," *School and Society*, Vol. LXXVI, No. 1967 (August 30, 1952), pp. 129-132.

Mills, C. Wright, Clarence Senior, and Rose Kihn Goldsen. *The Puerto Rican Journey*. New York, 1950, 238 pp.

Mirkin, Sydney. "The Puerto Rican Problem," *Daily News*, January 3, 1955, pp. 3, 29.

———. "The Puerto Rican Problem: Island Fights for Better Living," *Daily News*, January 5, 1955, pp. 2, 32.

———. "The Puerto Rican Problem: They Change Her, Island Feels," *Daily News*, January 4, 1955, pp. 3, 24.

Monserrat, Joseph. *School Integration: A Puerto Rican View*. San Juan, Commonwealth of Puerto Rico, Department of Labor, Migration Division, 1963, 16 pp.

———. "A Puerto Rican Family," Natural History, April, 1967 (On Lewis's *La Vida*).

Montag, Jennie, and Mary Finocchiaro. "Guidance and Curriculum for Puerto Rican Children," *High Points*, January, 1951, pp. 32-42.

Montes, Marta. "La Primera Escuela Puertoriquena en la Ciudad de Nueva York," *La Presna*, September 17, 1961.

"More Classes Set for Adults," *New York Sun*, November 25, 1947.

Muñoz Marín, Ines María Mendoza De. "Identidad Puertoriqueña," *La Prensa*, July 30, 1961.

Narvaez, Alfonso. "Beleaguered High School," *New York Herald Tribune*, December 26, 1965, p. 32.

"Need of the Puerto Rican Child," *New York Teacher News*, November 8, 1952, p. 3.

"Nuevo Método Para la Ensenañza de Idiomas," *El Diario de Nueva York*, February 26, 1952, p. 4.

New York City. Board of Education

A. Unpublished Materials

"Annual Report of the Commissioner of Education." n.d., 4 pp.

Board of Education Statement on the Decentralization of the New York City School System." June 14, 1965, 7 pp.

Bureau of Curriculum Research. "Puerto Ricans in New York City," 1965, 8 pp.

———. "A Resource Unit: Understanding Our Fellow American Citizens, the Puerto Ricans." N.d., 9 pp.

"Comparison of Special Programs, Classes, and Materials for Puerto Rican Students in Eighteen Schools." N.d., 8 pp.

"Curriculum Development: Notes for Discussion at Principals' Inservice Course." New York Board of Education, 1943.

Department of Speech Improvement. "Speech Problems of Puerto Rican Children." A Report of the Committee on Individualization, November, 1948, 13 pp.

Division of Elementary Schools. "Education of the Non-English Speaking Child." New York, 1962, 2 pp.

———. "Highlights of the Non-English Program." New York, 1963, 3 pp.

———. "Proposed Revision of Policy on Operation Understanding." New York, 1963, 9 pp.

———. "Record Sheets, Rating Sheets, and Instructional Aids for the Education of the Non-English Speaking Child," 11 pp.

Division of Elementary Schools. "The Substitute Auxiliary Teacher," 1958, 4 pp.

Division of High Schools. "Number of Candidates for Graduation —June, 1962," 5 pp.

———. "Report on Graduates—January, 1962, 2 pp.

———. "Non-English Program, Schools Having 25 or More Students Rated as Non-English Speaking in the Census of October, 1958, October, 1959, October, 1962, October, 1963," 30 pp.

———. "Some Resources Recommended for Use in the Education of Non-English Speaking Students." May, 1960, 9 pp.

Division of Junior High Schools. "Minutes of a Conference Related to an Educational Program for Puerto Rican Children." February 10, 1953, 3 pp.

———. "The Puerto Rican Bulletin: An Aid to Teachers and Supervisors of Puerto Rican Children." N.d., 30 pp.

———. "Some Facts and Figures about Puerto Rico and Puerto Ricans." 1952. Unpaged.

Donavan, Bernard E., and Benjamin J. Stern. "Memorandum of Pupils Whose Native Language Is Not English." March 20, 1953.

Pinocchiaro, Mary. "The Role of the Foreign Language Teacher in an Educational Program for Puerto Rican Children." N.d., 6 pp.

In-Service Course, Spring Term, 1963, Course C-886. "Prectical Techniques for Teachers of Spanish Working with Puerto Rican Pupils, Questions Submitted by Members of the Class," 11 pp.

New Release, July 12, 1965, 2 pp.

———. July 13-14, 1965, 2 pp.

———. July 21, 1965, 3 pp.

The Puerto Rican Study. Announcements, Correspondence, Minutes. In the *Covello Papers—Personal Files.*

The Puerto Rican Study. "Follow-Up Study of the Graduating Classes of Two Junior High Schools." A report prepared by Maria Luisa Rodriguez, September 20, 1955, 34 pp.

———. Project for Transitional-Stage Puerto Rican Pupils in the High School, Helping the Transitional Stage Pupil in the Subject Class." May 16, 1956, 6 pp.

———. "The Puerto Rican Study News Exchange," No. 1, November 4, 1954. Unpaged.

———. "The Puerto Rican Study News Exchange," No. 2, December 8, 1954. Unpaged.

———. "The Puerto Rican Study News Exchange," No. 6, April 21, 1955. Unpaged.

———. "A Report on School-Puerto Rican Parent Relations, 1955-6." A report prepared by Frances Low. New York, 1957, 61 pp.

———. "Who Are the Puerto Rican Pupils in the New York City Public Schools? Report No. 1: Educational and Familial Background." A report prepared by Samuel M. Goodman, New York, 1954, 27 pp.

Sanguimetti, Carmen. "The Puerto Rican School Child in Puerto Rico and in New York City." An address given at in-service course for teachers of Puerto Rican adults. New York, November 17, 1960, 9 pp.

"Special Census of School Population Classification of 'Non-English Speaking' Pupils, October 31, 1963." A report prepared by Bertha Leviton. May, 1964, 13 pp.

"Statistics on Regular Day Schools—Pupils Newly Arrived from Places Outside New York City and Leading Sources of Immigration." 1955, 3 pp.

Union Settlement. "College Readiness Program." 1965, 1 p.

Wolk Elsie. "A Summary Report of Reading Disabilities of Children Learning English as a Second Language." New York, 1963, 4 pp.

B. Published Materials

Bureau ofCurriculum Research. *Foreign Language Revision for Secondary Schools, Spanish, Level 5.* 1965, 47 pp.

Division of Elementary Schools. *Handbook,* 1964-1965, 221 pp.

———. *Handbook,* 1964-1965. 268 pp.

———. *Teaching Children of Puerto Rican Background in New York City Schools: Suggested Plans and Procedures.* 1954, 76 pp.

Donavan, Bernard E. *Implementation of Board Policy on Excellence for the City's Schools.* April 28, 1965, 34 pp.

Educating Students for Whom English Is a Second Language. December, 1965, 105 pp.

A Five-Year Crash Program for Quality Education. October 22, 1964, 16 pp.

Hillson, Henry T., and Florence Myers. *The Demonstration*

Guidance Project, 1957-1962: Pilot Project for Higher Horizons. 1963, 31 pp.

Interviewing Puerto Rican Parents and Children in Spanish: A Guide for School Personnel. N.d., 10 pp.

Landers, Jacob. *Higher Horizons: Progress Report.* January, 1963, 109 pp.

Portals to the Future, Annual Report of the Superintendent of Schools, 1959-1960. 78 pp.

Puerto Rican Profiles. Curriculum Bulletin No. 5, 1964-1965 Series, 96 pp.

The Puerto Rican Study, 1953-1957. J. Cayce Morrison, Director, 1958, 265 pp.

The Puerto Rican Study. *Developing a Program for Testing Puerto Rican Pupils in the New York City Public Schools.* 1958, 143 pp.

———. *A Letter to Friends of Puertorican Children.* October 1, 1955, 8 pp.

The Puerto Rican Study. *The Future Is Now.* N.d., 32 pp.

———. *Our Children from Puerto Rico, A Report on Their Island Home by the Visiting Puerto Rican Workshop of 1955.* 1957, 72 pp.

———. *Resource Units for Classes with Puerto Rican Pupils in the First Grade.* 1955, 145 pp.

———. *Resource Units for Classes with Puerto Rican Pupils in the Fifth Grade.* 1956, 174 pp.

———. *Resource Units for Classes with Puerto Rican Pupils in the Fourth Grade.* 1955, 143 pp.

———. *Resource Units for Classes with Puerto Rican Pupils in the Second Grade.* 1956, 119 pp.

———. *Teaching English to Puerto Rican Pupils in Grades Five and Six.* 1957, 274 pp.

———. *Teaching English to Puerto Rican Pupils in Grades Three and Four.* 1957, 216 pp.

———. *Who Are the Puerto Rican Children in the New York City Public Schools?* 1956, 88 pp.

Report of the Joint Planning Committee for More Effective Schools to the Superintendent of Schools, May 15, 1964, 19 pp.

School Districts 11 and 18, Benjamin E. Strumpf, Assistant Superintendent. *Your American Pupil from Puerto Rico. . . .* September, 1956, 12 pp.

Sixtieth Annual Report of the Superintendent of Schools, City of New York, Statistical Section, School Year 1957-1958. 1959, pp. 69-72.

Toward Greater Opportunity, A Progress Report from the Superintendent of Schools to the Board of Education, Dealing with Implementation of Recommendations of the Commission on Integration, June, 1960. 196 pp.

Working with Pupils of Puerto Rican Background, A Guidance Manual. 1965, 87 pp.

New York State Commission for Human Rights, Division of Research *The Puerto Rican Populations of the New York City Area: Populations of New York State: 1960 Report No. 2.* May, 1962, 22 pp.

"Niños Borícuas Usarán Aquí Libros Preparados en la Isla," *El Diario de Nueva York,* March 6, 1951, p. 1.

"N. Y. U. Rinde Homenaje a Dos Puertoriquenos" (Editorial), *El Diario de Nneva York,* April 17, 1952, p. 11.

"New York: World They Never Made." Reprinted from *Time,* June 12, 1950, 2 pp.

"Oportunidad de Estudiar el Inglés que puede Malograrse por Indiferencia" (Editorial), *La Prensa,* January, 1954.

Osuna, Juan J. *A History of Education in Puerto Rico.* Rio Piedras, P.R., 1949.

Ortiz, Ernesto, *et al.* Letter. "En Defensa de los Niños Puertoriquenos," *El Diario de Nueva York,* April 15, 1954.

Padilla, Elena. *Up From Puerto Rico.* New York, 1958, 317 pp.

"Parents, Children to Attend School," *The New York Times,* June 25, 1949, p. 8.

Passow, Harry A. (ed.). *Education in Depressed Areas.* New York, 1963, 359 pp. (See "Introduction," *supra.*)

Perlman, Ruth. "The American School: Cultural Crossroads," *The Elementary School Journal,* November, 1958, pp. 82-86.

La Prensa. Suplemento Educativo, September 17, 1961, 8 pp.

Probst, Nathan, and Sophia A. Olmsted. "The Rising Puerto Rican Problem," *Bar Bulletin* (New York County Lawyers Association), Vol. IX, No. 5 (March, 1952), pp. 5-12.

"Program a de Orientación Educativa para Ninos Hispanos," *El Diario de Nueva York,* September 30, 1951, pp. 4, 14.

"Proponen Intensificar la Ensenañza de Inglés," *La Prensa,* January, 16, 1961, pp. 3, 9.

"Puerto Rican Adults Taught." *New York Sun,* November 13, 1947.

"Puerto Ricans Bid for More Schools," *The New York Times,* August 6, 1967.

"The Puerto Rican Child," *New York Teachers' News*, November 29, 1952, pp 2, 7.

"The Puerto Rican Child," *Teacher News*, November 29, 1952, p. 227.

"Puerto Rican Children," *New York Teachers' News*, April 3, 1954, p. 4.

"Puerto Rican Committee Reactivated," *Better Times*, Vol. XXXII, No. 10 (December 1, 1950), p. 1.

Puerto Rican Community Development Project: A Proposal for a Self-Help Project to Develop the Community by Strengthening the Family, Opening Opportunities for Youth and Making Full Use of Education. New York, Puerto Rican Forum, 1964.

"Puerto Rican Conference on City Needs," *The New York Times*, April 17, 1967.

The Puerto Rico Forum, Inc. *Aspira*. 1965, 4 pp.

Puerto Rican Graduates of Morris High School June, 1961. Migration Division, Commonwealth of Puerto Rico, 1963, 23 pp.

"Puerto Ricans and Inter-American Understanding," *The Journal of Educational Sociology*, Vol. XXXV, No. 9 (May, 1962), pp. 385-440.

"The Puerto Ricans in New York City: Background Information for Teachers," *Curriculum and Materials*, Vol. XVIII, No. 3 (Spring, 1964), pp. 6-7.

"Puerto Rican Migration," *Real Estate News*, March, 1949, 1 p.

"Puerto Ricans Pose Problems in Education," *The Sun*, November 12, 1947, pp. 1-39.

"Puerto Rican Problem Cited," *Daily News*, November 11, 1947.

"Puerto Ricans Seek Better Jobs Here," *The New York Times*, June 16, 1948.

"Puerto Ricans Start Up Labor Ladder," *Business Week* (Reprint), May 2, 1953, 3 pp.

"Pupils from Puerto Rico," *The Elementary School Journal*, November, 1958, p. 74.

Quintero, Babby. "Del Ambiente Hispano," *La Prensa*, December 4, 1951, p. 3.

Raisner, Arnold. "New Horizons for the Student of Spanish-Speaking Background," *High Points*, February, 1966, pp. 19-23.

Rand, Christopher. *The Puerto Ricans*. New York, 1958, 178 pp.

"Report on Puerto Rico Schools: McCloskey Describes Difficulties and Accomplishments of Island Educators." *New York Sun*, July 24, 1948.

Reissman, Frank. *The Culturally Deprived Child*. New York, 1962, 140 pp.

Rogers, Melvin L. "For Puerto Rican Pupils: Crash Program in Reading," *The Elementary School Journal*, November, 1958, pp. 87-89.

Samuels, Gertrude. "Puerto Rico: Land of Paradox," *The New York Times Magazine*, October 30, 1955, pp. 18, 62, 64, 67.

Sanchez, Jose M. "Más Maestros Hispanos," *El Diario de Nueva York*, June 15, 1952, p. 7

Sayers, Raymond S. "New York Teachers in Puertorican Schools," *High Points*, November, 1957, 12 pp.

Santolala, Irene Silva. "Los Padres y el Escolar," *El Diario de Nueva York*, June 15, 1952, p. 7.

"Schools to Develop Puerto Rican Programs," *New York World Telegram and Sun*, August 28, 1953, p. 40.

"Se Crea Comité de Padres Hispanos de la Escuela No. 29 de Brooklyn, *El Diario de Nueva York*, June 22, 1952, p. 7.

"Seek Better School Program for NYC Puerto Rican Youth," *New York Teacher's News*, May 31, 1952, p. 4.

"L Semana de la Educación," *La Prensa*, November 1, 1953.

Senior, Clarence. "Schools, Newcomers and Community," *Problems and Practices in New York City Schools*. 1963 Yearbook of the Society for the Experimental Study of Education. Parts II and III, pp. 107-11. New York: Society for the Eperimental Study of Education, 1963.

————. *The Puerto Ricans: Strangers—Then Neighbors*. Quadrangle Edition. Chicago, 1965, 128 pp.

Sexton, Patricia Cayo. *Spanish Harlem: Anatomy of Poverty*. New York, 1965, 208 pp. (See Cordasco, *supra*.)

Shaw, Frederick. "A Follow-Up Study of the 1963 High School Graduates," *High Points*, November, 1965, pp. 31-56.

Slotkin, Aaron N. "The Treatment of Minorities in Textbooks: The Issues and the Outlook," *Strengthening Democracy*, Vol. XVI, No. 3 (May, 1964), pp. 1-2, 8.

Smith, Richard C. "This School Solves Its Own Problems," *The Elementary School Journal*, November, 1958, pp. 75-81.

"Spanish Endorsed for U.S. Schools," *The New York Times*, July 22, 1967, p. 54 (Senate Bill 428).

"Special Study for Migrants: Arts and Crafts Material for Puerto Ricans," *New York Sun*, December 16, 1947.

"Speech Training for Migrants," *New York Sun*, June 23, 1948.

"Sra. Collazo Dice Son Totalmente Falsa Palabras que se le Atribuyen," *El Diario de Nueva York*, July 30, 1952, p. 4.

"Statement of Policy: 'Excellence for the Schools of New York City,'" *Staff Bulletin* (Special Supplement), May 7, 1965, 4 pp.

"Superintendente Escuelas de N.Y. Pide Más Respeto Para los Borícuas," *El Diario de Nueva York*, January 16, 1961, p. 2.

Taylor, Carol. "A Better Era for Puerto Ricans: Obstacles of Mass Migration Are Disappearing for Our Newest New Yorkers," *New York World Telegram and Sun*, May 23, 1963, Second Section, p. 17.

"Teaching the Puerto Rican Child, *New York Teachers' News*, February 23, 1953, p. 3.

"Teaching Puerto Ricans in New York," *The New York Times*, December 17, 1950.

"10 Maestros para 11,900 Alumnos en Escuelas N.Y.," *El Diario de Nueva York*, April 10, 1952.

Treatman, Paul. "Operation-Understanding for Principals," *K-Six Magazine*, Issue 2 (1963-1964), pp. 19-24.

"Una Noche en P. Rico," *El Diario de Nueva York*, March 2, 1953, p. 6.

Wakefield, Dan. *Island in the City*. Boston, 1959, 278 pp.

Weales, Gerald. "New York's Puerto Rican Dilemma," *The New Leader*, March 7, 1955, pp. 8-10.

Weitzman, Judy. "Reheating the Melting Pot," *The New Leader*, June 28, 1954, pp. 11-12.

Welfare Council of New York City, Committee on Puerto Ricans in New York City. *Puerto Ricans in New York City*. New York, 1948, 60 pp.

White, Trumbull. *Puerto Rico and Its People*. Stokes, 1937.

Wolk, E. "The Teahing of English as a Second Language in the Elementary Schools of New York City," *Hispania*, Vol. 49 (May, 1966), pp. 293-296.

Young, Marguerite. "Schools in City Fit Courses to Puerto Ricans," *The New York Herald Tribune* (Reprint), November 16, 1947.

FRANK M. CORDASCO *is Professor of Educational Sociology at Jersey City State College and Educational Consultant, Migration Division, Commonwealth of Puerto Rico.*

LEONARD COVELLO *is Educational Consultant, Migration Division, Commonwealth of Puerto Rico, and former Principal, Benjamin Franklin High School, East Harlem, New York City.*

Doctoral Research
on
Puerto Rico and Puerto Ricans

Jesse J. Dossick
Professor of Social Studies Education
School of Education
New York University

TABLE OF CONTENTS

Page

DOCTORAL RESEARCH ON PUERTO RICO AND PUERTO RICANS

Jesse J. Dossick

None of the three major institutions of higher learning on the Island of Puerto Rico — the University of Puerto Rico in Rio Piedras and Mayaguez, Catholic University in Ponce, and Inter-American University in San German — have established schools of advanced studies in the arts and sciences and education accredited to grant a degree of Doctor of Philosophy or Doctor of Education.[1] During the past sixty-eight years of Puerto Rico's association with the United States, however, 320 doctoral dissertations dealing with Puerto Rico and Puerto Ricans have been completed and accepted in universities on the mainland. The number is respectable as a measure of interest in a geographical region of Puerto Rico's size and population. While 50 percent of this doctoral research has been carried out by Puerto Ricans, the conclusion should not be drawn, however, that this constitutes the total amount of doctoral research in which Puerto Ricans have been engaged up to the present. Many doctorates have been granted to Puerto Ricans whose research projects in the humanities and sciences have been in areas in which Puerto Rico per se does not figure.[2]

A thorough examination of the entire Canadian and British output of doctoral dissertations reveals only two titles on Puerto Rico — one approved in economics at Edinburgh in 1961 and the other in education at London in 1963. No attempt has been made to determine the extent of research and the number of dissertations on Puerto Rico produced in European institutions of higher learning such as the Universities of Madrid, Salamanca, and Paris; in Caribbean universities such as the University of Havana; and in the universities of Middle and South America, such as the University of Mexico. An additional list of these studies would be desirable and valuable.

Of the 57 mainland universities in which the listed doctoral research on Puerto Rico has been completed, seven universities alone account for half the output — Columbia, New York, Chicago, Cornell, Northwestern, Michigan, and Harvard. Columbia University has produced the largest number by far, with New York University in strong second place.

Advanced graduate research on Puerto Rico in American universities was negligible during the first forty years of this century, with a total of 26 dissertations being completed, 18 of which were accepted during the 1930's. The next decade produced 42 titles. The marked acceleration in output with

---

[1] The Department of Spanish Studies in the University of Puerto Rico recently established a graduate program leading to the degree of Doctor of Philosophy. Three doctoral dissertations approved in 1966 are included in this listing.

[2] These will be identified in a study to be published shortly by the Journal of Caribbean Studies on doctoral dissertations completed by citizens of the Caribbean area.

more than 250 dissertations being accepted since 1950 is a reflection of growth in doctoral research everywhere. It is worth noting also that where the bulk of the early research had been carried on by mainlanders, the number of Puerto Ricans who have been successful in earning their doctorates has also increased markedly. In addition, whereas the nature of the early research had been primarily concerned with the geology and geography of the Island, today we find that while interest in these areas is still retained more interest is displayed in its education, economics, sociological-anthropological areas, and history.

The fact that the largest number of dissertations, almost a third of the total, have been written in the field of education and have been written mostly by Puerto Ricans is not surprising, since teachers comprise the major group on the Island intent upon pursuing graduate studies for purposes of advancement in their profession. An examination of the education titles reveals that most of the studies are functional and are concerned with immediate and pressing problems on all levels in the field of education.

Students of Puerto Rican affairs will note for themselves the areas in which further study should be encouraged, for example, Puerto Rican art, in which area not one dissertation has been completed.

Supplementary items referred to as "auxiliary theses" have been appended to several classifications. These dissertations are not concerned primarily with Puerto Rico and Puerto Ricans, but they do contain enough relevant information of interest and value — in various chapters or sections — to warrant their inclusion.

AGRICULTURE

Bonnet, Juan A. "The Nature of Laterization as Revealed by Chemical, Physical, and Mineralogical Studies of a Lateritic Soil Profile from Puerto Rico," Wisconsin, 1950.

Bowman, Robert G. "Soil Erosion in Puerto Rico," California, 1942.

Burgos Macías, Rafael. "Potassium Availability in Puerto Rican Soils," Pennsylvania State, 1940.

Capó, Bernardo G. "Available Nutrient Contents of Puerto Rican Soils as Determined by Pot Tests," Cornell, 1943.

Imus, Harold R. "The Mayaguez Area: A Study in Farm Economy Analysis," Northwestern, 1951.

Lugo López, Miguel A. "The Moisture Relationship of Puerto Rican Soils," Cornell, 1950.

Nadal, Grau, Reynaldo. "Reproductive Behavior of the Dairy Goat, Capra Hircus, Under Puerto Rican Conditions," Ohio State, 1955.

Nolla, José A. "The Damping of Tobacco and its Control in Puerto Rico," Cornell, 1932.

Oliver-Padilla, Otis. "The Role of Values and Channel Orientations in the Diffusion and Adoption of New Ideas and Practices: A Puerto Rican Dairy Farmer's Study," Michigan State, 1965.

Rivera Brenes, Luis. "Economic Aspects of Roughage Production and Conservation in Puerto Rico," Minnesota, 1953.

Swisher, Carl L. "Agricultural Development Regions and Subregions of Puerto Rico," Northwestern, 1958.

Tosi, Joseph A., Jr. "Forest Land Utilization in Western Puerto Rico," Clark, 1959.

Wadsworth, Frank H. "The Development of the Forest Land Resources of the Luquillo Mountains, Puerto Rico," Michigan, 1950.

ANTHROPOLOGY

Icken, Helen M. "From Shanty Town to Public Housing: A Comparison of Family Structure in Two Urban Neighborhoods in Puerto Rico," Columbia, 1962.

Koss, Joan D. "Puerto Ricans in Philadelphia: Migration and Accommodative Processes," Pennsylvania, 1965.

Landy, David. "Culture, Family and Childhood in Rural Puerto Rico," Harvard, 1956.

Manners, Robert A. "Culture and Agriculture in an Eastern Highland Community of Puerto Rico," Columbia, 1950.

Maxwell, Thomas J. "Las Poincianas: A Puerto Rican Housing Project," Indiana, 1962.

Mencher, Joan P. "Child Rearing and Family Organization Among Puerto Ricans in Eastville, El Barrio de Nueva York," Columbia, 1958.

Mintz, Sidney W. "Cañamelar: The Contemporary Culture of a Rural Puerto Rican Proletariat," Columbia, 1951.

Murrill, Rupert I. "Racial Blood-Pressure Studies: A Critique of Methodology, with Especial Reference to the Effect of Age, Nutrition, Climate, and Race Blood-Pressure in Puerto Rico," Columbia, 1955.

Padilla, Elena. "Nocora: An Agrarian Reform Sugar Community in Puerto Rico," Columbia, 1951.

Peña, Joan Finkle de. "Standards of Growth and Development for Puerto Rican Children," Indiana, 1958.

Wolf, Eric A. "Culture Change and Culture Stability in a Puerto Rican Coffee Community," Columbia, 1951.

ARCHAEOLOGY

Rainey, Froelich G. "Archaeological Findings in Puerto Rico," Yale, 1935.

BOTANY

Almodóvar, Luis R. "The Fresh Water and Terrestrial Cyanophyta of Puerto Rico," Florida State, 1959.

Asenjo, Conrado F. "Studies of the Medicinal Plants of Puerto Rico," Wisconsin, 1940.

Bird, Piñero, Julio. "Mosaic of Jatropha Gossypifolia in Relation to the Leaf-Curl Virus of Tobacco in Puerto Rico," Minnesota, 1957.

García Molinari, Ovidio. "Grassland and Grasses of Puerto Rico, Nebraska, 1948.

González-Más, Arturo. "A Taxonomic and Ecological Study of the Cyperaceae of Puerto Rico," Florida State, 1959.

Roure, Luis. "The Rusts of Puerto Rico," Louisana State, 1962.

Tió, Marco A. "Photoperiodic Responses of Sugar Cane in Puerto Rico," Pennsylvania State, 1953.

Vélez, Ismael. "Vegetation of the Southwestern Part of Puerto Rico," Louisiana State, 1940.

ECONOMICS

Airov, Joseph. "Location Factors in the Synthetic Fiber Industry with Special Reference to Puerto Rico," Harvard, 1957.

Akin, Wallace E. "The D iry Industry of the San Juan Area, Puerto Rico," Northwestern, 1952.

Anderson, Jean R. "The Marketing of Non-Food Products in Puerto Rico," Radcliffe, 1953.

Andic, F. M. "Distribution of Income in Puerto Rico," Edinburgh, 1961.

Aponte Vásquez, Juan B. "An Analysis of Government Retirement Systems for the Commonwealth of Puerto Rico," Pennsylvania, 1962.

Ballesteros, Pauline A. "External Capital in Puerto Rico's Industrial Development," Illinois, 1959.

Barela, Federico M. "The Puerto Rico Labor Relations Act: A State Labor Policy and Its Applications," North Carolina, 1963.

Batchelder, Robert B. "Subhumid Plain of Northwestern Puerto Rico: Study in Rural Land Utilization," Northwestern, 1951.

Berríos González, Eliseo. "A Study of the Impact of Population Growth in Puerto Rico on Natural Resources, Including a Suggested Program for Improvement," New York, 1945.

Bonnick, Gladstone G. "The United States Sugar Acts: Effects on Puerto Rican Sugar-Cane Output," Chicago, 1965.

Bothwell, Lynn D. "Capital Formation in Puerto Rico, 1950-1960," George Washington, 1964.

Branson, Robert E. "The Structure and Efficiency of Food Marketing in Puerto Rico: A Study of Marketing Efficiency in an Underdeveloped Economic Area," Harvard, 1954.

10

Carpenter, Bruce R. "Puerto Rico's Planned Development of Tourism,"
American, 1964.

Chenault, Lawrence R. "The Puerto Rican Migrant in New York," Columbia,
1938.

Curtis, Thomas D. "Pre-Conditions to Land Reform: A Comparison of Pre-
Revolutionary America with Pre-Reform Puerto Rico," Indiana, 1965.

Díaz Rojas, Amando. "Financing Economic Development in Puerto Rico from
1942 to Date," New York, 1964.

Esteves, Vernon R. "Economic Policy for Puerto Rico," Harvard, 1948.

Fleisher, Belton M. "Some Economic Aspects of Puerto Rican Migration to
the United States," Stanford, 1962.

Freyre, Jorge Fabio. "External and Domestic Financing in the Economic Development of Puerto Rico: Analysis and Projections," Yale, 1966.

Friedlander, Stanley L. "Labor Migration and Economic Growth: A Case Study
of Puerto Rico," Massachusetts Institute of Technology, 1964.

Gaztambide, Juan B. "An Inquiry into the Possibilities of Local Planning in
Puerto Rico," Harvard, 1954.

González, Luis M. "The Economic Development of Puerto Rico from 1898 to
1940," Florida, 1964.

Gosfield, Amor. "Input-Output Theory and Its Application, with Special Reference to an Underdeveloped Economy: The Case of Puerto Rico," Pennsylvania,
1965.

Gray, Lois S. "Economic Incentives to Labor Mobility: The Puerto Rican Case,"
Columbia, 1966.

Griffith, Rosemary C. "Factors Affecting Continental United States Manufacturer
Investment in Puerto Rico," Radcliffe, 1961.

Haring, Joseph E. "External Trade, Capital Imports, and Economic Growth:
The Case of Puerto Rico," Columbia, 1959.

Helfeld, David. "Wage and Price Policy in Puerto Rico," Yale Law, 1954.

Hernández, Nicolás. "The Entrepreneurial Function of the Government of
Puerto Rico," Rutgers, 1965.

Imus, Harold R. "The Mayaguez Area: A Study in Farm Economy Analysis,"
Northwestern, 1951.

Lee, Hy Sang. "The Entrepreneurial Activities of the Government in the Economic Development of Puerto Rico," Wisconsin, 1965.

MacPhail, Donald D. "The Cattle Industry of the South Coast of Puerto Rico," Michigan, 1953.

Mann, Karl Otto. "Minimum Wages in the Puerto Rican Economy," Cornell, 1955.

Mears, Leon A. "Private Investment and Puerto Rican Development: Inducements and Impediments," California, 1954.

Mudie, John Howard. "The Role of the Government Development Bank in Puerto Rico's Economic Program," Texas, 1960.

Okuda, Kenji. "The Industrial Development Program in Puerto Rico, 1942-1953," Harvard, 1955.

Ortíz, Julio B. "The Two Per-Cent Sales Tax in Puerto Rico," Boston, 1939.

Padilla-Escabí, Salvador M. "A Plan for the Improvement of Puerto Rico's Highway System, Cornell, 1958.

Rivera, Héctor J. "Income Tax Development and Procedure in Puerto Rico," New York, 1959.

Rottenberg, Simon. "Labor Cost and Productivity in the Puerto Rican Economy," Harvard, 1951.

Saenz, Michael. "Economic Aspects of Church Development in Puerto Rico," Pennsylvania, 1961.

Sánchez Arán, Frank. "Financial Aspects of Economic Development in Puerto Rico," New York, 1963.

Serra, Guillermo. "An Economic Study of Family Sized Farms in Puerto Rico," Cornell, 1948.

Silva Recio, Luis F. "Public Wage Fixing and Its Effects on Collective Bargaining and the Labor Movement in Puerto Rico," Wisconsin, 1962.

Stone, Leroy O. "Some Demographic Concomitants of Economic Change in Sub-Regions of Puerto Rico: 1950-1960," Pennsylvania, 1965.

Taylor, Milton C. "Industrial Tax Exemption in Puerto Rico," Wisconsin, 1954.

Torres Peralta, Sarah Esther. "The Labor Management Relations Act and the Puerto Rico Labor Relations Act: A General Comparison," Illinois, 1956.

Torruellas, Luz M. "The United States Commercial Policy Towards Puerto Rico: An Inquiry into Its Impacts on the Puerto Rican Economy and Trade," Radcliffe, 1950.

Vélez Montes, Manuel J. "Government Strategy for Economic Development," Rutgers, 1965.

Vietorisz, Thomas. "Regional Programming Models and the Case Study of a Refinery-Petrochemical-Synthetic Fiber Industrial Complex for Puerto Rico," Massachusetts Institute of Technology, 1956.

White, Byron. "Cuba and Puerto Rico: A Case Study in Comparative Economic Development Policy," Texas, 1959.

EDUCATION

General

Mellado, Ramon Antonio. "Culture and Education in Puerto Rico," Teachers College, Columbia, 1947.

Mueller, John F. "A Survey of the Educational Program of Catholic Elementary and Secondary Schools in the San Juan Diocese of Puerto Rico," Teachers College, Columbia, 1954.

Porrata, Oscar Emilio. "A Suggested Policy for the Administration and Control of Public Education in Puerto Rico," Pennsylvania State, 1947.

Riestra, Miguel A. "Puerto Rico: Culture and Education in a Transitional Era," Illinois, 1962.

Rodríguez, Oscar. "A Proposal for a Church Program of Education for Family Living in Puerto Rico," Teachers College, Columbia, 1952.

Rodríguez Díaz, Manuel. "Conceptions Involved in Replanning Rural Education in Puerto Rico," Cornell, 1948.

Rosado, Domingo. "A Philosophical Study to Propose Objectives for Education in Puerto Rico," New York, 1959.

Serrano, Irma García de. "The Puerto Rican Teachers' Association and Its Relationship to Teacher Personnel Administration," New York, 1966.

Administration and Supervision

Bryant, Bill. "Certification Requirements for Elementary School Principals in the United States and Puerto Rico," Texas, 1961.

Cartagena Colón, Demetrio. "An Evaluation of the Policies and Procedures Used in Puerto Rico in Planning and Constructing Public School Buildings," New York, 1960.

Gómez, Laura. "Suggestions for Improving the Work of the Principal in the Elementary Schools of Puerto Rico," Teachers College, Columbia, 1951.

Piñero, Europa González de. "An Analysis of the Current Role of the Assistant Superintendent of Schools in Puerto Rico and How He Might Work More Effectively in the Commonwealth's Educational Program," New York, 1965.

Quiñones, Leo M. "Supervision in the Catholic High Schools of Puerto Rico," Nebraska, 1965.

Adult and Community Education

Dávila, Cecilia. "A Proposal for Community Education in Selected Resettlements in Puerto Rico," New York, 1955.

Keimig, Joseph F. "The Use of Adult Education in the Emergence of a New Order in Puerto Rico," Chicago, 1964.

Marcano-Blanco, Rafael. "Training Interests, Importance Given to Training and other Related Factors in Adult Education in Public Agencies of Puerto Rico," Indiana, 1965.

Murphy, Marcelino. "Educational and Social Action Programs in Government Sponsored Rural Communities in Puerto Rico," Teachers College, Columbia, 1953.

Rodríguez Robles, Juan. "Manual in Community Problems for Puerto Rican Schools," New York, 1950.

Agricultural and Vocational Education

Martínez Acevedo, Reinaldo I. "A Comparison of the Attitudes of Educators Toward the Future Development of Young and Adult Farmer Instruction in Vocational Agriculture in Puerto Rico," Pennsylvania State, 1955.

McElheny, John Richard. "Industrial Education in Puerto Rico: An Evaluation of the Program in 'Operation Bootstrap' from 1948 to 1958," Ohio State, 1960.

Meléndez, Juan Roberto. "A Study of the Puerto Rican Technical Cooperation Program in Selected Vocational Schools," Tennessee, 1962.

Urgell, Francisco Carlos. "The Development and Contemporary Problems of Vocational Education in Puerto Rico," Pennsylvania State, 1942.

Education of Puerto Ricans in the New York Metropolitan Area

Bucchioni, Eugene. "A Sociological Analysis of the Functioning of Elementary Education for Puerto Rican Children in the New York City Public Schools," New School for Social Research, 1965.

Crespo, Patria Cintrón de. "Puerto Rican Women Teachers in New York: Self Perception and Work Adjustment as Perceived by Themselves and Others," Columbia, 1965.

Kriedler, Charles. "A Study of the Influence of English on the Spanish of Puerto Ricans in Jersey City, New Jersey," Michigan, 1958.

Mayans, Frank Jr. "Puerto Rican Migrant Pupils in New York City Schools; A Comparison of the Effects of Two Methods of Instructional Grouping on English Mastery and Attitudes, Columbia, 1953.

Perlman, Ruth. "Our Mobile Population and the Schools: Some Problems of Teaching Immigrant Children in Metropolitan School Districts," Teachers College, Columbia, 1953.

Robinson, Gertrude A. "A Case Study of Puerto Rican Children in Junior High School 65, Manhattan, New York City, New York," New York, 1956.

Rosenthal, Alan G. "Pre-School Experience and Adjustment of Puerto Rican Children," New York, 1955.

Ruíz, Arreche, Paquita. "Vocational Needs of the Puerto Rican Migrant in New York City," Fordham, 1946.

Ryan, Louise T. "Common Errors in English Language Usage Made by Spanish-speaking Pupils," New York, 1950.

Sanguinetti, Carmen. "Adapting Science Instruction in New York City Junior High Schools to the Needs of Puerto Rican Background Pupils," Teachers College, Columbia, 1956.

Schwartzberg, Herbert. "The Effect of a Program of Choral Speaking on the Silent Reading Achievement of Sixth Grade Bilingual Puerto Rican Children in the New York City Elementary Schools," New York, 1963.

Stambler, Ada. "A Study of Eighth Grade Puerto Rican Students at Junior High School 65 Manhattan, with Implications for Their Placement, Grouping and Orientation," Teachers College, Columbia, 1958.

Wachs, William. "A Study of the Extent to Which Textbooks Teaching English to Foreign-born Hispanic Adults in New York City Help Them Comprehend the Daily English Newspapers They Read," New York, 1946.

Weissman, Julius. "An Exploratory Study of Communication Patterns of Lower Class Negro and Puerto Rican Mothers and Pre-School Children," Teachers College, Columbia, 1966.

Willis, Robert. "An Analysis of the Adjustment and Scholastic Achievement of Forty Puerto Rican Boys Who Attended Transition Classes in New York City," New York, 1961.

Elementary Education

Blanco Colón, R. "Permanent Withdrawals from Grades Four, Five and Six in Puerto Rico," George Peabody College, 1947.

Cruz Aponte, Ramon A. "Promotion Policies and Practices in the Public Elementary Schools of Puerto Rico," North Carolina, 1965.

Rodríguez, Antonio, Jr. "The Second Unit and the Rural School Problem of Puerto Rico," Indiana, 1944.

Health Education

Delgado-Murphy, Cristela. "The Development of Health Education in Puerto Rico: A Study with Particular Reference to Health Educator Roles in the Island-wide Program," North Carolina, 1962.

Higher Education

Aponte Hernández, Rafael. "The University of Puerto Rico: Foundations of the 1942 Reform," Texas, 1966.

Batista, Adelaida. "Occupational Preference Among Students at the College of Education, University of Puerto Rico," Teachers College, Columbia, 1966.

Cáceres, José Antonio. "Proposed Modification of Courses in the Social Foundations of Education at the University of Puerto Rico," Teachers College, Columbia, 1956.

Cole, James E. "A Study of School Service Bureaus in Selected Colleges and Universities in the United States, Puerto Rico and Hawaii," Utah, 1952.

Colón, Jesús M. "The Construction and Validation of Scales for Predicting Graduation from the Normal Diploma Program in the College of Education, University of Puerto Rico," Houston, 1964.

García, Marion. "The Guidance of the Normal School Student. Proposals for a Program of Staff Participation at the College of Education, University of Puerto Rico," Teachers College, Columbia, 1953.

González, William. "The Construction and Validation of a Scale to Predict Success in the College of Education of the University of Puerto Rico," Houston, 1964.

Heth, Edward Leon. "A Plan for Revising and Augmenting the Music Curriculum of the Polytechnic Institute of Puerto Rico," Teachers College, Columbia, 1950.

Keller, Richard F., Jr. "An Exploratory Study of the Needs for a Public Community College in an Area of Ten Puerto Rican Municipalities," Michigan State, 1963.

Méndez, Adela Marguerite. "The Reorganization of the Basic Course in English at the University of Puerto Rico," Teachers College, Columbia, 1953.

Nieves Falcón, Luis. "Recruitment to Higher Education in Puerto Rico; with Special Reference to the Period 1940-1960," London, 1963.

Preston, Faith. "A Plan of Administrative Organization for Puerto Rico Junior College," Teachers College, Columbia, 1964.

Putman, Ivan J., Jr. "Admission Data and the Academic Performance of Foreign Graduate Students at Columbia University," Columbia, 1953.

Quintero, Angel Guillermo. "A Critical Analysis of the General Studies Program of the University of Puerto Rico and a Plan for Its Development," Chicago, 1949.

Ramírez López, Ramon. "A Comparative Study of the Values of Teachers, Students of Education and Other University Students in Puerto Rico," Texas, 1957.

Riccio, Robert A. "A Proposed Course in Humanities for the College of Agriculture and Mechanical Arts of the University of Puerto Rico," Teachers College, Columbia, 1957.

Sáez, Florencio. "Democratizing Organization and Administration in the Evangelical Seminary of Puerto Rico," Teachers College, Columbia, 1947.

Sambolín, Luis F. "A Proposed Guide for Developing an Undergraduate Professional Curriculum in Recreation at Inter-American University of Puerto Rico," Teachers College, Columbia, 1962.

Torres, Josephina T. "Proposal for Associate Degree Pre-Service Nursing Education in Puerto Rico," Teachers College, Columbia, 1965.

Auxiliary Theses

Cajoleas, Louis Peter. "The Academic Record, Professional Development, and Return Adjustment of Doctoral Students from Other Lands: A Study of Teachers College Alumni 1946-55," Columbia, 1958.

Nash, Willard Lee. "The Stated Aims and Purposes of the Departments of Military Science and Tactics and Physical Education in the Land-Grant Colleges of the United States," Teachers College, Columbia, 1934.

Wellons, Ralph D. "The Organizations Set Up for the Control of Mission Union Higher Educational Institutions," Teachers College, Columbia, 1927.

History of Education

Anttila, Earl Urlo. "United States Educational Policy in the Caribbean," Texas, 1953.

Cafouros, Angeles Pereles. "The History of Elementary Education in Puerto Rico Under the American Government, 1898-1951," Indiana, 1951.

Carlin, Francis Maureen, Sister. "The Educational Work of the Amityville Dominicans in Puerto Rico (1910-1960)," Fordham, 1961.

Mendoza, Antonio Cuesta, Rev. "La Historía de la Educación en Puerto Rico (1512-1826)," Catholic, 1937.

Osuna, Juan F. "Education in Porto Rico," Teachers College, Columbia, 1923.

Reid, Charles. "Education in the Territories and Outlying Possessions of the United States," Teachers College, Columbia, 1941.

Auxiliary Thesis

Messina, Salvatore M. "Martin Grove Brumbaugh, Educator," Pennsylvania, 1965.

Language in Education

Cebollero, Pedro Angel. "Suggestions for a Language Policy for the Public Schools of Puerto Rico," Teachers College, Columbia, 1937.

Cruz, Aida S. Candelas de. "Linguistic Principles Underlying the Experiment in the Teaching of English as a Second Language in Puerto Rico," Teachers College, Columbia, 1953.

Epstein, Erwin H. "Value Orientation and the English Language in Puerto Rico: Attitudes Toward Second Language Learning Among Ninth Grade Pupils and Their Parents," Chicago, 1966.

Kavetsky, Joseph. "The Development of an English Reader for Puerto Rican Adults," Teachers College, Columbia, 1954.

Méndez, Adela Marguerite. "The Reorganization of the Basic Course in English at the University of Puerto Rico," Teachers College, Columbia, 1953.

Mergal, Margaret Z. "Structural Problems in the Written Use of English by Puerto Ricans," Teachers College, Columbia, 1959.

Nine-Curt, Judith. "A Pronounciation Course on the Vowels of American English, with Audio-Visual Aids for Native Speakers of Spanish," Teachers College, Columbia, 1966.

Planadeball, Marta Josephina. "Problems in Reading English as a Second Language at the University of Puerto Rico with Suggestions for Improvement," Teachers College, Columbia, 1955.

Roca, Pablo. "The Construction of an Interest Inventory for Students of Different Linguistic and Cultural Backgrounds, " Texas, 1952.

Rodríguez Bou, Ismael. "A Study of Parallelism of English and Spanish Vocabularies," Texas, 1944.

Rojas, Pauline. "A Critical Analysis of the Vocabulary of Three Standard Series of Pre-Primers and Primers in Terms of How the Words Are Used; with Special Reference to the Language Problem of the Spanish-speaking Children of Puerto Rico," Michigan, 1946.

Varona-Cartada, Laudalina Fernández. "Some Procedures for Using Pictures in Teaching English as a Second Language," Teachers College, Columbia, 1956.

Secondary Education

Cáceres, Ana María Carillo de. "Group Activities in the Secondary Schools of Puerto Rico, a Handbook for Teachers," Teachers College, Columbia, 1957.

Crespi, Alberta R. "Secondary School Teachers in the Territories and Posessions of the United States," Fordham, 1942.

Del Toro, José E. "The Expressed Interests and Concerns of Puerto Rican Youth in 1948-49; What They Suggest for Secondary Education," Teachers College, Columbia, 1961.

Hamill, Charles O. "A Proposed Plan to Evaluate the Public Secondary Schools of Puerto Rico," California, Berkeley, 1963.

Lopátegui, Miguelina Nazazario de. "Needs and Problems of Puerto Rican High School Students Related to N Variables," Purdue, 1957.

Moreno Marrero, José Agapito. "An Art Curriculum for the Junior High Schools of Puerto Rico, Colorado, 1944.

Zapata Rivera, Lucila. "A Geography of the Commonwealth of Puerto Rico for Secondary Schools," Teachers College, Columbia, 1958.

Auxiliary Thesis

Martin, Richard P. "The Adjustment of Latin American Male Students in Selected Private Secondary Schools in the United States," Northwestern, 1954.

Teacher Education

Grana, Lydia L. Díaz de. "A Study to Determine the Professional Problems of the Elementary School Cooperating Teachers of the University of Puerto Rico," New York, 1965.

Irizarry, Leila Victoria Tossas de. "Introducing a Program of Laboratory Experiences in the Basic Course in Elementary Education at the Inter-American University of Puerto Rico," Teachers College, Columbia, 1957.

López, Concepción Rodríguez de. "A Program for Training Teachers for the Puerto Rican Elementary Schools in the Teaching of Arithmetic," Teachers College, Columbia, 1961.

Otero, Ana L. Rodríguez de. "An Evaluation of the Methods Employed by the Department of Education in Helping Teachers Understand the Principles and Procedures Involved in School Health Programs in Puerto Rico," North Carolina, 1957.

Pastor, Angeles. "Learning To Write Through Experience: A Guide for Elementary School Teachers in Puerto Rico," Teachers College, Columbia, 1955.

Rexach, María G. "Improving Teacher Education for the Teaching of English as a Second Language in Puerto Rico," New York, 1961.

Robles, Juan. "The Effects of a Special Program of Teacher Education and Supervision upon Job Satisfaction of Vocational Agriculture Instructors of Puerto Rico," Pennsylvania State, 1959.

Rodríguez Surillo, Nicolás. "A Comparison of the Perceptions First Year Teachers, Practice Teachers, and Seniors Without Teaching Experience Hold of the Problems Facing Beginning Teachers in Puerto Rico," Michigan State, 1964.

Vázquez, Herminia. "The Role of the College of Education in the Reorientation of Secondary Education in Puerto Rico," Teachers College, Columbia, 1953.

Vergne, Aida Almenas de. "Improving In-Service Education for Beginning Elementary Teachers in Puerto Rico," Teachers College, Columbia, 1951.

Wellman, Coe Rushford. "A Plan for In-Service Training of Teachers and Leaders in the Methodist Church Schools in Puerto Rico," Teachers College, Columbia, 1936.

ENGINEERING AND PHYSICS

Biaggi, Nelson. "Studies on Rum Distillery Wastes in Puerto Rico," Michigan, 1957.

Carlson, Herbert C., Jr. "Ionospheric Heating by Magnetic Conjugate Point Photoelectrons as Observed at Arecibo," Cornell, 1966.

Deere, Don U. "Engineering Properties of the Pleistocene and Recent Sediments of the San Juan Bay Area, Puerto Rico," Illinois, 1955.

Padilla-Escabí, Salvador M. "A Plan for the Improvement of Puerto Rico's Highway System," Cornell, 1959.

Thome, George D. "A Study of Large-Scale Traveling Disturbances in the Ionosphere Using the Arecibo U.H.F. Radar," Cornell, 1966.

GEOGRAPHY

Augelli, John P. "Geography of Agriculture and Settlement in Interior Puerto Rico: Problems of the Upper Loíza Basin," Harvard, 1951.

Batchelder, Robert B. "Subhumid Plain of Northwestern Puerto Rico: Study in Rural Land Utilization," Northwestern, 1951.

Beishlag, George A. "Trends in Land Use in Southeast Puerto Rico," Maryland, 1953.

Blount, Stanley F. "A Regional Analysis of the Changes from 1950 to 1961 in Rural Land Use in the Isabela Irrigation District Northwestern Puerto Rico," Northwestern, 1963.

Brockmann, Vernon W. "Physical Land Types and Land Utilization in the Caguas-San Lorenzo Region of Puerto Rico," Northwestern, 1950.

Burchfield, William W., Jr. "The Geography of the Pineapple Industry of Puerto Rico," Maryland, 1953.

Campbell, David S. "The Geography of the Coffee Industry of Puerto Rico," Chicago, 1947.

Carey, George W. "The Application of Vectors and Correlation Analysis to the Study of the Urban Economic Geography of Mayaguez, Puerto Rico," Teachers College, Columbia, 1964.

Courtney, Dale Elliott. "Problems Associated with Predicting Land Use in Low Latitude Humid Regions: A Case Study of the San Sebastián-Rincón Area, Puerto Rico," Washington, Seattle, 1959.

Doerr, Arthur H. "The Relationship of Human Activities in Southwestern Puerto Rico to the Semi-arid Climate," Northwestern, 1951.

Dyer, Donald R. "The Development of Geographic Survey Techniques for the Rural Land Classification Program of Puerto Rico," Northwestern, 1950.

Gulick, Luther H., Jr. "Rural Occupance in Utado and Jayuya Municipios, Puerto Rico," Chicago, 1952.

Laidig, Kermit M. "Land Use in Southeastern Puerto Rico," Nebraska, 1955.

Lewis, Laurence A. "The Relations of Hydrology and Geomorphology in a Humid Tropical Steam Basin-the Rio Grande de Manatí, Puerto Rico," Northwestern, 1965.

Lobeck, Armin Kohl. "The Physiography of Puerto Rico," Columbia, 1917.

Lonsbury, John F. "Types and Patterns of Rural Settlements in Puerto Rico," Northwestern, 1951.

Netzer, Donald L. "Climate and Agricultural Crop-Land Use in Puerto Rico," Illinois, 1954.

Picó, Rafael. "The Geographic Regions of Puerto Rico," Clark, 1938.

Smith, Richard Vergon. "Characteristics and Locational Problems of Puerto Rican Industrialization," Northwestern, 1957.

Swisher, Carl Laverne. "Agricultural Development Regions and Sub-Regions of Puerto Rico," Northwestern, 1958.

Tosi, Joseph Andrew, Jr. "Forest Land Utilization in Western Puerto Rico," Clark, 1959.

Uttley, Marguerite E. "Land Utilization in the Canovanas Sugar District, Puerto Rico," Chicago, 1938.

Zapata Rivera, Lucila. "Geography of the Commonwealth of Puerto Rico for Secondary Schools," Teachers College, Columbia, 1958.

GEOLOGY

Almy, Charles C., Jr. "Parguera Limestone, Upper Cretaceous Mayaguez Group, Southwest Puerto Rico," Rice, 1965.

Heminway, Caroline E. "The Tertiary Foraminifera of Porto Rico," Indiana, 1941.

Hodge, Edwin. "The Geology of the Coamo-Guayama District, Porto Rico," Columbia, 1917.

Hubbard, Bela. "The Geology of the Lares District, Porto Rico," Columbia, 1924.

Lidiak, Edward G. "Petrology of the Andesitic Spilitic and Keratophyric Lavas, North Central Puerto Rico," Rice, 1963.

Mattson, Peter. "Geology of the Mayaguez Area, Puerto Rico," Princeton, 1957.

Meyerhoff, Howard A. "Geology of Puerto Rico," Columbia, 1934.

Mitchell, Graham J. "The Geology of the Ponce District, Puerto Rico," Columbia, 1918.

Norton, Matthew Frank. "Mineralogy of the Puerto Rico Trench: An Environmental Study," Columbia, 1958.

Otalora, Guillermo. "Geology of the Barranquitas Quadrangle, Puerto Rico," Princeton, 1961.

Pessagno, Emile H., Jr. "Geology of the Ponce-Coamo Area, Puerto Rico," Princeton, 1962.

Semmes, Douglas R. "The Geology of the San Juan District, Porto Rico," Columbia, 1917.

Slodowski, Thomas R. "Geology of the Yauco Area, Puerto Rico," Princeton, 1956.

Williams, Richard S. Jr. "Geomorphology of a Portion of the Northern Coastal Plain of Puerto Rico," Pennsylvania State, 1965.

HISTORY AND POLITICAL SCIENCE

Anderson, Robert W. "Parties, Groups, and Government in Puerto Rico," California, Berkeley, 1960.

Beck, Earl Ray. "The Political Career of Joseph Benson Foraker," Ohio State, 1943.

Boyd, William M. "The Administration of Territories and Island Possessions by the United States," Michigan, 1944.

Brownback, Annadrue H. "Congressional and Insular Opposition to Puerto Rican Autonomy," Alabama, 1966.

Chiles, Paul N. "The Puerto Rican Press Reaction to the United States, 1888-1898," Pennsylvania, 1942.

Cravens, Raymond L. "The Constitutional and Political Status of the Non-contiguous Areas of the United States," Kentucky, 1958.

Custer, Watson S. "A Decade of Church-State Relations in Puerto Rico, 1952-1962," Temple, 1965.

Díaz Soler, Luis M. "Historía de la Esclavitud Negra en Puerto Rico," Louisiana, 1950.

Eblen, Jack E. "The Governor in the United States System of Territorial Government," Wisconsin, 1966.

Fischman, Jerome I. "The Rise and Development of the Political Party in Puerto Rico Under Spanish and American Rule and the Historical Significance of the Subsequent Emergence and Growth of the Popular Party," New York, 1962.

Fitzgerald, William A. "A Survey of Religious Conditions in Puerto Rico, 1899-1934," Fordham, 1934.

Gould, Lyman Jay. "The Foraker Act: The Roots of American Colonial Policy," Michigan, 1958.

Hall, John D. "The Administration of United States Territories and Island Possessions," Syracuse, 1948.

Heikoff, Joseph M. "Federal Aid to Slum Clearance in Puerto Rico, 1950-56," Chicago, 1959.

Honcy, John C. "Public Personnel Administration in Puerto Rico," Syracuse, 1950.

Hunter, Robert J. "The Historical Evolution of the Relationship Between the United States and Puerto Rico, 1898-1963," Pittsburgh, 1964.

Kidder, Frederick E. "The Political Philosophy of Luis Muñoz Rivera (1859-1916) of Puerto Rico," Florida, 1965.

López Baralt, José. "The Policy of the United States Towards Its Territories with Special Reference to Puerto Rico," Cornell Law School, 1933.

Lugo Silva, Enrique. "The Tugwell Administration in Puerto Rico," Ohio State, 1949.

Mathews, Thomas G. "Puerto Rican Politics and the New Deal," Columbia, 1957.

McIntosh, William. "The Development of Political Democracy in Puerto Rico," Minnesota, 1953.

McNeil, Robert L. "The United States and Self-Government for Puerto Rico', 1898-1952," Fletcher, 1956.

Mergal Llera, Angel. "Féderico Degetau, un Orientador de su Pueblo," Columbia, 1943.

Morales Carrión, Arturo. "Puerto Rico and the Non-Hispanic Caribbean: A Study in the Decline of Spanish Exclusivism," Columbia, 1952.

Muñiz, Dolores. "Puerto Rico Under the Administration of Governor Yager, 1913-1921," Michigan, 1945.

Muñoz Amato, Pedro. "Executive Reorganization in the Government of Puerto Rico Under the Executive Governor Act of 1947," Harvard, 1950.

O'Leary, Daniel H. "The Development of Political Parties in Puerto Rico Under American Occupation," Boston College, 1936.

Perkins, Ernest R. "The Development of the Colonial Policy of the United States (To the Passage of the Jones Act for the Philippines and Porto Rico, 1916 and 1917)," Clark, 1930.

Perkins, Whitney T. "American Policy in the Government of Its Dependent Areas; A Study of the Policy of the United States Toward the Inhabitants of Its Territories and Insular Possessions," Fletcher, 1949.

Reuter, Frank T. "Church and State in the American Dependencies, 1898-1904: A Study of Catholic Opinion and the Formation of Colonial Policy," Illinois, 1960.

Santana, Arturo F. "The United States and Puerto Rico, 1797-1830," Chicago, 1954.

Senff, Earl K. "Puerto Rico Under American Rule," Kentucky, 1948.

Snyder, William H. "Caribbean Relations of the United States; the Content for a New College Course," New York, 1933.

Stern, David Sachs. "The Constitutional History of the Commonwealth of Puerto Rico," New York, 1960.

Thomas, David Y. "A History of Military Government in Newly Acquired Territory of the United States," Columbia, 1904.

Torres-Peralta, Sarah Esther. "The Labor-Management Relations Act and the Puerto Rico Labor Relations Act: A General Comparison," Illinois, College of Law, 1956.

Valentine, Elvin L. "The American Territorial Governor," Wisconsin, 1928.

Walters, Everett. "Joseph Benson Foraker, An Uncompromising Republican," Columbia, 1950.

HOME ECONOMICS

Busquets, Carmen Teresa Pesquera. "Differential Adoption of Homemaking Practices in Family Financial Management Recommended in Farm and Home Development in Puerto Rico," Cornell, 1961.

Lacot, Maria Socorro. "Freedom in Making Personal Decisions as Perceived by Puerto Rican Ninth-Grade Girls," Iowa State University of Science and Technology, 1962.

Stefani, Rosa Luisa. "An Exploratory Study of Values and Practices in Child Rearing Among Urban Laboring Class Families in Puerto Rico," Cornell, 1955.

LANGUAGE

Hull, Adrian L. "The Linguistic Accommodation of the Game of Baseball, a Cultural Innovation in the Spanish of Puerto Rico," Teachers College, Columbia, 1963.

Jones, Morgan E. "A Phonological Study of English as Spoken by Puerto Ricans Contrasted with Puerto Rican Spanish and American English," Michigan, 1962.

Kriedler, Charles. "A Study of the Influence of English on the Spanish of Puerto Ricans in Jersey City, New Jersey," Michigan, 1958.

Ponce, Engracia Cerezo de. "La Zona Lingüística de Aguadilla," Puerto Rico, 1966.

Ramírez, María del Tránsito Vaquero de. "Estudio Linguistico de Barranquitos," Puerto Rico, 1966.

Sáez, Mercedes de los Angeles. "Puerto Rican-English Phonotactics," Texas, 1962.

Velázquez, Mary D. Rivera de. "Contrastive Analysis of English and Puerto Rican Spanish," Indiana, 1965.

LITERATURE

Carrino, Frank Gaetano. "Manuel Fernández Juncos: Pivotal Force in the Insular Movement of Puerto Rico Through 'El Buscapie,'" Michigan, 1956.

Duffy, Kenneth J. "Luis Llorens Torres, Poet of Puerto Rico," Pittsburgh, 1941.

Hansen, Terrence L. "The Types of the Folktale in Cuba, Puerto Rico, the Dominican Republic, and Spanish South America," Stanford, 1952.

Lugo, Nilda Sofía Ortiz de. "Vida y Obra de Luis Llorens Torres," Puerto Rico, 1966.

Parrish, Robert T. "A Study of the Personality and Thought of Eugenio Mario de Hostos," Wisconsin, 1940.

MUSIC

Heth, Edward Leon. "A Plan for Revising and Augmenting the Music Curriculum of the Polytechnic Institute of Puerto Rico," Teachers College, Columbia, 1950.

Muñoz, María Luisa. "Music in Puerto Rico," Teachers College, Columbia, 1958.

PHILOSOPHY

Díaz, Vicente M. "Orientaciones en el Pensamiento Filosofico de Eugenio Mario de Hostos," Northwestern (completed, although not accepted because death of writer predated acceptance).

Parrish, Robert T. "A Study of the Personality and Thought of Eugenio Mario de Hostos," Wisconsin, 1940.

Sisler, Robert. "Eugenio Mario de Hostos y Bonilla: A Comparative Study of the Educational and Political Contributions of this Antillean Philosopher and Reformer," New York, 1962.

PSYCHOLOGY

Bolotin, Max. "The Use of Human Figure Drawings in Evaluating Children and Adolescents of Special Educational and Cultural Background: An Examination of the Effectiveness of Current Diagnostic Criteria with the Draw-a-Person Test as Applied to Puerto Rican Children and Adolescents," New York, 1959.

Bouquet, Susana. "Acculturation of Puerto Rican Children in New York and Their Social Attitudes Towards Negroes and Whites," Columbia, 1962.

Concepción, Abigail Díaz de. "Resources in the Lives and Culture of Puerto Rican Students Which Will Aid in the Understanding and Use of Basic Concepts in Social Psychology," Teachers College, Columbia, 1960.

Drusine, Leon. "Some Factors in Anti-Negro Prejudice Among Puerto Rican Boys in New York City," New York, 1955.

Hernández, Carlos. "The Spanish Revision of the S.R.A. Junior Inventory, Form A," Purdue, 1958.

Marín, Rosa C. "The Relationship of Three Psychological Tests to Grades Earned in Classroom Courses in the School of Social Work of the University of Puerto Rico," Pittsburgh, 1953.

Martínez, Juan N. "The Attitudes and Concepts of Puerto Rican Professionals Regarding Mental Illness: An Exploratory Study of a Group of Puerto Rican Professionals; Medical Doctors, Social Workers, Nurses, Teachers, and Religious Workers," New York, 1957.

Oliver-Padilla, Otis. "The Role of Values and Channel Orientations in the Diffusion and Adoption of New Ideas and Practices: A Puerto Rican Dairy Farmer's Study," Michigan State, 1964.

Puig Aruelo, Héctor. "A Quantitative Cross-Cultural Study of Job Satisfaction in the United States, Italy and Puerto Rico," Michigan State, 1960.

Schaefer, Dorothy F. "Prejudice in Mentally Retarded, Average and Bright Negro and Puerto Rican Adolescents," Columbia, 1965.

Sobrino, James F. "Group Identification and Adjustment in Puerto Rican Adolescents," Yeshiva, 1965.

Stoval, Franklin L. "A Study of Scaled Scores with Special Reference to the Inter-American Tests," Texas, 1945.

Suraci, Anthony. "Reactions of Puerto Rican and Non-Puerto Rican Parents to Their Mentally Retarded Boys," New York, 1966.

Vincenty, Nestor Isaac. "Racial Differences in Intelligence as Measured by Pictorial Group Tests with Special Reference to Porto Rico and the United States," Harvard, 1930.

PUBLIC HEALTH

Brown, Myrtle Irene. "Changing Maternity Care Patterns in Migrant Puerto Ricans," New York, 1961.

RELIGION

Custer, Watson S. "A Decade of Church-State Relations in Puerto Rico 1952-1962," Temple, 1965.

Fitzgerald, William A. "A Survey of Religious Conditions in Puerto Rico, 1800 1934," Fordham, 1934.

Seda, Angel Luis. "Implications for Puerto Rico in a Study of the Hospital Chaplaincy in the United States," Teachers College, Columbia, 1958.

SOCIOLOGY

Puerto Rico

Amundson, Robert H. "Population Problems and Policies in Puerto Rico, India, and Japan," Notre Dame, 1956.

Cofresí, Emilio. "Differential Fertility in Puerto Rico," Duke, 1949.

Combs, Jerry W., Jr. "Human Fertility in Puerto Rico," Columbia, 1954.

Díaz, María E. "Public Assistance in Puerto Rico, A Case Study of the Transplantation of a Social Institution," Pittsburgh, 1954.

Feldman, Arnold S. "Social Structure and Fertility in Puerto Rico," Northwestern, 1956.

Hernández, Joseph W. "The Sociological Implications of Return Migration in Puerto Rico: An Exploratory Study," Minnesota, 1964.

Hernández Ramírez, Martín, Jr. "A Socio-Economic Study of Southwestern Puerto Rico," Cornell, 1947.

Macisco, John J., Jr. "Internal Migration in Puerto Rico, 1955-1960," Brown, 1966.

Maunez, Juan José. "A Program for Coordinating Community Agencies in the Control of Juvenile Delinquency in San Juan, Puerto Rico," New York, 1962.

McGinnis, Robert B. "A Family Pattern and Fertility in Puerto Rico," Northwestern, 1955.

Ríos, Trinidad Rivera de. "Two Experiences in the Use of a Time-Limited Pre-Discharge Casework Service in Two Institutions for Emotionally Disturbed Children; The Esther Loring Richards Childrens' Center in Owing Mills, Maryland and the State Home for Boys in Guayanabo, Puerto Rico," Pennsylvania, 1962.

Rogler, Charles C. "Comerío: A Sociological Study of an Inland Puerto Rican Town," Kansas, 1936.

Seda Bonilla, Edwin. "The Normative Patterns of the Puerto Rican Family in Various Situational Contexts," Columbia, 1958.

Stone, Leroy O. "Some Demographic Concomitants of Economic Change in Subregions of Puerto Rico, 1950-60," Pennsylvania, 1964.

Stycos, J. M. "Family and Fertility in Puerto Rico," Columbia, 1956.

Vázquez, José L. "The Demographic Evolution of Puerto Rico," Chicago, 1964.

Vázquez, Pablo B. "Casteñer; A Study of a Planned Rural Community in Puerto Rico," Wisconsin, 1951.

Puerto Ricans in Chicago and Philadelphia

Koss, Joan D. "Puerto Ricans in Philadelphia: Migration and Accommodation," Pennsylvania, 1965.

Lennon, John J. "A Comparative Study of the Patterns of Acculturation of Selected Puerto Rican Protestant and Roman Catholic Families in an Urban Metropolitan Area (Chicago)," Notre Dame, 1963.

Puerto Ricans in New York City

Chartock, Sarah K. "A Descriptive Study of the Programs Undertaken by the Riverside Neighborhood Assembly to Further Democratic Integration on the West Side of Manhattan," New York, 1957.

Goldsen, Rose K. "Puerto Rican Migration to New York City," Yale, 1953.

Gosnell, Patria Arán. "The Puerto Ricans in New York City," New York, 1945.

Jenkins, Shirley. "Reciprocal Empathy in Intergroup Relations: An Exploratory Study of Puerto Rican and Negro Groups in New York City," New York, 1957.

Pérez Jusino, David. "A Suggested Human Relations Program for Puerto Ricans in Spanish Harlem," Teachers College, Columbia, 1952.

Rosner, Milton S. "A Study of Contemporary Patterns of Aspirations and Achievements of the Puerto Ricans of Hells Kitchen," New York, 1957.

Tendler, Diana. "Social Service Needs in a Changing Community: A Study of the Use of Voluntary Social Agencies by Puerto Rican Clients," New York, 1965.

TROPICAL MEDICINE

Palacios de Borao, Gonzalo. "An Epidemiological Study of Leprosy in Porto Rico, With Special Reference to Topographic and Climate Factors," Columbia, 1929.

ZOOLOGY

Biaggi, Virgilio, Jr. "Studies in the Life History of the Puerto Rican Honey Creeper, Coereba Flaveola Portoricensis," (Bryant), Ohio State, 1949.

Candelas Reyes, Gustavo Antonio. "Studies on the Freshwater Plankton of Puerto Rico," Minnesota, 1956.

Connor, Robert Sherman. "Studies on Some Digenetic Trematodes Parsitic in Shore Birds of Puerto Rico," Purdue, 1956.

Cromroy, Harvey Leonard. "A Preliminary Survey of the Plant Mites of Puerto Rico," North Carolina State College, 1958.

Danforth, Stuart T. "An Ecological Study of Cartagena Lagoon, Porto Rico, With Special Reference to the Birds," Cornell, 1925.

García Díaz, Julio. "An Ecological Survey of the Fresh Water Insects of Puerto Rico. I — The Odonata: With New Life Histories," Cornell, 1937.

LeZotte, Lloyd A., Jr. "Studies on Marine Digenetic Trematodes of Puerto Rico; The Family Bivesiculidae, Its Biology and Affinities," Purdue, 1954.

Martorell Dávila, Luis F. "A Survey of the Forest Insects of Puerto Rico," Ohio State, 1943.

Pérez Escolar, Mario E. "The Gummosis of Pineapple in Puerto Rico and Its Control," North Carolina State, 1955.

Ramos, Jose Antonio. "Review of the Auchenorhyncous Homoptera of Puerto Rico. Part III — Kinnaridae, Cercopidae, Mebracidae and Cicididae," North Carolina State, 1956.

Siddiqi, Ather Husain. "Digenetic Trematodes of Marine Fishes of Puerto Rico, A Monographic Study," Purdue, 1959.

Vélez, Manuel J., Jr. "The Taxonomy, Distribution, and Certain Ecological Aspects of the Diplopoda of Puerto Rico," Michigan, 1965.

INDEX

D (Cont.)

Díaz Soler, Luis M., 23
Díaz, Vicente M., 26
Doerr, Arthur H., 21
Drusine, Leon, 26
Duffy, Kenneth J., 25
Dyer, Donald R., 21

E

Eblen, Jack E., 23
Epstein, Erwin H., 17
Esteves, Vernon R., 10

F

Feldman, Arnold S., 28
Fischman, Jerome I., 23
Fitzgerald, William A., 23, 27
Fleisher, Belton M., 10
Freyre, Jorge Fabio, 10
Friedlander, Stanley L., 10

G

García, Marion, 15
García Díaz, Julio, 30
García Molinari, Ovidio, 8
Gaztambide, Juan B., 10
Goldsen, Rose K., 29
Gómez, Laura, 13
González, Luis M., 10
González, William, 16
González-Más, Arturo, 9
Gosfield, Amor, 10
Gosnell, Patria Arán, 29
Gould, Lyman Jay, 23
Grana, Lydia L. Díaz de, 19
Gray, Lois S., 10
Griffith, Rosemary C., 10
Gulick, Luther H., Jr., 21

H

Hall, John D., 23
Hamill, Charles O., 18
Hansen, Terrence L., 26
Haring, Joseph E., 10
Heikoff, Joseph M., 23
Helfeld, David, 10
Heminway, Caroline E., 21

Hernández, Carlos, 27
Hernández, Joseph W., 28
Hernández, Nicolás, 10
Hernández Ramírez, Martín, Jr., 28
Heth, Edward Leon, 16, 26
Hodge, Edwin, 21
Honey, John C., 23
Hubbard, Bela, 22
Hull, Adrian L., 25
Hunter, Robert J., 23

I

Icken, Helen M., 7
Imus, Harold R., 7, 10
Irizarry, Leila Victoria
Tossas de, 19

J

Jenkins, Shirley, 29
Jones, Morgan E., 25

K

Kavetsky, Joseph, 17
Keimig, Joseph F., 13
Keller, Richard F., Jr., 16
Kidder, Frederick E., 23
Koss, Joan D., 8, 29
Kriedler, Charles, 14, 25

L

Lacot, María Socorro, 25
Laidig, Kermit M., 21
Landy, David, 8
Lee, Hy Sang, 11
Lennon, John J., 29
Lewis, Laurence A., 21
LeZotte, Lloyd A., Jr., 30
Lidiak, Edward G., 22
Lobeck, Armin Kohl, 21
Lonsbury, John F., 21
Lopátegui, Miguelina
Nazazario de, 18
López, Concepción Rodríguez de, 19
López Baralt, José, 23
Lugo, Nilda Sofía Ortiz de, 26
Lugo López, Miguel A., 7
Lugo Silva, Enrique, 23

PUERTO RICAN MIGRATION

A Preliminary Report

Prepared for:
U.S. Civil Rights Commission

By:
Puerto Rican Research and
Resources Center, Inc.

I. Sources and Quality of the Data

Births, deaths and migration are the three basic components of population dynamics. The first two have had the greatest influence on population in terms of size, growth and composition in the majority of modern countries. However, in the case of Puerto Rico, migration is the most important factor. From the beginning of the 1950's, Puerto Rico has experienced one of the greatest population out-flows in modern history. Approximately 135,000 persons migrated during the 1945-49 period and 430,000 between 1950 and 1959.

The lack of reliable data on internal and external migration patterns stands in sharp contrast to the comprehensive data available on the other two population components and, even more so, to the highly accurate and reliable macro-economic statistics compiled by the Planning Board of Puerto Rico.

Such a monumental oversight cannot be accidental. Migration is a difficult phenomenon to measure, particularly in the case of Puerto Rico where the local government has no legal authority to regulate external migratory population movements. However, the magnitude of the problem is, in itself, the best argument for the development of a comprehensive data-gathering system on the Puerto Rican migrant. The development of such a system would be facilitated by the fact that Puerto Rico is an island and virtually all its external population movements take place by air. After more than 25 years of a massive migratory movement to the United States and an internal migration which has transformed the human geography of Puerto Rico (a move from rural to urban regions and particularly, the astounding population growth of the greater San Juan area), it seems inexcusable that, as late as 1972 no significant progress has been made in the systems used for gathering data on migration.

In order to establish a public policy aimed at meeting the social and economic problems which confront the migrant within and outside Puerto Rico, it is essential that a comprehensive survey of migration considering all relevant factors (social, economic, cultural and political which have influenced internal and external population movements) be undertaken.

Appendix A treats at length the methods used by the Planning Board, Port Authority and Department of Health to gather data on migration. None of the methods presently used provide complete, accurate or reliable data. Innumerable questions in this area remain unanswered. Because of the scarcity of information, many of the answers to these questions are based on speculation.

We must, therefore, begin our discussion with this warning. The following study is based on the information available to us and is, therefore, necessarily flawed by the paucity and inaccuracy of information.

II. Conditions in Puerto Rico

In order to understand Puerto Rican migration to the United
States it is necessary to know the historical, political and economic
circumstances which underlie this demographic movement. An inquiry in
this direction will necessarily lead to the consideration of two factors:
1) the circumstances "pushing" Puerto Ricans to migrate, and 2) the demand
for, and accommodation of, the Puerto Rican migrants in those regions to
which they migrate. Examination of the first factor requires a
discussion of the economic situation of the island, beginning with
the period preceeding migration, and concluding with an assessment of the
relationship between present trends of the Puerto Rican economy and
migration. The second factor calls for a discussion of the existing
conditions within the labor market in the United States, specifically the
demand for a certain type of labor, as well as the social conditions
encountered by the migrant in his new setting.

A. Pre-Development Period: 1945 and Before

Puerto Rico is a tropical island, approximately 100 miles from
east to west, and 35 miles from north to south. The population was
roughly 2,000,000 in 1940, or 600 persons per square mile (even then, one
of the most densely populated areas in the world). The birth rate was
39 per thousand, and the death rate 18.2 per thousand, giving a rate of
natural increase of 21 per thousand.[1] Public health improved somewhat
following the American occupation in 1898, but still left much to be
desired as evidenced by the high death rate. After the American

occupation, certain production changes were introduced which brought about
changes in the insular social structure. A rudimentary rural capitalism
was replaced by an industrial, high finance capitalism. The characteristic
social type of the former economy -- the individual and independent
"hacendado" working his family farm -- gave way to the managerial hier-
archy of the corporate sugar factory. Statistics show the change. In
1894, 205 sugar "haciendas" marketed the island crop; by 1945, they
had been reduced to 35 central stations, twelve of which were in the
hands of the four leading corporations which accounted for
some 39% of the total output.[2] This trend resulted in the decline of
an entire social class and of its way of life; the highland
"jibaro" and the sugar workers of the coastal plains became daily wage
earners (those who could obtain work at all).
They became propertyless, too, in the classical sense, since by 1930
some 150,000 workers with 600,000 dependents, owned no land at all. The
employee was dependent upon the agricultural corporation for credit,
employment, and housing.

Approximately 44% of all those employed depended
directly on agriculture. Sugar cane accounted for more than 50% of
agricultural production which made the economy extremely vulnerable, since
it depended for survival solely on the price of sugar in the world market.
The high production costs, plus the competition provided by Cuba, Hawaii
and the Philippines made the problem more acute. On the other hand, the
cultivation of coffee and tobacco (comprising most of the remaining 50%
of agriculture) was on the decline. The tobacco industry had concentrated
on production of filler tobacco for cigars, and was severely damaged
by the increasing popularity of the cigarette. The coffee industry
lost its international markets during the Second World War. Aside from

agriculture, the other source of employment was manufacturing, especially the needle trades. The economic situation was alarming. Unemployment had acquired an almost absolute dimension: "a population of about 2,200,000 depending on the production of some ≠630,000 employed persons -- less than 30% of the population."[3] The distribution of income accurately reflects the situation: 13% of the families accounted for 60% of the total personal income, while the remaining 87% accounted for only 40%.[4] The gross domestic investment was $23 million, only 8% of the gross product. Thus, most of the income left the island: some as profits for absentee owners, the rest as payment for imported goods. The economy was essentially an open one: imports amounted to 47% of the net income, while exports were around 40% of the insular income. A deficit of $40.1 million existed in the balance of payments, that is, 7% of the gross product.[5] The low level of real income was the result of low productivity, which resulted from the lack of capital for dynamic investments. The latter was due to an absence of savings, caused by excessive consumption, the classic closed circle of poverty.

The social consequences of the economic situation described above were deplorable. "In general," observed Perloff in his 1949 study of the situation, "the poverty, the crowding, the prevalance of diseases, the malnutrition, the lack of adequate educational, recreational and cultural facilities -- in short, the conditions under which the vast majority of Puerto Ricans live -- are not conducive to a high degree of individual development. As is true in so many other places, the poverty of the Puerto Ricans creates the very conditions which are in large measure the cause of their poverty. To break this circle and create the conditions for human improvement is the goal toward which strenuous efforts in Puerto Rico are currently being directed."[6]

It is at this historical junction that the mass migration of Puerto Ricans to the United States begins. Later, we shall see how this demographic movement was generated. We will offer a general chronology of migration as well as an analysis of its most salient trends.

B. Operation Bootstrap: Beginnings of Industrialization

The period after 1945 marks the turning point in the Puerto Rican transformation. Experience gained in the work of wartime organizations had helped train a corps of administrative assistants who could become the timber of Luis Muñoz Marin's cabinets. The institutional machinery appropriate to organizing a radically fresh balance between output and people in an underdeveloped economy, and to replacing stagnation with growth, had been set up by means of the far reaching legislative program of 1942. The University of Puerto Rico made its own valuable contribution to the general problem with the publication of special studies in the areas of labor economics, manpower analysis and occupational structure.[7] What remained to be done was to direct all this into the creation of new income-producing processes by means of a planned industrialization program. This, was the purpose of "Operation Bootstrap." The "battle for production" gathered its momentum slowly after 1945 and entered into a relatively rapid rate of growth by the middle 1950's, to become the main stimulus in transforming a declining agrarian economy into an expanding industrial structure.

Operation Bootstrap was essentially a governmental program of aids and incentives aimed at mobilizing capital for the island's economic development. The program can be viewed as consisting of two distinct stages. The first phase, from 1942 to about 1950, was characterized by government-built and operated plants (cement, glass bottles, shoes, etc.) undertaken primarily as a means of proving to private capital the feasibility of profitable industrial enterprise on the island. These plants were financed by the remission of federal excise tax collected on the sale of Puerto Rican rums in the American market. In this fashion, $160 million was collected. The Puerto Rico Industrial Development Company (PRIDCO) was created in 1942 to manage the established industries. However, by 1948, after more than five years of governmental effort, and after investing more than $20 million, PRIDCO had created less than 2,000 factory jobs-- when at least 100,000 were needed.[8] The income generated by manufacturing was still low--$70 million out of a total of $557 million, or 14.7% of the total income.[9] Agriculture continued to account for most of the national income, $137 million (of a total of $557 million), and was employing 41.7% of the labor force.[10] Per capita income had increased moderately, but it was still low; it rose from $121 in 1940 to $256 in 1948. Unemployment was reduced slightly

It was clear that government efforts were not producing the necessary results. The government had to make a choice between two alternatives. The first alternative was a hard, long-term one, requiring perhaps a quasi-socialist regime and a framework of political and economic independence: the second alternative was less austere, a short-term one requiring less effort from the government, but involving a high level of economic dependency on the inflow of foreign capital (since there was not enough capital in the local economy). For institutional reasons which go beyond the scope of this report, the second alternative was chosen. This marked the beginning of the second phase in the economic development of the island. PRIDCO gave way to the Economic Development Administration known as "Fomento." This last agency was put in charge (and still is) of the industrialization program.

In order to attract the urgently needed foreign capital, a series of incentives had to be provided. This led to the enactment of income-tax exemption legislation. Since 1947, firms or individuals establishing various kinds of enterprises (manufacturing and hotels) have been exempt from taxes on business income and property, and from minor municipal levies. In most instances, this exemption holds for a period of ten years (especially since 1954). These laws, enacted in 1947, also provide exemption from taxes to any firm or individual who leases property to industries qualifying under it.

In 1963, an additional income-tax exemption incentive aimed at attracting industries toward areas of high unemployment, was passed. The new act concedes to every elegible business similar tax exemptions ranging from 10 to 17 years: 10 years in "developed" zones; 12 years in zones of "intermediate development;" and 17 years in "underdeveloped zones." Under a new provision, any business may pay 50% of its income tax for a period of 20, 24 or 30 years, depending on its location. This also applies to municipal levies, property taxes and the distribution of dividends and benefits. The Development Administration provides the prospective   firm with feasibility studies on its operation; it also finances the training of production workers.

The attractiveness of the tax-exemption incentive to investors is shown by the figures compiled by the Commonwealth government. In 1963, tax exempt manufacturing firms earned tax-free profits amounting to 22%

of their average equity investment, as compared to 7.1% in the United States after taxes.[12] In fact, according to a pamphlet published by the Economic Development Administration, profits after taxes in Puerto Rico are on the average four times greater than those derived by companies in the United States.[13]

The new development program was successful in attracting outside capital to the island. The flow of industrial investments was to have enormous influence in the shaping of events to come.

C. The Present: The Impact of Operation Bootstrap

By the end of 1950, 83 firms had been established under the Fomento program; between 1950 and 1960, 525 new firms were established, and by the end of 1966, there were 1,280 firms operating under the program. The manufacturing sector accounted for most of the growth of the economy; a growth rate of total and per capita output, which as Lloyd G. Reynolds observes, "is one of the highest of the world."[14] Real gross national product per capita rose at the following rates since 1950.[15]

```
1950-55  -  5.8
1955-60  -  3.9
1960-66  -  6.9
```

According to James C. Ingram, "this growth record compares favorably with records established in other rapidly growing economies such as Canada in 1900-13, Japan in 1880-1920 and Germany after World War II."[16]

The trend towards industrialization was well on its way. In fact, manufacturing increased its share of the island's income at a frantic pace:

from 12% in 1940 to 15.9% in 1948, to 23.3% in 1966. By 1955, it had already established itself as the most important sector of the economy. Meanwhile, agriculture dropped from 32% in 1940 to 7.2% in 1966.[17] In absolute terms, manufacturing income increased from $27 million in 1940 to $612 million in 1966 (an increment of 2,166%). The manufacturing structure was increasingly diversified; the most notable shift has been in the share of sugar in manufacturing income, which dropped from 37% in 1947 to 5.1% in 1966. New products account for more than 60% of the national income. The most radical shift was from a heavy dependence on hand-made products, prepared by thousands of home-workers, to machine-made apparel manufactured in industrial plants, a trend most noticeable in textiles.

The advent of industrialization was accompanied by changes in the social structure. The rigid two-class structure which existed before the 1940's, slowly gave way to a new configuration; a middle sector developed, which has been growing at a very fast pace. This sector consists essentially of the new professions in process of formation, the occupational types which have grown up under the influence of new economic and social institutions: the government school teacher, the office worker, the technician, the civil servant, the professional salesman, etc. The emergence of this sector was made possible by the widespread availability of educational facilities. As Tumin and Feldman[18] show in their study of stratification in the island, education has been (and still is) the main vehicle for upward social mobility. Puerto Rico has one of the highest rates of students per capita in the world.

A classical corollary of industrialization, namely, the conflict between traditional and modern values, is present in Puerto Rico.

The island, as the authors of The People of Puerto Rico conclude
at the end of their exhaustive study, is changing from an agrarian
two-class orientation to a modern industrial society. The capital basis
is shifting from the ownership of land to industrial, bureaucratic,
and commercial activity as preferred styles of economic activity. Socio-
logically this means the displacement of the traditional ruling groups
such as the non-corporate sugar "hacendados", and the older type of rural
middle class, by new groups whose members have had little difficulty in
adjusting their style of life to the changing trends. Culturally, it
means the gradual diffusion of American-style cultural practices to the
point where they begin to create new uniform patterns of behavior and
attitude characterized, collectively as a process of "Americanization." The
entire insular society is being forcibly repatterned by the institutional
changes wrought by modernization. "All socio-cultural segments of the
island," the Columbia study acknowledges, "are becoming more alike in
their cash-mindedness, their dependence upon wages, the purchase of manufactured goods, the decline of home industries, their stress on individual
effort, their utilization of national health, educational, and other
services...the diffused traits are those of industrial civilization,
especially in their American forms."[19]

We have provided a general description of the economic situation of the island in an effort to provide a basis for the discussion of
Puerto Rican migration. As we shall see, the flow of Puerto Ricans
to the United States has been influenced from its beginning by two
principal factors: 1) the employment situation in Puerto Rico and,
2) the demand within the U.S. labor market. There is a direct relationship between the net flow of Puerto Rican migrants to the United States
and the volume of business activity in the American economy, as the
following graph indicates.

U.S. NATIONAL INCOME
(BILLIONS OF DOLLARS)

NET MIGRATION
FROM PUERTO RICO
(THOUSANDS)

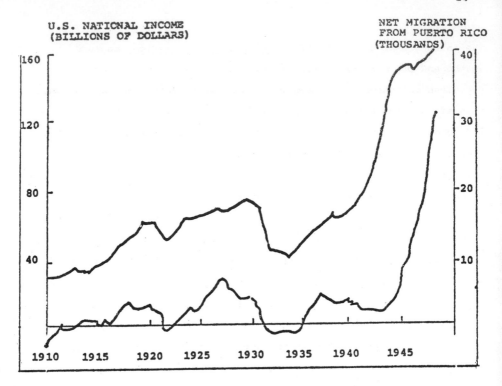

Relation of Emigration from Puerto Rico to Economic
Conditions in the U.S.

(U.S. National Income in Current Dollars: All Data for Fiscal Years)

Key: U.S. National Income --
        Puerto Rican Net Migration
Source: Harvey S. Derloff's, "Puerto Rico's Economic Future
        University of Chicago Press, 1946

The correlation between migration and business cycles has
been used by some authors[20] to substantiate the claim that it is the
"economic pull" of the American labor market, rather than conditions on the island, that constitutes the basic force behind
Puerto Rican migration. We consider this only one element affecting
migration which, in itself, fails to explain the total situation. In order
to understand the process, one must focus on the interaction between
the two factors. For even if a strong incentive exists in the form of
a "pull" from a distant market, it is a fact that human beings show
rather strong attachments to their socio-cultural reality, and
resist within reasonable limits any drastic changes in that reality.
Thus, even if a "pull" is present, it will be ineffective without a
corresponding "push". In the case of Puerto Rico, that factor must
be searched for in the interal contradictions within its economy.

The Puerto Rican economy is expanding at an accelerated pace --
gross product increased from $1,681 million in 1960 to $4,607 million
in 1970 (that is, 2.74 times) and gross domestic investment increased,
during the same period, from $397 million to $1,449 million (that is, 3.64
times)[21]. Nonetheless, this growth has not generated an employment
volume sufficiently large to absorb the existing surplus of the labor
force. During the 1960-70 period, total unemployment increased from
82,000 to 89,000. During the same period, the unemployment rate decreased
from 13.2 to 10.8 per cent, not as a result of an expansion in total
employment, but rather as the result of a relative stabilization of
the participation rate. The decrease occurred because a large number of

persons, frustrated by the difficulty of finding a job, decided
not to enter the working force. The result was a slight
increase in the participation rate from 45.2% in 1960 to 46.4% in
1970: an astounding fact if we consider that economic growth usually
generates a substantial increase in the participation rate in all
the countries that have experienced some economic expansion.

Two factors seem to have weighed heavily in limiting employment
opportunities: First, even though minimum wages in Puerto Rico are
much lower than in the United States, they have risen more rapidly
than on the mainland. In Puerto Rico, as a whole, manufacturing
wages have increased by approximately 6 per cent per year since 1960.
Manufacturing wages in the U.S., during the same period, have increased
only by approximately 3 per cent per year. As the wage differential
between the two economies has decreased, new investments in Puerto Rico
have tended to concentrate on capital intensive industries. In the
case of industries already established, the tendency has been to
introduce labor-substitution techniques. Second, the massive decline
of the agricultural sector (Its participation in the net income was
reduced from 13.3% in 1960 to 4.8% in 1970 and its participation
in the total volume of employment decreased from 22.8 per cent in
1960 to 10.2% in 1970), also contributed to holding down
the employment level.

It is not surprising, then, that the employment market in the
United States holds considerable attraction for the Puerto Rican
working class, particularly among its younger members, among whom
the unemployment rate is highest. It is not true that the young

migrants, due to their limited educational attainment, were unable to
meet the standards of their Puerto Rican employers. Statistics show that
approximately half of these migrants have completed eight or more years
of schooling, compared to six years for the total Island population.[22]

Therefore, there is evidence that migration of Puerto
Ricans to the United States has been due to structural crises in the
island's economy. Neither demographic characteristics nor the degree
of available human resources were taken into account at the time when
the industrial development program was initiated by the Commonwealth
Government. The meeting of short-range needs seems to have prevailed.
The lack of integrated planning consequently led to a reliance on the
export of Puerto Ricans as the key factor in achieving economic growth.

We repeat that the inability of Puerto Rico's development program to reduce unemployment is at the very basis of the demographic
movement of Puerto Ricans to the United States. According to
data gathered by the Department of Labor of Puerto Rico, the rate of
unemployment has remained constant (in the neighborhood of 12%)
since 1947. This has been so in spite of the fact that the
population increase has been moderated by the exodus of workers
to labor markets in the United States.

Unemployment Rates in Puerto Rico

Selected Years

Year	rate*
1947	11.8
1950	14.7
1955	14.3
1960	12.0
1965	11.3

*Percent of unemployed within the
labor force. Source: Bureau of
Labor Statistics, Puerto Rico
Department of Labor

III. Migration

Migration is not a phenomenon new to Puerto Rico. Although migration reached its greatest heights only after the Second World War, it is estimated that between 1899 and 1944 approximately 75,000 Puerto Ricans migrated to the United States.[23] As a result of advances attained in air transportation during the war, and the demand for workers in the United States market, there began in 1945 one of the largest population movements ever recorded in modern history. As a result of the 1940-1960 migration, the population of Puerto Rico in 1960 was one million less than it would have been without migration.[24]

The greatest number of migrants was registered in the period 1950-54. This was due to the lack of workers in the United States during the Korean War. As can be seen in the table, net migration has declined sharply in the last six years. We will analyze this recent trend below.

NET MIGRATION FROM PUERTO RICO: CALENDAR YEARS 1945-1965

Period or Year	Number of Migrants to U.S.	Yearly Average	% of Population
1945-49	135,000	27,000	1.3
1950-54	237,000	47,500	2.2
1955-59	193,000	38,600	1.7
1960-65	39,000	6,500	0.2
1960	16,000	**	0.7
1961	-2,000	**	-0.1
1962	12,000	**	0.5
1963	-5,000	**	-0.2
1964	1,000	**	0.0
1965	17,000	**	0.6

**Does not apply

Source: Files of the Demographic Register, Department of Health
        of Puerto Rico.

The last column of the above table shows why Puerto Rican
migration to the United States is considered one of the greatest
peacetime population movements recorded in contemporary history. During the
1950-1960 decade the yearly migration average was equivalent to
two per cent of the island's population -- an extraordinary
movement of people if we consider that during the same decade the
population of the island increased at the rate of 2.7% per year.

The migrational currents have resulted from differences between the
distressed social and economic conditions at the point of origin and the
much better situation at the receiving point. In addition, the
currents were made possible by the fact that Puerto Ricans,
as North American citizens, have free entry into
the United States. In addition, the costs of transportation between the two
countries have been extremely low. It appears that the unemployment
situation in Puerto Rico has had the greater influence on
the migratory current, while the employment opportunities in the
United States have provided an additional pressure. The coefficient
of correlation between unemployment in Puerto Rico and migration
to the United States for the period 1946 to 1965 is 0.63 This
indicates that the greater the unemployment in Puerto Rico the
higher the migration. On the other hand, the correlation between
unemployment in the United States and migration in Puerto Rico
is -0.79, which, in turn, indicates that migration tends to increase when unemployment decreases in the United States and vice-
versa.[25]

As we previously pointed out, net migration to the U.S. has

decreased considerably during the last years. Migration balances
have been visible now and then (years 1961, and 1967).[26] This
recent reduction in the migration balance can be explained in the
following ways:

1-The unemployment situation in the United States has
   worsened considerably during recent years and/or

2-The level of unemployment in Puerto Rico has decreased
   notably during recent years.

An analysis of the situation in the United States shows that
unemployment increased between 1956 and 1961 and has decreased
consistently ever since, reaching a 4.6% level in 1965, the
lowest rate since 1956. In the case of Puerto Rico
a slight decrease in the rate of unemployment occurred between 1960 and
1964 but an increase took place in 1965. It appears that changes
in the levels of unemployment in the United States have been the
most important factor in the decreased migration since
1957. As will be seen later, these changes are not the only
explanation.

In 1958 the Department of Labor of Puerto Rico began to gather
data on the place of birth and origin of the migrants. As can be
seen in the table below, in spite of the decrease observed in the
net balance, the migration of native Puerto Ricans to the United
States seems to have remained at high levels. It appears
that there has been a considerable increase in the

migration to the island of persons not born in Puerto Rico.

PLACE OF BIRTH AND ORIGIN OF THE MIGRANTS*
FISCAL YEARS 1958-59 and 1961-62
(IN THOUSANDS)

Place of birth	1961-62	1960-61	1959-60	1958-59
Puerto Rico	-66.3	-50.8	-46.6	-45.5
Outside of Puerto Rico	+53.4	+34.1	+24.5	+11.3
Of Puerto Rican Parents	+14.1	+ 9.7	- -	- -
Of Non-Puerto Rican Parents	+39.3	+24.4	- -	- -
Did not reply	- 0.2	- 1.1	- 0.6	- 0.0
Total	-13.1	-17.8	-22.7	-34.1

*A minus sign is equivalent to a migration balance, while a plus
sign signifies net migration.

Among the individuals not born in Puerto Rico, there is
one group whose parents (one or both) are Puerto Rican and another
group (which appears to be larger), made up of individuals
whose parents are not Puerto Rican.

The figures indicate that there exist two migrational currents in Puerto Rico: one of migration to the United States
by natives of Puerto Rico, and a current of migration
to Puerto Rico by children of Puerto Rican migrants and non-
Puerto Ricans.

According to the 1960 census data, during the period 1950-60
Puerto Rico had a total immigration of about 42,000 persons who
were not born in Puerto Rico. Of these, about 39,000 were

North Americans. This immigration of North Americans and other non-Puerto Ricans seems to have been much more intense during the latter part of the decade.

The data gathered by the Planning Board since 1962 reveals a similar trend. The current of movement to the United States seems to have remained at high levels while the movement to the Island seems to have increased.

THE TWO CURRENTS OF THE MIGRATION MOVEMENT IN
PUERTO RICO: 1962-63 to 1964-65

Year	Migration to the U.S.	Migration to Puerto Rico	Net Migration to the U.S.
1962-63	53,000	40,000	13,000
1963-64	43,000	51,000	- 8,000
1964-65	66,000	50,000	16,000

Source: Planning Board, Economic Report to the Governor, 1965
        p. 191.

According to the 1960 census data, during the period 1955-60 Puerto Rico received an average of 6,000 non-Puerto Ricans per year. The Planning Board data also indicate that during the last five years the annual average increased to 9,000 and to 11,000 during the last year.[26]

It is evident that the migration of Puerto Ricans to the United States has not decreased, as the total net balance would seem to indicate. Our people continue to migrate in large numbers to the United States while the children of Puerto Rican migrants,

North Americans, and other non-Puerto Ricans move
to the Island in ever increasing numbers.

IV. <u>Demography of the Migrant: Age, income, education and skill.</u>

We have previously stated that the population growth of Puerto
Rico has been conditioned, to a large extent, by the external migratory
movement, more specifically, by the movement of Puerto Ricans to the
U. S. In the last few years migration patterns have been complicated by two additional migratory currents: return migration to Puerto
Rico and the influx of non-Puerto Ricans to the island (a group composed mostly of North Americans, Cubans, and Dominicans). The social
impact of <u>internal</u> migration cannot be underrated. Internal migratory
movements (mainly from rural to urban areas) have resulted in a considerable redistribution of the Island's population, as is revealed by
the fact that <u>while the average</u> yearly growth of the total population during
the 1960-70 decade was only 1.4%, urban population growth was 3.5%.[27]
Accordingly, the population density of the north coast censual region
(which includes several metropolitan areas) increased from 881 persons per
square mile in 1940 to 1,771 persons per square mile in 1970. During
this same period, the total population density of Puerto Rico increased
from 546 to 792 persons per square mile.[28]

An in-depth study of all the factors influencing internal migratory movements has never been undertaken. The available statistics on
these movements are even less reliable than those on external migration.
We can, however, identify several factors that have influenced the
massive population movement to the San Juan Metropolitan area and to
other areas of rapid development, such as Ponce and Mayaguez. They
include: an increase in job supply in urban areas due to a high
concentration of Fomento factories and government offices[29];
the persistent crisis in the agricultural sector which

continues to diminish in importance as a source of employment and income.

In this paper, we are principally concerned with the external migratory movement of Puerto Ricans, particularly to the United States. Virtually all research studies that have been made on the Puerto Ricans residing in the U.S. identify four basic characteristics common to all:

a) a low educational achievement level

b) an average age level between 14 and 44 years

c) a majority were urban residents in Puerto Rico

d) a majority are males

Many of these studies were prepared in the 1950's and relied on very rudimentary data. Nevertheless, some of the conclusions reached coincide with those of more recent documents prepared by the Government of Puerto Rico. We will now examine some of these conclusions.

As has been pointed out, Puerto Rican migrants (considered as immigrants in the United States) have a low level of educational attainment. Based on that assumption, it was asserted that migrants were not representative of the Puerto Rican population, since they generally constituted the less priviledged groups within Puerto Rican society. Recent data tends to contradict this assumption. As the Planning Board of Puerto Rico has stated, "It has been observed that migrants ...have a better education than the population in general."[30] As a matter of fact, according to the same source, approximately half of the migrants have completed eight or more years of schooling, compared with six years for the population in general. The percentage distribution of migrants by level of schooling can be observed in the following table:

YEAR 1966

| Grades | AGE | | | | |
Approved	6-13	14-24	25-44	45 or more	Total
None	22.5	1.7	6.6	13.2	4.7
1-3	22.1	4.8	21.3	23.9	10.5
4-7	49.9	33.9	19.6	32.9	31.9
8-11	5.5	40.9	19.6	10.3	32.4
12		16.5	21.4	3.3	15.5
13 and over	--	0.6	4.9	6.7	1.9

The educational attainment of the majority of Puerto Rican migrants compares very unfavorably with that of native born U.S. residents and probably with that of earlier immigrants -- Norwegians, French, etc. It is sufficient to remember that in 1960 the educational attainment level in the United States averaged 10.6 years.[31]

The structural crisis of the Puerto Rican economy, resulting from an increasing income level and a constant employment rate, has caused a surplus in the labor force. This surplus, consisting mainly of younger people, is not necessarily made up of persons of low income, or who have a low educational attainment level, by comparison to the rest of the island's population.

More recent data tends to confirm that migration continues to be strongest among younger members of the labor force. For

example, of the 79,600 persons who migrated in 1966, a total of 51,404
were between the ages of 14 and 24, while 14,701 were between 25 and 44
years of age; that is, 83.1% were between the ages of 14 and 44.[32]
This continuing trend appears to be related to the relative stabilization
of the participation rate in the labor force in Puerto Rico. The participation rate is greater among young groups, particularly among the
20-24, 25-34, 35-44 age groups. If a considerable percentage of the
younger members of the labor force migrate, the rate of participation
declines or tends to stabilize. The latter has been true in Puerto Rico.
Consequently, migration has been a relief valve for the economy of Puerto Rico.

The age distribution of the Puerto Rican population (with a median
age of 18 years) is incompatible with the type of industrial development
prevalent on the island. Labor intensive industries are being replaced
by capital intensive industries. Such substitution decreases the possibility of providing employment for the surplus of the existing labor
force. Another factor which we must take into account is the increase
of women in the labor force. In 1950 there were 17,000 women in the
force; in 1967, there were 220,000. In spite of special incentives
offered to industries which employ males, the industries established
under the Fomento program have employed more females.

Another assumption regarding the basic characteristics of the Puerto
Rican migrant is, as stated above, that they came mostly from urban
areas in Puerto Rico, especially from the San Juan metropolitan area.
This assumption has been contradicted by recent data not available
to earlier researchers in this field. The table below is quite
revealing:

PERCENTAGE DISTRIBUTION OF MIGRANTS BY
AGE AND PLACE OF RESIDENCE: 1966

Age Group	Rural Area	Urban Area	Total
6	57.6	42.4	100.0
6-13	72.2	27.8	100.0
14-24	65.7	34.3	100.0
25-44	63.8	36.2	100.0
45-64	60.5	39.5	100.0
65 or over	30.5	69.5	100.0
Total	64.1	35.9	100.0

Source: Planning Board, I Economic Report to the Governor,
       1967, p. 5-29.

The decline of the agricultural sector, as a source of income
and employment and the massing of manufacturing industries in urban
areas are two factors which account for the migration of young
people from rural areas in Puerto Rico to the United States.
In fact, the same factors which explain the high rate of internal
migration also account, in part, for external migration.

V. The Puerto Rican Experience in the United States:

Throughout this essay, we have dealt with the structural factors influencing the migration of Puerto Ricans to the United States.

Economic factors play a fundamental role in spurring a migration,
but we should not overemphasize them. Migration is above all a human
problem and cannot be reduced to a mere discussion
of the laws of supply and demand in the labor market. It would also
be absurd to assume a fatalistic attitude toward the myriad of
social problems that emerge as a consequence of the massive movement
of people we have been describing thus far--a movement that has brought
over a million people out of a predominantly agricultural island and
into a country with a radically different cultural makeup.

A. A Profile

Before we can begin a profile of the Puerto Rican population on
the mainland we must point out that there is no up-to-date accurate
data on the total number of people of Puerto Rican origin living in
the United States. This figure may be well over two
million people; however, we will have to wait until the 1970 census
figures are published in order to make any definite statement. It is,
however, also necessary to stress that the 1970 figures might not
be as reliable as we might wish. Partly because of the publicity
given to the new treatment used by the 1970 Census regarding Puerto
Ricans in the various communities, a widespread boycott of the Census
among Puerto Ricans took place. In addition, mail census inquiries
elicit extremely law responses among Puerto Ricans.

We again repeat that what follows is hampered, as was our discussion about the process of migration, by the scarcity of availab
data. We will have to place an undue emphasis on a profile of the New
York Puerto Rican community since it was only in New York City that
we were able to find extensive data.[34]

In 1960, nearly 900,000 Puerto Ricans--born either on the island
or in the states to Puerto Rican parents--lived in the United States.
Persons born in Puerto Rico were first recorded as residents of the
states by the United States Census of 1910, when 1,500 were
enumerated. Their numbers increased so that by 1940 almost 70,000
lived in the 48 states. By 1950 Puerto Rican born persons numbered
226,000. In the following decade the net gain due to migration
from the island amounted to nearly 390,000.

The census of 1950 recorded the beginning of the second generation of Puerto Ricans in the United States--those born on the continent to parents who came from the island. They numbered 75,000 in
1950 and 272,000 ten years later. By 1960, three out of every ten Puerto
Rican stateside residents had been born on the continent.

With the great post-war migration there began a reversal of the historic
trend of Puerto Ricans living in New York City. In 1910 only a
little more than a third of the migrants lived in New York
City, but by 1940, 88 per cent made New York their home. Since then,
a dispersal to other areas has occurred. The percentage in New York
City for those born in Puerto Rico dropped to 83 in 1950 and 70 in
1960. The dispersal probably is continuing, although Puerto
Ricans in the United States still are overwhelmingly New Yorkers.
More than two-thirds of the migrants and their children live in
New York.

Among Puerto Ricans located in New York City, more than 47 per
cent of the males and 45 per cent of the females were under 20 years
of age in 1960. The aged are few in the Puerto Rican community.
Just 1.5 per cent of the men and 2.5 per cent of the women were 65 or
over in 1960. As a result of the number of children among them, a
relatively small part of the Puerto Ricans are at their prime working
ages. Only 51.1 per cent of the men and 52.4 per cent of the women
were aged 20 through 64 in 1960.

In New York City only 13 per cent of the Puerto Rican men and
women 25 years of age and older in 1960 had completed high
school: 87 per cent were dropouts. The deficiency in the educational
preparation of the Puerto Rican population is dramatically revealed
by the numbers who had not even completed a grade-school education. In
1960, more than half--52.9 per cent--of Puerto Ricans in New York City
25 years of age and older had less than an eighth grade education. In
contrast, 29.5 per cent of the nonwhite population had not finished
the eighth year, and only 19.3 per cent of whites had so
low an academic preparation.

The males and females born in Puerto Rico at every age level
exhibit very high percentages of school-dropouts. These figures
range from 84 to 97 per cent. Those Puerto Ricans born in the
United States, however, have considerably fewer
school droupouts. In the youngest age group -- 25 through 35 -- the
differential between the two generations is largest, amounting to
34 percentage points for females and 25 for males. Among this
relatively mobile population, birth and present residence in the
United States do not necessarily mean that all education was ac-

quired in stateside schools. Moreover, an unknown number of Puerto
Ricans educated on the mainland have returned to the Commonwealth.
So differences in educational attainment by place of birth is
probably not a satisfactory indicator of the impact of the
mainland's educational system.

If the educational attainment of Puerto Ricans born in the
United States is strikingly better than that of those born in the
Commonwealth, it so far has had small weight in the statistics for the
total adult Puerto Rican community in New York City. The numbers
in the second generation who have reached adult years is still
small, only 6.4 per cent were 20 years of age and older in
1960.

There is evidence that Puerto Rican youth, more than any other
group, has difficulty achieving an education in the
New York City public schools. In 1961 a study of a Manhattan neighborhood showed that fewer than 10 per cent of Puerto Ricans in the
third grade were reading at their grade level or above. Moreover,
the degree of retardation of Puerto Rican youth was extreme. Three
in ten were retarded one and one-half years or more. In the
middle of their third school year, they were reading at a level
appropriate for entry into the second grade. By the
eighth grade the degree of reading retardation was even
more severe. While 13 per cent of the Puerto Rican youth were
reading at grade level or above, almost two-thirds were retarded
more than three years.

Puerto Rican graduates from New York City high schools with
academic diplomas still are rare. Of the nearly

21,000 academic diplomas granted in 1963, only 331 went to Puerto
Ricans. This is only 1.6 per cent of the total academic diplomas.
By contrast, Puerto Ricans received 7.4 per cent of the vocational
school diplomas. As a result, only 20 per cent of the small number
of Puerto Ricans completing high school in 1963 were prepared to begin
higher academic education.

In 1960, 70.6 per cent of the employed Puerto Rican males were
in low-income occupations (operators and kindred workers, non-
household service workers, private household workers, and laborers).

Of the employed Puerto Rican women, 78.2 per cent worked in
the low-status occupations. Employed Puerto Rican and nonwhite
women were concentrated in the low-status occupations to a greater
degree than were Puerto Rican and nonwhite males.

The Puerto Ricans employed by agencies of New York city's
government also are in the least desirable jobs to a greater degree than are Negroes and others. Three of every four Puerto Rican
city employees are at the level of operators or below. In other
words, only 25 per cent of the Puerto Ricans are employed as foremen, clerical workers, professionals or officials on the city pay-
roll.

Overall, only 3 per cent of city employees are Puerto Rican.
As a result, the Puerto Rican proportion in each occupational category is small, the largest being 6.4 per cent of service workers.
The most striking differences are between ethnic proportions of the
craftsmen and foremen employed by New York City, only 3.7 per cent
were Negroes and only six-tenths of one per cent were Puerto Ricans;
of the influential category of officials, only one-half of one per

cent (44) were Puerto Ricans.

Comparisons of 1960 with 1950 show modest changes in occupations of Puerto Ricans. In 1950, 37.2 per cent of the employed males 14 years old and over were operators and kindred workers; 28.4 per cent more were non-household service workers; 5.2 per cent were laborers. Among better-paying jobs, 11.1 per cent of these men were craftsmen, foremen, and kindred workers; 10 per cent were clerical, sales and kindred workers; 5.4 per cent were managers, officials, and proprietors; and 2.6 were professionals, technicals, and kindred workers.

The employed women in 1950 were even more highly concentrated in a few occupational categories. Of these, 77.5 per cent were operators and kindred workers; 9.2 per cent were clerical, sales, and kindred workers; 5.9 were non-household service workers; and 2 per cent were professional, technical, and kindred workers. None of the other occupational categories employed as many as 2 per cent of the Puerto Rican females.

The percentage distribution of Puerto Ricans among major occupational groups in 1960 showed changes, even though Puerto Ricans remained predominantly in low-status jobs. For males 14 years and older the percent in non-household service occupations declined from 28.4 to 20.5; the percentage of managers, officials, and proprietors dropped from 5.4 to 3.7; professional, technical, and kindred workers declined slightly as a proportion of the total. However, it should be remembered that the number of Puerto Ricans in New York had increased considerably between 1950 and 1960. Even though certain job categories showed a drop in the proportions of Puerto

Ricans, in every instance the absolute number of persons
increased. Among the males in 1960, the percentage employed as
laborers (5.9) and as craftsmen, foremen, and kindred workers
(11.3) remained about the same as in 1950. Clerical, sales, and
kindred workers showed a modest increase, from 10 to 12.3 per cent.
The greatest increase, however, was registered in the category of
operators and kindred workers, in which 44.1 per cent of the
employed Puerto Rican males worked in 1960, compared with 37.2
percent in 1950. In spite of these shifts, the occupational distribution of employed Puerto Rican males over-all showed no improvement in the decade. In 1950, 70.9 per cent of them were in the
lowest income occupations (operators, private household workers,
non-household service workers, and laborers)· In
1960 the comparable figure was 70.6 per cent.

Changes in the decade between censuses were somewhat
more favorable for employed Puerto Rican females, though at both points
in time they were employed in low-status jobs in greater pro-
protions than were Puerto Rican males. In 1950, 85.9 per cent of the
employed females were in the lowest income occupations (listed above)
compared with 70.9 per cent of the men. By 1960, only 78.2 per
cent of the females were so employed, compared with 70.6 per cent
of the males. The gap between males and females narrowed from 15 to
7.6 percentage points during the decade.

Improvement in the occupational situation of Puerto Rican women
occurred chiefly through their employment as clerical, sales, and
kindred workers. Of the total, 9.2 per cent were so employed in
1950; by 1960 the proportion in this category had increased to 15.9

per cent. A slight gain was also registered by professional, technical, and kindred workers.

Examination of the separate data for the first and second-
generation Puerto Ricans shows even more clearly an improvement of
the occupational status of employed Puerto Rican women relative to
Puerto Rican men. The employed men and women 14 years of age and
older born in Puerto Rico were, of course, heavily engaged in low-
status occupations at the beginning and at the end of the 1950-1960
decade. Of the employed Puerto Rican-born men in 1950, 71.9 per
cent were in low-status jobs (as defined above). The number changed
only slightly--to 72.4 per cent--by 1960. The employed women born
in Puerto Rico, however, improved their occupational positions to a
more striking degree, even though they began (and remained) in a
disadvantaged occupational situation relative to the men. In 1950,
89.1 per cent of these women were in the low-status occupational
categories, but by 1960 the percentage had fallen to 82.3. Thus,
due to improvement in the occupations of females, the percentage-
point difference between men and women born in Puerto Rico dropped
from 17.2 to 9.9 over the decade.

Among the employed Puerto Ricans born in the United States the
females began with an occupational distribution more favorable than
that of the men in 1950, and they widened their advantage during the
decade. However, the occupational situation of both men and women
improved significantly. In 1950, 57.7 per cent of the men and 51.7
per cent of the women were in low-status occupations. By 1960 the
figures had dropped to 48.4 per cent for the males and 34.2 per cent
for the females. Thus the female occupational distribution improved

to a greater degree than did that of the men. As a result, the
female percentage-point advantage increased from 6.0 in 1950 to
14.2 in 1960.

The occupational advance for both men and women of the second
generation was achieved in similar ways -- through increasing
participation as professional, technical, and kindred workers, and
as clerical, sales, and kindred workers. The proportion of men
who were craftsmen, foremen and kindred workers also rose.
The most dramatic increase in the proportion was of women employed in
clerical, sales, and kindred tasks, which rose from 39.4 per cent in
1950 to 56.0 per cent in 1960. The greatest percentage-point
losses for the men were in the operator and non-household service
categories and, for women, in the operator category--from 40.9
per cent in 1950 to 24.4 per cent in 1960.

The occupational distributions do not tell the entire story,
for of the 147,495 Puerto Rican males 14 years old and over in
New York City's labor force in 1960, 14,507 -- or 9.9 per cent --
were unemployed. This unemployment was heavily concentrated among
youth. Of the Puerto Rican male labor force 14 to 19 years of age,
19.7 per cent were unemployed, as were 19.0 per cent of the non-
white males of the same ages. (The figures for age groups are for
New York City and Nassau, Suffolk, Rockland, and Westchester
counties combined and probably understate the unemployment then
prevalent in New York City.) Among females of the same age group,
the unemployment rate of 14.7 for nonwhites was virtually the same
as the Puerto Rican rate of 15.0. Unemployment was also high among
the labor force 20 to 24 years of age: 10.7 per cent of the Puerto

Rican males and 12.4 per cent of the females; for nonwhites, 9.7
per cent of the males and 9.2 per cent of the females. Rates of
unemployment at older ages were lower, but for no male Puerto
Rican age group did it fall below 7.7 per cent.

In summary, the occupational statistics for Puerto Ricans in
New York City show that they largely had low-status, low-
income occupations in 1950 and in general remained in them in
1960. The over-all unemployment rate for Puerto Rican males has
consistenly exceeded that of any other racial or ethnic group in
the City. A considerable upgrading is apparent in the occupations
of the generation born in the United States relative to those who
migrated here. However, the proportion of the second generation
that has reached labor-force age is still small. Among both the
first and second generation a trend is evident in the improvement
of the occupational status of employed women relative to that of the
employed men of the same generation. If the trend continues, it
may have unfavorable implications for the stability of traditional
Puerto Rican cultural patterns of family life.

The low educational attainment of the Puerto Rican population
and the low-status jobs at which they work are reflected in the evident
poverty of their families. Poverty is significantly more pronounced
among Puerto Ricans than among any other identifiable racial and
ethnic group at least in New York City.

In 1959, 33.8 per cent of Puerto Rican families had incomes
of less than $3,000, and more than half (53.7 per cent) had less
than $4,000. The nonwhites in the city were better off, although
not in an enviable situation. In this group, 27.1 per cent had

incomes below $3,000 and 43.6 per cent had less than $4,000. The
other whites were least disadvantaged. Only 11.8 per cent of their
families had incomes of less than $3,000; 19.2 per cent had less
than $4,000.

Because of the youthfulness of the Puerto Rican population
in comparison with nonwhites and other whites, the children and
youth in the Puerto Rican communities are struck more severely
than any other group by massive conditions of poverty and deprivation.

As newcomers, Puerto Ricans entered the competition for housing
later than did the nonwhite and other white populations. This is
reflected in the statistics on the year in which household heads
moved into the units in which they resided in 1960. Among Puerto
Ricans, 46.5 per cent had moved in during the period from 1958 to
March, 1960. Only 30 per cent of the nonwhites and 22.8 per cent
of the whites had occupied their units so recently. Puerto Rican
heads of households were under-represented as long-term occu-
pants of housing units. While just 18.7 per cent of them had moved
into their 1960 unit in 1953 or earlier, 41.1 per cent of the non-
white and more than half (53.6 per cent) of the other white household heads were long-term residents.

In New York City, where owner-occupants of housing units
are a distinct minority, those with household heads of Puerto Rican
birth or parentage were least represented in the ownership group.
Of the Puerto Rican families in the City, 95.3 per cent rented the
unit where they lived, compared with 86.8 per cent of those with
nonwhite heads and 75.6 per cent of those with other white heads

of households. As the lowest-income population in the city, Puerto Ricans also paid less rent for renter-occupied units, but only slightly less than did the nonwhites. The median gross rent (the "middle" rent, with half the rents less, and half exceeding it) for Puerto Ricans was $62; that for non whites was $66. In comparison, the other whites in general paid substantially higher rents. Their median was $76.

The Puerto Rican households are concentrated in the oldest residential structures in New York City. Of the households, 87.3 per cent were in structures built in 1939 or earlier, whereas 84 per cent of the nonwhite households and 79.2 per cent of the other white households were in the older buildings. The Puerto Rican homes also are more frequently in structures with larger numbers of units than are the homes of the nonwhites and the other whites. Of Puerto Rican households, 85.4 per cent were in structures with five or more units, compared with 70.5 per cent for the nonwhites and 61.1 per cent for the other whites.

Though a significant number of Puerto Rican households are in large, low-income public-housing projects where physical standards are maintained, 40.1 per cent of their households were in deteriorating and dilapidated structures. While 10.4 per cent of the Puerto Rican households and 8 per cent of the nonwhite lived in "dilapidated" units, (as the term is defined by the U.S. Bureau of the Census), only 1.8 per cent of the other whites were so housed.

Puerto Ricans residing in these households were crowded to a degree not true of the nonwhites and other whites. Of

the households with a Puerto Rican head, 38.6 per cent were in units
with 1.01 or more persons per room. Thus, the information about the
housing of Puerto Ricans parallels that characterizing their population. Just as they are the least educated, most frequently out of a
job and looking for work, most concentrated in low-status occupations,
and have the least family income of any identifiable ethnic population in
New York City, so do they live in housing units that are the most
deteriorated or dilapidated, and the most crowded. For this they pay
slightly lower rents.

According to public health records, Puerto Ricans in New York City
consistently maintain an intermediate health rate relative to that of
nonwhites and other whites. This is shown by statistics on infant
mortality, active tuberculosis, and infectious venereal diseases.[35]

The mortality rate for Puerto Rican infants--the number of deaths
under one year of age per 1,000 live births--has hovered around 30
for the past decade. The actual rate for 1963 was 28.4, but annual
fluctuations have produced almost this low a rate in prior years
followed by higher rates. Thus, the pattern for the decade has been
a rate of about 20 for the other whites, 30 for the Puerto Ricans, and
40 for the nonwhites.

Similar relationships are pointed up in statistics on newly
reported cases of active tuberculosis, all forms, in 1963. Puerto
Ricans comprise 7.9 per cent of New York City's population, but
account for 13.8 per cent of new tuberculosis cases. Thus, the
proportion of Puerto Rican cases was not quite twice the percentage of
Puerto Ricans in New York's population. As in infant mortality rates,
then, Puerto Ricans are between the other whites and the nonwhites in

rate of new cases of tuberculosis.

Data on rates of infection with syphilis and gonorrhea are much less adequate, but they also show Puerto Rican rates in excess of those for whites and lower than those for nonwhites. However, these statistics should be interpreted as suggesting the possibility of ethnic differences in true rates, not as establishing them. In the first place, the data reflect only the cases diagnosed in public clinics. It is highly likely that many cases diagnosed by private physicians are not reported and that this particularly minimizes the rates for whites. Second, Puerto Ricans are identified only by a judgment that the name on the record "sounds" Spanish. The degree of error thus introduced is unknown and may be very large. It is safer merely to state that a serious problem of veneral infection exists in New York City, than to emphasize differences in rates among ethnic groups.

A recent study indicates that a high rate of mental disability may exist among Puerto Ricans in New York City. Based on responses to a list of symptoms, rather than past or present treatment for disability, nearly half--48.8 per cent--of the sample of persons born in Puerto Rico were classified as ranking in the highest of three groups in degree of mental disability.

We have thus far attempted to profile the Puerto Rican on the mainland. We have, however, only been able to describe those Puerto Ricans residing in urban areas, and particularly, in New York City. We must now briefly turn to the case of the agricultural migrant.

The Puerto Rican worker who migrates to the agricultural

fields of the United States is one of the least known and least
studied human qroups of our society. His departure for the United
States is a temporary act that is repeated every year. As a rule,
the Puerto Rican aqricultural miqrant is forced to live about six months
out of every year away from home. Generally, he leaves Puerto Rico
starting in the month of April and returns six months later. In 1970,
approximately 50,000 Puerto Ricans went to work in the aqricultural
sector in the United States.

The majority of those workers go to farms in the North-
east reqion of the United States, particularly those in the states
of New Jersey, New York, Connecticut, Delaware, Massachusetts, Ohio
and Pennsylvania. The Puerto Rican miqrant's participation in U.S.
agriculture has become an essential factor in those areas of the
nation where local aqricultural workers are scarce and where, in spite
of mechanization, agricultural workers are still necessary. As was
pointed out earlier, the increasinq deterioration of the aqricultural
sector in Puerto Rico has made agricultural laborers more obsolete
and unnecessary every day.

For this reason, the Puerto Rican agricultural worker is unemployed
or holds temporary low-paying jobs durinq the months he remains on
the island. In view of this, U.S. aqricultural employers have been successful in their efforts to recruit Puerto Rican farm workers.

The recruitment of Puerto Ricans for aqricultural tasks in the
United States has been carried out in two ways. First, the
agricultural worker himself, following instructions
from his employer, informally contracts the services of other workers.
Second, a special office of the Commonwealth Government recruits

workers to go to the mainland.

In spite of the direct intervention of the Commonwealth Government in the recruitment effort, the information available on the Puerto Rican agricultural migrant in the United States is fairly scarce. Occasionally, either local or mainland newspapers publish a statement of a political leader or of a migrant spokesman which describes some aspect, usually negative, of agricultural migration, such as living conditions on the farms, the absence of unemployment insurance, the lack of unions, and the arbitrary systems of compensation by units. But, on the whole, the invisible migrant Puerto Rican farmworker is little known in his own country.

B. The Problems of the Puerto Ricans in the U.S.

The problems of Puerto Ricans on the mainland stem basically from two sources; one, the conditions which exist in the United States affecting the poor and those racial and cultural groups which are rejected or relegated to the lower eschelons of society. The other source is the problems created by conditions and characteristics of the Puerto Rican migrant himself.

It is not necessary to show that at this point in the history of this country persons who are black or who possess visible characteristics of the Negro race will be discriminated against in employment, housing, schools and in receiving equal treatment. Puerto Ricans, in general, are darker in color than other Americans. Some Puerto Rican migrants are white, some are black, but the majority of the group is racially mixed.

In the scheme of discrimination in the United States some cultural origins are less desirable than others and a hispanic cultural

origin with evident mixtures of African and Indian traits (exactly the components of most Puerto Rican migrants) ranks very high in the degree
of undesirability. Spanish-speaking persons (unless they are from
Spain) are also low on the prestige ladder. Puerto Ricans speak Spanish
but in the mind of educators and other professionals in the U.S.
their Spanish is classified as "Puerto Rican".

School systems in the United States have been found to segre-
gate by color and by certain cultural-racial groups (Mexican-American,
Indian and Puerto Rican). These segregated parts of the school systems operate under inferior conditions and impart an inferior
education. These conditions have been fully described by innumerable
research studies and books, and have been litigated in courts. The reality
of segregation has been recognized by various American social scientists
and other students of the problems of American education.

The majority of Puerto Ricans on the mainland live in the
ghettos of most large Northeastern cities of the United States. They
suffer from the physical as well as spiritual conditions attendant to
poverty in these cities. They also suffer from the powerlessness
and voicelessness of recent arrivals in cities. These cities have
well developed   intricate patterns of power blocks and organizational life. Puerto Ricans arrive in cities which are being
abandoned by the middle class. What the Puerto Ricans inherit
are the deteriorated services which these abandoned cities can
still offer.

In short, the conditions and characteristics of the Puerto
Rican in the United States which determine the group's
problems can be enumerated as follows:

1) Puerto Rican migrants are the bearers of a culture with different patterns of behavior and values from those found in the United States.

2) Puerto Rican migrants come from a basically rural environment and arrive in the most urbanized areas in the United States.

3) Most Puerto Ricans migrants possess either no skills or very rudimentary skills

4) Puerto Rican migrants possess the lowest educational level of any of the ethnic or color groups with w om they share the cities.

The exodus to the United States has brought the Puerto Ricans face to face with the massive gulf that separates the American dream from the American reality. Unlike earlier migrant groups of European descent, Puerto Ricans have been unable to become acculturated to the American way of life. Today, after more than two generations of direct contact with the American way of life, Puerto Ricans are still a highly "visible" group within the American society.

The Puerto Rican migrant arrives at a time when the American economy has ady bsorbed the European migrants, and when the only available openings are at the very bottom of the social and economic structure. After the termination of World War II, the American economy experienced an enormous growth following the opening of new markets which created a tremendous demand for labor. This growth forced the economy to use up most of its labor surplus, namely, the ethnic and racial minorities, in order to keep pace.

The Puerto Rican migrant entered the American scene at a time when the existing   conditions made social mobility very difficult since the demands of the economy could not be met effectively by the skills he had to offer. As production followed its logical trend, that of increased mechanization, the demands of the economy became more specialized, and the supply of labor increased in the unskilled sectors in which the Puerto Rican migrant is forced to compete. The result was a higher unemployment rate among Puerto Ricans, and a deterioration of living conditions.

Prominent among the factors which hamper the assimilation of Puerto Ricans is the fact that Puerto Ricans are a racially mixed people. The racism of the receiving society is perhaps the first indication the migrants have of being in a different and hostile world.[36]

As Gordon K. Lewis pointed out, there has been, from the very moment of American occupation of the island, a strong fear among many Americans of Puerto Rican "penetration" and a powerful effort to keep the islander "in his place" as a second class citizen.[37] The high degree of "visibility" of Puerto Ricans within the American society has led some commentators to label Puerto Ricans as a "problem".

Finally, the colonial situation of Puerto Rico has been a major factor in defining the treatment accorded the islanders in the United States. The political relationship between the U.S. and Puerto Rico has deprived the Puerto Rican migrant in various intangible, and subjective ways, of the dignity and respect accorded to previous migrant groups who came from sovereign nation-states.

APPENDIX A

Brief examination of the present state of the data available on migration. Various methods are being used to compile
migration data, none of which is either accurate or reliable.
The first of these methods is employed by the Balance of
Payments Office of the Bureau of Economic and Social Analysis
within the Planning Board of Puerto Rico. The method consists
of interviews with airline passengers to determine whether or not
they are residents of Puerto Rico. One of every four persons
interviewed is further asked his destination, the purpose of his
trip, his occupation, etc.

According to a report prepared by the firm of Peat, Marwick,
Mitchell and Co.[38] the above survey is carried out by one person and the information gathered is tabulated by the Planning
Board every year. It is noted that the number of people working
on the survey is inadequate and there is no electronic processing
of the data. Consequently, there are considerable delays in the
publication of the information obtained from the surveys.

The second method, used by the Ports Authority,
tabulates information provided by airline and shipping companies.
The information obtained from the airlines is submitted in connection with a tax payable by the airlines on each ticket sold.
This method omits passengers who do not pay for their
tickets, and furthermore, since the method used is not uniform,

the analysis of the data gathered requires considerable time. The
survey emphasizes only global movement and volume of passengers.
It makes no attempt to distinguish between resident and non-
resident passengers, nor does it include information regarding
sex, age or occupation of passengers.

The airlines' information is submitted to the
Balance of Payments Office to be used (after the addition of non-
resident figures) in the preparation of population estimates. The
data thus obtained from the airlines makes no distinction between
tourists, businessmen, or migrants and is, therefore, not
an adequate measure of the outflow of Puerto Ricans to the mainland, nor the inflow of non-Puerto Ricans to the island.

Just as unreliable as the above-mentioned methods is the
attempt made by the Planning Board to obtain information about
migrants by using the Department of Labor's household survey. This
survey is used by the Planning Board as the basis for determining
the Island's rates of employment and unemployment. In the course
of this survey, the interviewer asks whether any members of the
household who were residing in Puerto Rico at the time of the
survey last year are now living outside Puerto Rico. This is
equivalent to asking who emigrated during the preceding year.
The survey also tries to determine which members of the households
were living outside Puerto Rico during the preceding year. Thus,
the attempt is made to determine the number of immigrants to the
island.

The household survey is useful in determining three principal
types of migratory movements: 1) from rural to urban areas; 2)

from one municipality to another (particularly from low-density to high-density municipalities; 3) emigration to the mainland. 4) immigration to the island by non-Puerto Ricans (principally North Americans, Cubans, Dominicans). The survey covers 8,000 households, which constitute a sub-sampling of the 48,000 households included in the Department of Labor's sampling.

There are a number of serious deficiencies in the use of the household survey to determine the volume of migration and the characteristics of migrants. First, there is no way of obtaining any information in the case where an entire household has migrated. Thus, the method underestimates the actual number of migrants. Second, the survey does not take into account, as a characteristic, whether members of the household are owners or tenants.

A fourth method being used to obtain migration data is based on changes in population between successive censuses and on birth and death rate figures. Through the use of these censuses and of a component or residual formula and its variations one can indirectly obtain reliable estimates on migration data for the period between two successive censuses. Commonly known as "vital statistics method," the accounting equation used is the following:

$$P_1 = P_o + N - D + M$$

P_1 is the population at the time of the last census, P_o is population at the time of the prior census, N stands for births which occurred between the two censuses, D represents deaths, and finally, M is net migration occurring during the period between the two censuses.

The equation can be reformulated as follows:

$$M = P_1 - P_0 - N + D$$

In other words, net migration during the period between two censuses is equal to the population at the time of the last census minus the population at the time of the prior census, minus births occurring during the period between the two censuses, plus the number of deaths occurring between the two censuses.

Before 1960, the vital statistics method yielded information on the balance of the net migration of each municipality, with no indication as to whether migrants were moving to other municipalities or outside Puerto Rico. Since 1960, the census has been recording the municipalities where people live at the time of the census and the municipalities in which they were born. This additional data helps to estimate net internal migration between municipalities during the period between the two census. In this manner, we can obtain net total external migration for each municipality by subtracting net internal migration from total net migration (obtained through an application of the above-mentioned equation).

The vital statistics method is of rather limited usefulness. It does not produce current information. For example, the

necessary data from the 1960 census was not available until 1963.
The method, furthermore, does not register annual changes
in migration patterns.

REFERENCES CITED

1 - Puerto Rico Planning Board, Economic Report to the Governor, 1966, p. 2.

2 - Gordon K. Lewis, Puerto Rico, Freedom and Power in the Caribbean. New York, Monthly Review Press, 1963, p. 93.

3 - Harvey S. Perloff, Puerto Rico's Economic Future, The University of Chicago Press 1949

4 - Santos Negrón Díaz, "Crítica al Desarrollo Económico de Puerto Rico," in Pabellon, 1966, p. 13.

5 - Puerto Rico Planning Board, op. cit., Table I

6 - Perloff, op. cit., p.53.

7 - Lewis, op. cit., p. 167

8 - Negrón Díaz, op. cit., p. 14

9 - Puerto Rico Planning Board, op. cit., p. 53

10- ibid, table XXI

11- ibid, table XVIII

12- Negrón Díaz, op. cit. p. 15

13- ibid, p. 15

14- Lloyd G. Reynolds, "Wages and Employment in a Labor Surplus Economy", American Economic Review, December 1965.

15- Puerto Rico Planning Board, op. cit., p. 2

16- James C. Ingram, "Regional Payments Mechanisms: The Case of Puerto Rico," The University of North Carolina Press, 1962, p. 134

17- ibid, table I.

18- Melvin M. Tumin and Arnold S. Feldman, Social Class and Social Change in Puerto Rico, Princeton University Press, 1961.

19- Julian Stewart, ed., The People of Puerto Rico, New York, 1949,

p. 487

20- see: C. Wright Mills et. al. The Puerto Rican Journey, Harper and Brothers Publishers, New York, 1950. First edition. Also Clarence Senior, The Puerto Ricans: Strangers--Then Neighbors, Quadrangle Books, 1965

21- Puerto Rico Planning Board, Economic Report to the Governor, 1970. Table II, A-4

22- Puerto Rico Planning Board. Economic Report to the Government, 1967 pp 5-29

23- A.J. Jaffe, People Jobs and Economic Development, The Free Press, 1959, pp. 64-65

24- Of this million, around 700,000 were migrants and 300,000 the sons of migrants who would have been born in Puerto Rico had their parents not migrated. See: José L. Vázquez Calzada, The Demographic Evolution of Puerto Rico, Unpublished doctoral dissertation. The University of Chicago, 1964, chapter IV

25- These coefficients can be considered relatively high since a perfect association between two variables given a correlation coefficient of 1.0 (or -1.0 in the case of an inverse relation); the coefficient is 0 when there is no association between two variables.

26- The trend described continues from 1965 to the present; in 1969 we find a reverse flow (to Puerto Rico) similar to the ones encountered in 1961 and 1963. In order to explain these reverse flows it would be necessary to have data on the existing demand for labor in certain industries within the American economy, as well as specific data on the migrants returning to Puerto Rico. See Appendix A for a discussion of the problems presented by the data collection methods being used by the Puerto Rican government.

27- Puerto Rico Planning Board, Economic Report to the Governor, 1965,
   p. 193.

28- Puerto Rico Planning Board, Report on Human Resources to the Governor,
   1970, p. 53

29- ibid., p. 11

30- ibid., Table 17, A-22 It must be remembered that the Government
   of Puerto Rico employs around 113 thousand people, that is 15.3% of
   all people employed in the econmy.

31- ibid., p. 62

32- U.S. Department of Commerce, Census, 1960.

33- Puerto Rico Planning Board, Economic Report to the Government, 1967
   pp. 5-27

34- See Puerto Rican Forum, Inc., 1964 Study of Poverty Conditions in
   the New York Puerto Rican Community, passim.

35- El Mundo, San Juan, October 31, 1970 and tho San Juan Star, January
   17, 1971.

36- Luis Nieves Falcón, Diagnóstico de Puerto Rico, Rio Piedras, Puerto
   Rico (1971), p. 249.

37- See Gordon K. Lewis, op. cit.

38- Peat, Marwick, Mitchell and Company, Methodology for the Study of
   Internal and External Migration of Puerto Rico: a Report Prepared
   for the Puerto Rico Planning Board (February, 1971).

THE IMPACT OF PUERTO RICAN MIGRATION ON GOVERNMENTAL SERVICES IN NEW YORK CITY

Edited by

Martin B. Dworkis

RHODA H. BERKOWITZ
MARY ALICE BRITTON
LEONARD BRODSKY
RAFAEL COTTO
DAWN ARLENE ELKIN
ENID RUTH HAMMER
LEON I. SALOMON
BERTRAM WEINER
DANIEL X. WELSH

FACULTY ADVISORY COMMITTEE

DR. WILLIAM J. RONAN, Chairman
*Dean of the Graduate School of Public Administration
and Social Service, and Professor of Government.*

DR. FRANK COHEN
Director of Student Services, Social Service Program

DR. CHARLES E. REDFIELD
Lecturer in Administrative Communication

DR. STERLING D. SPERO
Professor of Public Administration

DR. PAUL STUDENSKI
Professor of Economics

MR. JAMES R. WATSON
Lecturer in Public Administration

PROJECT DIRECTOR AND EDITOR

DR. MARTIN B. DWORKIS
Associate Professor of Public Administration

THE IMPACT OF PUERTO RICAN MIGRATION ON GOVERNMENTAL SERVICES IN NEW YORK CITY

GRADUATE SCHOOL OF PUBLIC ADMINISTRATION
AND SOCIAL SERVICE, NEW YORK UNIVERSITY

NEW YORK UNIVERSITY PRESS●1957
NEW YORK
Washington Square

CONTENTS

INTRODUCTION

This volume is the result of an inquiry by a group of graduate students of Public Administration in the academic year 1953-54. The topic was selected by a faculty committee, but the rest of the study, its planning, programming, field and library research, was developed by the student group itself. The faculty project director and the faculty supervisory committee acted as consultants.

The student group included recent college graduates in their first year of graduate study and some younger civil servants, who had taken leave of their government posts to spend a year in academic study for the Master of Public Administration degree. Participation in the project was accepted in substitution for the traditional individual master's thesis and was part of a full academic program in the field of public policy and administration.

The study is one of a series of group field research projects, undertaken by the faculty of the Graduate School of Public Administration and Social Service, as an experimental program in education, growing out of the conviction of the faculty that group experiences constitute excellent preparation for a career in governmental administration.

In selecting the topic, the faculty had in mind the utilization of such resources of the New York metropolitan area as a laboratory, the interests of the students, the light that could be shed upon an important area of civic responsibility, and the possibility of completion within an academic year.

While accepted research devices were utilized, the faculty did not hesitate to assist the project staff in discarding such devices when the group considered them unnecessary or unduly binding. There were sought the subtleties of the educational process in working together, arguing conclusions, debating experiences, adjusting to differences, and adapting schedules and outside interests. To the faculty, the results were apparent in the intangible but forceful and recognizable growth in personality and character of the project staff.

1

As the project developed, the research on the effects of Puerto Rican migration to the city became progressively specialized. At the beginning of the study, governmental and private sources were able to provide general written material. Near the end, original and often unpublished data had to be secured from individuals or agencies. In the first meetings, orientation lectures were utilized to cover the general background of the Puerto Rican migrant, and, in addition, guest speakers provided the group with names of significant leaders of pertinent public and private organizations.

Throughout the year, staff members were urged to attend public meetings of Puerto Rican groups and associations. The contacts that were developed were valuable in securing information of an original nature.

The difficulties involved in interviewing had, from the very beginning, been emphasized by the faculty, and various means were utilized in training the researchers. Role-playing sessions were held with faculty and staff acting out the parts of interviewer and interviewee. Apprentice interviews were arranged for in which a few staff members accompanied the project director and held "critiques" after the interview to evaluate the approaches used. While primarily intended for training, the apprentice interview on several occasions resulted in the accumulation of valuable information. These accordingly developed a well-defined pattern for the conference-type of interview, held in roundtable fashion, with an informal sequence of questions, note-taking, and the reporting and comparison of results.

The administrative aspects of organizing for the study were also utilized, as means of educating the students for group work. The students devised the means of recording and storing data. The exchange of information being vital to the success of the study, the student researchers worked out means of avoiding either a time-consuming, complex system or a useless, haphazard system. Control sheets for the cataloguing of materials, trips, and interviews were utilized to avoid duplication of effort and to keep informed of colleagues' activities. A correspondence register controlled incoming and outgoing mail.

Staff reporting was done through regularly scheduled meetings and by frequent informal staff "get-togethers." As a member of a committee, that is, a subgroup, each staff member co-operated on two or more principal aspects of the study. The entire group worked together on the final writing and editing and defended the methods, findings, and conclusions at a formal presentation session before the faculty committee.

The generous responses of the many city officials and officials of the Commonwealth of Puerto Rico, to whom the school is deeply indebted, provided the project members with invaluable insights. The group was materially aided by, and is cordially appreciative of, the assistance of many leaders of civic, fraternal, education- al, institutional, and political groups. While the ideas and obser- vations of the people interviewed have been utilized as fully as possible, all errors of omission and commission are the sole responsibility of the project group and, for data after mid-1954, of the project director.

The project was materially assisted by a grant from the Car- negie Corporation of New York. In the opinion of the faculty, the outstanding success of this and similar projects in other aca- demic years has resulted in the incorporation of this method in the regular curriculum, no longer as an educational experiment but as an integral part of the training for the public service, for a selected group of graduate students.

THE PUERTO RICANS

COME TO NEW YORK CITY

For over a century New York City has been the focal point of waves of immigration from Europe. Now, in the mid-twentieth century, the city has experienced a new type of immigration—not of aliens but of American citizens from the Caribbean island of Puerto Rico. Unlike the European arrivals, most of whom dispersed themselves to the four corners of the United States, the vast majority of Puerto Ricans have remained in the city of their arrival, thus creating unique and special problems for both the city and the state.

The Puerto Rican influx began to snowball shortly after World War II.(1) During the decade 1944-1953, an annual average of 36,354 Puerto Ricans arrived in the United States. Most of them came by air because of the cheap transportation, and since there are nonstop flights between the island and New York, most of them arrived in New York—and have stayed there. By the end of 1956, there were approximately 600,000 migrants from the island and their children in New York City. Since 1950, there have been more Puerto Rican men than women arriving, though in the over-all migration figures the women predominate. By 1948, only 5 per cent of the arrivals had settled outside New York City; by 1956, 20 per cent were living elsewhere in the country, and there are now people of Puerto Rican birth or origin in every state. The greatest increases have occurred in industrial states: California, New Jersey, Pennsylvania, and Illinois.

---

1. The Puerto Rican migration is relatively small compared to the total cross-state migration of Americans, about 1.2 per cent of the 21 million in the 1950-1955 period. The situation, however, is complicated by the concentration in New York City, and the difference in language and cultural background of the island's American citizens.

The Puerto Rican population of New York is increasing by
over 1,000 migrants a week. Since the newcomers are almost all
young—very few over forty-five—and consequently at the period
of greatest fertility, their high birth rate, higher than on the island,(2) increases their numbers. The birth rate among Puerto
Ricans in New York is 49.1 per thousand as compared to the general birth rate of 18.7 per thousand, and a birth rate among nonwhites, excluding Puerto Ricans, of 29 per thousand.(3) The relative youth of the Puerto Rican group, coupled with a great reduction in infant mortality, results in a death rate that is almost as
low as that on the island. As the Puerto Ricans become a larger
part of the population, they will have a greater effect on the general population trends and rates. In 1950, Puerto Ricans constituted approximately 3 per cent of the city's total population; in
1955, almost 7 per cent. Taking into consideration the above statistics and current trends, it is forecasted that, by 1960, New
York's Puerto Rican population will be 9 per cent of the city
total.(4)

The Puerto Rican is an American citizen. He is free to travel
at will from the island to any part of the United States. Any plan
to arbitrarily limit the number entering the United States would
be impossible to carry out, without a drastic change in the relationship between the United States and the Commonwealth of

---

2. The island birth rate, among the highest in the world, is about
   35 per thousand (almost 85,000 births per year in a population
   of 2,264,000). The rate of natural increase—births over deaths—
   is 26.6 per thousand. See, Puerto Rico Department of Labor,
   Bureau of Labor Statistics, Estimates of the Population Size and
   Characteristics. See also The New York Times, January 3, 1956,
   p. 54.
3. A. J. Jaffe, Puerto Rican Population of New York City (New York:
   Bureau of Applied Social Research, Columbia University, 1954),
   p. 34; in 1955-1956, the birth rate among Puerto Ricans dropped
   somewhat to 42 or 43 per thousand, while the over-all city-wide rate
   went up to 20 per thousand.
4. The New York City Planning Department forecast predicts an increase from 246,306 Puerto Ricans (the Census of 1950) to 740,000
   in 1960 and 1,160,000 in 1970. The percentages, in terms of the
   total city population predicted, would be 3.1 per cent (the Census of
   1950), 8.9 per cent in 1960, and 13.5 per cent in 1970. See The New
   York Times, November 22, 1954, p. 25. These are very conserva-
   tive figures, based upon a drop in net migration from 350,000 in the
   1950-1960 period to 250,000 in 1960-1970 and a drop in the Puerto
   Rican birth rate from its 1955 rate of 42.6 per thousand, to 30 per
   thousand in 1960 and 23 per thousand in 1970. Other reliable
   sources indicate a Puerto Rican population as high as 12 per cent of
   a 1960 total in the city of 8,250,000.

Puerto Rico. Those with communicable diseases could possibly
be barred by health and police regulations, but any attempt to in-
spect every migrant would doubtless be met by a storm of pro-
tests, particularly if those inspections were confined to Puerto
Rican arrivals. The Puerto Rican's American citizenship, the
nearness of the island to the mainland, and the relatively cheap
and quick air transportation—which also make it easy for him to
return to the island if he wishes—are all motivating factors in
the influx.

The Puerto Rican leaves the island for three reasons: low
wages and unemployment, poor living conditions, and overpopulation—662 persons to the square mile. Economically harassed,
the average Puerto Rican pictures the United States as a land of
opportunity and vast wealth; and many of them think this wealth
is easily obtained. The Puerto Rican migrant, unlike the European immigrant, does not come for political or religious reasons,
but entirely for economic reasons, and thus the arrivals represent families in economic stress: men and women who often
think their cares will disappear overnight, once they land in New
York. As stated by Felipe Torres, a New York State Assembly-
man of Puerto Rican origin: "They come here with no intention
of remaining here permanently. They come here because they
have to for economic reasons." When times are good and jobs
plentiful, especially in New York City, the influx increases; but
if there is a slump and the labor market is tight, it slackens. At
times there has even been a net out-migration, as in the last
three months of 1953, when there was a net reverse flow of
14,690 from the United States to the island.(5)

Members of the professional classes in Puerto Rico are well
off and do not come to the United States, except for professional
training, and they return to the island when this is completed.
This results in a serious lack of trained Puerto Ricans to interpret the new way of life to their fellow countrymen in the United
States, and to form a much-needed core of leadership; the lack
of which is one of the most striking obstacles in the attempt at
the coincident adjustment of the community and its new residents.
This lack is especially felt in social work and the medical field.

The majority of Puerto Ricans migrate in a standard pattern.
One family member, generally a male, comes alone to New York.
He takes the first job he can find, rents a room in which to sleep,

---

5. The New York Times, February 17, 1954, p. 35; the approximate net
   Puerto Rican migration to the mainland is as follows: 1945 - 14,000,
   1946 - 40,000, 1947 - 25,000, 1948 - 33,000, 1949 - 26,000, 1950 - 35,000,
   1951 - 50,000, 1952 - 60,000, 1953 - 70,000, 1954 - 21,000, 1955 - 46,000,
   1956 - 60,000 (anticipated); The New York Times, March 5, 1956, p. 33.

and soon sends for his family to join him. He writes enthusiastic
letters to relatives and friends in Puerto Rico, telling them how
splendidly he is getting on and what a wonderful place New York
is, thus stimulating a desire in them to come to New York too.
Since Puerto Ricans are clannish and like to have their own people about them, the one in New York often arranges employment
for his relatives or friends; and when they arrive, he gladly puts
them up in his own home—even though it may be one room—until
they can get quarters of their own. This is a contributing factor
to the overcrowded living conditions of the Puerto Ricans in New
York.(6)

The Puerto Rican woman, subservient to the male on the island,
finds New York offering her a different and vastly improved role
in society. Although the majority have not taken advantage of the
many opportunities offered them, the city presents a multitude of
social contacts and diversions outside the home. Also, the Puerto
Rican woman finds that New York's light industries and service
industries, all demanding little physical strength, make many
more jobs available to her than to the Puerto Rican man. She
finds it easy to get a job, the pay is far better than on the island,
and her new wage-earning ability raises her status in the family
to the point where she is equal, and sometimes superior, to the
male.(7)

---

6. See Chapter II.
7. See Chapter III.

THE IMPACT

ON HOUSING

Contrary to the opinion widely held by New Yorkers after World War II that the influx of Puerto Ricans caused the severe housing shortage, that situation actually developed from building inactivity over a period of many decades. The lack of low-income dwelling units was already felt in the twenties—one of the effects of World War I. Puerto Ricans, far from causing the housing shortage, are as much victims of it as are others in the city.

The Puerto Rican's most immediate and critical need when he arrives in New York City is shelter for himself and his family. Often he finds accommodations with relatives or friends already established, but frequently he is left to his own resources. In his search for adequate facilities he is confronted with the inhibiting pressures of discrimination, language differences, inflated rentals, and his own low economic status. He gravitates to crowded and poor neighborhoods where other people of his own background live.

Table 1 illustrates the pattern of Puerto Rican concentration in New York City as of 1950. In 96.4 per cent of the city's census tracts, 35.4 per cent of the Puerto Ricans live. The remaining 64.6 per cent are concentrated within only 3.6 per cent of the tracts. However, in comparison with the Negro population, which has lived in the city longer, the Puerto Ricans seem to be better off. In 89.1 per cent of the tracts reside 8.4 per cent of the Negro population. The remaining 91.6 per cent call but 10.9 per cent of the tracts home.(1) Both these groups are subjected to discriminatory housing and rental practices, but the lighter-skinned Puerto Ricans seem freer to move about. Although the conditions under which Puerto Ricans live in New York are su-

---

1. The City of New York, City Planning Commission, Tenant Relocation Report (January 20, 1954), Table 37.

TABLE 1

CONCENTRATION PATTERN OF THE PUERTO RICAN
POPULATION OF NEW YORK CITY, 1950

	Distribution of Populated Census Tracts, Per Cent of Puerto Ricans in Total Population				
	Under 10%	10-24.9%	25-49.9%	50% and over	Total
New York City					
Number of populated census tracts ...	2,277	59	21	5	2,362
Percentage of city's census tracts ...	96.4	2.4	0.9	0.3	100.0
Number of Puerto Ricans	87,175	61,772	60,671	36,688	246,306
Percentage of Puerto Ricans in city ..	35.4	25.1	24.6	14.9	100.0
Manhattan					
Number of populated census tracts ...	241	27	8	4	280
Percentage of borough's census tracts	86.0	9.7	2.8	1.5	100.0
Number of Puerto Ricans	43,457	33,303	28,950	32,797	138,507
Percentage of Puerto Ricans in borough	31.4	24.0	20.9	23.7	100.0
The Bronx					
Number of populated census tracts ...	400	11	7	1	419
Percentage of borough's census tracts	95.4	2.6	1.7	0.3	100.0
Number of Puerto Ricans	15,775	16,280	25,978	3,891	61,924
Percentage of Puerto Ricans in borough	25.5	26.3	41.9	6.3	100.0
Brooklyn					
Number of populated census tracts ...	836	20	6	0	862
Percentage of borough's census tracts	96.9	2.4	0.7	0	100.0
Number of Puerto Ricans	22,624	11,932	5,743	0	40,299
Percentage of Puerto Ricans in borough	56.1	29.6	14.3	0	100.0
Queens					
Number of populated census tracts ...	691	0	0	0	691
Percentage of borough's census tracts	100.0	0	0	0	100.0
Number of Puerto Ricans	4,836	0	0	0	4,836
Percentage of Puerto Ricans in borough	100.0	0	0	0	100.0
Richmond					
Number of populated census tracts ...	111	1	0	0	112
Percentage of borough's census tracts	65.2	34.8	0	0	100.0
Number of Puerto Ricans	483	257	0	0	740
Percentage of Puerto Ricans in borough	65.3	34.7	0	0	100.0

Source: The City of New York, City Planning Commission, "Tenant Relocation Report," Table 38.
Table derived from figures of the United States Bureau of the Census and the New York
City Department of City Planning.

perior to those they had been accustomed to on the island, as a
whole they desire improved accommodations. A survey taken in
the Washington Heights, East Harlem, Lower East Side, and
Chelsea-Lowell areas of Manhattan showed that 85 per cent of
those interviewed wished to move. They liked Manhattan but they
preferred to live in quieter and cleaner neighborhoods.(2)

Puerto Ricans are particularly overcrowded. If, by a process
of interpolation with the estimates for 1960, the 1950 census figures are extended to 1954, it will be found that the Puerto Rican
household consists of 3.83 persons, or 0.59 persons more than
white households—a "household" being defined as "one occupied
dwelling unit." This seemingly small difference acquires greater significance when the density per room occupied by both
groups is considered. In 1950, 10 per cent of all Puerto Rican
households and but 4 per cent of all white households contained
upwards of 1.51 persons per room.(3) It was estimated that 22
per cent of all Puerto Rican households lacked private toilets
or baths and hot running water, as compared with 10 per cent
for all white households.(4)

Puerto Ricans as a group are relegated to the oldest housing
in the city, with the most dilapidated plumbing facilities. Tables
2, 3, 4, and 5 illustrate these conditions, as well as Puerto Rican
rent levels and the extent of excessive density.

Despite the poor housing conditions under which they live,
Puerto Ricans pay rents far higher in proportion to services obtained than any other group. Instances of severe exploitation are
far from isolated. Landlords, unscrupulous Puerto Ricans among
them, violate legal obligations to avail themselves of undeserved
benefits. Too frequently, Puerto Rican tenants, unfamiliar with
these restrictions and unaware of their right to obtain redress,
fail to report owners and violations. In most cases, however,
irresponsible landlords rely on the firm legal bases of outdated
housing and building codes to reap their undue profits. A study,
conducted by the Kings County Grand Jury,(5) illustrates this.
Four sample houses, built in 1899 for one-family occupancy,
were later converted into "class B" multiple dwellings.(6)

---

2. Manny Diaz, Earl Finch, Larry Gangware, et al., The Attitudes of
   Puerto Ricans in New York City to Various Aspects of Their
   Environment (Project No. 4317, New York School of Social Work,
   June, 1953).
3. City of New York, City Planning Commission, op. cit., Table 32.
4. Ibid.
5. Second Grand Jury Presentment, County Court, County of Kings,
   March 3, 1953, Appendix II.
6. A "class B" multiple dwelling is defined as: "a multiple dwelling

Collectively, their 77 rooms, subdivided into 65 apartments, excluding the superintendent's apartment, contained 91 adults and
158 children, or an average of 3.23 persons per room. Only eight
units had private toilets and four had private showers; the others
shared common facilities. From four to six persons cooked, ate,
and slept in one room and shared a toilet with many others.
Monthly proceeds to the landlord came to $4,380.93, an exorbi-
tant average rate of $56.86 per room.

Puerto Ricans, lowest in the economic strata, can ill afford
these rentals. Often the Department of Welfare, in spite of its
avowed preference for less expensive housing provisions for its
clients, is forced to accede to landlords' demands. In the case
cited above, 41 of the 65 households were sustained in part or in
full through public assistance. Rents in these cases ranged from
$43.33 to $112.66 monthly, the majority at the higher rates.

Puerto Ricans face severe discrimination in housing. Legislation, in both the City and State of New York, is among the most
advanced in the country, in prohibiting segregation and discrimination in public and public-assisted housing. The law forbids
discrimination against an individual seeking housing, if the land
or structure is wholly or partially exempt from city taxes, or if
the city has supplied funds or other financial assistance, or if
the land was acquired by the city through eminent domain. But
private operators are not subject to these restrictions.

More subtle discriminatory practices continue to thrive, even
in the face of legal provisions. Certain public and private individuals and organizations have successfully used pressure to
keep low-rent housing projects, in which Negroes and Puerto
Ricans live in significant numbers, out of various areas of the
city. It is perhaps more than coincidence that the boroughs of
Queens and Richmond, with 18.2 per cent and 59.7 per cent of the
city's vacant land, respectively, contain only 6,869 and 967 low-
income dwelling units.

There is little discrimination of any type in New York City Housing Authority projects. Tenant selections are made from International Business Machine cards, containing no information regarding race, color, or creed. On the other hand, selection practices
of public-assisted private developments are open to question.

Housing discrimination has far-reaching implications for
_____

which is occupied, as a rule transiently, as the more or less temporary abode of individuals or families who are lodged with or without
meals....This class shall also include dwellings, designed as private
dwellings, but occupied by one or two families with five or more
transient boarders, roomers, or lodgers in one household." Multiple
Dwelling Law, art. I, sec. 4, sub. 9.

TABLE 2

HOUSING CONDITIONS IN NEW YORK CITY CENSUS TRACTS HAVING SUBSTANTIAL PUERTO RICAN POPULATION, 1950

1. CONDITION AND PLUMBING FACILITIES

Areas*	No. of Dwelling Units Reporting		No Private Bath or Dilapidated		Per cent of Dwelling Units	No Running Water or Dilapidated		Per cent of Dwelling Units
New York City	2,333,151	100.0%	223,706	100.0%	9.6	112,117	100.0%	4.8
2%+ Puerto Rican Tracts	498,104	21.3	91,286	40.8	18.3	51,124	45.6	10.3
5%+ Puerto Rican Tracts	303,976	13.0	61,755	27.6	20.3	37,566	33.5	12.4
10%+ Puerto Rican Tracts	163,703	7.0	34,823	15.6	21.3	24,564	21.9	15.0
20%+ Puerto Rican Tracts	75,044	3.2	14,991	6.7	20.0	11,742	10.5	15.6

2. AGE OF HOUSING

Areas*	No. of Dwelling Units Reporting		Year Built								1919 Per cent of Dwelling Units
			After 1940		1930-39		1920-29		1919 & Previous		
New York City	2,302,675	100.0%	193,305	100.0%	256,435	100.0%	721,915	100.0%	1,131,020	100.0%	49.1
2%+ Puerto Rican Tracts	489,045	21.2	4,780	2.4	17,630	6.9	75,360	10.4	391,275	34.6	80.0
5%+ Puerto Rican Tracts	303,480	13.2	2,695	1.4	9,595	3.7	41,805	5.8	248,385	22.0	81.8
10%+ Puerto Rican Tracts	164,200	7.1	805	0.4	4,435	1.7	19,565	2.7	139,570	12.3	85.0
20%+ Puerto Rican Tracts	74,485	3.2	110	0.1	1,740	0.7	9,525	1.3	63,110	5.6	84.7

3. OVERCROWDING AND RENT LEVELS

Areas*	Overcrowding: No. of Dwelling Units Reporting		No. of Dwelling Units with 1.01 or More Persons per Room		Per cent of Dwelling Units	Higher Median Rent than N.Y.C.†		Lower Median Rent than N.Y.C.†		Per cent of Dwelling Units in Tracts—Rent below N.Y.C. Median
						Tracts	Dwelling Units	Tracts	Dwelling Units	
New York City	2,318,553	100.0%	386,167	100.0%	16.7	—		—		—
2%+ Puerto Rican Tracts	500,758	21.6	99,962	27.2	20.0					
5%+ Puerto Rican Tracts	311,500	13.4	66,196	17.1	21.3					
10%+ Puerto Rican Tracts	168,772	7.3	38,374	9.9	22.7					
20%+ Puerto Rican Tracts	77,797	3.4	20,722	5.3	26.6					

* Tracts containing housing projects or other substantial public institutions are excluded in all areas except New York City totals. "2%+ Puerto Rican Tracts" means Census Tracts containing over 2% Puerto Ricans, etc.

† Data not comparable.

Source: Data was determined by combining Tables 3, 4, and 5 and data for Queens and Richmond, as determined from 1950 Census, Report PD-37. Percentage of Puerto Rican population calculated from Population of Puerto Rican Birth or Parentage, New York City: 1950 (Welfare and Health Council of New York City).

TABLE 3

HOUSING CONDITIONS IN MANHATTAN CENSUS TRACTS HAVING SUBSTANTIAL PUERTO RICAN POPULATION, 1950

1. CONDITION AND PLUMBING FACILITIES

Areas*	No. of Dwelling Units Reporting		No Private Bath or Dilapidated	Per cent of Dwelling Units	No Running Water or Dilapidated	Per cent of Dwelling Units	Per cent of Dwelling Units
Manhattan	598,856	100.0%	110,979	100.0%	55,424	100.0%	9.3
2%+ Puerto Rican Tracts	288,472	48.2	61,332	55.3	30,537	55.1	10.6
5%+ Puerto Rican Tracts	180,540	30.1	43,427	39.1	23,771	42.9	13.2
10%+ Puerto Rican Tracts	90,107	15.0	22,164	20.0	14,295	25.8	15.9
20%+ Puerto Rican Tracts	37,522	6.3	9,356	8.4	7,179	13.0	19.1

2. AGE OF HOUSING

Areas*	No. of Dwelling Units Reporting		After 1940	Per cent of Dwelling Units	1930–39	Per cent of Dwelling Units	1920–29	Per cent of Dwelling Units	1919 & Previous	Per cent of Dwelling Units	1919 Per cent of Dwelling Units
Manhattan	587,065	100.0%	35,370	100.0%	35,880	100.0%	101,300	100.0%	414,515	100.0%	70.6
2%+ Puerto Rican Tracts	280,640	47.8	4,110	11.6	12,915	36.0	41,065	40.1	222,550	53.7	79.3
5%+ Puerto Rican Tracts	179,295	30.5	2,340	6.6	7,365	20.5	21,055	20.8	148,535	35.8	82.8
10%+ Puerto Rican Tracts	90,565	15.4	800	2.3	3,460	9.6	7,785	7.7	78,695	19.0	86.9
20%+ Puerto Rican Tracts	36,800	6.3	105	0.3	1,065	3.0	2,605	2.6	33,025	8.0	89.7

3. OVERCROWDING AND RENT LEVELS

Areas*	Overcrowding: No. of Dwelling Units Reporting		No. of Dwelling Units with 1.01 or More Persons per Room	Per cent of Dwelling Units	Higher Median Rent than Manhattan		Lower Median Rent than Manhattan†		Per cent of Dwelling Units in Tracts—Rent below Manhattan Median
					Tracts	Dwelling Units	Tracts	Dwelling Units	
Manhattan	606,266	100.0%	99,846	16.5	—	—	—	—	—
2%+ Puerto Rican Tracts	292,535	48.3	54,799	18.7	51	131,520	66	148,845	53.1
5%+ Puerto Rican Tracts	185,831	30.7	38,159	20.5	20	57,703	55	119,132	67.4
10%+ Puerto Rican Tracts	94,472	15.6	20,174	21.4	11	25,967	26	63,533	71.0
20%+ Puerto Rican Tracts	39,693	6.5	10,775	27.1	2	6,599	13	30,532	82.2

*Tracts containing housing projects are excluded in all areas except Manhattan (also other substantial public institutions) totals. "2%+ Puerto Rican Tracts" means Census Tracts containing over 2% Puerto Ricans, etc.

† Manhattan Median Rent is $42.27. Only tracts reporting median rent included.

Source: Data was determined from 1950 Census, Report PD-37. Percentage of Puerto Rican population calculated from Population of Puerto Rican Birth or Parentage, New York City: 1950 (Welfare and Health Council of New York City).

TABLE 4

HOUSING CONDITIONS IN BROOKLYN CENSUS TRACTS HAVING SUBSTANTIAL PUERTO RICAN POPULATION, 1950

1 CONDITION AND PLUMBING FACILITIES

Areas*	No. of Dwelling Units Reporting		No Private Bath or Dilapidated		Per cent of Dwelling Units	No Running Water or Dilapidated		Per cent of Dwelling Units
Brooklyn	786,347	100.0%	65,734	100.0%	8.4	32,079	100.0%	4.1
2%+ Puerto Rican Tracts	96,126	12.2	16,536	25.2	17.2	8,741	27.2	9.1
5%+ Puerto Rican Tracts	49,005	6.2	9,931	15.1	20.3	6,522	20.3	13.3
10%+ Puerto Rican Tracts	26,336	3.3	6,377	9.7	24.2	4,701	14.7	17.9
20%+ Puerto Rican Tracts	9,546	1.2	3,343	5.1	35.0	2,693	8.4	28.2

2. AGE OF HOUSING

Areas*	No. of Dwelling Units Reporting		Year Built								1919 Per cent of Dwelling Units
			After 1940		1930–39		1920–29		1919 & Previous		
Brooklyn	781,335	100.0%	43,675	100.0%	73,670	100.0%	235,480	100.0%	428,510	100.0%	54.8
2%+ Puerto Rican Tracts	96,630	12.4	440	1.0	1,565	2.1	6,520	2.8	88,105	20.6	91.2
5%+ Puerto Rican Tracts	49,515	6.3	225	0.5	735	1.0	2,460	1.0	46,095	10.8	93.1
10%+ Puerto Rican Tracts	26,475	3.4	0	0.0	145	0.2	1,105	0.5	25,225	5.7	95.3
20%+ Puerto Rican Tracts	9,665	1.2	0	0.0	30	†	40	†	9,595	2.2	99.3

3. OVERCROWDING AND RENT LEVELS

Areas*	Overcrowding: No. of Dwelling Units Reporting		No. of Dwelling Units with 1.01 or More Persons per Room		Per cent of Dwelling Units	Higher Median Rent than Brooklyn ‡		Lower Median Rent than Brooklyn ‡		Per cent of Dwelling Units in Tracts—Rent below Brooklyn Median
						Tracts	Dwelling Units	Tracts	Dwelling Units	
Brooklyn	785,278	100.0%	138,369	100.0%	17.6	—	—	—	—	—
2%+ Puerto Rican Tracts	95,186	12.1	19,610	14.2	20.1	15	14,149	75	69,555	83.1
5%+ Puerto Rican Tracts	48,658	6.2	10,649	7.7	21.9	6	5,082	39	37,324	88.0
10%+ Puerto Rican Tracts	26,114	3.3	6,521	4.6	24.2	3	2,365	23	21,383	90.0
20%+ Puerto Rican Tracts	9,511	1.2	2,637	1.9	27.7	0	—	10	8,886	100.0

*Tracts containing housing projects are excluded in all areas except Brooklyn totals. "2%+ Puerto Rican Tracts" means Census Tracts containing over 2% Puerto Ricans, etc.

†Less than 0.05%.

‡Brooklyn Median Rent is $40.49.

Source: Data was determined from 1950 Census, Report PD-37. Percentage of Puerto Rican population calculated from Population of Puerto Rican Birth or Parentage, New York City: 1950 (Welfare and Health Council of New York City).

TABLE 5

HOUSING CONDITIONS IN BRONX CENSUS TRACTS HAVING SUBSTANTIAL PUERTO RICAN POPULATION, 1950

1. CONDITION AND PLUMBING FACILITIES

Areas*	No. of Dwelling Units Reporting		No Private Bath or Dilapidated		Per cent of Dwelling Units	No Running Water or Dilapidated		Per cent of Dwelling Units
Bronx	417,605	100.0%	19,664	100.0%	4.7	15,220	100.0%	3.6
2%+ Puerto Rican Tracts	108,467	26.0	11,774	59.9	10.9	9,961	65.5	9.2
5%+ Puerto Rican Tracts	74,431	17.8	8,397	42.7	11.3	7,273	47.8	9.8
10%+ Puerto Rican Tracts	47,260	11.3	6,282	31.9	13.3	5,568	36.6	11.9
20%+ Puerto Rican Tracts	27,976	6.7	2,292	11.7	8.2	1,870	12.3	6.7

2. AGE OF HOUSING

Areas*	No. of Dwelling Units Reporting		Year Built								1919 Per cent of Dwelling Units
			After 1940		1930–39		1920–29		1919 & Previous		
Bronx	413,270	100.0%	31,835	100.0%	52,865	100.0%	173,240	100.0%	155,330	100.0%	37.6
2%+ Puerto Rican Tracts	106,745	25.8	140	0.4	2,520	4.8	25,695	14.8	78,390	50.5	73.4
5%+ Puerto Rican Tracts	74,670	18.1	130	0.4	1,495	2.8	18,290	10.6	53,755	34.6	72.0
10%+ Puerto Rican Tracts	47,160	11.4	5	†	830	1.6	10,675	6.2	35,650	23.0	75.6
20%+ Puerto Rican Tracts	28,020	6.8	5	†	645	1.2	6,880	4.0	20,490	13.2	73.1

3. OVERCROWDING AND RENT LEVELS

Areas*	Overcrowding: No. of Dwelling Units Reporting		No. of Dwelling Units with 1.01 or More Persons per Room		Per cent of Dwelling Units	Higher Median Rent than Bronx‡		Lower Median Rent than Bronx‡		Per cent of Dwelling Units in Tracts—Rent below Bronx Median
						Tracts	Dwelling Units	Tracts	Dwelling Units	
Bronx	420,536	100.0%	90,811	100.0%	21.6	—	—	—	—	—
2%+ Puerto Rican Tracts	110,707	26.3	25,141	27.7	22.7	2	1,980	48	99,934	98.6
5%+ Puerto Rican Tracts	77,011	18.3	17,388	19.1	22.6	1	675	31	70,685	99.1
10%+ Puerto Rican Tracts	48,186	11.5	11,879	13.1	24.7	0	—	18	45,145	100.0
20%+ Puerto Rican Tracts	28,593	6.8	7,310	8.0	25.6	0	—	10	26,837	100.0

*Tracts containing housing projects or other substantial public institutions are excluded in all areas except Bronx totals. "2%+ Puerto Rican Tracts" means Census Tracts containing over 2% Puerto Ricans, etc.

†Less than 0.05%.

‡Bronx Median Rent is $42.63. Only tracts reporting median rent included.

Source: Data was determined from 1950 Census, Report PD-37. Percentage of Puerto Rican population calculated from Population of Puerto Rican Birth or Parentage, New York City: 1950 (Welfare and Health Council of New York City).

Puerto Ricans. As long as it persists, the concentration of that group will continue. Slum condemnation programs have, at best, placed Puerto Ricans in an already limited market. Were they allowed unrestricted mobility, the Puerto Ricans' integration would be hastened greatly.

Public housing is increasingly fulfilling the shelter needs of Puerto Ricans in New York City. Although the city's population has increased by 400,000 since World War II, and over 280,000 dwelling units are substandard, construction starts between 1946 and 1953 numbered but 203,750 units. Of this total, 145,146, or 71.2 per cent, were privately financed, and 58,604 utilized public funds.(7) Private construction during this period produced 10,000 fewer units than in the same number of semidepression years preceding the war, and 300,000 fewer than in the seven-year boom in the twenties.(8) Construction costs have played a major role in this curtailment. It has been impossible for private industry to supply low-rent housing to the 1,558,800 families and individuals earning less than $3,500 a year.(9) According to the 1950 census, 96,440 Puerto Rican wage earners, or 94.5 per cent, had incomes of less than $3,500. Their average income of $1,647 compared unfavorably with the city average of $2,410.(10)

Table 6 lists the rental distribution and apartment costs for sampled private construction. It is readily seen that these rentals are prohibitive for Puerto Ricans, most of whom have large families (11) and low incomes. Public housing, on the other hand, has indeed helped to fill in the gap for these people. Tenant selections are made on the basis of prescribed eligibility requirements. Legal families of limited income—including clients of the Department of Welfare—who cannot afford available private housing of adequate standards, and who have lived in the city for at least two years, may be admitted to Housing Authority projects. Preference is given to veterans and to persons displaced by slum clearance.

The proportion of Puerto Rican tenants in public housing projects is on the increase. In February, 1953, 5.4 per cent of the tenants in Authority-operated projects were Puerto Ricans; in May, 1954, 8 per cent; and in February, 1956, 14 per

7. City of New York, City Planning Commission, op. cit., Table 23.
8. Memorandum from Mayor Vincent R. Impellitteri to Federal Housing Administrator Arthur Cole, October 8, 1953.
9. City of New York, City Planning Commission, op. cit., Table 27.
10. Ibid., Table 39.
11. A survey in the Manhattanville area of Manhattan, by the Women's City Club, indicates that 30 per cent of Puerto Rican families had five or more members.

cent. Slum clearance in areas formerly inhabited by Puerto
Ricans, as well as the group's increasing ability to meet residence requirements, mainly accounts for their rising proportion

TABLE 6

RENTAL DISTRIBUTION OF NEW PRIVATE HOUSING

(Housing completed between January—March, 1951)

Rental	Percentage
less than $50	0%
$50-60	1
$60-70	1
$70-80	13
$80-90	22
$90-100	16
$100-110	9
$110-120	15
over $120	23

APARTMENT SIZES AND AVERAGE RENTS
OF PRIVATE HOUSING

(Completed between October—December, 1950)

Size	Average Rent	Percentage
5 or more rooms	$160	4%
4—4-1/2 rooms	116	35
3—3-1/2 rooms	101	48
2—2-1/2 rooms	86	10
less than 2 rooms	99	3

Source: Bureau of Labor Statistics, New Housing in Metropolitan Areas,
Bulletin 115 (September, 1952), Tables 26A, 28A and B.

in the projects. Because of the requirement that residents must
be legally constituted families, consensuality among Puerto
Ricans often bars some families(12); others fall short of the
two-year residence requirement.

---

12. Consensuality, a family arrangement without the benefit of a formal

Puerto Rican tenants do not cause project managers major concern. Managers report that on the whole Puerto Ricans pay their rent promptly, and that once they understand what is expected of them, their housekeeping habits are not objectionable. One characteristic peculiar to Puerto Ricans, which derives from their tropical background and persists to the chagrin of project managers, manifests itself in the form of "condensation." Contrary to the advice of project staffs, Puerto Ricans keep casement windows tightly shut during cold weather. The resulting condensation of water vapor (from steam-heated rooms) on walls and ceilings causes telling damage to paint and plaster. But the matter does not rest there. Puerto Ricans, unaware of the cause of this condition, complain volubly to the management that their walls leak.

The housing problems of Puerto Ricans: slum clearance, redevelopment, and relocation are all closely related to, and are indeed outgrowths of, the city's ineffective planning machinery. New York City has never had a master plan. Housing projects, schools, recreational facilities, transportation, zoning, and all the other aspects of community living have not been laid out with an eye toward integration. Puerto Ricans have suffered particularly from this deficiency. Their assimilation has been immeasurably hampered by the complexities that grow out of poor planning.

If, for example, more middle-income housing were available, Puerto Ricans, as well as other groups, might well be in a position to occupy those decent quarters, vacated by people who are able to pay higher rents in better neighborhoods. Thus, Puerto Ricans might be scattered more evenly throughout the city. Consequently, more housing projects designed to accommodate the low-middle-income groups should be built.

Slum clearance without good planning for neighborhood conservation means nothing. Slums grow faster than others can be removed. Slum demolition by itself is not the answer to blight. As long as poor planning remains the order of the day in New York City, Puerto Ricans, as well as all slum dwellers, will continue to suffer.

---

ceremony, is more common on the island than among Puerto Ricans on the mainland. "Approximately one quarter of Puerto Rico's married couples live without legal bonds," J. Mayone Stycos, Family and Fertility in Puerto Rico (New York: Columbia University Press, 1955), pp. 107-108.

CHAPTER III

THE IMPACT

ON EMPLOYMENT

The majority of Puerto Rican migrants who leave the island because of limited job possibilities enter the economic life of New York City. Lack of skills, language difficulties, and unfamiliarity with New York's complex environment restrict these newcomers to the more menial jobs in various industries. As of mid-1953, there were an estimated 100,000 Puerto Rican men and about 55,000 women in the New York City labor force. (See Table 7.) The overwhelming majority are engaged in manual labor. More than three fourths of the women are operatives, and about two thirds of the men are operatives and service workers.(1) Most of the women classified as operatives run simple machines in the garment industry. Almost forty thousand needle-trade workers, constituting 10 per cent of the total labor force of the industry, are Puerto Rican women. The men do not seem to be concentrated in any one industry. The male operatives hold less skilled jobs in metal trades, electric plating, paper goods, and auto trades. Those in the service occupations are primarily bus boys, kitchen and pantry workers, dishwashers, and laundry workers.

Most of the migrants who come to New York City have no special kind of work in mind but will accept any jobs they can get. They arrive with very little money and must find some source of income immediately.(2) Many obtain jobs through relatives or

1. Jaffe, op. cit., p. 20.
2. Contrary to some ideas, "labor contractors do not bring the Puerto Ricans to New York....91 per cent arrived in New York without any prior arrangement, 6 per cent had a job lined up before arrival by friends in New York, 3 per cent came through labor contract." Nathan Probst and Sophia A. Olmsted, "The Rising Puerto Rican Problem," Bar Bulletin (New York County Lawyers Association), IX (March 1952), p. 10.

TABLE 7

PERCENTAGE DISTRIBUTION OF EMPLOYED PUERTO RICANS IN NEW YORK CITY, 1950

(By Occupation and Sex)

	Male			Female		
	Puerto Rican	Non-white	Total New York City	Puerto Rican	Non-white	Total New York City
Total employed	100.0%	100.0%	100.0%	100.0%	100.0%	100.0%
White collar	17.8	21.5	45.2	12.2	16.1	56.4
Professional, technical, and kindred workers	2.6	3.3	9.9	2.0	5.0	11.2
Managers, officials, and proprietors	5.3	4.9	15.2	1.0	1.1	4.2
Clerical, sales, and kindred	9.9	13.3	20.1	9.2	10.0	41.0
Manual	82.2	78.5	54.8	87.8	83.9	43.6
Craftsmen, foremen, and kindred	11.0	10.5	17.2	1.7	1.3	1.8
Operatives	36.8	25.9	19.2	76.8	31.2	24.5
Private household workers	*	1.7	0.2	1.6	35.5	7.0
Service workers	28.1	24.3	11.3	5.9	13.5	8.7
Laborers, except farm and mine	5.1	14.0	5.6	0.9	0.9	0.5
Farmers and farm laborers	*	0.4	*	*	*	*
Occupation not reported	1.2	1.7	1.3	0.9	1.5	1.1

* Less than one half of 1 per cent.

Source: Based on the 1950 United States Census of Population, Special Report P.E. No. 30, as interpreted in A. J. Jaffe, op. cit., p. 23.

friends or without any outside assistance. It is difficult to determine to what extent they use the facilities of private employment
agencies, but the proportion is probably greater among the newly
arrived migrants than among those familiar with other, and free,
services in the city. The agency fee and incidence of exploitation
have discouraged some, but the need of acquiring a job immediately still draws many to private agencies. An increasing number are using the placement services of the Puerto Rico Commonwealth Office, which runs an employment bureau, and the New
York State Employment Service.

Assisting Puerto Ricans to find jobs is the main activity of the
Commonwealth Office. About 80 per cent of the people who come
to this office are served by the employment section. For the
most part, this bureau handles those applicants who have a poor
knowledge of English and would encounter difficulty using the New
York State Employment Service, while those without language
difficulty are encouraged to use the state agency. Employers
call upon the Commonwealth Office directly to supply them with
Spanish-speaking typists, stenographers, and other clerical help.
The section has also found openings for applicants in which a
knowledge of English is not required. Like other nonprofit agencies, the Commonwealth Office receives clearance orders, i.e.,
notices of job openings, through the New York State Employment
Service.

The New York State Employment Service charges no fee for
its placement service for employers and employees. In terms of
case loads, the impact of the Puerto Rican migration on the State
Employment Service has been heaviest in the needle-trades, industrial, and service offices; but since the service cannot ask
questions pertaining to race or nationality, no statistics are
available.

The language difficulty constitutes the major problem in providing employment services for Puerto Ricans. The problem is
twofold. There is the difficulty of interviewing and communicat-
ing with non-English-speaking job seekers, and then there is the
problem of placing them. Since the interview involves the gathering of detailed and precise information about the applicant's
skills and previous experience, the language barrier makes the
procedure slow and difficult. Some interviewers suspect that
Puerto Rican applicants understand English but are unable to
express themselves or, if they can, prefer not to. Many applicants bring a friend or relative to interpret for them, but this
practice has proved unsatisfactory. Frequently the interpreter
has less command of English than the applicant. Also, the interpreter, in his eagerness to help the applicant, may not give an

accurate description of his skills or a clear interpretation of the interviewer's questions. For these reasons the employment offices prefer an applicant to come without an interpreter. The needle-trades office, in order to handle the increasing number of Spanish-speaking people seeking jobs in the garment industry, gave a refresher course to those interviewers who had studied Spanish in school or college. About 15 of the 150 interviewers at this office speak Spanish, but at times these interviewers are unable to serve all the Spanish-speaking applicants. The bilingual interviewer attempts to conduct the interview in English first, but if this proves unsuccessful, Spanish is used.

Though to some extent it is possible to find employment for non-English-speaking applicants, the large majority of jobs available through the New York State Employment Service require a knowledge of English. In some places—for example, large hotel and restaurant kitchens—the use of English is not necessary for the direction of simple tasks, but the number of such jobs is limited. When the work is more than mere routine, the employer wants only those workers with whom he can communicate, no matter how skilled Spanish-speaking workers may be.

Lack of skills is another formidable barrier to the placement of Puerto Ricans. The migrant is not prepared by his previous training and experience to fit immediately into the complex and highly specialized economy of New York City. Most of these people are unskilled.(3) Those Puerto Ricans who do have some degree of skill are confronted by the difference between Puerto Rican and mainland job standards. For example, a Puerto Rican who may be a good machinist on the island may not possess the skills required for the same sort of task in New York.

A high degree of manual dexterity is commonly found among Puerto Ricans. This has enabled the New York State Employment Service to place many of them in light assembly jobs in the costume jewelry, toy manufacturing, and electric plating industries. Most Puerto Rican women have done household sewing on the island and some have learned to operate simple machines;

---

3. This is not to imply that the Puerto Ricans who migrate are unemployables. As a matter of fact, "of the labor force among the migrants 71 percent had been gainfully employed in Puerto Rico for at least the full 24 month period before coming to New York, and fully 85 percent gave up jobs in Puerto Rico in furtherance of the desire to migrate." Probst and Olmsted, op. cit., p. 10. Also see Clarence Senior, Strangers and Neighbors (New York: Anti-Defamation League, 1952), pp. 107-108, to the effect that migrants were above the average in Puerto Rico in education, occupational rating, and skill.

consequently, many find work in the garment industry, and after
a week or so of training, are able to operate machines. There
are some jobs for which Puerto Ricans are unable to qualify,
not only because of the language difficulty but also because of
their limited knowledge of the city, such as delivery and mes-
senger work. Domestic service is another area which Puerto
Ricans have not entered. The New York State Employment Service a few years ago tried to encourage Puerto Rican women to
accept domestic work by establishing a household-training project. The service brought some 250 girls from Puerto Rico and
placed them in Westchester County homes as domestics.
But they were handicapped by their lack of English and their unfamiliarity with the use of modern household appliances. Most of
them left the job within three weeks and the program was abandoned. An additional reason causing Puerto Rican women to shun
household jobs is the attraction of higher wages in industry.

There is general agreement among officials of the New York
State Employment Service that Puerto Ricans would be integrated
more readily into the employment market of New York City if
they had some preparation on the island. Interviewers recom-
mend that Puerto Ricans who practiced some trade on the island
should bring their tools with them, and those who were licensed
to carry on any business should seek immediate certification in
New York. It is suggested that vocational training on the island
should be expanded, and that the English terminology for industrial processes and tools be taught in the trade schools.

The New York State Employment Service is under the aegis of
the Federal Bureau of Employment Security. One function of the
Bureau is the co-ordination and development of farm placement
programs. There is a shortage of farm labor in various parts
of the United States during the harvesting season. Since 1947,
part of the farm labor force needed on the eastern seaboard has
been secured from Puerto Rico. In 1953, 6,000 migrant laborers
from Puerto Rico entered New York State. The number of Puerto
Rican farm workers on the mainland had increased to 20,000 in
1954 and 1955 and was expected to total almost 40,000 in 1956.(4)
Many of these farm laborers come to the mainland on their own
and travel up and down the coast with the main stream of migratory workers. This supply is supplemented by others brought
from Puerto Rico through a contract program of the Federal
Bureau of Employment Security. A contract covering wages,
hours, and other conditions of employment is drawn up between
the worker and the farmer. The farmer arranges for the trans-

---

4. The New York Times, March 5, 1954, p. 12; September 9, 1955, p. 3.

portation of the workers from the island, the cost of which is deducted from future wages.

Farmers are generally satisfied with Puerto Rican farm laborers. Most of them are family men who are eager to do their work and return to the island. Drinking and other disorderly conduct are not as common among these people as among other migratory workers.

It is difficult to determine how many Puerto Rican contract workers return to the island at the termination of the contract. The director of the Puerto Rico Commonwealth Office in New York thinks that practically all these contract laborers return to the island. Some interviewers in the New York State Employment Service, however, believe that at least half of them come to New York City. The Federal Bureau of Employment Security estimates that 15 per cent remain on the mainland.

Puerto Rican migrants receive higher wages and better their working conditions, when they obtain jobs in New York City (5); but often their wages still fall below minimum levels prescribed by law. Both New York State and the federal government have jurisdiction over wages, hours, and other working conditions in New York City. The United States Wage and Hour Division found that Puerto Rican employees are involved in a majority of the serious violations which come to its attention. Puerto Ricans also make up a substantial portion of the work load of the New York State office. It has been estimated by the office that, in the 1952—1955 period, half of the money collected for workers who had failed to receive the minimum wage, or time and a half for overtime had been collected on behalf of Puerto Rican workers.

Many Puerto Ricans are unaware of their rights under federal and state laws; others, although aware of government regulations, hesitate to report violations for fear of losing their jobs—they do not know that the complainant's name is not made known without his written consent.

There is usually less reliance upon governmental agencies for the protection of workers' rights in areas where unions are strongly entrenched. Unionization is widespread in Puerto Rico, with about 52 per cent of the labor force organized, compared with 25 per cent on the mainland. Unions on the island are loosely organized, and their activities are less extensive than those on

---

5. The median earnings in 1949 of Puerto Ricans and nonwhites in New York City were about the same — $1,700 per person. Jaffe, op. cit., p. 240. The median in 1955 is estimated at $2,400 compared to the over-all city-wide median of $3,780. Interpolated from U.S. Bureau of Labor Statistics reports.

the mainland. In New York City, 30 per cent of the Puerto
Rican workers belong to unions, the same percentage as for the
entire labor force of the city. Some unions, in industries with
large numbers of Puerto Rican workers, have adapted their programs by using Spanish-speaking organizers and interpreters,
printing material in Spanish in union newspapers, providing
counseling services, and holding English classes for the Puerto
Rican membership. One of the more effective approaches has
been made by the International Ladies' Garment Workers' Union.
All information sent out by the union is also printed in Spanish,
and a Spanish-language newspaper, Justicia, is published monthly.
The Shirtmakers Union, Local No. 23, which has more Puerto
Rican members than any other local, has undertaken an extensive
educational program. The audio-visual method of teaching English
is used in the two classes which meet twice a week each semester.
The union accommodates about 150 Puerto Ricans a year in this
program. Attendance of Puerto Rican workers at union meetings
has steadily increased. The election of six Puerto Ricans to the
executive board of the local indicates the extent of Puerto Rican
participation.

It is difficult to determine whether Puerto Ricans are discriminated against by potential employers because there are so few
reported cases. Between 1945 and 1953 only twenty-one cases
were reported to the New York State Commission Against Discrimination. Many other alleged cases of discrimination were
found to be merely misinterpretations of contracts and lack of
understanding of job requirements. There does not seem to be
any evidence that Puerto Ricans have been subject to discrimination in employment. However, despite the lack of reports, some
Puerto Ricans feel they are discriminated against, and this feeling impedes their integration into the community. Dark-skinned
Puerto Ricans encounter the same discrimination as do mainland
Negroes who seek white-collar positions. However, since very
few migrants have qualifications for clerical jobs, the problem
does not often arise.

CHAPTER IV

THE IMPACT

ON WELFARE SERVICES

Throughout the peak years of the postwar Puerto Rican migrations, considerable fear, resentment, and hostility toward the new group were aroused through the widespread circulation of unfounded rumors. These were rooted in the belief that the primary motivation for the migration was the desire of Puerto Ricans to obtain public assistance from the City of New York. Most of these rumors also hinted strongly at a sinister connection between the Puerto Rican influx and the political activities of former Congressman Vito Marcantonio of the American Labor party. According to one widely accepted theory, the "revolving-fund" theory, Marcantonio financed Puerto Ricans' transportation to New York in return for their votes. It was further alleged that he would exert his personal influence to put them on relief. The congressman was supposed to have been repaid from their welfare allotments, and thus enabled to finance the transportation of more and more islanders to New York.

Admittedly, some few Puerto Ricans do make the Department of Welfare their first stop when they reach New York; nevertheless, the opinion held by responsible officials of the department, and also by the Puerto Rico Commonwealth Office, is that most Puerto Ricans do not come with the intention of going on relief but rather to improve their economic status by their own efforts. This opinion prevails in the governmental and nongovernmental agencies throughout the city. Similarly, the authorities give little credence to reports of improper activities by Marcantonio. They contend that Puerto Ricans never received public assistance in such significant amounts—even during the period of Marcantonio's political dominance—as to make credible the existence of an organized machinery for bringing them to New York and putting them on relief. While it is true that Marcantonio exerted a considerable influence within the Department of Welfare prior to

1948, the stringent eligibility requirements for assistance pre-
cluded fraudulent use of the relief rolls for the political purposes
of any individual.

However, the large-scale migration of economically under-
privileged Puerto Ricans, and the rumors that resulted from it,
focused public attention on the internal and external operations
of the Department of Welfare to a greater extent than ever before.
The question has been raised whether needy Puerto Ricans turn
to the department. Many do not for various reasons. First, their
lack of experience with welfare services on the island has not
conditioned them to seek or to expect the degree of governmental
aid New York City offers. Public assistance in Puerto Rico is
granted only in extreme cases of destitution. The cash allowance
is very limited, amounting to about $9.00 a month, and no supple-
mentary assistance is provided to employed persons. Some
Puerto Ricans, assuming that the same conditions prevail in New
York, consider it futile to apply for relief. Second, many are not
even aware of the existence of social-welfare facilities. Third,
many other Puerto Ricans, discouraged by reports that some
applicants for aid have received abrupt or inconsiderate treatment from the department, turn to other community resources,
such as the Catholic Charities, the New York City Mission Society, or the Hudson Guild. Fourth, the Puerto Ricans' strong
sense of pride inhibits some from seeking aid through the Department of Welfare and other community agencies. Even among
those who do turn to the department or to private agencies, there
is a relative reluctance to remain public charges. The Department of Welfare's experience has been that on the whole the
Puerto Rican case load has a higher turnover than that of any
other group.

Department of Welfare figures indicate that the number of
Puerto Ricans on relief varies somewhat from month to month,
and the proportion is directly affected by the business outlook.
Just before the Korean War, in June, 1950, when business conditions were relatively poor, the relief rolls reached a peak of
353,000 persons, with 35,000 Puerto Ricans, or roughly 10 per
cent, receiving public assistance.(1) In February, 1953, a period
of relative prosperity, it was estimated by the department that
about 20,000 Puerto Ricans, or 7.5 per cent of the 267,000 persons on the rolls, were relief recipients. As of March, 1954, a
period of increasing unemployment, the department's estimate
was that about 27,000 Puerto Ricans, or 10 per cent of the entire
case load, a higher proportion than that of any other ethnic group,

---

1. Jaffe, op. cit., p. 47.

were receiving public assistance—to meet varying degrees of
need, from supplementary assistance to full support. In mid-
1955, however, the number of Puerto Ricans on relief was cited
by one source as 72,000 out of an estimated 500,000 in the city.
This accounts for 25 per cent of the over-all total of 287,473 persons on relief, while 37 per cent of them comprise the clients in
home relief and aid to dependent children.(2)

Puerto Ricans on relief come generally from the younger,
more employable group. For the most part, they receive their
assistance under aid to dependent children and home relief. In
the Non-Residence Welfare Center, which provides assistance
for needy eligible persons who have not resided in New York
State for one year, the figures are as follows: 95 per cent of the
case load is Puerto Rican, out of 2,323 cases for December,
1953; 48 per cent were cases of aid to dependent children; 35 per
cent, home relief; 9 per cent, aid to the disabled; 7 per cent, old-
age assistance; and 1 per cent, aid to the blind. The categorical
distribution of cases in other welfare centers differs with the
percentage of Puerto Ricans to the entire case load, but for the
Puerto Rican clientele the same pattern of concentration is
evident.

The need for aid to dependent children among Puerto Ricans
arises primarily because of the parents' youth and consequent
fertility, resulting in their characteristically large families,
and low incomes. In addition, such aid is sometimes sought by
mothers of children whose husbands or consensual partners
have deserted them. The consensual relationship, part of the
mores of Hispanic societies, is among the cultural patterns which
a good many Puerto Ricans in New York retain.

Home relief for the Puerto Rican is necessitated by the peculiar complications of his employment situation.(3) The Puerto
Rican's language and his lack of skills, which limit his job opportunities, often render him incapable of providing for his family. Even if he is not out of work, he may still require assistance
to supplement an insufficient income. Moreover, many Puerto
Ricans, because of the seasonal nature of their employment, are
not eligible for unemployment insurance benefits and may require
public assistance during jobless periods.

The Puerto Rican relief client presents particular and peculiar
problems. When he arrives in New York City his clothing is, at
best, ill adapted to the rigors of the northern climate. Money for
clothing, supplied by the Department of Welfare, is often spent on

2. New York Post, June 8, 1955, p. 4.
3. See Chapter III.

impractical items, the preference for which grows out of Puerto
Rican cultural acceptance. For example, bright-colored gar-
ments, which soil easily, are likely to be chosen instead of dark-
colored and more durable ones. The Puerto Rican's clothing,
often an array of loud, unblending colors, tends to create an unfavorable impression on prospective employers, who are apt to
place a premium on a worker's appearance. Similarly, money
given to buy food is often spent on nonessential and nonnutritious
items. The Puerto Rican continues to eat what he ate on the island, despite the difference in climate and the fact that he is
leading a much more active life. He knows nothing of the nutritional values of food. This is an especially serious matter,
since there is a prevalence of tuberculosis among Puerto Ricans.
   Social investigators and home economists in the Department
of Welfare advise clients on dietary problems and distribute
Spanish-language pamphlets on the subject. The Department of
Health works with the Department of Welfare on the matter of
tuberculosis, certifying cases for care in the home. In such
cases the Department of Welfare grants special dietary allow-
ances and makes other necessary provisions to render aid.(4)

---

4. See Chapter VI.

CHAPTER V

THE IMPACT

ON EDUCATIONAL SERVICES

The Puerto Rican migration to New York City has further complicated a school system already plagued with problems.

In October, 1952, the elementary schools in Manhattan had 24,437 Puerto Rican pupils; Bronx elementary schools had 12,226; and Brooklyn elementary schools had 9,189.(1) In some schools the Puerto Rican enrollment was 50 per cent or more.

The Puerto Rican population and its concentration have been on the increase. For example, in Districts 1, 2, 3, and 4 in Manhattan on the Lower East Side, there was an increase of 1,234 Puerto Ricans in the elementary schools from May to September 1953. Puerto Ricans in the total school enrollment increased from 23 per cent to 27 per cent. In Districts 15 and 16 in the Bronx, Puerto Ricans in 1953-1954 constituted only 19.2 per cent of the elementary school population. Of this number, 25.7 per cent, or 1,222 of 4,875 Puerto Ricans, had been in the New York City school system less than fourteen months, and 587 had been admitted directly from Puerto Rico between September 8 and November 18, 1953. In Districts 25 and 27 in Brooklyn, a significant increase in Puerto Ricans is also noted. As of October, 1953, 826 of a total enrollment of 2,401 Puerto Ricans had been in the city's schools less than fourteen months. Even though many newcomers are replacing pupils who have returned to the island, the growth is very significant.

The increase of New York's Puerto Rican population, and the increasing mobility of Puerto Ricans within the city, have demonstrated a great need for better planning on the part of the Board of Education. Yet the migration has added problems which make planning for building facilities very difficult. It is virtually impossible to foresee future areas of population con-

---

1. The New York Times, February 25, 1953.

centration, and to foresee where the Puerto Ricans are going to settle. The city opened Public School 108 in East Harlem, Manhattan, in 1951. The population of the area grew so rapidly that by 1953 the first and second grades were on a split schedule; lunch had to be served in three shifts; and classroom space was so limited that the introductory classes for Puerto Ricans had to be held in a converted stock room. Another school, less than ten years old, Public School 118, in Manhattan, became so crowded that, as of the 1953-1954 school year, five different sessions were necessary to accommodate all the children.

This crowding came about through changes in the neighborhood, as buildings were converted into rooming houses. The result was an increase in the enrollment of Puerto Ricans to 14 per cent in 1951, 28 per cent in 1952, and 32 per cent in 1953. The 4 per cent increase from 1952 to 1953 is actually larger numerically than it would seem, since the total enrollment of the school had increased.

The influx of Puerto Ricans and their mobility are not the only factors complicating planning, and are not the original cause of the poor planning that prevails in the city's school system.

Teachers also feel the increased pressure, as the numbers in, and the composition of, their classes change almost from day to day. The situation throughout the city is changing so fast that it is extremely hard to avoid some sort of "trouble" area. Nevertheless, teachers strive to move into "better" schools if they can effect a transfer. As a result, in most schools with a significant Puerto Rican student body, the teachers are apt to be young and inexperienced. This turnover constitutes a major administrative problem. Public School 108, in Manhattan, gives an illustration of the influence of Puerto Ricans on this trend. As of 1953, only three out of fifty-two teachers had ten years' experience; twenty-three were on probation, which means less than three years' experience; twelve were substitutes pressed into full-time service; and eight had just completed their probation period.

In one large high school with a large number of Puerto Ricans the turnover has reached even the administrative level, there having been six principals in two years. Again, this problem is not due solely to Puerto Ricans but also to the generally low socioeconomic level of areas of Puerto Rican concentration. The evidence, however, clearly indicates that the problems presented by the Puerto Ricans contribute very substantially to the teacher turnover.

The smooth functioning of the school system is made even more difficult by the mobility of the Puerto Ricans. A number of children who have had some schooling in New York City return to the island and are replaced by an even larger number from the island who have had no schooling. This means that there will continue to be a large proportion who do not speak English and therefore must have special instruction of some kind. For example, in Districts 15 and 16, in the Bronx, 1,593 out of 4,875 Puerto Ricans were non-English-speaking as of the fall of 1953. In Districts 25 and 27, Brooklyn, 1,226 out of 2,401 were non-English-speaking. This ratio is much the same throughout the city.

Not only do Puerto Ricans travel to and from the island, but they are extremely mobile within the city. It is difficult to isolate the turnover rate of Puerto Rican children, but a look at the figures for Public School 108, in Manhattan—approximately 98.8 per cent Puerto Rican—will give some indication. In 1952, with an enrollment of 1,500, there was a turnover of 1,106—674 admitted and 432 discharged. From September through November, 1953, Public School 39, in the Bronx, with 50 per cent Puerto Ricans, had a turnover of 869 in a base school enrollment of 2,000. These were not all Puerto Ricans, but of 62 admissions in November, 1953, 40 were Puerto Ricans. Public School 50, in Brooklyn, reported that in the shortened school month of December, 1953, there was a turnover of 26 in a total Puerto Rican enrollment of approximately 375. Throughout the city, school administrators have reported a very high turnover rate among the newcomers.

The fact that Puerto Ricans move so frequently has an effect on the Bureau of Attendance. Often a child leaves school without proper notification of the authorities. As a result, school records are not changed for some time. Meanwhile, the bureau must make an investigation to determine the family's new address. The situation is further confused by the Hispanic custom of using the mother's name as the child's last name. The child may have registered in the first school using the Puerto Rican form of the name. The family later Anglicizes the name, and when the pupil goes to another school, this form is used. Thus, while the Bureau of Attendance is looking for the child under the old name, he may be attending another school under his new name. These occurrences, though exceptional, happen often enough to make this an administrative problem.

A 1953 survey conducted by a special service committee set up by the Board of Education showed that the attendance record in schools with a large Puerto Rican enrollment is not appreciably lower than in others. Indications are that the attendance records of Puerto Ricans may be 1 or 2 per cent lower than the rest of the school population. The slight difference may possibly be caused by: 1) a lack of knowledge of city laws, procedures, and facilities; 2) the fact that in most cases both parents work and often older children must stay home to care for younger members of the family; 3) the need for older children to work; 4) health problems resulting from poor living conditions; 5) a lack of warm clothing for cold weather. The Bureau of Attendance has created the position of Substitute Auxiliary Attendance Officer, to try to handle the attendance problems of children who are not literate in English and have a different cultural background. As of December, 1953, there were twenty-one of these officers.

The placement of the large number of Puerto Rican children entering New York's educational system constitutes a serious problem because of the lack of a valid test for measuring their intelligence. The Inter-American Test was tried by the Bureau of Educational Research, but it proved unsuccessful with the Spanish-speaking youngsters. Other nonverbal tests, such as Pintner and Davis-Eels, have been experimented with, but all were found lacking because they utilize experiences unfamiliar to Puerto Ricans.

For the most part, Puerto Rican children are placed in schools with pupils of their own age. Since they are slight in build, however, and lack knowledge of English, the Board of Education allows them to be placed one, or possibly two, grade levels below their age group.

If a Puerto Rican is under sixteen years of age, he is put in junior high school. He is not permitted in senior high school unless he has a junior high school diploma from the island, because it is felt that he will not adjust properly if he cannot compete with his fellow students. It has been recommended that new arrivals who are fifteen or sixteen years old should either be admitted directly to senior high school without restriction as to the length of time of previous schooling or reading achievement or that a tenth year be added to junior high school for pupils who are close to sixteen and seventeen years of age.

The lack of education(2) among Puerto Ricans has caused school administrators to develop various techniques for integrating the youngsters and for developing their facility in English, so that they can absorb the regular curriculum.

One of these new developments is the "C" class, or orientation class especially organized for newly admitted Puerto

---

2. The migrant group is considerably superior, however, in comparison to the general population of Puerto Rico. Illiteracy is less than 3 per cent among Puerto Ricans in New York, as compared to 12 per cent in San Juan. The median education among the 10 to 45 year old group in New York is approximately seven years, compared to a little over nine years for the city as a whole.

Ricans to orient them to city life and to give them a working knowledge of English.(3) One class on each grade level
is the ideal, but this is seldom achieved because the Puerto Rican population is constantly changing, their percentage in the
schools varies, and the number of Puerto Ricans in various age
groups differs. The Board of Education prefers to limit these
classes to twenty-five, although the number sometimes runs as
high as forty. In any orientation class, practically all levels of
previous educational experience will be found. Also, since the
Puerto Rican population is in a state of flux, students enter and
leave the class all through the year; thus, at any one time the
teacher will have been teaching different members of the class
for different periods of time.

The size of the "C" classes is further increased because they
are set up according to the Puerto Rican enrollment in June.
Since warm weather and availability of jobs attract Puerto Ricans in greater numbers during the summer, a very large number
of Puerto Rican children apply for admission to the schools in
September. Special planning is necessitated to meet this situation. One possible solution to this problem is for schools with a
high enrollment of Puerto Ricans to leave at least one class in
each grade unfilled to provide room for new admissions in September.

A variation of the orientation class is found in Public School
108, in Manhattan, where 98.8 per cent of the pupils are Puerto
Rican. Students who have been in the school a year or more, and
who, it is felt, have not made sufficient progress, are placed in this
orientation class to speed their adjustment. The school has the
customary introductory class to teach the newest arrivals English and to acquaint them with New York City life. This variation
of the orientation class is felt to be most practicable.

In the junior high schools, the "C" class is supplemented with
transition classes. Joan of Arc Junior High School has a series
of twelve class levels which are called "vestibule classes," or
"V" classes. The "V" classes are organized on skill levels
from V-1 to V-12, with the children gradually progressing up
the ladder. The V-1 class is comparable to a "C" class, since
the new arrivals are placed there and the teaching is essentially
the same. There is no set pace for this program; students move
up when they are ready. Many children, for instance, are illit-
erates in both languages, and will have to remain in V-1 for some

---

3. It is estimated that half of the Puerto Rican children in the public
   primary schools need language training, in addition to all the other
   fundamentals of learning.

time. Some already know English and can progress as soon as
they can be encouraged to use it. Still others will progress
slowly because of the security they feel in speaking Spanish. In
Public School 50, Brooklyn, another junior high school, just one
transition class is used. After a child has progressed somewhat
in the "C" class, he is moved to the transition class, which has
special curriculums to help in the integration of the children.
The program includes government (city, state, and national) and
group guidance, along with language and other basic subjects.
The group guidance sessions are conducted in Spanish, which is
permissible because it is not a subject-matter class.

Another technique in helping Puerto Rican children adjust to
the city is that of taking them from their regular classes period-
ically, for one or two hours of instruction, by a special teacher
assigned to the school, to assist in the program for the Puerto
Ricans. This technique may be used exclusively, or it may supplement the orientation classes. Where the technique is used
exclusively, the emphasis may be on English or on orientation to
the city. Usually these subjects are combined, so that English is
taught through the discussion of city life. Where the technique is
used as a supplement to the orientation class, it serves as a substitute for the transition class.

Using the philosophy of letting one child help and teach another, some schools utilize the "buddy system." In this technique,
a Puerto Rican youngster who has been in the city long enough to
have made a substantial adjustment is assigned to help a newcomer. This is merely a formalization of a system already prevailing. Whether assigned for that purpose or not, the Puerto
Rican child usually tries to help his neighbor, who is experienc-
ing the same problems he had faced earlier. The "buddy system" is also used alone to implement or supplement the "C"
classes or special lessons.

In its attempt to speed and smooth the adjustment of Puerto
Rican children, the Board of Education assigns special teachers,
called Substitute Auxiliary Teachers (SAT), to schools having a
significant Puerto Rican enrollment. These SATs are of Spanish-
American background and have all the other qualifications for
teaching, but cannot pass the speech test required for the regular
license. The exact duties of an SAT are left to the principal of the
assigned school to determine, although it is understood that a
substantial portion of the time will be given to liaison between
the school and the child, and between the school and the parents.
At James Otis Junior High School the SAT teaches the "C" class,
and at Public School 141, in Brooklyn, he spends all his time as
a community co-ordinator. At Public School 108, in Manhattan,

the SAT spends part of his time working on the introductory program and the rest on parent and community problems. Even when the SAT is assigned to the teaching phase of the program, parents of Puerto Rican pupils and members of the community will come to him for guidance. As of mid-1953, only twenty of these teachers had been appointed. Considering the influx of Puerto Ricans, this is not a sufficient number. The main reason for the small number is that the SATs cannot obtain regular licenses because of their accent, regardless of how well they know English. Since it is almost impossible to lose an accent completely, this regulation gives the SAT only temporary status. Because of the high demand for professionals in Puerto Rico, there is little incentive for these people to come to New York for SAT positions.

Schools with large Puerto Rican enrollments receive additional teaching help from the Board of Education. These teachers, who are of the group called OTP (Other Teaching Position), perform the same function as the SATs but hold a regular license. They are assigned because of special skills in languages and in handling non-English-speaking groups.

Two co-ordinators for the Puerto Rican program, one for the elementary schools and one for the junior high schools, have been appointed. Their task is to provide central direction and advice for schools with a large number of Puerto Ricans. The work has been purely of a staff nature in that it has consisted of advice and suggestions. Because the co-ordinators work out of the central office, however, their recommendations carry considerable weight. Any assistance in this area is helpful, and the work of these co-ordinators has certainly been of value. They have collected information from those teaching Puerto Ricans and have disseminated this information throughout the school system. So far as they provide a vehicle for the exchange of information and the establishment of an awareness of the problems and efforts to solve them, the co-ordinators fulfill their purpose. Knowingly or unknowingly, however, they seem to give the impression to some school staffs that the communications they issue provide the only answers. Passive acceptance of the information supplied by their officials may result from a lack of strong leadership in some schools, since certainly other schools have sought their own answers in the light of their own experience, along with the experience of others.

Since most Puerto Ricans are Roman Catholics, parochial schools have also felt the impact of the migration. The Archdiocese of New York has established one school exclusively for Puerto Ricans, Commander Shea School, annex to St. Cecilia's School, in East Harlem. This school has 840 students and attempts to pro-

vide for the emotional and economic lacks which have developed
with the migration to the mainland. Some Puerto Ricans prefer
to have their children in parochial schools, because the religious
bond is a tie to the island culture.

Commander Shea School has two classes for newcomers. In
the upper grades, they are placed with a teacher who is a graduate of the University of Puerto Rico and thus understands the
environmental background of her pupils. She works with them
individually for one year, and then they are placed in their regular class level. First-grade children with no knowledge of English are put in a special class with the same type of teacher.
After one year of learning the language, and of training in the
·school's methods of study, they are ready to start the regular
first-grade work. These youngsters thus spend two years in the
first grade.

Since parochial schools are private, they can be more selec-
tive in their student body. They do not accept new entrants in
the latter part of a term, but if the pupil reapplies at the start of
a new term, he will be admitted. These schools require evidence
of church membership, usually a baptismal certificate.

The average class size at Commander Shea School is large,
forty-five to fifty pupils. But the orientation classes never have
more than thirty. The authorities feel that the stricter discipline
in parochial schools permits the larger classes to be effectively
handled. The greater respect for the sister-teacher also makes
truancy less of a problem.

Before students graduate from Commander Shea School, they
are given an intelligence test. Most of the boys go to Chelsea
Vocational High School after graduation, but some attend other
schools. A large number of the girls enroll at Cathedral High
School, where they are given a special program, including a
double period of English daily in place of the required foreign
language.

In both public and parochial schools the question of curriculum is one of great concern. Much study has been done on this
problem but few obvious changes have taken place. There is
greater concentration on English and remedial speech, a large
proportion of class time being given to language improvement.
There is greater emphasis on social studies, and at times the
English and social studies instructions are merged to form one
core program. Less obvious changes have come about in regular class programs. The courses have been modified by teachers to accommodate members of the class who do not have the
educational background to follow the regular pace.

Teachers have found that in classes with a large proportion

of Puerto Ricans, changes must be made in the level of instruction because of the variation in educational experience and the difference in ages. In adjusting programs to meet the needs of Puerto Rican students, teachers have had to adopt new teaching devices. Experiential methods are utilized extensively. Everyday experiences of the children are used for class discussion purposes. Charts made by teachers on these discussions replace ordinary textbooks. Trips about the city are used as tools. These tours perform a dual function: they familiarize students with the city and provide interesting subjects for class discussion. Visual aids are utilized as part of the modern teaching methods, because the Puerto Ricans may be familiar with an article or action but not familiar with the English word for it.

Textbooks suitable for Puerto Rican pupils are difficult to obtain. The books must deal with material appropriate to their social maturity and yet use simple English. Some educators also feel that it is necessary to get books without grade markings, because such markings often cause feelings of inferiority in children. This, however, appears to be leaning over backward in trying to adapt the schools to Puerto Ricans. A teacher with any kind of rapport with his class could explain this easily. The Board of Education has given extra allotments for textbooks and materials to schools with large Puerto Rican enrollments.

Language is the key factor in the difficulties involved in the adjustment and education of Puerto Rican youths. It is this which necessitates special instruction and materials for these pupils. Practically every phase of the program is designed to get Puerto Rican children to learn and use English. Teaching them the language is easier than getting them to use it in their everyday contacts, because they tend to live in areas which are predominantly Hispanic. These children study, play, and live with other Puerto Ricans, with whom they converse in Spanish. Most of the youngsters will use English only when absolutely necessary. Schools try to promote the speaking of English by mixing Puerto Rican students with other students in assembly, shop, and gym programs, but generally this has not been very effective.

Puerto Rican children, when first entering New York schools, tend to be very shy, because of their unfamiliarity with the city. Also they have a timidity toward school authorities, acquired on the island, where discipline is much stricter. Once the extreme shyness disappears, they are quite volatile. This does not constitute a problem in itself, but there is danger that they will take advantage of their new-found freedom.

The Board of Education considers the adjustment of the children at least as important as teaching them a few subject-matter

courses. This is one of the reasons for the "C" classes. It is
felt that these give the children a chance to adapt themselves
gradually to a completely strange environment. They obtain a
feeling of security which they would not get if forced to compete
immediately with native New Yorkers. Some Puerto Ricans, on
the other hand, contend that they are discriminated against because their children are placed in separate classes. It appears
that the children themselves do not hold this view. They seem
relieved to be among people with whom they feel at home.

In connection with the adjustment problem, some educators
follow the philosophy that the family, not the child, is the education unit. Treating the family as a unit helps eliminate conflicts
between the old Puerto Rican culture and the new mainland culture.

School officials were stunned by the suddenness of the Puerto
Rican impact. It meant that they had to meet all the children's
needs, not only to educate them but to safeguard their nutrition,
security, and mental health. A large number of the children are
seriously disturbed in moving from the island to the mainland.
Many of their problems arise from the conditions which the
youngsters face in New York—poor housing, health, and sanitary
conditions in the home. The Bureau of Child Guidance, which
works with disturbed children, consists of 23 units, each having
one psychiatrist, four psychologists, and four social workers.
Two units work with mentally retarded children, which leaves
21 to work with other child guidance problems of the schools.
Only about one sixth of the schools can be covered, and even in
these schools only the most serious cases can be treated.

The bureau must work very closely with teachers to help in
mental hygiene development. Consultation with teachers is necessary to find cases of emotional maladjustment. The social
worker must get to know the children and help the teacher to
know them as individuals, thus bringing the teachers and the
children together. Many teachers seriously question the amount
of progress they are making with Puerto Rican pupils, because
the students tend to grow restless and undisciplined. Feelings of
frustration often appear among teachers. This is sometimes tied
in with the relative inexperience of teachers in schools with a
high Puerto Rican enrollment. One school had what was termed
a crisis in January, 1954. Apparently due to the Christmas va-
cation and a heavy snowfall, the pupils became completely uncon-
trollable. A conference between teachers and social workers was
necessary to convince teachers that the outbreak was not due to
a deficiency in their work. The social worker responsible for
this school must cover ten other schools, and she can devote

only one full day a week to this school. It is obvious that a full-
time social worker is needed for this school, and for many others
as well. A case worker in a Puerto Rican section, who was able
to spend four days a week in the school, remarked that it needed
15 full-time workers. He averages 40 cases, which are only the
most serious ones, and only 20 or 30 of these can receive the intensive treatment they need.

One cause of disturbance among Puerto Ricans is the color problem. Often some members of one family are darker than others, and
the children get confused ideas. This stems from what they see of
discrimination. Another difficulty is that of the second generation:
the conflict between the Hispanic culture of the parents and the
new American culture which the children are absorbing. Parental discipline is often upset when the mother is employed and the
father cannot find work, since the Puerto Rican culture is predominantly patriarchal. The language barrier works its hardship here as elsewhere. It is reported that the diagnostic difficulties of the Children's Court and Family Court have been tri-
pled by this cause. The court began group diagnosis to overcome the language difficulties.

Health education is a great need of Puerto Ricans, and the
basic principles of hygiene and sanitation are taught to newcomers in the schools. Malnutrition is widespread among the
children. The school tries to ensure at least one good meal a
day through the school lunch program. The meal consists of a
hot dish (soup), a sandwich, dessert, and milk. A large percentage of Puerto Ricans participate in this program and most of
them receive it free, since any family earning less than a prescribed amount for its particular size is entitled to have its
children receive free lunches. In Puerto Rico all elementary
schools not on a split-session program provide free lunches.
In New York the children have to accustom themselves to different and new foods served in the lunches. Most of them do not like
any kind of fish. Since the city does not serve meat because of
Jewish dietary laws forbidding meat and milk at the same meal,
the Puerto Ricans sometimes refuse to eat the lunch. The Bureau of School Lunches points out that since the Puerto Ricans
are only one segment receiving school lunches, and since the
meals are prepared in a central kitchen, menus cannot be designed especially for them. Spanish-speaking personnel are employed at lunchroom counters, and signs about food and eating
habits are posted in both English and Spanish.

The lunch period, along with gym, assemblies, manual training
classes, etc., give the Puerto Ricans an opportunity to mingle
with other students, which they hesitate to do when they first enter

school. After school hours, of course, the type of neighborhood
in which they live determines their friends. If it is a Puerto Rican neighborhood, they are apt to stick together; if the Puerto
Ricans are in a minority, they are forced to mingle with others.
Extracurricular activities in secondary schools help draw Puerto
Ricans out, but unfortunately many students work after school and
this leaves them little time for these programs.

Puerto Ricans will become better adjusted if they enter a vocational field for which they are fitted and which they like. Junior high schools provide some vocational guidance. The counselors, however, usually have meager information about the individual students, so they try not to interfere with proposed vocational plans unless it is obvious that the choice is extremely
poor. If the students have no plans, they are generally advised
to attend a vocational high school. After a year of general training, they can choose the specialized training they prefer.

With the increase of Puerto Ricans in the schools, the Board
of Education has urged teachers to take training to improve their
understanding and teaching of these youngsters, and courses in
Spanish have also been offered. The response, however, has not
been as great as desired, since many teachers do not want as-
signment to schools with large Puerto Rican enrollments.

The migration to New York has resulted in a large increase in
enrollment of adult education classes, particularly in the English
classes for non-English-speaking persons. In the elementary
grades of the adult education classes it is assumed that the students may be illiterate in both Spanish and English, and therefore
Spanish is not used. Authorities feel that even those who have had
a little English will profit more by strengthening their foundation
and by using English from the start. It has been noted that
Puerto Ricans tend to remain in the schools for shorter periods
of time than other students. Quite often they remain only long
enough to learn sufficient English to get along in their jobs.

The place of private agencies in adult education is an important one. Many Puerto Ricans prefer to attend classes at settlement houses, churches, or with their fellow employees at union
halls, because of the informality of the programs and their familiarity with the other students. The system of formal examinations for diplomas is valuable in the adult education scheme,
because it sets standards for instruction while allowing the
people to choose their schools. It also permits them to proceed
at their own pace and to spend a minimum number of years in
school.

New York's public library system also plays its part in the education of both adults and children. Libraries in areas with large

Puerto Rican populations have geared their activities and adapted their services to help the newcomers. Classes from the public schools visit the libraries, where the services are explained and the pupils registered. The most difficult problem of the libraries is to get the Puerto Ricans to use them. Many, of course, are illiterate, but even those who could use libraries take little advantage of their services. Sometimes this is due to ignorance of the services the libraries provide; other times it is because the Puerto Ricans think there is a charge for library services. The number of Spanish books available at libraries is severely limited, and this also curtails the effectiveness of the library service. An example of what a fresh supply of books can do is presented by the Woodstock Branch Library, where the Spanish circulation doubled when Spanish books were purchased with a special allotment from the city.

The city's educational system, generally speaking, has not been successful in getting Puerto Rican parents to participate actively in school life and affairs. The need is not merely to get parents to attend social gatherings of the parents' associations, but to get them to participate in other activities. Some interesting experiments have been tried. At Benjamin Franklin High School, a separate parents' association was formed for the Puerto Ricans in the belief that more could be accomplished this way. The initial response was very good, but when the original leaders left, the group disintegrated and the idea was abandoned. This innovation, while appearing to involve discrimination, actually showed an understanding of how to help these new people help themselves. At Public School 11, in Manhattan, an information service was set up, not exclusively for Puerto Ricans, but used chiefly by them. This had considerable success.

The Parents' Association at Public School 108, in Manhattan, has an exceptionally active record. Through the influence of this group, the school, located in East Harlem, with a 98.8 per cent Puerto Rican enrollment, was opened in the summer of 1953. When funds for the summer of 1954 were not forthcoming, the association raised the money itself. The influence of this type of activity on the school community is evident. The school has become the center of community activities of many forms. It has close ties with such organizations as the Council of Spanish-American Organizations and the East Harlem Council for Community Planning. There is great respect for the school among parents and pupils alike, and there is an extremely small amount of vandalism, such as broken windows, stealing, etc.

Many schools use the children both to attract the parents to school activities and to encourage them to perform useful com-

munity services themselves. The Borrinquen Club at Benjamin
Franklin High School is an excellent example. Members of the
club act as interpreters for the mobile tuberculosis X-ray
trucks and also publicize the services offered by these units.
Club members co-operated with the Sanitation Department in a
clean-up campaign in the East Harlem area. There seems to be
much promise in this type of activity, which helps children to
become useful members of the community.

Some schools are further utilized for community purposes as
all-day neighborhood schools. In these schools, clubs and other
supervised activities are provided for children after school
hours. Only children whose parents are working are eligible.
These schools provide an important service in keeping children
off the streets and occupied. Unfortunately, existing facilities
are not adequate to meet the needs. At Public School 141,
Brooklyn, there is not enough equipment or personnel to handle
the needs of those who are enrolled. At Public School 108, Manhattan, 100 per cent of the school population is enrolled and
there is a long waiting list.

No co-ordinated program exists for the education of Puerto
Ricans in New York and it is not clear that there should be one.
But since any individual program depends on the Board of Education for support, financial or otherwise, close supervision is
necessary to ensure that the children get the best education possible for the money available. The Ford Foundation has made a
grant for studying the educational program for non-English-
speaking children. It is hoped that this study will provide some
answers, so that an integrated program can be developed for the
education of Puerto Ricans. However, this study, begun in the
fall of 1953, will not be completed for several years. In the interim, the Board of Education is deferring most new action.
This means that, for the time being, the Puerto Ricans must continue their schooling under the present inadequate system.

CHAPTER VI

THE IMPACT ON HEALTH AND HOSPITAL SERVICES

The Puerto Rican migrant faces health problems similar to those of almost every group coming into New York City from a foreign land. However, his cultural background and status as an American citizen create other health situations which are unique to his group. As an American citizen, he is not subject to federal immigration laws. In the opinion of some authorities, there is definite need for a strict physical examination of all Puerto Ricans entering the mainland. On the other hand, there is a strong view held by many that forcing him to submit to such examination would be contrary to the Constitution.

Low economic conditions, inadequate housing and sanitary facilities, and poor diet standards found on the island affect the Puerto Rican's health. Since 1940, the health and sanitary conditions on the island have greatly improved, but still are not comparable to mainland standards. There are various cultural differences, aside from the language barrier, that impede the Puerto Rican's integration into the mainland population. Among these, in the field of health, are climatic change, clothing differences, dietary and sanitary habits, and different familial living patterns.

Puerto Rico's climate is temperate, averaging 78° F all year round. Therefore the clothing needs on the island are much less complex than in New York—where there are extreme changes from torrid to zero weather. The island clothing is light in weight and small in quantity. When the Puerto Rican migrates to New York, he is often unaware of the sharp difference in temperature and seasonal changes. It is not at all unusual for many of the migrants to wear summer clothing in bitter cold weather.

Customs brought from the island and a lack of familiarity with modern sanitation facilities and mechanical appliances cause

45

many Puerto Ricans to continue some primitive habits which affect their own health and the sanitation of the community. Many
use such appliances as gas stoves, electric and kerosene heaters,
and gas refrigerators, but often do not know that they are dan-
gerous when not properly used and cared for. Their ignorance
in these matters has often caused some serious accidents. In
several cases Puerto Ricans have lost their lives, sometimes a
whole family has been killed. Many Puerto Ricans do not report
violations to the Department of Health because of their inability
to communicate in English. Also they fear the loss of their living
quarters if they cause trouble for the landlord.

Overcrowded and unsanitary living conditions lead to additional health problems, such as rat infestation and the spread of disease. The new migrants are at the lowest socio-economic level
and tend to settle in already depressed housing areas.(1) The
apartments in these localities are susceptible to rodent infestation due to many openings or breaks in pipes or walls. In addition, the doubling and tripling up of families into one apartment, often just one room, places an increased strain on garbage disposal facilities. Unhygienic methods of disposal are
common, such as leaving garbage in inadequate containers in
rooms and hallways, or throwing it down air shafts or out of
windows. This is partly due to habits which the migrant practiced in rural island communities, where garbage was thrown
out the window to be eaten by farmyard animals.

The New York City Department of Health has distributed information on the prevention of rat bites to all groups living in
depressed areas, because an average of 500 cases each year
were reported to the department from 1947 to 1953. Since a high
percentage of these cases were in Puerto Rican families, some
of the leaflets were printed in Spanish.

Each spring the New York City Department of Sanitation em-
barks on a full-scale campaign to inform the people in congested
areas of the importance of following good sanitation methods.
The department sends floats and sound trucks into these neighborhoods. In Puerto Rican sections the information is broad-
cast in Spanish. Spanish translations of sanitation regulations
are also distributed.

Susceptibility to disease is increased by poor, overcrowded
housing conditions and deficient knowledge regarding health
care and sanitation practices. These problems exist in an acute
manner for the Puerto Ricans in New York. Between 1949 and
1951 there were 474 reported cases of tuberculosis per 100,000

---

1. See Chapter II.

Puerto Rican residents.(2) The Puerto Ricans, estimated at about 5 per cent of the city's population, accounted for 10 per cent of all newly reported cases of tuberculosis in 1952. In the same year, the Puerto Ricans comprised 9 per cent of the roster, which contained 18,286 active cases.(3) Of the total tuberculosis cases reported during the first ten months of 1953, 10 per cent were Puerto Ricans.

Opinions differ regarding the Puerto Ricans' contraction of tuberculosis. Some medical officials believe that a number of Puerto Ricans come to New York City with advanced stages of the disease. These seek medical attention immediately or shortly after their arrival. Others feel that the migrants, living in conditions of poverty, overcrowding, and poor sanitary facilities, contract the disease after being in the city for a short time. The evidence is inconclusive. Some tuberculosis is a type of disease which takes time to incubate; some individuals might retain it in its latent stages while living on the island, where the climate is warm and the living tempo slow. When these Puerto Ricans migrate to New York, they are thrown into an increased work tempo, requiring a substantial diet, which they fail to get. This, plus congested living quarters, tends to lower their resistance to tuberculosis.

There are several heavily populated Puerto Rican districts in the city where tuberculosis is very prevalent. These districts are the Navy Yard area in Brooklyn and the East Harlem and Upper East River Drive areas in Manhattan. Figures for the East Harlem area show that the tuberculosis rate in this district is approximately one and one-half times that of the city's overall rate. The Puerto Rican population, which lives in one third of the area, contributes more than one half of the cases for the entire district. (See Table 8.)

Puerto Ricans are actively attending city clinics for chest X-rays. There is a three-way relationship between the New York City Department of Health, the New York Tuberculosis and Health Association, and the neighborhood organizations. These groups encourage people to have chest X-rays and to seek treatment if necessary. This over-all approach is used throughout the city.

The existence of a language handicap necessitates a different approach in dealing with many Puerto Ricans. One committee, the Washington Heights District Committee, set up a program using Puerto Rican volunteers to go into the community to dis-

2. Jaffe, op. cit., p. 42.
3. Ibid.

seminate printed information in Spanish; to bring the people to
the clinics for X-rays; and to act as interpreters. The use of
volunteers who are familiar with Puerto Rico has proved extremely effective in this area.

TABLE 8

REPORTED CASES OF TUBERCULOSIS
IN EAST HARLEM AREA, 1952

Cases		District Population (Approximate)
Foreign-born and native white	144	120,000
Nonwhite	94	30,000
Puerto Rican	271	70,000
Total	510	220,000

Source: Brooklyn Council for Social Planning, Report of Workshop Con-
         ference on Puerto Ricans (October, 1953), and East Harlem
         Health Center figures.

     The Department of Health and the Tuberculosis and Health
Association both distribute information in Spanish on the prevention of tuberculosis. While it is often not difficult to per-
suade Puerto Ricans to go to the clinics for X-rays and minor treatment, the greatest problem lies in long-term hos-
pitalization. When tuberculosis is contagious and requires extensive treatment, patients have to be isolated from family,
friends, and the immediate community. They face the problems of loss of earning power, depletion of savings, and the
possibility of the family's requiring financial assistance for
some time. These factors are true for all tuberculosis patients. The Puerto Rican cultural background and family ties
make it even more difficult for the migrants to adjust to
long-term hospital treatment. Thus a number of Puerto Rican patients tend to check out of tuberculosis wards before
treatment has been completed. In such cases, provision
must be made for home treatment and out-patient care.
Some Puerto Ricans, known to have tuberculosis, refuse to
enter hospitals or submit to any treatment. They present an

extremely serious problem, for they endanger the health of their families.(4)

Many differences exist in relation to skills, interests, and values involved in rehabilitating tubercular patients. They appear among Puerto Ricans as among other groups in New York. There are two additional problems—language difficulties and lack of skill—in the rehabilitation of this group. When patients leave the hospitals, they are eligible for assistance from the New York State Division of Vocational Rehabilitation, which aims at training and placing its clients. The TB-Cardiac Unit of the division has had an increasing number of Puerto Ricans seeking its services. Since tuberculosis patients are not eligible for aid from the state agency until discharged from the hospital, the New York Tuberculosis and Health Association set up a rehabilitation division in June, 1943. This offers long-term counseling services to patients, between sixteen and forty-five, who are still under hospital care, and also to those who have been discharged. Attempts have been made to deal with the language and adjustment problems of Puerto Ricans by teaching them English in the hospitals and providing referral service in aftercare treatment. Direct advisory service to health workers and hospital staffs is also given. The community itself does not provide sufficient rehabilitation services for tuberculosis patients.

Malnutrition is a strong influencing factor in lowering resistance to disease. Since many Puerto Ricans tend to retain the same dietary patterns formed on the island, they often exist on a diet insufficient for the climate and tempo of life in New York City. For example, because of a lack of green vegetables on the island and occasional dangers of eating raw vegetables there, they continue to shun them in New York. The Health Department's nutrition clinics are particularly aware of this matter and attempt to remedy it. Instead of trying to make complete changes in the Puerto Ricans' eating habits, the emphasis is placed on strengthening their present diet with proper and essential additions. The clinics distribute literature in both English and Spanish. Reliance on illustrative material is even more successful because some of the migrants are not literate in either language. Food models, multicolored pictures, and bar charts are used to show the advantages of eating more health-giving foods. The use of these charts has been very effective in encouraging Puerto Ricans to drink more citrus juices. The

---

4. The increased use and effectiveness of new drugs (streptomycin, isoniazid, and others) have made out-patient care the normal rather than the exceptional mode of treatment. See Building Better Government (Second Annual Report of the Mayor, 1955), pp. 55 and 57.

comparative vitamin contents are illustrated by showing the bar
for orange juice much larger than bars for other juices.

Puerto Rican migrants come from a tropical area where parasitic diseases are prevalent, and thus they add to the case load of
tropical diseases in New York. The two principal ones found among
Puerto Ricans are schistosomiasis and amoebiasis. In 1952, there
were 166 cases of schistosomiasis reported for persons coming
from the island.(5) Schistosomiasis is the less serious of the two
diseases because it is not directly transmittible and is not con-
tractible in New York.(6) Its harm is restricted to the person affected; in its advanced stages it causes chronic tiredness, loss of
weight, and eventual liver damage, which limits the individual's
working capacity. If left untreated, the patient can become a
chronic invalid and in later years a public charge.

The amoebiasis patients present a more serious health problem,
for this parasitic disease is transmitted through contaminated "foods,
fluids, fingers, and flies." In a 1950 study of the examination of 709
food handlers; it was found that there were 250 from tropical American countries, of these 140, or 56 per cent, either had amoebiasis
or were carriers.(7) However, the city's Health Department does
not feel that parasitic diseases are of great consequence in New
York, and when detected, they are easily treated and cured.

New York City maintains two tropical disease clinics, established during World War II, which provide for examinations and
give treatment for diagnosed cases.

Puerto Rican children seem especially prone to asthma and
other respiratory diseases. They also tend to have poor teeth.
The State of New York has aided the city by supplying funds for
dental work among children.

Although there is a popular impression that venereal diseases
are widespread among Puerto Ricans, there are no available data
by which this group can be compared with the total city population.
Alcoholism does not constitute a health problem. Only a minute
number of cases of this type have been found by the city's doctors
and hospital staffs. Employers also have noted a definite absence
of drunkenness among Puerto Ricans as compared with other low-
income groups.

It is suspected that there is a greater rate of emotional maladjustment and mental disturbance among Puerto Ricans than has
been reported. Some use city and state psychiatric services, but

5. Workshop Conference on Puerto Ricans (Brooklyn Council for Social
   Planning Report, October, 1953), p. 11.
6. Jaffe, op. cit., p. 44.
7. Workshop Conference on Puerto Ricans, op. cit., p. 8.

the majority are unfamiliar with the entire concept of mental hygiene. Since mental hygiene is a fairly new concept to most Puerto Ricans, they are generally unaware of the need for psychiatric help. Not understanding these concepts, there is a fear of seeking psychotherapy. Although Puerto Ricans are readily availing themselves of other medical services in the city, they seldom use psychiatric services.

Many feel insecure in their new environment. Overcrowded living quarters, poor socioeconomic conditions, and a feeling of nonintegration with the rest of the community contribute to this sense of insecurity. The language barrier and the difference in mores make it even more difficult for Puerto Ricans to adjust to the new environment. Coming into a community where people are more color-conscious than on the island tends to make some Puerto Ricans sense and fear discrimination. This results in their maintaining their island culture for fear that with integration they might be confused with other minorities.

American-born children of first-generation Puerto Ricans are particularly affected by environment and adjustment difficulties. They learn the language and mainland patterns of living more easily than their parents. The parents thus tend to depend on the children and lose their status in the home. This leads to strained relations in the household, because of conflict between the first and second generations. A form of spiritualism is practiced by some Puerto Ricans. While it may offer temporary compensation to the individual seeking emotional relief, it is doubtless the cause of much anxiety and insecurity among children.

It is difficult to evaluate the health of the city's population, and evaluating one single group is even more complicated. Health and hospital records of diseases cannot be accepted as complete because many diseases are treated privately and are not always reported. The crude death rate from 1949 to 1951 shows that the mortality rate among Puerto Ricans in New York City was lower than for whites and nonwhites: whites, 10.0 per thousand; nonwhites, 9.6 per thousand; Puerto Ricans 4.2 per thousand.(8) The rate is low because the Puerto Rican population contains a smaller percentage of older people, not because the group is healthier. Most of the deaths in the city occur among persons 45 years and older. Since the majority of Puerto Ricans are under this age, the crude death rate does not show a true picture. It is better to compare age-specific rates than crude or even age-adjusted rates. In comparing age-specific rates, it is found that the Puerto Rican death rate for those suffering from the young-age diseases, i.e., infectious

8. Jaffe, op. cit., p. 35.

and respiratory diseases, is almost three times that of the same age group in the rest of the population. The group also suffers from a higher ratio of deaths associated with pregnancy. This is caused by the higher birth rate combined with a low standard of living and lack of understanding of prenatal care. A strong attempt is being made by the Department of Health to encourage pregnant women and young mothers to use the city's prenatal clinics. Several doctors have reported that young Puerto Rican mothers are beginning to use these facilities, and the clinics have noted a marked rise in Puerto Rican clientele.

The New York City Department of Health carries on its work in district health centers servicing 352 areas of the city. It has taken definite steps to serve the increasing number of Puerto Rican patients. The language barrier is the greatest handicap facing doctors, nurses, and other workers dealing with Puerto Ricans in the health centers and clinics. Many Spanish-speaking patients use fellow patients or relatives as interpreters, but in most cases this has been found unsatisfactory.

In the period following World War II, New Yorkers became more conscious of preventive medical care and hospital care, which caused the increased use of available hospital facilities. Overcrowding resulted, and in 1948, the over-all average occupancy of the city's general hospitals reached 102.4 per cent. In 1952, the average occupancy was 95 per cent, and in 1955 it was 87 per cent.(9) The ideal standard of maximum occupancy is 85 per cent. During these years the city started a major hospital construction program, increasing the number of hospital beds, and at the same time building new hospitals and replacing old ones.

The Department of Hospitals has no over-all program for serving any one group in the city. However, it does face particular difficulties in dealing with the large number of the city's newest migrants. Since Puerto Ricans tend to settle in specific areas and use the city's hospitals there, the department has tackled the problems of this new group on a hospital-by-hospital basis. One major problem has been caused by an increase in the number of patients who cannot speak or understand English. Communication between patients and staff becomes difficult. Hospital staffs are badly curtailed. Nurses are especially needed. The Hospital Department tries to assign Spanish-speaking personnel to hospitals where the percentage of Spanish-speaking patients is high. In September, 1953, in conjunction with the Board of Education, a program was instituted to teach the Spanish language and cultural background to hospital staffs. Though 2,000 members volunteered for this special

9. Annual Report (Department of Hospitals, City of New York, 1952),
   p. 11; Building Better Government, op. cit., p. 59.

instruction, only four classes were given and enrollment was
limited, making it possible for only 160 staff members to attend.
Further effort is being made to alleviate the language problem in
some hospitals by recruiting Puerto Rican women as volunteer interpreters. These also help at bedsides in feeding and patient care.
This program, begun in 1952, is conducted on a small scale. Increased numbers of Puerto Ricans are being employed on the
custodial and attendant levels in hospitals, and they are occasionally used as interpreters.

Metropolitan Hospital on Welfare Island has a large percentage of Puerto Ricans using its facilities. In 1952, 62 per cent of
the tuberculosis ward patients were Puerto Ricans, and in January, 1953, this figure had risen to 65 per cent. To cope with the
high percentage of Spanish-speaking people, the hospital's signs
and directions are printed in both Spanish and English. Although
the institution has a limited number of Spanish-speaking nurses,
it was successful in obtaining two Spanish-speaking social workers,
one recruited from the island. Metropolitan Hospital has also
worked out a program with the Board of Education to teach civics
and English two days a week to Spanish-speaking tuberculosis patients, as part of their rehabilitation. This program, however, has
not been entirely effective because the teacher employed spoke and
understood English only and patients showed a lack of enthusiasm
in participating.

Many questions arise about the material effect of the Puerto
Ricans on the city's hospital services. Because of their low economic level, the migrants tend to make greater use of the city's hospitals
than of voluntary and private ones. Those hospitals which have
noted an increased number of Puerto Ricans using hospital facilities and out-patient clinics are Bellevue Hospital Center, Lincoln,
Metropolitan, Welfare Island Dispensary, Harlem Hospital, Mt.
Sinai, Sydenham, Morrisania, Sea View Tubercular, and Kings
County Tubercular. Some hospital staffs maintain that many of
the Puerto Rican patients are new arrivals who have quickly
availed themselves of the city's hospital services. The Department of Hospitals, however, considers this only a minute percentage and claims that the facilities are adequate to accommodate the
newcomers. With the constant expansion of physical facilities, the
department can serve the influx but it cannot provide adequate
staffs. Department officials say that the need for expanded facilities is not due to the Puerto Rican migration, but is the result of
a generally expanding population and lengthening average life span
—caused by the improvement in the control of disease and use of
medical facilities.

THE IMPACT

ON CRIME AND DELINQUENCY

The rapid growth of New York City's population in the postwar period, partially attributable to the Puerto Rican migration, has been accompanied by a sharp increase in crime and delinquency. Among the charges leveled at the Puerto Rican newcomers is that of contributing unduly to this upsurge. Of the eleven high delinquency areas in which the New York City Youth Board concentrates its efforts, seven have a large Puerto Rican population: Upper West Side, East Harlem, and Park West in Manhattan; Mott Haven-Longwood and Morrisania-Belmont in the Bronx; and South Brooklyn and Williamsburg in Brooklyn. For example, in the Park West area, Puerto Ricans comprise 5.8 per cent of the population, but the Puerto Rican case load of the Youth Board is between 35 and 40 per cent. In the Harlem area, with 4 per cent Puerto Rican inhabitants, these people account for about 39 per cent of the case load.

In general, delinquency is linked with such conditions as economic deprivation, with all its ramifications--lack of recreational facilities, family breakdown, personal maladjustment, and lack of community status. The Puerto Ricans, as the city's newest migrants, are particularly subject to the pressures arising from these factors. Their socioeconomic condition has relegated them to the already depressed areas of the city. The consequent overcrowding, superimposed upon existing deterioration, creates an atmosphere conducive to the breeding of juvenile delinquency.

While social life in Puerto Rico is oriented about the family, the extremely overcrowded living conditions in New York City preclude use of the home as a center of social activities. Moreover, the transition from the island to the mainland culture has had a pronounced effect on the basic family relationship. The conflicts arising between the bicultural children and their slower-

to-acclimate parents culminate in serious maladjustments. The
parents lose status in the home and parental guidance is often
lacking. Serious emotional maladjustment is frequently attributable to strife between parents and, among many Puerto Rican
youngsters, to an awareness of the consensual relationship of the
parents, which confronts them with the new-found stigma of ille-
gitimacy.

The lack of community status of Puerto Ricans has its roots
in the mutual distrust among the various racial and ethnic
groups. Nonacceptance of Puerto Ricans, by the greater part of
the community, is a result of prejudicial conceptions concerning
their color, morals, cleanliness, and contribution to neighborhood
deterioration. Puerto Ricans, in turn, having become aware of
mainland racial views, place continued reliance upon their Hispanic culture to differentiate themselves from American Negroes.

A serious lack of suitable recreational facilities in heavily
populated Puerto Rican districts, particularly in Spanish Harlem
and Morrisania, forces many Puerto Rican youths to spend their
leisure time playing in streets, vacant lots, etc. If the weather
is bad, they seek such outlets as bars, motion-picture theaters,
dance halls, or poolrooms.

Police authorities maintain that Puerto Rican youths become
involved in antisocial behavior of a minor nature, such as truancy, vandalism, incorrigibility, petty thievery, and minor sex offenses. However, these officials have tended to minimize unduly
Puerto Rican participation in more serious offenses such as gang
depredations, narcotics addiction, prostitution, and serious sex
crimes. For some teen-age Puerto Ricans the gang serves as
substitute for a satisfactory family relationship, as a bulwark
against discrimination, as a release for pent-up energies and
emotions, and as a source for a strong sense of in-group security. Unless such associations are channeled along constructive
lines, the gang members may engage in destructive and illegal
activities, ranging from school disturbances to the commission
of felonies. Furthermore, when gangs are strongly organized in
an area, particularly on an ethnic or racial basis, wars between
rival gangs erupt, posing a serious threat to the property and
physical well-being of the people in the neighborhood. Although
a few strongly knit gangs exist among Puerto Rican teen-agers,
the over-all pattern is one of loosely organized groups with fluid
membership.

Recognizing the latent value of the gang as a socializing force,
the New York City Youth Board, through its Council of Social
and Athletic Clubs, has sought to divert the activities of these

groups toward more wholesome pursuits. To accomplish this the council sends out "gang workers," i.e., group workers concerned with the activities of gangs, who establish an informal relationship with the gang and gain the confidence of its members. The board's East Harlem Council has seven members—six Puerto Ricans and one Italian—working with gangs of from 300 to 350 youths each. Similar efforts along these lines are made by other organizations such as the Casita Maria, a unit of Catholic Charities, located on East 107th Street, and the First Spanish Evangelical Church of the Good Neighbor, on East 106th Street.

One serious criticism of this novel approach is that the gang worker, in order to gain the confidence of the group, tends not to report illegal activities. It is also questionable whether this program has succeeded in diverting a substantial number of potential delinquents from committing unlawful actions. The short period of time during which this program has been in effect makes evaluation difficult. The Youth Board, however, reports that the delinquency rate has decreased in areas in which the plan has been carried out. The board does not regard its efforts as a panacea; but as patterns of gang behavior change, it will adapt its approach accordingly.

In the late forties and early fifties the courts, police officials, social agencies, school authorities, and physicians became aware of the alarming increase in drug addiction among the city's teen-agers. The emotional instability of many Puerto Rican youths, and the rather easy availability of drugs in Harlem, contributed to an increased use of narcotics among these adolescents. Many Puerto Rican addicts have been brought to the attention of the authorities through the commission of such crimes as burglary, purse snatching, mugging, car stripping, procuring, and prostitution. Many of these crimes were committed as a means of financing their addiction.

The extent of the use of narcotics among the youths of this group, as compared to the city's youth as a whole, is a matter of conjecture. The problem of narcotics use and addiction is more acute than many public agencies, such as the Board of Education, are willing to admit. In 1951, there were 7,500 boys and girls under 21 who were addicts, and the use of narcotics by teen-agers on the Lower East Side is increasing.(1)

In 1952, Riverside Hospital, a unit of the city Department of Hospitals, located on North Brother Island, and specializing in treatment of narcotic addicts, treated an average of 150 patients. Approximately 11 per cent of the addicts were Puerto Rican.

---

1. The New York Times, May 24, 1951, p. 29.

In 1953, with the inauguration of a narcotics' term of the City
Magistrates Courts, services at the hospital were provided for
an average of 200 youths, 18 per cent of whom were Puerto
Rican. The hospital estimates that this percentage will rise
because of the use of drugs among this group, and because of
the greater awareness of facilities available for treatment. Although Riverside Hospital provides post-institutional treatment,
the majority return to their original corrupting environment and
become subject to the same pernicious influences.

The extent of delinquency among Puerto Rican youths is not
precisely measurable, but fairly accurate figures on the number
of delinquents who come to the attention of the authorities are
available. In the Children's Court of the Domestic Relations
Court, which handles delinquency and neglect cases of children
under sixteen, Puerto Ricans accounted for 10 per cent of all
delinquency petitions filed in 1950. In 1953, when the number
of Puerto Rican children in the age group over which the court
had jurisdiction had doubled, the proportion rose to 15.6 per
cent.(2)

A general and popular misconception which has actually pene-
trated the judiciary was expressed by Presiding Justice John
Warren Hill of the Domestic Relations Court in the court's
twentieth annual report. He stated that:

"Twenty-seven per cent of all children who came to our court
in Manhattan last year as delinquents were the children of Puerto
Rican migrant parents, a figure out of all proportion, since the
ratio of Puerto Rican-born citizens to the total city population
is about 5 per cent."(3)

The correlation of Judge Hill's figures is in error. A valid
comparison would relate the proportion of Puerto Rican delinquents appearing in the court to the ratio of Puerto Rican
youths in Manhattan, rather than to the total Puerto Rican
population of the city. His use of figures is also invalid because
he does not take into consideration the heavy concentration of
Puerto Ricans in Manhattan, nor the large percentage of them
in the young age bracket. (See Table 10.)

In 1952, the youth term of City Magistrates Courts, which
handles cases of young people over sixteen, reported that out
of 2,509 arraignments, 524, or 21 per cent, were youths with
Spanish names.

Beginning in 1950, through the central register of the New
York City Youth Board the city attempted to estimate the

---

2. Jaffe, op. cit., p. 52.
3. The New York Times, April 27, 1953, p. 25.

actual rate of delinquency and to provide for an unduplicated case count of delinquent young people in the New York City area. Reports were compiled from such public agencies as the Children's Court, the Juvenile Aid Bureau, the Bureau of Attendance, City Magistrates Courts, and selected private youth-serving agencies. Figures obtained from March, 1951, to March, 1952, indicate that 7.3 per cent of the delinquents were of Puerto Rican origin.(4) The over-all 7.3 percentage is broken down further in Table 9.

While the rate of juvenile delinquency among Puerto Rican youths is slightly higher than that of the general population in the same age group, the picture is not of such alarming proportions as has been generally assumed. The restricted economic and social position of this group, coupled with the strains of a culturally disturbed family relationship, promotes tendencies toward social noncompliance.

TABLE 9

EXTENT OF DELINQUENCY AMONG PUERTO RICAN YOUTHS
IN NEW YORK CITY, 1951, 1952

Area	Puerto Rican Youths Age 5-20	Percentage of Total Youths	Puerto Rican Delinquent Youths	Percentage of Total Delinquent Youths
New York City	73,202	4.7	2,147	7.3
Bronx	18,404	5.9	517	8.7
Brooklyn	11,977	2.1	359	3.6
Manhattan	41,164	13.2	1,238	13.1
Queens	1,437	.5	30	.8
Richmond	1,220	.5	3	.5

Source: Paul J. Reiss, "Backgrounds of Puerto Rican Delinquency in New York City" (Master's thesis, Fordham University, 1954), p. 95.

Encountering a higher rate of delinquency within this group, various agencies have felt the need to change their programs in order to offer constructive help. There have been general attempts to secure Spanish-speaking personnel in preventive agencies serving Puerto Rican areas. The Police Athletic League has some Spanish-speaking workers and operates an over-all policy of matching the backgrounds of its staff with the clientele of its neighborhood centers. The program also emphasizes the integration of all children, regardless of background, into the community life through play activities. Since Puerto Rican youngsters are quick to learn English, and the recreational setting is ideal for developing language facility, PAL need not be overdependent on

---

4. The nativity of the parents was known in only 75 per cent of the total cases. See Jaffe, op. cit., p. 53.

Spanish-speaking recreational workers. It has developed the commendable practice of spotting at least one Spanish-speaking worker in fair-to-heavily populated Puerto Rican neighborhoods. The children derive a sense of security from the presence of a staff member who is able to understand them, and, in addition, they are shown an integrated pattern of living. The Juvenile Aid Bureau and the New York City Youth Board, both more directly involved in the treatment of Puerto Rican delinquents and their immediate families, employ bilingual workers in their programs.

An increasing number of Puerto Rican youths are appearing in Children's Court, but since the court makes public very little information concerning its cases, it is impossible to ascertain fully the impact of this group. Delinquent youths are remanded by the court to one of the temporary detention homes, pending a hearing or commitment to other institutions. The temporary detention homes for youthful offenders, between seven and sixteen years of age, are known as Boys' Youth House and Girls' Youth House. Children in both centers remain on an average of from three to five weeks. During that time they are given thorough physical and psychiatric examinations. In April, 1954, the capacity of Boys' Youth House was 165, with the Puerto Ricans averaging approximately 15 per cent. In February, 1954, at Girls' Youth House, Puerto Ricans comprised 22 per cent of the total of 94 inmates.

The distinct difference between Puerto Rican boys and girls committed lies in the nature of the offenses. The delinquency of Puerto Rican boys does not differ from that of youthful offenders in general; but the girls are more apt to have been involved in sex delinquencies.

While it has been possible to derive some insight into the problem of juvenile delinquency the extreme reluctance of the New York City Police Department to divulge any information on crimes committed by adult Puerto Ricans has seriously hampered a complete evaluation of this issue. Under the circumstances there can be no accurate assessment of Puerto Rican participation in criminal activities. However, information of a general nature has been obtained from the courts, probation departments, other governmental and private agencies, and also from press accounts.

As nearly as can be ascertained, Puerto Ricans are involved in such major offenses as homicide(5), assault, statutory rape, narcotics offenses, and theft, and in minor violations of city ordinances and motor-vehicle laws. The minor offenses are committed unwittingly as a general rule, because of the newcomers' ignorance

---

5. Homicides, suicides, and accidents accounted for 12.5 per cent of the deaths among New York's Puerto Ricans in 1952. See Jaffe, op. cit., p. 41.

of local laws and the English language. Crimes such as homicide and aggravated assault generally are not committed for gain but stem from the highly emotional volatile Latin American temperament and can be classified under the heading of crimes of passion. The relatively high incidence of statutory rape arises from the differences between the laws and mores of New York and those of the island. In Puerto Rico the age of consent is fixed at fourteen years, as compared to eighteen years in New York. The widespread practice of premarital and consensual relationships among Puerto Ricans accounts for most of the charges of statutory rape brought against them.

Narcotics offenses of Puerto Rican adults are confined as a rule to possession, use, and small-scale peddling of dope, rather than to involvement in interstate or international traffic. The Federal Bureau of Narcotics is not especially interested in or concerned with this group but concentrates its efforts on apprehension of persons in the upper echelons of the narcotics traffic. The type of violation found among Puerto Ricans is considered a matter for local authorities.

The New York City Police Department has studiously avoided any discussion of the Puerto Rican impact upon its operations. In order to develop better relations between the police and Puerto Ricans, it was recommended that in the human relations course initiated in 1953 at the Police Academy, special emphasis be given to Puerto Rican problems. Increasing awareness of the problem is demonstrated also by the fact that when the city's Bureau of Training and Career Development offered two Spanish-language courses in 1956, designed to accommodate 150 policemen, over 1,200 applied

Puerto Ricans are appearing in increasing numbers in the county courts of Manhattan, Bronx, and Brooklyn, which have jurisdiction over felonies in their respective areas. In Kings County Court, where the Probation Department maintains an excellent reporting system, some indication of the number of Puerto Rican defendants can be obtained from Table 10.

Since Puerto Ricans have not yet settled in appreciable numbers in either Richmond or Queens, the county courts there have little contact with this group. In Queens County Court, for example, between 1,000 and 1,500 cases were heard in 1953, and only seven involved Puerto Rican defendants. Of these, three required interpreters.

The courts have attempted to overcome the language problem by using regular staff members who have some knowledge of Spanish, or by utilizing Spanish-speaking personnel. The City Magistrates Courts, with about fifteen interpreters, have done

TABLE 10

PERSONS PLACED ON PROBATION IN KINGS COUNTY COURT, 1944 and 1952

	1944			1952		
	Total	Puerto Rican	Percentage of Puerto Rican Total	Total	Puerto Rican	Percentage of Puerto Rican Total
Homicide	21	0	0	55	10	18.2
Robbery	111	4	3.6	249	9	3.6
Burglary	235	7	2.9	372	23	6.2
Assault	218	8	3.7	224	17	7.6
Larceny	157	3	1.9	293	2	.7
Auto thefts	150	0	0	179	7	3.9
Sex offences	137	1	.7	151	16	10.6
Offences against family	24	1	4.2	23	2	8.6
Miscellaneous	17	0	0	61	2	3.3
Youthful offences	51	0	0	43	6	14.0
Narcotics	-	-	-	122	6	4.9
Total	1,121	24	2.1	1,772	100	5.6

most in this direction. Certain parts—Night, Mid-Manhattan, Bay Ridge, and Traffic Court—have many Puerto Rican cases, and in about 90 per cent of these an interpreter is required.

Most law-enforcement agencies in New York City are cognizant of the problems created by increasing pressures from this new migrant group, and they have made efforts to adjust programs and procedures within their organizational framework and financial limitations.(6)

---

6. It is interesting to note that in 1954, of 800,000 young people between the ages of 5 and 21 in Puerto Rico, there were 2,246 cases registered as delinquent or pre-delinquent. In New York City there were an estimated 43,300 cases in the same age group, which numbered 1,732,000. It is evident that juvenile delinquency is not a Puerto Rican import. See Gertrude Samuels, "Puerto Rico: Land of Paradox," The New York Times Magazine, October 30, 1955, pp. 18ff.

CONCLUSIONS

AND RECOMMENDATIONS

The impact of Puerto Rican migration on the government of the City of New York has been considerable. The problems of serving these new New Yorkers and of integrating them into the community are likely to increase in the near future.

1. The socioeconomic conditions in Puerto Rico will continue to impel migration. The birth rate in Puerto Rico remains spectacularly high, 35 per thousand in 1955(1), and life expectancy is on the increase.(2) The mortality rate has dropped from 18 per thousand in 1940 to 7 per thousand in 1955.(3) Over twenty thousand persons enter the labor market each year (4) out of a potential of 45,000.(5) Of a total labor force of 636,700, over 97,000 are unemployed (6) and possibly as many as 200,000 underemployed.(7)

The combination of high fertility and a decreasing death rate would alone negate the island's excellent attempts at industrialization and increased living standards. Despite an increase of 334 per cent since 1910 in the island's gross product,(8) it is manifestly impossible for the government to anticipate the elimination of unemployment and underemployment.(9)

1. The New York Times, January 3, 1956, p. 54.
2. Clarence Senior, Strangers and Neighbors (New York: Anti-Defamation League, 1952), p. 30.
3. Puerto Rico: Indices of Social and Economic Progress, 1940 and 1955 (Commonwealth Economic Development Administration, 1956).
4. The New York Times, June 5, 1955, p. 119; March 5, 1956, p. 33.
5. Ibid, March 5, 1956.
6. Puerto Rico: Indices ..., op. cit.
7. The New York Times, June 5, 1955, p. 119.
8. Economic Development Administration, Puerto Rico Reports Economy Trebled, 1940 to 1955.
9. The goal is for 800 new industrial plants by 1960, to provide direct employment for 85,000 and indirect jobs for 50,000 more. See Gertrude Samuels, op. cit., pp. 18ff.

These factors, coupled with the willingness of Puerto Ricans to move and their desire to improve their occupational opportunities, their economic status and the educational opportunities for their children(10), will undoubtedly result in a continued high level of migration from the island. Indeed, many experts consider such migration essential to the welfare of the island.(11)

2. Unless induced otherwise, most Puerto Rican migrants will settle in New York City. From the viewpoint of Puerto Rican migrants, the United States mainland is far superior to any other area—including Spanish-speaking Latin America—in which they would seek to improve their status. Despite considerations and inducements to settle in Latin America, only negligible numbers of migrants have gone outside of the continent.(12)

Prosperity on the mainland is the key attraction for Puerto Rican migrants. With the domestic economy booming by 25 per cent in the decade between 1950 and 1960(13), the contrast with conditions on the island may result in an increased movement to the mainland. While consumer prices have gone up 15 per cent since the base period of 1947-1949, the median income in the United States has risen 34 per cent in the same base period.(14)

Despite many hopes to the contrary(15), the preponderance of Puerto Rican migrants will settle in New York City. The virtual elimination of seaborne passenger traffic and the ease of airline passage to New York City and Miami make these two cities terminal points. For most Puerto Ricans, the northern city is preferable, both for employment and social conditions. If direct air

---

10. Paul K. Hatt, Background of Human Fertility in Puerto Rico (Princeton University Press, 1952), passim.
11. Clarence Senior, Puerto Rico Emigration (University of Puerto Rico, 1947), p. 119; U. S. House of Representatives, Committee on Insular Affairs, Investigation of Political, Economic and Social Conditions in Puerto Rico (Government Printing Office, 1945).
12. Ibid., p. 41.
13. America's Needs and Resources (Twentieth Century Fund, 1955); Joint Committee on the Economic Report, Potential Economic Growth During the Next Decade (Government Printing Office, 1954).
14. U. S. Department of Labor, Bureau of Labor Statistics, Consumer's Price Index (April, 1956); U. S. Department of Commerce, Bureau of the Census, Consumer Income (December, 1955).
15. City of New York, Mayor's Committee on Puerto Rican Affairs, Interim Report (1953), p. 10; Dora Tannenbaum, Sara McCaulley, and H. Daniel Carpenter, The Puerto Rican Migration (New York, 1955), p. 5; Charles Abrams, Chairman of the New York State Commission Against Discrimination, as reported in The New York Times, February 26, 1956, p. 74.

transportation were provided to other northern industrial communities—Boston, Detroit, Philadelphia, Cleveland—the possibilities of a greater dispersion would be materially increased. As of mid-1956, however, passengers from Puerto Rico had to change planes in order to reach some metropolis other than Miami, New York, and Chicago.

If the number of migrants continues at the rate of 35,000 to 50,000 per year, some 75 per cent may be expected to settle in New York City. This would represent a decrease in the 1948-1953 rate but is in line with the expectations of both official and civic agencies.(16) Nevertheless, between 26,000 and 37,000 new migrants may be expected in New York City as an annual average over the next decade. This expectation will be realized even if the number of manufacturing jobs drops sharply from the total of 968,050 in 1955. As positions do open for operatives and service workers, Puerto Rican migrants and Negroes—both being on the increase numerically—will continue to fill the needs and to move up the economic ladder as well.

3. Governmental Agencies in New York City will have to meet the special needs of the Puerto Rican migrants. In general, the needs of Puerto Ricans in New York City are much the same as those of any American citizen—employment, housing, education, leisure, recreation, etc. The special needs of this one group, however, are directly related to the language and cultural differences which they possess.(17) It is expected that these differences will enrich the cultural life of the New York community and add, in the long run, to the appreciation of the Hispanic tradition. While this process is going on, there is also the process of integrating the migrants and their families into the community's laws, mores, and folkways. These two processes, interrelated and joined, call for positive and comprehensive action on the part of the "City Fathers" to provide and foster patterns of acceptance and understanding on the part of all municipal officials and the citizenry.

Puerto Rican migrants need employment counseling and vocational guidance from people who can speak their language and evaluate their skills.(18) They need public officials and union officials who will be watchful and helpful in preventing illegal exploitation of their lack of understanding of the labor laws.

They and their families need housing. In the light of a shortage

---

16. City of New York, Mayor's Committee ... , op. cit., pp. 4, 16, 19; Puerto Rico, Department of Labor, Migration Conference, 1953, p. 1; Senior, Strangers and Neighbors, op. cit., p. 16; The New York Times, November 22, 1954, p. 25; Samuels, op. cit., p. 18.
17. See Chapter I.
18. See Chapter III.

of low-cost housing, it becomes imperative for city officialdom to prevent rent gouging, and crowded and unsanitary conditions. Strengthened laws and strengthened enforcement may result in decreasing available housing facilities, but the alternatives, in terms of community deterioration, are totally unacceptable.(19)

The migrants' children need education. Spanish-speaking teachers will be necessary for many years before the language situation is resolved.(20) The children will need community centers, parks, playgrounds, and all forms of recreational facilities—and Spanish-speaking counselors and instructors to go with them.

In many other areas of municipal and civic endeavor, Puerto Rican migrants will have special needs.(21)

4. The impact of Puerto Rican migration on governmental services in New York City will be greater in the decade to come.

---

19. See Chapter II.
20. See Chapter V.
21. See Chapters IV, VI, VII.

INDEX

INDEX

56TH CONGRESS, { SENATE. { DOCUMENT
2d Session. { { No. 222.

LIBRARY OF CONGRESS,

DIVISION OF BIBLIOGRAPHY.

A

LIST OF BOOKS

(WITH REFERENCES TO PERIODICALS)

ON

PORTO RICO.

BY

A. P. C. GRIFFIN,

CHIEF OF DIVISION OF BIBLIOGRAPHY.

MARCH 2, 1901.—Presented by Mr. LODGE, referred to the Committee on
Library, and ordered to be printed.

WASHINGTON:
GOVERNMENT PRINTING OFFICE.
1901.

INTRODUCTION.

In the compilation of this list no effort has been made to go beyond the resources of this Library.

It embodies a considerable collection of native literature gathered by Dr. Friedenwald upon the occasion of a visit to the island in 1898.

Appended is a list of Porto Rican administrative documents, reports of local organizations, etc.

The spelling "Porto Rico" is in conformity with the rule adopted by Congress and accepted by the Board on Geographic Names.

A. P. C. GRIFFIN,

Chief of Division of Bibliography.

HERBERT PUTNAM,

Librarian of Congress.

3

PORTO RICO.

BOOKS RELATING TO PORTO RICO.

Abad, José Ramon. Puerto Rico en la Feria-exposicion de Ponce en 1882. Memoria redactada de orden de la junta de la misma.
Ponce, P. R.: Establ. tip. "El Comercio," 1885. 351 pp. 8°.

Abbad y Lasierra, Iñigo. Historia geográfica, civil y política, de la isla de S. Juan Bautista de Puerto Rico. Dala á luz Don Antonio Valladares de Sotomayor. Con Privilegio real.
Madrid: MDCC. LXXXVIII. En la imprenta de Don Antonio Espinosa. viii, 403 pp. 8°.

———— Historia geográfica, civil y política de la isla de San Juan de Bautista de Puerto Rico. Dala a luz Don Antonio Valladares de Soto Mayor.
Impresa en Madrid: Año de M.DCC.LXXXVIII. Puerto Rico: Año 1831. Reimpresa en la oficina del gobierno a cargo de D. Valeriano de Sanmillan.
>   (*In* Cordova, Pedro Tomas: Memorias geograficas . . . de la isla de Puerto Rico . . . vol. 1. Puerto Rico: En la oficina del gobierno; a cargo de D. Valeriano de Sanmillan, 1831. 8°.)

———— Historia geografica, civil y natural de la isla de San Juan Bautista de Puerto Rico. Nueva edicion, anotada en la parte histórica y continuada en la estadística y económica por José Julian de Acosta y Calbo.
Puerto-Rico: Imprenta y libreria de Acosta, 1866. 568 pp. Facsimile. 4°.

The Abolition of slavery in Cuba and Porto Rico, by several Cuban and Porto-Rican abolitionists.
New York: Wm. C. Bryant & Co., printers, 1866. 34 pp. 8°.

Acosta, José Julian. Apuntes para la historia de Puerto-Rico. Artículos publicados en "El Agente." Con motivo del proyecto de "Escuela filotécnica" en la ciudad de Mayagüez.
Puerto-Rico: Imprenta y libreréa de Acosta, 1879. 22 pp. 12°.

Acosta, José Julian.　Discurso leido el dia 28 de Noviembre de 1882 en la solemne apertura del instituto civil de segunda enseñanza de la provincia de Puerto-Rico.

Puerto-Rico : Imprenta y librería de Acosta, 1882.　10 pp.　8°.

────── Discurso leido en la solemne apertura del curso académico de 1883–84 del Instituto civil provincial de segunda enseñanza de Puerto-Rico.

Puerto-Rico : Imprenta de "El Asimilista," 1883.　12 pp. 8°.

────── Tratado de agricultura teorica.　Con aplicacion a los cultivos intertropicales.　.　.　.　Tomo 1.

Puerto Rico: Acosta, 1862.　8°.

El Agente.　El proceso de "el Agente.　Articulo denunciado, defensa, sentencia (absolutoria).

Puerto-Rico : Imp. de el Agente, 1881.　29 pp.　16°.

Alfan y Baralt, Antonio.　Los partidos Antillanos.　Estudio politico.

Puerto Rico: José Gonzalez Font, 1886.　23 pp.　8°.

Amadeo y Antomarchi, Jesus Maria.　Una plaga social y la plegaria de una virgen.　Ensayo científico social.

Puerto-Rico: Tip. "La Correspondencia," 1894.　314 pp. 16°.

American Art Association, New York.　Catalogue of 500 large photographs .　.　.　views taken by the special photographic outfit with the United States Army during 1898 and 1899, illustrating the scenic beauty of Porto Rico.　.　.　.

New York: American Art Association, 1899.　54 pp.　Plates. 8°.

Angelis, Pedro de.　Miscelaneas puertorriqueñas.　Colección de articulos históricos biográficos.

Puerto Rico: Tip. de Ferreras, 1894.　65 pp.　12°.

Apuntes para la flora y fauna de Puerto-Rico.

(*In* Anales de la Sociedad Española de historia natural, vol. 10, 1881.)

Arecco y Torres, Domingo.　Recopilación de disposiciones oficiales. Contiene esta obra las leyes, reales ordenes y disposiciones mas notables, publicadas en la "Gaceta oficial" desde el 1° de Enero de 1878 hasta fin de Diciembre de 1887 arregladas per orden alfabético y de materias, con su indice correspondiente.　Tomo I.

Mayagüez : Imprenta de Arecco hijo, 1889.　F°.

Asenjo y Arteaga, Federico. El catastro de Puerto Rico. Necesidad de su formacion y posibilidad de elevarlo a cabo.
Puerto-Rico: C. B. Meltz, 1890. 148 pp. 8°.

Baldorioti de Castro, Roman. Las facultades omnímodas en 1811 y los diputados de Puerto Rico en 1869. Reminiscencia.
Madrid: Imp. de la Gaceta de los Caminos de Hierro, 1869. 16 pp. 4°.

> (Asuntos de Puerto-Rico. Reconstitucion social, política y económica de la isla. vol. 2. Sept., 1869.)

Baldwin, James. Our new possessions: Cuba, Puerto Rico, Hawaii, Philippines.
New York: American Book Co., 1899. 32 pp. Illus. 8°.

Berniér, Félix Matos. Recuerdos benditos.
Ponce, Puerto Rico: Tip. "El Telégrafo," 1895. 314, vi pp. 8°.

Bidwell, C. T. Account of the aborigines of the island of Porto Rico. Compiled by C. T. Bidwell, Her Majesty's consul, from "La Historia geográfica, civil y politica de Puerto Rico," by Fray Iñigo Abbad; published at Mexico in 1788.

> (*In* Great Britain. Parliament. Sessional papers, 1879, vol. 72. Reports of Her Majesty's consuls, vol. 26, pp. 1616–1622.)

―――― Report by Consul Bidwell on the trade and commerce of the island of Puerto Rico, and on the produce and trade of the province for 1878, with reference to preceding years.

> (*In* Great Britain. Parliament. Sessional papers, 1879, vol. 72. Reports of Her Majesty's consuls, vol. 26, pp. 1622–1660.)

Blanch, José. Directorio comercial e industrial de la isla de Puerto Rico para 1894.
Puerto Rico: Tip. al vap. de la Correspondencia, 1894. 190, (2) pp. Folded map. 8°.

Blanco y Sosa, Julián E. Enmiendas á la constitucion organica del partido autonomista Portorriqueño presentadas a la asemblea de Mayaguez que debera celebrarse el 1° de Abril.
Ponce: Tipografia de la Revista de Puerto-Rico, 1891. (2), 137 pp. 16°.

―――― Veinte y cinco años antes, apuntes para la historia, coleccion de artículos publicados en El Progreso y La Voz del País. . . .
Puerto Rico: Sucesion de J. J. Acosta, 1898. viii, 253 pp. 2 portraits. 8°.

Boletin Eclesiastico de la diócesis de Puerto Rico. 1860, no. 1,
2; 1861–64; 67–68. Semi-monthly.
Puerto Rico: D. I. Guasp, [1861–68]. 6 v. in 3. 8°.

Brau, Salvador. Las Clases jornaleras de Puerto Rico . . .
memoria . . . premiada en el certamen del Ateneo
puerto-riqueño . . .
*Puerto Rico: Imprenta del "Boletin Mercantil," 1882. (4),
86 pp. 12°.*

—————— Ecos de la batalla. Artículos periodísticos. Primera serie.
Con un prólogo-semblanza del Manuel Fernandez Juncos.
*Puerto-Rico: Impr. y libreria de J. G. Font, 1886. xviii,
282, (2) pp. 8°.*

—————— Lo que dice la historia. Cartas al señor ministro de ultramar por el director de " el Clamor del País." . . .
*Madrid: Tip. de los Hijos de M. G. Hernández, 1893. 45
pp. 12°.*

—————— Dos factores de la colonizacion de Puerto-Rico. Conferencia
pública en el Ateneo de San Juan.
Puerto-Rico: Sucesion de J. J. Acosta, 1896. 30 pp. 12°.

Bryan, William S. Our islands and their people as seen with camera
and pencil; introduced by . . . J. Wheeler, with
special descriptive matter and narratives by J. de Olivares
. . . Photographs by W. B. Townsend . . . Parts
1–24.
*St. Louis, New York: N. D. Thompson Pub. Co., [1899–
1900]. 24 pts. Plates. Portraits. Map. F°.*

Una Campaña parlamentaria. Coleccion de proposiciones presentadas y discursos pronunciados en las Córtes españolas de
1872–73. Por la diputacion radical de Puerto-Rico.
*Madrid: Imprenta de M. G. Hernandez, 1873. 395, (4) pp.
8°.*

> Contents: Al lector, (signed) Varios amigos de la reforma colonial;
> A los electores de Puerto Rico (memorandum), por Rafael M. de
> Labra. Discursos: Las elecciones de Puerto Rico, discurso por
> Joaquin M. Sanromá, 10 Oct. 1872; La casacion criminal en
> ultramar, por José F. Cintron y R. M. de Labra; El codigo en
> ultramar, por R. M. de Labra; La diputacion de Puerto-Rico ante
> las reformas ultramarinas, por R. M. de Labra; La abolicion de
> la esclavitud en Puerto-Rico, discursos por Joaquin M. Sanromá,
> José F. Cintron, R. M. de Labra y José Alvarez Peralta; Los
> sucesos de Camuy por R. M. de Labra; La reforma electoral, por
> Luis Padial y R. M. de Labra; Publicacion de leyes y reglamentos,
> por R. M. de Labra; Proposiciones de ley y dictámenes.

Campos, Ramón Morel. Guía local y de comercio de la ciudad de Ponce . . .
Ponce: "El Telégrafo," 1895. 113 pp. 8°.

El porvenir de Utuado, estudio, historico, descriptivo y estadistico . . . con un prólogo de Marcelino Andino.
Ponce: "El Vapor," 1896. 245 pp. 8°.

Canini, Italo Emilio. Four centuries of Spanish rule in Cuba; or, why we went to war with Spain. A historical sketch, with illustrations from old and modern authorities, and the latest official statistics about Cuba, Porto Rico, and the Philippines.
Chicago: Laird & Lee, 1898. 220 pp. 16°.

Cardénas, Francisco. Estado de la poblacion y del trabajo en las islas de Cuba y Puerto Rico.
(In Memorias de la Real academia de ciencias, vol. 4, pp. 419–454. Madrid, 1883.)

Carroll, Henry K. Report on the island of Porto Rico, its population, civil government, commerce, industries, productions, roads, tariff, and currency, with recommendations . . . Respectfully submitted to Hon. William McKinley . . . October 6, 1899.
Washington: Government printing office, 1899. 813 pp. 8°.

Cepeda, Francisco. Propaganda autonomista. Conferencias de Abuli celebradas con el jefe de la minoria autonomista parlamentaria Rafael M. de Labra sobre politica Antillana. . . .
Ponce: Tip. de la " Revista de la Puerto-Rico," 1890. xxxii, 304 pp. 16°.

Chicago. **Exposición universal de Chicago de 1893.** Adición al catálogo de la sección Española comprende las islas de Cuba, Puerto-Rico y Filipinas, publicada por la Comisión general de España.
Madrid: Imprenta de Ricardo Rojas, 1894. 14, (2), 124 pp. 8°.

Church, A. M., *editor.* Picturesque Cuba, Porto Rico, Hawaii, and the Philippines: a photographic panorama of our new possessions . . .
Springfield, Ohio: Mast, Crowell & Kirkpatrick, 1898. 121 pp. Illus. 4°. (Farm and fireside library, no. 168.)

Clifford, George, *3d Earl of Cumberland.* The voyage to Saint John de Porto Rico, by the Right Honorable, George, Earle of Cumberland, written by himselfe.

> (*In* Purchas His pilgrimes. The fourth part. (Liber vi.) Chapter II. pp. 1150–1154. London: Printed by William Stansby for Henrie Fêtherstone, and are to be sold at his shop in Paul's Church-Yard, at the Signe of the Rose. 1625. F°.)

Coggeshall, George. Thirty-six voyages to various parts of the world, made between 1799 and 1841. Selected from his ms. journals of eighty voyages. 3d edition with illustrations. In one volume. Revised, corrected and enlarged, with additional notes and explanations.

New York: published by and for the author, 1858. 583 pp. Plates (lithographs). 8°.

> Contains accounts of several voyages to Cuba and Porto Rico.

Coll y Toste, Cayetano. La ciudad de San Juan.

> (*In* Infiesta, A. Lealtad y heroismo de la isla de Puerto Rico. pp. 307–333, Plan of Puerto Rico. Puerto Rico: 1897.)

——— Colón en Puerto Rico. Disquisiciones histórico-filológicas. *Puerto Rico: Tip. al vapor La Correspondencia, 1893. viii, 195 pp. 8°.*

——— Crónicas de Arecibo (Apuntes históricos). *Arecibo: Salicrup y Co., 1891. iv, 95 pp. 8°.*

Contreras, J. M. González. Guía oficial general de Puerto Rico. *Puerto Rico: Imprenta de La Gaceta, 1897. 636 pp. Portraits. 8°.*

Copeland, Thomas Campbell. American colonial handbook. A ready reference book of facts and figures, historical, geographical, and commercial, about Cuba, Puerto Rico, the Philippines, Hawaii, and Guam. *New York and London: Funk & Wagnalls Co., 1899. 180, (1) pp. Maps. 16°.*

Córdova, Pedro Tomas de. Memorias geográficas, históricas, económicas y estadísticas de la isla de Puerto Rico.. *Año de 1831–1833. En la oficina del gobierno a cargo de D. Valeriano de Sanmillán. Puerto Rico. 6 vols. 8°.*

> Vol. 1, 1831, contains a reprint of "Historia geográfica, civil y política de la isla de San Juan Bautista de Puerto Rico, por Fray Iñigo Abbad y Lasierra . . . Madrid, 1788." Vols. 2–6 (Puerto Rico. 1831–1833.) contain Sr. Córdova's continuation of Fray Iñigo's work up to the year 1833.

Cortón, Antonio. Las Antillas. Cuba, Puerto-Rico, La Martinica, Santo Domingo, Haiti, Jamaica, Guadalupe, San Thomas, Trinidad.
Barcelona: Jaime Jepús, 1898. (2), *80 pp.* 8°.
Puerto Rico, pp. 19–40.

Davis, Richard Harding. The Cuban and Porto Rican campaigns. Illustrated.
New York: Charles Scribner's Sons, 1898. xiii, (1), 360 pp. Folded map. 8°.

Dewell, James D. Down in Porto Rico with a kodak.
New Haven: The Record Pub. Co., 1898. 102 pp. Illus. Map. 8°.

Diaz Agero, Ricardo. Discurso leido por Ricardo Diaz Agero, Presidente de la Audiencia territorial de Puerto Rico, en el solemne acto de la apertura de los tribunales de la isla en 2 de Enero de 1891.
Puerto Rico: Tipografia del "Boletin Mercantil," 1891. 25, (5) pp. 2 folded sheets. 8°.

Diaz Caneja, Ignacio. La cuestión ultramarina; bosquejo crítico é histórico, político y gubernativo, administrativo y económico.
Puerto Rico: Imprenta del "Boletin Mercantil," 1885. xi, (1), 337 pp. 8°.

———— Las reformas del Sr. Maura. Estudio crítico.
Puerto Rico: Tip. del "Boletín Mercantil," 1893. 66 pp. Port. 8°.

———— Waterloo político: examen crítico de las principales teorias sobre que descansa el edificio político moderno.
Puerto Rico: Tip. del Boletín Mercantil, 1891. (8), 200 pp. 8°.

Dinwiddie, William. Porto Rico: Its condition and possibilities. With illustrations from photographs by the author.
New York: Harper & Bros., 1899. vii, (3), 299 pp. 8

Dumont, Enrique. Ensayo de una historia médico-quirúrgica de la isla de Puerto Rico. T. 1, 2, entrega 1–4.
Habana: Imp. "La Antilla," de N. Cacho-Negrete, 1875–76. 2 v. 8°.
Vol. 2 lacks all after p. 160.

Eden, Charles Henry.   The West Indies.
>   *London: Sampson Low (etc.), 1880.   viii, 239 pp.   Folded*
>   *map.   16°.   (Foreign countries and British colonies.)*
>   The islands of Cuba and Puerto Rico, pp. 145–171.

Elias, José.   "La vacuña."   Revista que en conmemoracion del primer
>   centenario de su descubrimiento.   (Puerto Rico, 14 de mayo
>   de 1896.)
>   *Puerto Rico: Imp. del "Boletin Mercantil," 1896.   23 pp.*
>   *Portrait.   8°.*

Elzaburu, Manuel.   El Ateneo.   Discurso leido en el Ateneo puerto-
>   rriqueño   .   .   .   el dia 29 de Enero de 1887; con motivo
>   de la distribución de premios obtenidos en los certámenes
>   de aquel centro correspondientes á 1885 y 86.
>   *Puerto Rico: J. G. Font, 1888.   19 pp.   8°.*

——— La instrucción de enseñanza superior de Puerto-Rico.   Dis-
>   curso leido en el Ateneo puertorriqueño   .   .   .   la noche
>   del 10 de octubre de 1888   .   .   .
>   *Puerto-Rico: Imprenta de José Gonzalez y Font, 1888.   48 pp.*
>   *8°.*

——— Una relacion de la historia con la literatura; discurso leido en
>   el Ateneo puertorriqueño   .   .   .   la noche del 20 de
>   Febrero de 1888   .   .   .
>   *Puerto Rico: J. G. Font, 1888.   18 pp.   8°.*

Enamorado Toral, Julio.   Carnet del dependiente de comercio.
>   Colección de reglas, tablas y demás datos utíles á los que se
>   dedican á tareas comerciales en la isla de Puerto Rico.
>   *Yauco, P. R.: Est. tip. "Borinquen," 1896.   57 pp.   2*
>   *tables.   16°.*

Eves, Charles Washington.   The West Indies.   Published under the
>   auspices of the Royal colonial institute.   4th edition.
>   *London: 1897.   xxxi, (1), 354 pp.   Plates (photographs).*
>   *Folded maps.   16°.*
>   Porto Rico, pp. 288–289.

Fénix (El).   Periódico local, instructivo, mercantil y de avisos.
>   (Weekly.)   Oct. 13, 1855; April 26, 1856; May 24, 1856;
>   July 12, 1856–June 27, 1857; July 4, 1857–Dec. 26, 1857;
>   Jan. 2, 1858–Dec. 23, 1858.
>   *Ponce, Puerto-Rico, 1855–59.   4°.*
>   With El Ponceño, Ponce, Puerto-Rico, 1854.   4°.

Fernandez Juncos, Manuel.   (Galería Puerto-Riqueña.)   Costum-
>   bres y tradiciones.
>   *Puerto Rico: El Buscapie, 1883.   viii, 232 pp.   8°.*

Ferrer Hernandez, Gabriel. La instrucción pública en Puerto-Rico. Su pasado, su presente y modo de mejorarla en lo futuro. *Puerto-Rico: Imp. de José Gonzalez Font, 1885. 206 pp. 16°.*

—— La mujer en Puerto-Rico. Sus necesidades presentes y los medios mas faciles y adecuados para mejorar su porvenir. *Puerto Rico: El Agente, 1881. xvi, 72 pp. Sq. 12°.*

Fisher, H. N. Principles of colonial government adapted to the present needs of Cuba, Porto Rico, and of the Philippines. *Boston: L. C. Page & Co., 1900. 56 pp. 8°.*

Fiske, Amos Kidder. The West Indies. A history of the islands of the West Indian archipelago, together with an account of their physical characteristics, natural resources, and present condition. *New York: G. P. Putnam's Sons, 1899. xii, (2), 414 pp. Plates (photo-gravures). Folded maps. 8°.*

> Contains chapters on the physical characteristics of Puerto Rico; history and Spanish government of Puerto Rico; ports and towns of Puerto Rico; social and economic conditions in Puerto Rico; Puerto Rico in American hands.

Fleites, José Rodríguez. Manual de procedimientos en materia criminal, para los funcionarios y agentes de policia, guardia civil, jueces y fiscales municipales y juzgados de instrucción, con apéndices de distintas leyes y disposiciones vigentes . . . 1ª ed. *Puerto Rico: Imp. del "Boletín Mercantil," 1896. 207, (5) pp. 1 tab. 4°.*

Flinter, George Dawson. An account of the present state of the island of Puerto Rico. Comprising numerous original facts and documents illustrative of the state of commerce and agriculture, and of the condition, moral and physical, of the various classes of the population in that island, as compared with the colonies of other European powers; demonstrating the superiority of the Spanish slave code, the great advantages of free over slave labour, etc. *London: Longman, Rees, Orme, (etc.), 1834. 392 pp. 8°.*

—— Examen del estado actual de los Esclavos de la Isla de Puerto Rico bajo el gobierno español: en que se manifiesta la impolítica y peligro de la prematura emancipacion de los esclavos de la India Occidental. *Nueva-York: 1832. 124 pp. 8°.*

Flinter, George Dawson. A view of the present condition of the slave population in the island of Puerto Rico, under the Spanish government. Showing the impolicy and danger of prematurely emancipating the West India slaves. With observations on the destructive tendency of injudicious reform and revolutionary principles on the prosperity of nations and colonies.
Philadelphia: Printed by Adam Waldie, 1832. (2), 117 pp. 8°.

Franck, —. Margarita. Escenas de la vida intima.
Mayagüez, P. R.: Imp. de Arecco hijo, 1889. 174, (3) pp., 2 l. 8°. (Biblioteca puerto-riqueña.)

Gage, Thomas. The English-American; his travail by sea and land: or a new svrvey of the West-India's, containing a journall of three thousand and three hundred miles within the main land of America. . . . Also a new and exact discovery of the Spanish navigation to those parts, and of their dominions, government, religion, forts, castles, ports, havens, commodities, fashions, behaviour of Spaniards, priests and friers, blackmores, mulatto's, mestiso's, Indians; and of their feasts and solemnities. With a grammar, or some few rudiments of the Indian tongue.
London: Printed by R. Cotes, and are to be sold by Humphrey Blunden, and Thomas Williams, 1648. (10), 218, (12) pp. F°.

——— A new survey of the West India's: or the English-American, his travail by sea and land : containing a journal of three thousand and three hundred miles within the main land of America. Second edition enlarged by the author, and beautified with maps.
London: Printed by E. Cotes, M.DC.LV. (10), 220, (12) pp. Maps. F°.

Gandía, Zeno. La Charca. Crónicas de un mundo enfermo.
Ponce: M. López, 1894. 291, (2) pp. 8°.

Gautier Benítez, José. Poesías de José Gautier Benítez.
Puerto Rico: Sucesión de J. J. Acosta, 1892. (4), 176, (3) pp. Portrait. 3 plates. 12°.

George, Marian M. A little journey to Puerto Rico. For intermediate and upper grades.
Chicago: A. Flanagan company, [1900]. 95 pp. Illustrated in text. 12°. (The plan book series.)
List of reference books on p. 80.

Goenaga, Francisco R. de. Los sepultureros de España en Puerto-Rico ó sea Macías, su Ayudante Cervera, Camó y su tiempo.
Puerto Rico: Boada y Comp., *1899. 92 pp. 12°. (Notas para la historia.)*

Gómez, J. G., and **Sendras y Burin**, A. La isla de Puerto-Rico. I. Bosquejo histórico desde la conquista hasta principios de 1891.
Madrid: José Gil y Navarro, 1891. (2), 199, (9) pp. 8°.

Granier de Cassagnac, A. Voyage aux Antilles.
Paris: Dauvin et Fontaine, 1842, 1844. 2 vols. 8°
Vol. 2, pp. 185–200 on Puerto Rico.

Great Britain. *Foreign office.* Annual series, 1891, no. 816. Report for the year 1889 on the trade of Porto Rico.
London: 1891. (2), 7 pp. 8°.

——— ——— 1893, no. 1306. Report for the year 1891.
London: 1893. (2), 9 pp. 8°.

Hall, A. D. Porto Rico; its history, products, and possibilities.
New York: Street & Smith, [1898]. 171 pp. 12°. (Historical series, no. 3.)

Halstead, Murat. Our new possessions. Natural riches, industrial resources . . . of Cuba, Porto Rico, Hawaii, the Ladrones, and the Philippine Islands . . .
Chicago: The Dominion Co., 1898. 400 pp. Plates. Portraits. Map. 8°.

——— Pictorial history of America's new possessions, the isthmian canals and the problem of expansion . . . with chapters on the policy of American expansion, contributed by W. McKinley, G. Cleveland . . . and others.
Chicago: The Dominion Co., 1898. 681 pp. Illus. 4°.

Hamm, Margherita Arlina. Porto Rico and the West Indies.
London and New York: F. T. Neely, [1899]. 230 pp. Plates. Portrait. 12°.

Hardie *brothers.* Photo-gravures of picturesque Puerto Rico.
1899. Hardie brothers, San Juan, Puerto Rico. 72 plates. obl. 12°.

Henry, Guy V. Remarks on the financial administration of colonial dependencies [Puerto Rico].
(*In* American social science association. Journal, Dec., 1899, pp. 158–163.)

Herrera y Tordesilla, Antonio de. Cronica general de las Indias. Lo referente á la isla de Puerto Rico. Desde la decada 1ª hasta la 5ª.

> (*In* Tapia y Rivera (Alejandro), editor.   Biblioteca historica de Puerto Rico . . . pp. 91–121. Puerto Rico: Imprenta de Marquez, 1854. 8°.)

Herrmann, Carl Stephen. From Yauco to Las Marias, being a story of the recent campaign in western Puerto Rico by the Independent Regular Brigade, under command of Brigadier-General Schwan.
> *Boston: Richard G. Badger & Co., 1900.   Plates, and port. of Theodore Schwan.   109 pp.   8°.*

Hill, Robert Thomas. Cuba and Porto Rico, with the other islands of the West Indies. Their topography, climate, flora, products, industries, cities, people, political conditions, etc.
> *New York: Century Co., 1898.   xxviii, 429 pp.   Plates.   8°.*

——— Notes on the forest conditions of Porto Rico.
> *Washington: 1899.   48 pp.   Maps and plates.   (United States Department of Agriculture, Division of Forestry.   Bulletin No. 25.)*

Hitchcock, Frank H. Trade of Puerto-Rico.
> *Washington: Government printing office, 1898.   84 pp.   8°. (United States.   Department of Agriculture, Section of foreign markets.   Bulletin no. 13.)*

[Imray, James]. A sailing directory for the West India islands; containing instructions for navigating among the islands of Porto Rico, Hayti, Jamaica, Cuba, &c., and for the various ports in the Bay of Honduras and the Gulf of Mexico. Carefully compiled from the most recent surveys made by order of the British, French, American, and Spanish governments.   6th edition.
> *London: James Imray, 1851.   viii, 279 pp.   8°.*

——— Sailing directions for Porto Rico and the Caribbee islands: compiled from the latest English, French, and Spanish surveys.   3d edition.
> *London: James Imray, 1852.   iv, 100 pp.   8°.*

Infantes y Pérez, Leopoldo López. Guía de la policía judicial ante los delitos públicos en las islas de Cuba y Puerto Rico.
> *Matanzas: Establecimiento tipográfico "Galeria literaria," 1895.   103, (3) pp.   8°.*

Infiesta, Alejandro. La exposición de Puerto Rico. Memoria redactada, segun a cuerdo de la junta del centenario.
Puerto Rico: Imp. del "Boletín Mercantil," 1895. (2), 312 pp. Plates. Portraits. 8°.

> Contains: Part I.—Chapter I. Síntesis de los principales acontecimientos de la historia de Puerto Rico. II. Geografía de la isla, . . . geología. Meteorología. Fauna y flora . . . III. Población . . . Instrucción popular. Comercio, agricultura é industria. Riqueza de la isla.
> Part II.—La exposición. Chapter IV. Los certámenes. Obras premiadas por el Ateneo, la económica y el bien público . . . la antología puertorriqueña . . .
> Part III.— . . . Chapters II, III. Ciencias, literatura, música, imprenta. IV. Trabajo de mujer . . . V. Productos agrícolas. VI. Artes usuales, frutos tropicales. VII. . . . Instrucción pública. VIII. Comercio . . .

—— Lealtad y heroismo de la isla de Puerto Rico, 1897.
Puerto Rico: A. Lynne é Hijos de Pérez Moris, 1897. vii, 367 pp. Plates. Portraits. 8°.

—— Memoria con los cuadros de enseñanza y estadísticos correspondientes que sobre el estado de la instrucción primaria · en el distrito sud de esta provincia . . .
Puerto-Rico: Tip. "El Comercio." 1886. 2 parts in 1 volume. Folded sheets. F°.

Instituto de segunda enseñanza de Puerto-Rico. Memoria del curso de 1893 á 94, leida en la solemne apertura del de 1894 á 95 por Santiago Hita y Comas. Precedida del discurso . . . por Jaime Comas y Muntaner.
Puerto-Rico: Imprenta del "Boletín Mercantil," 1895. 219, (2) pp. 8°.

—— *Same.* 1894 á 1895.
Puerto-Rico: "Boletín Mercantil," 1896. 68, (2) pp. 12°.

—— *Same.* 1895 á 1896.
Barcelona: A. Lopez Robert, [1896]. 67, (1) pp. 8°.

—— Memoria correspondiente al curso académico de 1896 á 1897.
[Barcelona: A. López Robert, impresor, 1896.] 75, (2) pp. 8°.

Instituto geográfico y estadístico de España, Madrid. Reseña geográfica y estadística de España, por la dirección general del Instituto geográfico y estadístico.
Madrid: Imprenta de la Dirección general del Instituto geográfico y estadístico, 1888. xxiv, 1116, (1) pp. Folded map. F°.

> Puerto Rico, pp. 1065–1069, viz: Geography, geology, orography and hydrography, climate, flora; civil, judicial, military, maritime, ecclesiastic, and university divisions; population.

Instruccion para la cobranza por la via de apremio de los débitos á favor de los ayuntamientos y para la gestion de las diputaciones provinciales aprobada por Real decreto de 25 de Julio de 1885.

Ponce: Tip. de la Revista de Puerto-Rico, 1891. 8 pp. 16°.

Janer y Soler, Felipe.   Elementos de cosmografía y geografía particular de la isla de Puerto-Rico.

Puerto Rico: Gonzalez & Co., 1883. 101 pp. 12°.

Jefferys, Thomas.   A description of the Spanish islands and settlements on the coast of the West Indies, compiled from authentic memoirs revised by gentlemen who have resided many years in the Spanish settlements, and illustrated with thirty-two maps and plans.

London: 1762.   (6), xxiv, 106, (2) pp.   4°.

> Pp. 95–97 on Puerto Rico.   With plans, "San Juan" and "Aguada Nueva."

Kellogg, Eva M. C.   The war islands.   Cuba and other islands of the sea.   Edited by Larkin Dunton.

Silver, Burdett & company.   New York, 1898.   448 pp. Illus.   Maps.   12°.

Krug, L.   Indianische alterthümer in Porto Rico.

> (*In* Zeitschrift für Ethnologie, 1876.   Heft 6, pp. 428–437.)

Labra, Rafael Maria de.   A los electores de Sabana Grande (Puerto-Rico).   . . .

Madrid: M. G. Hernandez, 1873.   59 pp.   8°.

——— (Cuestiones de ultramar.)   La cuestion de Puerto-Rico.

Madrid: J. E. Morete, 1870.   119 pp.   8°.

Laët, Jan de.   Historia de nuevo mundo, ó descripcion de las Indias occidentales.   . . .

> (*In* Tapia y Rivera (Alejandro), editor.   Biblioteca historica de Puerto Rico   . . .   pp. 123–227.   Puerto Rico: Imprenta de Marquez, 1854.   8°.)

Lavallée, Francis.   Esquisse historique et géographique de l'île de Puerto-Rico.   Avec une carte.

> (*In* Bulletin de la Société de géographie.   5e série.   vol. 2.   pp. 81–96.   Paris, 1861.)

Layfield, John (?) *D. D.*   A large relation of the Porto Ricco voiage; written as is reported, by that learned man and reverend Divine Doctor Layfield, his Lordship's chaplaine and attendant in that expedition; very much abbreviated.

> (*In* Purchas His pilgrimes.   The fourth part.   (Liber vi.)   Chapter III.   pp. 1155–1176.   London: Printed by William Stansby for Henrie Fêtherstone, and are to be sold at his shop in Paul's Churchyard, at the signe of the Rose.   1625.   F°.)

Ledru, André Pierre. Reise nach den Inseln Teneriffe, Trinidad, St. Thomas, St. Cruz und Porto Rico . . . aus dem Französischen übersetzt. Mit einer Charte der Insel Porto-Rico.
Weimar: Verlag des II. S. priv. Land. Indust. Comptoirs, 1812. xx, 322 pp. Map. 8°.

> Pp. 195–305, Porto Rico.

—— Viage a la isla de Puerto Rico en el año 1797 ejecutado por una comision de sabios Franceses . . . con objeto de hacer indagaciones y colecciones relativas a la historia natural . . . traducido al castellano por D. Julio L. de Vizcarrondo.
Puerto-Rico: J. Gonzalez, 1863. 268 pp. 8°.

—— Voyage aux îles de Ténériffe, la Trinité, Saint Thomas, Sainte Croix, et Porto Rico . . . ouvrage accompagné de notes et d'additions par M. Sonnini. Avec très belle carte gravée par J. B. Tardieu, d'après Lopez.
Paris: Arthur Bertrand, 1810. 2 vols. 8°.

> Vol. 2, pp. 46–278, Porto Rico.

Leslie's official history of the Spanish-American war. A pictorial and descriptive record of the Cuban rebellion, the causes that involved the United States, and a complete narrative of our conflict with Spain on land and sea; supplemented with fullest information respecting Cuba, Porto Rico, the Philippines and Hawaii. Compiled from the official records at Washington.
[*Washington,*] [*1899*]. *612, (2) pp. Illus. F°.*

El Liberal. Periodico republicano-autonomista. June 30–December, 1886.
Mayaguez, P. R.: 1886. F°.

Lobo, Miguel. Historia general de las antiguas colonias Hispano-Americanas desde su descubrimiento hasta el año mil ochocientos ocho.
Madrid: Imp. de Miguel Guijarro, 1875. 3 vols. 8°.

> Vol. 1, pp. 304 *et seq.*, Puerto Rico.

Löfling, Peter. Reisebeschreibung nach den spanischen Ländern in Europa und America in den Jahren 1751 bis 1756, nebst Beobachtungen und Anmerkungun über die merkwürdigsten Gewächse, herausgegeben von Carl von Linné. Aus dem Schwedischen übersetzt von Alexander Bernhard Kölpin. Mit Kupferstichen. 2te Auflage.
Berlin: 1776. In Verlag Gottl. August Lange. 16, (16), 406, (2) pp. 8°.

López de Velasco, Juan.   Geografía y descripción universal de las Indias, recompilada por el cosmógrafocronista Juan López de Velasco desde el año de 1571 al de 1574, publicada por primera vez en el Boletín de la Sociedad geográfica de Madrid, . . . por Don Justo Zaragoza.
Madrid: Estab. tip. de Fortanet, 1894. xiii, (3), 808 pp. Folded map. 8°.

> Contents: Corografía de la isla de Cuba, pp. 110–119.   Descripción de la isla San Juan de Puerto Rico, pp. 126–134.   Corografía de las islas Filipinas, pp. 581–591.

Lopez Tuero, Fernando.   Isla de Puerto Rico.   Estudios de economía rural.
Puerto Rico: "Boletin Mercantil," 1893.   142 pp.   12°.

—— Isla de Puerto Rico.   La reforma agrícola.
Puerto Rico: Tip. del "Boletin Mercantil," 1891.   202 pp. (4).   8°.

—— Tratado de cultivos tropicales.   . . .   2ª edicion.
Puerto Rico: Imprenta del " Boletin Mercantil," 1896.   272 pp.   8°.

Luechetti, M.   Puerto-Rico.   Exposicion al congreso de Washington con respecto al regimen administrativo y economico que ha de establecerse en Puerto Rico.
Puerto-Rico: F. J. Marxuach, 1898.   39 pp.   Folded map. 8°.

MacGregor, John.   Hayti and the foreign West Indies.   (Commercial tariffs . . . of the several states of Europe and America . . . Part XX.)

> (*In* Great Britain.   Parliament.   Sessional papers.   1847.   vol. 64.
> London, 1847.)
> Pp. 119–144, Puerto Rico.

Magalhães, Miguel de, *compiler.*   Colonial business directory of the island of Puerto Rico.   (1898.)
New York: 1898.   8°.

Marin, Ramón.   La villa de Ponce considerada en tres distintas epocas. . . .   Editoriales publicados en el periodico "La Crónica." . . .
Ponce: "El Vapor," 1877.   146 pp.   16°.

Martín Sánchez, Francisco.   Discursos y rectificaciones . . . pronunciados en el congreso de los diputados. . . . 1895.
Madrid: Hijos de J. A. García, 1895.   48 pp.   12°.

Mason, Otis T.   The Latimer collection of antiquities from Porto Rico in the National Museum and the Guesde collection of antiquities in the Pointe-a-Pitre, Guadeloupe, West Indies. *Washington: Published by the Smithsonian Institution, 1899. v, 372-837 pp.   8°.*

(From the Smithsonian Reports for 1876 and 1884.)

Memoría de los trabajos realizados por la seccion Puerto Rico del Partido revolucionario Cubano, 1895 á 1896. *Imprenta de A. W. Howes, New York City: [1898].   249 pp. Plate.   8°.*

Memoria sobre las obras públicas de la isla de Puerto-Rico en el año de 1875 á 1876.

(*In* "Revista do obras públicas," vol. 6.   Madrid, 1878.)

Millspaugh, C. F.   Plantæ utowanæ.   Plants collected in Bermudas, Porto Rico, St. Thomas, Culebras, Santo Domingo, Jamaica, Cuba, the Caymans, Cozumel, Yucatan, and the Alcran shoals.   December, 1898, to March, 1899.   The Antillean cruise of the yacht *Mowana*. *Chicago: 1900.   110 pp.   Map.   8°.   (Field Columbian Museum.   Publication 43, Botanical series, vol. ii, no. 1.)*

"Botanical collections made on a yachting trip through the West Indies."

Minguella y Arnedo, T.   Carta pastoral que el ilmo. Sr. obispo de Puerto Rico, dirige al clero y fieles de su diocesis. *Puerto-Rico: Imprenta del Boletín Mercantil, 1897.   23 pp. 12°.*

Morris, Charles.   Our island empire.   A hand-book of Cuba, Porto Rico, Hawaii, and the Philippine islands. *Philadelphia: J. B. Lippincott company, 1899.   xii, 7-488 pp. Map.   8°.*

Möschler, H. B.   Die Lepidopteren-Fauna der Insel Porto-Rico. Mit dem Bildnisse des Verfassers und einer Tafel.

(*In* Senkenberger naturforschende Gesellschaft, Frankfurt a. M. Abhandlungen, vol. 16, 1890: 69–360.)

Un Negrófilo concienzudo.   Cuba y Puerto Rico.   Medios de conservar estas dos Antillas en su estado de esplendor, por . . . *Madrid: José Cruzado, 1866.   159 pp.   8°.*

Neumann-Gandia, Eduardo. Benefactores y hombres notables de Puerto-Rico. Bocetos biográficos-críticos, con un estudio sobre nuestros gobernadores generales. Obra exornada con fotograbados. Vol. I.
Ponce: 1896. "La Libertad." xi, (1), 404, (3) pp. Portraits. 8°.

―――― Gloriosa epopeya. Sitio de los Ingleses de 1797, con datos hasta ahora no publicados.
Ponce: "La Libertad," 1897. 52 pp. Portrait. 8°.

―――― Sitio de los holandeses.
In Infiesta, A. Lealtad y heroismo de la isla de Puerto Rico, pp. 261–274.

North-American and West Indian Gazetteer. Containing an authentic description of the colonies and islands in that part of the globe, showing their situation, climate, soil, produce and trade; with their former and present condition. Also, an exact account of the cities, towns, harbours, ports, bays, rivers, lakes, mountains, number of inhabitants, etc. Illustrated with maps. The second edition.
London: Printed for G. Robinson, 1778. (6), xxiv, (216) pp. 16°.

Ober, Frederick A. Puerto Rico and its resources. With maps and illustrations.
New York: D. Appleton and company, 1899. viii, (4), 282 pp. Plates (photogravures). Folded map. 12°.

―――― The storied West Indies.
New York: D. Appleton & Co., 1900. xx, 291 pp. 8°.

Osgood, Daniel. A letter on the yellow fever of the West Indies.
New York: Published by Elam Bliss, 1820. 72 pp. 12°.

Oviedo y Valdes, Gonzalo Fernandez de. Fragmentos de la historia general y natural de las Indias. Libro 16, y algunos capitulos de otros libros referentes a Puerto-Rico.
(*In* Tapia y Rivera (Alejandro), editor. Biblioteca historica de Puerto Rico. . . . pp. 7–90. Puerto Rico: Imprenta de Marquez, 1854. 8°.)

Packard, R. L. Education in Cuba, Porto Rico, and the Philippines.
(*In* United States Commissioner of Education. Report, 1897–98, vol. 1, pp. 909–967. Washington, 1899.)

Partido autonomista Puerto-riqueño. Exposicion que dirigen al Excmo. Sr. Presidente del consejo de ministros por conducto del Excmo. Sr. Gobernador general de Puerto Rico y del ministro de ultramar el directorio y la delegacion del Partido autonomista Puerto-riqueño.
Madrid: José Gil y Navarro, 1888. 49, (2) pp. 12°.

Partido revolucionario cubano. La seccion Puerto Rico. Memoria de los trabajos realizados por la seccion Puerto Rico del partido revolucionario cubano. 1895 á 1898.
A. W. Howes, New York City: [1898]. 250 pp. 8°.

Peñaranda, Carlos. Cartas Puerto-Riqueñas . . . 1878–1880.
Madrid: "Sucesores de Rivadeneyra," 1885. 195 pp. Portrait. 8°.

Perez Morís, José, y Luis **Cueto y Gonzalez Quijano.** Historia de la insurreccion de Lares, precedida de una reseña de los trabajos separatistas. . . .
Barcelona: Narciso Ramirez y Ca., 1872. xii, 13–342, (1) pp. 8°.

Porto Rico. Estadística general del comercio exterior de la provincia de Puerto-Rico correspondiente al año natural de 1890.
Puerto-Rico: 1891. (8), 193 pp. 4°.

——— Presupuestos generales de gastos é ingresos de la isla de Puerto Rico para el año económico de 1878–79.
Madrid: 1878. 115, (2) pp. 4°.

——— *Same.* 1886–87.
Madrid: 1886. 4°.

——— La situacion de Puerto-Rico; las falacias de los conservadores y los compromisos del partido radical. Por un Puerto-Riqueño.
Madrid: 1873. Imprenta de J. Noguera á cargo de M. Martinez. 79 pp. 8°.

——— *Dirección de instrucción pública.* Programas de Ingles para oposiciones al grado superior y elemental.
Puerto Rico: Boletin Mercantil, 1898. 10 pp. 16°.

——— *Junta insular de instrucción.* Teachers' manual for the public schools of Puerto Rico; issued under the authority of the Insular board of education, by the president of the board. Manual del maestro para las escuelas públicas de

Porto Rico—Continued.

> Puerto Rico; publicado bajo los auspicios de la Junta insular de instrucción, por el presidente de la junta.
>
> *Silver, Burdett & Co., New York: 1900.   xv, (1), 595 pp. Plates.   8°.*

Purdy, John.   The Columbian navigator.

> Volume I.   A sailing directory for the Bermuda Islands, the eastern and southern coasts of the United States, and the State of Texas.   Being Part II of the sailing directories for the eastern coasts and islands of America.   Second edition, improved and corrected from numerous sources, by Alexander Findlay.
>
> *London: Printed for Richard Holmes Laurie, 1847.   194 pp. Folded map.   Plates.   8°.*

> Volume II.   The Columbian navigator.   A sailing directory for the northern part of the West Indies, and the Mexican sea; comprising the islands of Porto Rico, Hayti, or St. Domingo, Jamaica, Cuba, and the Bahama Islands, and the coasts of the Yucatan and Mexico, from Cape Catoche to the Rio del Norte, including the description of the Florida or Gulf stream.   Being Part III of the sailing directories of the eastern coasts and islands of America.   Fourth edition, improved and corrected from numerous sources, by Alexander G. Findlay.
>
> *London: Printed for Richard Holmes Laurie.   Additions to 1856.   xx, 308 pp.   Plates.   8°.*

> Volume III.   The Columbian navigator; or, sailing directory for the American coasts and the West Indies.   Comprehending: 1. Descriptions of the winds, seasons, tides, and currents, and directions for the passages to and among the islands, and to the ports of Guyana, &c.   2. The general navigation of the Caribbean or Colombian sea, from leeward to windward, &c.   3. The island of Porto-Rico, the Virgin islands, and St. Croix.   4. The Caribbee or Windward islands, from Sombero to Trinidad.   5. The coast and rivers of Guyana, from the equator and the Maranon, westward, to the gulf of Paria.   6. The Colombian or Leeward islands, from Margarita westward.   7. The coast of Venezuela, from the gulf of Paria to La Guayra.   8. The coasts from La Guayra to St. Juan de Nicaragua.   9. The islands and shoals between Jamaica and Nicaragua.   10. Mosquitia or the Mosquito shore, from Nicaragua to Cape Honduras, 11. The Bay and Gulf of Honduras, &c., from Cape Hon-

Purdy, John—Continued.

duras to Cape Catoche and Cape Antonio, including the Golfo and Rio Dulce. 12. Temperatures of air and water in the West Indies: Preservation of health: Spanish names and pronunciation. Composed and arranged from a great variety of documents, as enumerated in the work, including most especially, a corrected translation of the ' Derrotero de las Antillas,' by Capt. Andr. Livingston, and the contributions of many other intelligent navigators. Second edition; materially improved, revised, and enlarged.

London: Printed for R. H. Laurie, 1839.   xxiv, 338 pp. Illus. (woodcuts).   Plate.   8°.

Quimones, Francisco Mariano.   Historia de los partidos reformista y conservador de Puerto Rico.

Mayagüez: Tip. Comercial, 1889.   iv, 61 pp.   8°.

Ramos, F.   Prontuario de disposiciones oficiales.   Redactado por . . . F. Ramos . . . Aprobado y dispuesto su publicacion por el gobierno superior civil de esta isla. Contiene las disposiciones mas notables del gobierno superior de la isla, desde el año de 1824 hasta fin de Marzo de 1865 . . .

Puerto-Rico: 1866.   Imp. de Gonzalez.   531 pp.   F°.

Rector, Charles H.   The story of beautiful Porto Rico. A graphic description of the garden spot of the world by pen and camera. Comprising the history, geography, soil, climate . . . Profusely illustrated.

Chicago: Laird & Lee, 1898.   184 pp.   Folded map.   12°.

La Reforma agrícola; órgano de la Asociación de agricultores de Puerto-Rico.

Puerto-Rico: 1896–97.   2 vols.   8°.

Regnault, Élias.   Histoire des Antilles et des colonies françaises, espagnoles, anglaises, danoises et suédoises.   Saint-Domingue, Cuba et Porto-Rico.   . . .

Paris: Firmin Didot frères, 1849.   (2), 160 pp.   8°. (L' Univers, vol. 26.)

Repertorio histórico de Puerto-Rico.   Año 1, Número 1–3, Noviembre, 1896–Dic 15, 1897.

Puerto Rico: Inc. J. J. Acosta, 1897.   4°.

Robinson, Albert Gardner.   The Porto Rico of to-day.   Pen pictures of the people and the country.

New York: Charles Scribner's sons, 1899.   xiv, (2), 240 pp. Plates (photogravures).   Maps.   12°.

Sama, Manuel María.   Bibliografía Puerto-Riqueña.
  Mayaguez, P. R.: Tipografía comercial, 1887.   159 pp.   8°.

Sanromá, Joaquín María.   Puerto-Rico y su hacienda.
  Madrid: T. Fortanet, 1873.   96 pp.   8°.

Santacilia, Pedro.   Lecciones orales sobre la historia de Cuba, pronunciadas en el Ateneo democratico Cubano de Nueva York.
  Nueva-Orleans: L. E. del Cristo, 1859.   xi, 220 pp.   8°.

Santaella, Herminio W.   Geografía astronómica y política de España
  y sus posesiones ultramarinas.   2ª edition.
  Ponce, Puerto Rico: M. Lopez, 1887.   131 pp.   16°.

Scherzer, Karl *von*.   Reise der österreichischen Fregatte "Novara"
  um die Erde . . . 1857–1859.   Statistisch-commercieller
  Theil.
  *Wien: K. K. Hof und Staatsdruckerei.   1865.   2 vols.   Map.
  8°.*
    Porto Rico, vol. 2, pp. 467–495 (with map).

Schoelcher, Victor.   Colonies étrangères et Haïti; résultats de
  l'émancipation anglaise.
  Paris: Pagnerre, 1843.   2 vols.   8°.
    Vol. I: pp. 309–345, on Porto Rico; pp. 349–358, Cuba.

Sichar y Salas, Mariano.   El porvenir de Ponce.
  Ponce: M. Lopez, 1889.   59 pp.   8°.

——— Viaje por la costa noroeste de la isla de Puerto-Rico . . .
  Conferencia leida en el circulo militar de la capital de la
  misma.
  Puerto Rico: "Boletín Mercántil," 1886.   55 pp.   8°.

Sievers, W.   Zur Kenntniss Puerto-Ricos.   Mit einer Karte.
    (*In* Mittheilungen der Geographischen Gesellschaft in Hamburg,
    1891–92.)

Simpson, Charles Torrey.   Distribution of the land and freshwater
  mollusks of the West Indian region and their evidence
  with regard to past changes of land and sea.
    (*In* U. S. National Museum.   Proceedings, vol. 17, pp. 413–450.
    Washington.   1895.   Plate.   8°.)

Situación (La) de Puerto Rico.   Las falacias de los conservadores y
  los compromisos del partido radical por un Puerto-Riqueño.
  Madrid: J. Noguero á cargo de M. Martínez, 1873.   79 pp.
  (*Propaganda reformista.*)

Spain. Aranceles generales para el cobro de derechos de importacion y exportacion en todas las aduanas de los puertos habilitados de la isla de Puerto-Rico, aprobados por S. M. en Agosto de 1849, y reformados con sujecion á las bases prescriptas en reales órdenes de 8 de igual mes de 1851 y 5 de Octubre del corriente año.
Puerto-Rico: Imprenta de Acosta, 1857. (92) pp. F°.

———— Constitucion autonomica. Decreto sobre igualdad de derechos politicos y ley electoral de Puerto-Rico.
Puerto-Rico: Imprenta "El Pais," 1898. (2), 29 pp. 16°.

———— Constitution establishing self government in the islands of Cuba and Porto Rico. Promulgated by royal decree of November 25, 1897. [Translated.] Division of customs and insular affairs, War Department, August, 1899.
Washington: Government Printing Office, 1899. 24 pp. 8°.

———— Instruccion reglamentaria aprobada por S. M., para el servicio de las aduanas en los puertos habilitados de la isla de Puerto-Rico. Mandada observar por real órden de 5 de Octubre de 1857.
Puerto-Rico: Imprenta de Acosta, 1857. (4), 51 pp. F°.

———— Ley para el ejercicio del derecho de asociacion mandada observar en las islas de Cuba y Puerto-Rico por real decreto de 13 de Junio de 1888.
Puerto-Rico: Imprenta de Gobierno, 1888. 6 pp. 8°.

———— *Ministerio de ultramar.* Régimen del gobierno y administracion civil de la isla de Puerto-Rico. Reformas planteadas con arreglo á la ley de bases de 15 de Marzo de 1895. Leyes y decretos. Edición oficial.
Madrid: Imprenta de la viuda de Minuesa de los Ríos, 1897. 206 pp. 8°.

———— Presupuestos generales de ingresos y gastos de la isla de Puerto-Rico para el año económico de 1878–79.
Madrid: Imprenta de Manuel Ginesta, 1878. 115, (2) pp. 4°.

———— *Same.* 1886–87.
Madrid: 1886. 4°.

———— Real decreto de 25 de Noviembre de 1897 adaptando la ley electoral de 26 de Junio de 1890 á las islas de Cuba y Puerto-Rico.
Habana: Imprenta del gobierno y capitanía general, 1898. 40 pp. 8°.

Spain. Reglamento provisional para la adaptación de la ley electoral
de 26 de Junio de 1890 á las islas de Cuba y Puerto-Rico.
Puerto-Rico: Tipografía de la Sucesión de J. J. Acosta, 1898.
(4), 31 pp.   8°.

———— Suplemento á la instruccion reglamentaria y aranceles generales que rijen en las aduanas de la isla de Puerto Rico,
mandado publicar y observar en las mismas aduanas por
disposicion de la intendencia. Edicion oficial.
Puerto Rico: Imprenta de Acosta, 1864.   71, (1) pp.   fol.

Stone, Roy.   Agriculture in Puerto Rico.
(*In* United States: Department of Agriculture, Yearbook, 1898.
pp. 505–514. Washington, 1899. 1 plate.)

Tapia y Rivera, Alejandro.   Biblioteca histórica de Puerto Rico que
contiene varios documentos de los siglos xv, xvi, xvii, y
xviii. . . .
Puerto Rico: Imprenta de Marquez, 1854.   587, 14 pp.   8°.

———— Camoens.   Drama original en tres actos.   Refundido y corre-
gido por el autor, para esta segunda edición: la primera fué
hecha en Madrid en 1868.
Puerto Rico: Est. tip. de Acosta, 1878.   75, (1) pp.   12°.

———— Conferencias sobre estética y literatura, pronunciadas en el
Ateneo Puerto-Riqueño.
Puerto Rico: Tip. de Gonzalez & Co., 1881.   311 pp.   12°.

———— Miscelánea.   Novelas, cuentos, bocetos y otros opúsculos.
Puerto Rico: González & Co., 1880.   (2), 260, (2) pp.   12°.

———— Noticia historica de D. Ramon Power, primer diputado de
Puerto Rico, con un apéndice que contiene algunos de sus
escritos y discursos.
Puerto Rico: Est. tip. de Gonzalez, 1873.   49 pp.   12°.

———— Postumo el transmigrado; historia de un hombre que resus-
citó en el cuerpo de su enemigo.
Puerto-Rico: J. G. Font, 1882.   2 parts in 1 vol.   8°.
NOTE.—Title of part 2 reads: "Postumo envirginiando; ó historia
de un hombre que se coló en el cuerpo de una mujer."

Tejada, L. de.   Descripción del huracán del 13 de Setiembre de 1876
en la isla de Puerto-Rico.
(*In* Revista de obras públicas, vol. 25. Madrid, 1877.)

Ubeda y Delgado, Manuel. Isla de Puerto Rico: estudio histórico, geográfico y estadístico.

Porto Rico: Establecimiento tip. del Boletin, 1878. 290 pp. 8°.

> "En tres secciones divide su obra el Sr. Ubeda. En la primera ocúpase de la historia de la isla desde su descubrimiento hasta nuestros días, consultando la Historia geográfica, civil y natural de Puerto Rico, del sabio benedicto Fray Iñigo Abad; las Memorias de Don Pedro Tomás de Córdoba, y la Historia de la insurrección de Lares. En la segunda sección trata de la organización de Puerto-Rico; y en la tercera ofrece una descripción geográfica de la isla en general, y datos estadísticos, históricos, etc. etc., sobre todos y cada uno de los pueblos en particular . . . "

United States. *56th Congress, 1st session. House document no. 594.* Relations of Puerto Rico to the Constitution. Letter from the Assistant Secretary of War, transmitting a reply to the resolution of the House of Representatives of March 30, 1900, relating to any opinion or opinions of a law officer of that department on the relations of the island of Puerto Rico to the Constitution. 17 pp. 8°.

——— ——— *House report 249.* Ways and means committee. Report of S. E. Payne submitting H. 8245, to regulate trade of Puerto Rico, as a substitute for H. 6883; with views of minority, Feb. 8, 1900. 32 pp. 8°.

——— ——— To regulate the trade of Puerto Rico, and for other purposes. [Mr. Payne's report from the committee on ways and means (to accompany H. R. 8245), with views of the minority.] Feb. 8, 1900. 32 pp. 8°.

——— *56th Congress, 2d session. House document no. 136.* Disbursements by the Treasurer of Porto Rico, May to September, 1900. 34 pp.

——— ——— *House document no. 137.* Reports of the Auditor of Porto Rico of receipts and disbursements, May to October, 1900. 142 pp.

——— ——— *House document no. 171.* Agricultural resources and capabilities of Porto Rico. Report by special agent in charge of agricultural investigations in Porto Rico. December 11, 1900. 32 pp. 7 plates. 8°.

——— *War Department.* Proclamation (to people of Porto Rico). Nov. 24, 1898.

Puerto Principe: 1898. Broadside. In Spanish and English.

(Proclamation concerning the overtaking of the government of the province of Puerto Principe by Brig. Gen. L. A. Carpenter.)

United States. *War Department. Adjutant-General's Office. Military Information Division.* Military notes on Puerto Rico.
Washington: Government Printing Office, 1898. 75 pp. 12 folding maps. Small 8°.

—————— *Department of Porto Rico.* Inauguration of the first civil governor of Porto Rico. May 1, 1900.
[*San Juan, Porto Rico.*] *Published by direction of the commanding general. Department of Porto Rico. 1900. 35*
Pp. 19–35 contain Spanish text with separate title-page.

—————— *Director of Census of Porto Rico.* Report on the census of Porto Rico, 1890. Lt. Col. J. P. Sanger, director. Henry Gannett, Walter F. Willcox, statistical experts.
Washington: Government Printing Office, 1900. 417 pp. Plates. Colored maps. 8°.

—————— Report of Brig. Gen. George W. Davis, U. S. V., on civil affairs of Puerto Rico, 1899.
Washington: Government Printing Office, 1900. 342 pp. 8°.

—————— Customs tariff and regulations for ports in Porto Rico in possession of the United States.
Washington: Government Printing Office, 1898. 42 pp. 8°.

—————— *Division of Customs and Insular Affairs.* Amended customs tariff and regulations for ports in Porto Rico.
Washington: Government Printing Office, 1899. 108 pp. 8°.

————————— Immigration regulations for the island of Porto Rico.
Washington: Government Printing Office, 1899. 9 pp. 8°.

————————— (Reports under Circular No. 10.) Puerto Rico, embracing the reports of Brig. Gen. George W. Davis, military governor, and reports on the districts of Arecibo, Aguadilla, Cayey, Humacao, Mayaguez, Ponce, San Juan, Vieques and the subdistrict of San German. Arranged by topics.
Washington: Government Printing Office, 1900. 94 pp. 8°.

————————— Translation. Laws relating to the civil administration and government of the island of Porto Rico.
Washington: Government Printing Office, 1899. 53 pp. 8°.

————————— Translation. Compilation of the organic provisions of the administration of justice in force in the Spanish colonial provinces, and appendices relating thereto. (1891.)
Washington: Government Printing Office, 1899. 170 pp. 8°.

United States. *War Department. Division of Customs and Insular Affairs.* Translation of the civil code in force in Cuba, Porto Rico, and the Philippines.
Washington: Government Printing Office, 1899. 322 pp. 8°.

————— ————— ————— Translation of the code of commerce in force in Cuba, Porto Rico, and the Philippines, amended by the law of June 10, 1897, including the commercial registry regulations, exchange regulations, and other provisions of a similar character, with annotations and appendices.
Washington: Government Printing Office, 1899. iv, 291 pp. 8°.

————— ————— ————— Translation of the notarial laws in force in Cuba and Porto Rico. 1888.
Washington: Government Printing Office, 1899. 58 pp. 8°.

————— ————— ————— Translation of the penal code in force in Cuba and Porto Rico.
Washington: Government Printing Office, 1899. 175 pp. 8°.

————— ————— ————— Translation of the provincial and municipal laws of Porto Rico.
Washington: Government Printing Office, 1899. 58 pp. 8°.

————— ————— Translation of the law of civil procedure for Cuba and Porto Rico, with annotations, explanatory notes . . .
Washington: Government Printing Office, 1901. x, (2), 544 pp. 8°.

————— ————— Translation of the law of railroads for the island of Puerto Rico, granted to the island by royal decree of December 8, 1887, and promulgated in Puerto Rico on January 10, 1888.
Washington: Government Printing Office, 1899. 45 pp. 8°.

————— ————— Translation of the mortgage law for Cuba, Puerto Rico, and the Philippines. (1893.)
Washington: Government Printing Office, 1899. 90 pp. 8°.

————— ————— Translation of the police law of railroads of Puerto Rico, and regulations for its application, promulgated on the 17th of February, 1898.
Washington: Government Printing Office, 1899. 37 pp. 8°.

————— ————— *Division of Insular Affairs.* Report of Brig. Gen. George W. Davis on the industrial and economic conditions of Puerto Rico.
Washington: Government Printing Office, 1900. 47 pp. 8°.

Valiente, Porfirio.   Réformes dans les îles de Cuba et de Puerto Rico.
   Paris: A. Chaix et cie., 1869.   xx, 412 pp.   8°.

Valle Atilés, Francisco del.   El campesino Puertorriqueño, sus condiciones físicas, intelectuales y morales. . . .
   Puerto Rico: José Gonzalez Font, 1887.   167 pp.   8°.

Valle, José G. del.   Un ciudadano modelo.   [F. Asensio y Arteaga.]
   *Puerto Rico: Tip. al vapor de " La Correspondencia," 1896.
   28 pp.   12°.   (Bibliografía portorriqueña.)*

——— Puerto Rico.   Chicago.   Trabajos descriptivos y de investigaciones críticas.   Prólogo de Alejandro Ynfiesta.
   [Puerto-Rico:] 1895.   xi, 233, (8) pp.   12°.

Valle, Rafael del.   Poesías.   Con un prologo de A. Valdivia.
   A. Salicrup, Arecibo, P. R.: 1884.   xix, 205, (8) pp.   8°.

Valle y Soriano, Sebastián del.   Manual para el puntual cumplimiento
   de varias de las obligaciones de los ayuntamientos de la
   provincia de Puerto Rico.
   Puerto Rico: Imprenta de Gonzalez, 1882.   xvii pp.   8°.

Viñes, Benito.   Apuntes relativos á los huracanes de las Antillas en
   setiembre y octubre de 1875 y 1876.   Discurso leido en la
   Real Academia de ciencias médicas, físicas y naturales de
   la Habana.
   Habana: Tipografía El Iris, 1877.   256 pp.   Folded map.   8°.

——— Investigaciones relativas á la circulacion y traslacion ciclónica
   en los huracanes de las Antillas.   Primera edicion.
   *Habana: Imp. del "Arrisador Comercial," de Pulido y Diaz,
   1895.   79 pp.   Portrait.   8°.*

Vivian, Thomas J., and **Smith**, Ruel P.   Everything about our new
   possessions.   Being a handy book on Cuba, Porto Rico,
   Hawaii, and the Philippines.
   New York: R. F. Fenno & Co., 1899.   182 pp.   12°.

Vizcarrondo, Julio L. de.   (Puerto Rico, geography and history.)
   Puerto Rico? [186–?]   106 pp.   12°.
      Title-page missing.

Walton, Clifford Stevens.   The civil law in Spain and Spanish America, including Cuba, Puerto Pico, and the Philippine islands;
   and the Spanish civil code in force; annotated and with
   references to the civil codes of Mexico, Central and South
   America. . . .
   *Washington: W. H. Lowdermilk & Co., 1900.   xix, 672 pp.
   8°.*

Wilson, H. M. Water resources of Puerto Rico.

*Washington: Government Printing Office, 1899.   48 pp.
Plates.   Maps.   8°.*

(United States Geological Survey.   Water supply and irrigation
papers, no. 32.)

Voyage aux Antilles espagnoles, à Porto-Rico, Cuba et au Mexique.
Considérations sur l'influence française dans ces régions.
(D'après le "B. S. Études colon. et marit.")   J. Claine.
*Bul. Union Géographique du Nord de la France, vol. 14:
241–243.*

ARTICLES IN PERIODICALS.

1834. Flinter's account of Porto Rico.
Monthly review, vol. 135 (Nov., 1834): 411.

1835. Flinter's account of Porto Rico.
Edinburgh review, vol. 60 (Jan., 1835): 328.

1844. Commerce with Porto Rico.
Hunt's merchants' magazine, vol. 10 (Apr., 1844): 327.

1847. Turnbull's Porto Rico and Cuba.
Southern quarterly review, vol. 12 (July, 1847): 91.

1883. Porto Rico. H. Eggers.
Nature, vol. 29 (Dec. 6, 1883): 129.

1888. Literature from Porto Rico.
Literary world, vol. 19 (June 9, 1888): 189.

1891–1892. Zur Kenntniss der Insel Puerto Rico.
Geographische Gesellschaft, Hamburg. Mittheilungen, 1891–1892, pp. 217–236.

1893. Porto Rico. J. Claine.
Tour du monde, vol. 66 (1893): 417–432. Ill. maps.
"A visit to Porto Rico in 1892, with numerous well-chosen illustrations."

1894. Le monde antilien: Cuba, Puerto-Rico. C. de Varigny.
Revue des deux mondes, 4° période, vol. 121 (Jan., 1894): 167.

1894. Depth of the ocean near Porto Rico. The physical condition of the ocean. W. J. L. Wharton.
Geographical journal, vol. IV (Sept., 1894): 255.

1896. Politische geographische Betrachtungen über Puerto Rico. E. Deckert.
Geographische Zeitschrift, vol. 2 (1896): 138.

1898. Le chalutage sur les côtes de Porto-Rico. A. Nobre.
Revue maritime (1898): 618–621.   *(War Department.)*

1898. Bombardment of San Juan. H. Martin.
Harper's weekly, vol. 42 (May 28, 1898): 507.

1898. With Admiral Sampson's fleet. The bombardment of San
Juan. C. T. Chapman.
Harper's weekly, vol. 42 (June 4, 1898): 538.

1898. The San Juan bombardment. E. Emerson, jr., and others.
Leslies' weekly, vol. 86 (June 9, 1898): 378.

1898. Porto Rico as seen last month [June, 1898]. E. Emerson.
American review of reviews, vol. 18 (July, 1898): 42.

1898. The economic condition of Porto Rico.
Board of trade journal, vol. 25 (July, 1898): 26–30.

1898. Porto Rico and the capture of San Juan. W. Winthrop.
Outlook, vol. 59 (July 16, 1898): 675

1898. Forcible annexation.
Nation, vol. 67 (July 28, 1898): 65.

1898. Porto Rico. A. Solomon.
Independent, vol. 50 (July 28, 1898): 254–255.

1898. Porto Rico: its natural history and products.
Scientific American supplement, vol. 46 (July 30, 1898): 18880.

1898. The island of Porto Rico. F. A. Ober.
Century, vol. 56 (Aug., 1898): 546–554; (Oct., 1898): 957.

1898. *Same. Article condensed.*
Living age, vol. 218 (Aug. 13, 1898): 478–479.
Public opinion, vol. 25 (Aug. 11, 1898): 169.

1898. The island of Puerto Rico. W. P. Wilson.
Current literature, vol. 24 (Aug., 1898): 140.

1898. Porto Rico: Spain's last outpost.
Gunton's magazine, vol. 15 (Aug., 1898): 95.

1898. Campaign in Porto Rico. With map.
Independent, vol. 50 (Aug. 4, 1898): 290–291.

1898. Our reception in Porto Rico.
Public opinion, vol. 25 (Aug. 11, 1898): 164.

1898. Imprisonment of W. F. Halstead.
Illustrated American, vol. 24 (Aug. 12, 1898): 105.

1898. The Puerto Rican expedition. T. D. Walker.
Harper's weekly, vol. 42 (Aug. 20, 1898): 827.

1898. Saint Thomas and San Juan. F. A. Ober.
Independent, vol. 50 (Aug. 25, 1898): 543–545.

1898. Alone in Porto Rico.   E. Emerson, jr.
Century, vol. 56 (Sept., 1898): 666–667.

1898. Our new island, Puerto Rico.   E. Deland.
Chautauquan, vol. 27 (Sept., 1898): 669–672.

1898. The commercial promise of Cuba, Porto Rico, and the Philippines.   G. B. Waldron.
McClure, vol. 11 (Sept., 1898): 481–484.

1898. Miles takes Porto Rico.   E. A. Walcott.
Overland, n. s., vol. 32 (Sept., 1898): 257.

1898. Porto Rico.   With map.
Journal of education, vol. 48 (Sept. 1, 1898): 140.

1898. Educating the Cubans and Porto Ricans.
Public opinion, vol. 25 (Sept. 1, 1898): 262.

1898. The occupation of Ponce.   C. T. Chapman.
Harper's weekly, vol. 42 (Sept. 3, 1898): 863.

1898. How the stars and stripes came to Arroyo.   C. T. Chapman.
Harper's weekly, vol. 42 (Sept. 3, 1898): 874.

1898. Dramatic reception of peace news.   W. E. W. MacKinlay.
Leslie's weekly, vol. 87 (Sept. 22, 1898): 234.

1898. A dramatic interruption.   T. D. Walker.   [The end of the
war in Porto Rico.]
Harper's weekly, vol. 42 (Sept. 24, 1898): 939–942.

1898. The Puerto Rico campaign.   J. M. A. Darrach.
Harper's weekly, vol. 42 (Sept. 24, 1898): 942.

1898. Porto Rico as a field for investors.   A. Solomon.
Independent, vol. 50 (Sept. 29, 1898): 903.

1898. Porto Rico as it is.
Current literature, vol. 24 (Oct., 1898): 338.

1898. Porto Rico.   New United States colony.   P. MacQueen.
National magazine, vol. 9 (Oct., 1898): 3.

1898. Peace in Puerto Rico.   T. D. Walker.
Harper's weekly, vol. 42 (Oct., 1, 1898): 958.

1898. Typhoid fever in Porto Rico.   N. Senn.
Scientific American supplement, vol. 46 (Oct. 1, 1898): 19032.

1898. Porto Rico to-day.   G. G. Baldwin.
Independent, vol. 50 (Oct. 6, 1898): 964.

1898. A snap-shot at Porto Rico. P. MacQueen.
Leslie's weekly, vol. 87 (Oct. 13, 1898): 295.

1898. From Guayama to St. John. M. Wilcox.
Harper's weekly, vol. 42 (Oct. 15, 1898): 1010.

1898. A glimpse of interior Porto Rico. P. MacQueen.
Leslie's weekly, vol. 87 (Oct. 20, 1898): 315.

1898. A Puerto Rican problem. The crowded prisons. M. Wilcox.
Harper's weekly, vol. 42 (Oct. 29, 1898): 1055.

1898. Occupation of Mayaguez. R. F. Zogbaum.
Harper's weekly, vol. 42 (Oct. 29, 1898): 1067.

1898. In Porto Rico with General Miles. W. P. Sutton.
Cosmopolitan, vol. 26 (Nov., 1898): 13–22.

1898. The closed door in Porto Rico. R. Ogden.
Nation, vol. 67 (Nov., 1898): 383.

1898. The Porto Rican campaign. R. H. Davis.
Scribner's magazine, vol. 24 (Nov., 1898): 515–527.

1898. Character of the Porto Rican market.
Public opinion, vol. 25 (Nov. 10, 1898): 604.

1898. The "black hand" in Puerto Rico. J. H. Thacher.
Harper's weekly, vol. 42 (Nov. 12, 1898): 1100–1102.

1898. The evacuation of Porto Rico. W. Dinwiddie.
Harper's weekly, vol. 42 (Nov. 19, 1898): 1139.

1898. The closed door in Porto Rico.
Nation, vol. 67 (Nov. 24, 1898): 383.

1898. Puerto Rico. The military road. W. Dinwiddie.
Harper's weekly, vol. 42 (Nov. 26, 1898): 1163.

1898. Puerto Rico and public instruction. C. E. Waters.
Education, vol. 19 (Dec., 1898): 239–242.
American review of reviews, vol. 19 (Jan., 1899): 92.

1898. Financial wrong in Porto Rico. C. Wiener.
North American review, vol. 167 (Dec., 1898): 754–755
Public opinion, vol. 25 (Dec. 29, 1898): 806.

1898. Cock-fighting in Puerto Rico. W. Dinwiddie.
Harper's weekly, vol. 42 (Dec. 3, 1898): 1174.

1898. Porto Rico, Cuba and the Philippines. H. A. Herbert.
Independent, vol. 50 (Dec. 8, 1898): 1646.

1898. Puerto Rico.   The home life of the people.   W. Dinwiddie.
Harper's weekly, vol. 42 (Dec. 10, 1898): 1211.

1898. Porto Rico, a mission field.   G. G. Groff.
Independent, vol. 50 (Dec. 22, 1898): 1881.

1898. The water works of·San Juan.   W. Dinwiddie.
Harper's weekly, vol. 42 (Dec. 24, 1898): 1271.

1898. Garrisoning Cuba and Porto Rico.   T. G. Steward.
Independent, vol. 50 (Dec. 29, 1898): 1927.

1898. The money of Puerto Rico.   W. Dinwiddie.
Harper's weekly, vol. 42 (Dec. 31, 1898): 1286.

1898. The book trade in Porto Rico.
Publisher's weekly, vol. 54 (Dec. 31, 1898): 1176.

1899. Hawaii and Porto Rico.
Independent, vol. 51 (Jan. 5, 1899): 77.

1899. Porto Rico.   Industrial possibilities of the island.   W. Dinwiddie.
*Harper's weekly, vol. 43 (Jan. 28, 1899): 101; (Feb. 4, 1899):
122.*

1399. The exploitation of electric tramways in Porto Rico.   A. Mattel
Lluveras.   With map.
Engineering magazine, vol. 16 (Feb., 1899): 799.

1899. School system of Porto Rico.   A. P. Gardner.
Forum, vol. 26 (Feb., 1899): 711.

1899. Archbishop Chapelle's mission.
Independent, vol. 51 (Feb. 2, 1899): 358.

1899. First missionaries to Porto Rico.   S. T. Willis.
Independent, vol. 51 (Feb. 2, 1899): 371.

1899. Church of Christ in our new possessions.
Independent, vol. 51 (Feb. 9, 1899):431.

1899. Coffee culture [in Porto Rico].   W. Dinwiddie.
Harper's weekly, vol. 43 (Feb. 11, 1899): 146.

1899. Observations in Porto Rico.   W. H. Ward.
Independent, vol. 51 (Feb. 16, 1899): 463.

1899. Catholic problem in Porto Rico and Cuba.
Independent, vol. 51 (Feb. 16, 1899): 499.

1899. Sugar-culture [in Puerto Rico]. W. Dinwiddie.
Harper's weekly, vol. 43 (Feb. 18, 1899): 167.

1899. Tobacco-culture [in Puerto Rico]. W. Dinwiddie.
Harper's weekly, vol. 43 (Feb. 23, 1899): 193.

1899. Porto Rico, the land and the people. W. H. Ward.
Independent, vol. 51 (Feb. 23, 1899): 543.

1899. The condition of Porto Rico. W. H. Ward.
American review of reviews, vol. 19 (Mar., 1899): 313.

1899. New customs tariff of Porto Rico.
Board of trade journal, vol. 26 (Mar., 1899): 321.

1899. Porto-Rico. Configuration and geology. R. T. Hill.
National geographical magazine, vol. 10 (Mar., 1899): 93.

1899. Gen. Henry's policy in Porto Rico.
Independent, vol. 51 (Feb. 2, 1899): 310; (Mar. 2, 1899): 643.

1899. Fruit-raising, market gardening and horticulture [in Puerto Rico]. W. Dinwiddie.
Harper's weekly, vol. 43 (Mar. 4, 1899): 217.

1899. Byways in Porto Rico. Anne Rhodes.
Outlook, vol. 61 (Mar. 4, 1899): 502–509.

1899. With General Miles in Porto Rico. B. T. Clayton.
Independent, vol. 51 (Mar. 9, 1899): 679.

1899. The church property in Porto Rico.
Independent, vol. 51 (Mar. 9, 1899): 711.

1899. Physical features of the island [Puerto Rico]. W. Dinwiddie.
Harper's weekly, vol. 43 (Mar. 11, 1899): 244.

1899. Military government in Porto Rico. S. S. Tuthill.
Independent, vol. 51 (Mar. 16, 1899): 745; (Mar. 23, 1899): 818.

1899. Puerto Rico's cabinet.
Harper's weekly, vol. 43 (Mar. 18, 1899): 258.

1899. Prevalent diseases in the island [Puerto Rico] and hygienic precautions. Geology. W. Dinwiddie.
Harper's weekly, vol. 43 (Mar. 18, 1899): 265.

1899. The great caves of Puerto Rico. W. Dinwiddie.
Harper's weekly, vol. 43 (Mar. 25, 1899): 293.

1899.   Puerto Rico and the Puerto Ricans.   W. H. Sloane.
Missionary review, vol. 22 (Apr., 1899): 253–258.

1899.   No church unity in Porto Rico.
Independent, vol. 51 (Apr. 6, 1899): 974.

1899.   Revenue and taxes.   W. Dinwiddie.
Harper's weekly, vol. 43 (Apr. 8, 1899): 345.

1899.   Destitution in Porto Rico.
Independent, vol. 51 (Apr. 13, 1899): 993.

1899.   Marriage reform in Porto Rico.
Independent vol. 51 (Apr. 20, 1899): 1099.

1899.   The peasants of Puerto Rico.   W. Dinwiddie.
Harper's weekly, vol. 43 (Apr. 29, 1899): 424.

1899.   Difficulties confronting the United States.   W. V. Pettit.
Atlantic monthly, vol. 83 (May, 1899): 634–644.

1899.   Burden-bearing in Puerto Rico.   W. Dinwiddie.
Harper's weekly, vol. 43 (May 6, 1899): 458.

1899.   Needs of the Porto Ricans.   L. M. Rivera.
Independent, vol. 51 (May 11, 1899): 1284.

1899.   Cities of Puerto Rico.   W. Dinwiddie.
Harper's weekly, vol. 43 (May 13, 1899): 481.

1899.   The value of Porto Rico.   R. T. Hill.
Forum, vol. 27 (June, 1899): 414–419.

1899.   Campaign in Porto Rico.   H. C. Lodge.
Harper's monthly, vol. 99 (June, 1899): 63–77.

1899.   The penal code of Cuba and Porto Rico.   Lloyd McKim
Garrison.
Harvard law review, vol. 13 (June, 1899): 124.

1899.   Americanizing Porto Rico.   G. V. Henry.
Independent, vol. 51 (June 1, 1899): 1475.

1899.   Trade with Porto Rico.
Independent, vol. 51 (June 8, 1899): 1585–1586.

1899.   The engineering development of Porto Rico.   Herbert M.
Wilson.
Engineering magazine, vol. 17 (July, 1899): 602–621.

1899.   The currency of Porto Rico.   J. D. Whelpley.
Forum, vol. 27 (July, 1899): 564–569.

1899. Need of good roads.
Munsey, vol. 21 (July, 1899): 486.

1899. Insular commission on church and state.
Independent, vol. 51 (July 13, 1899): 1894–1895.

1899. Insular police of Porto Rico. S. S. Tuthill.
Independent, vol. 51 (July 20, 1899): 1922.

1899. Case of Porto Rico.
Independent, vol. 51 (July 27, 1899): 2031.

1899. Porto Rico from a woman's point of view. Mrs. G. V. Henry.
American review of reviews, vol. 20 (Aug., 1899): 177–180.

1899. Americanizing the church in Cuba and Puerto Rico.
Harper's weekly, vol. 43 (Aug. 5, 1899): 777.

1899. Sanitary work in Porto Rico. L. P. Davison.
Independent, vol. 51 (Aug. 10, 1899): 2128–2131.

1899. People of Porto Rico. L. Amadeo.
Independent, vol. 51 (Aug. 24, 1899): 2285–2286.

1899. Puerto Rico's disaster. [The hurricane of July, 1899]. W. S. Post.
Harper's weekly, vol. 43 (Aug. 26, 1899): 850.

1899. Sanitary work in Porto Rico. L. P. Davison.
Scientific American supplement, vol. 48 (Aug. 26, 1899): 19787.

1899. The flag and trade: a summary review of the trade of the chief colonial empires. A. W. Flux.
Royal statistical society. Journal, vol. 62 (Sept., 1899): 489–522.
Porto Rico, pp. 512–513.

1899. Reise Eindrücke aus Puerto Rico. Th. Hübener.
Globus, vol. 76 (Sept. 2, 1899): 133–138.

1899. How shall Puerto Rico be governed?
Public opinion, vol. 27 (Sept. 7, 1899): 294.

1899. Future of Porto Rico.
Independent, vol. 51 (Sept. 28, 1899): 2633–2634.

1899. Geologic formation of Porto Rico.
Public opinion, vol. 27 (Sept. 28, 1899): 399.

1899. Porto Rico and the Portoricans.   M. W. Harrington.
Catholic world, vol. 70 (Nov., 1899): 161–177.

1899. How shall Puerto Rico be governed?   H. K. Carroll.
Forum, vol. 28 (Nov., 1899): 257–267.

1899. Our duty in Porto Rico.   G. V. Henry.
Munsey, vol. 22 (Nov., 1899): 233–249.

1899. Religious question in Porto Rico.   H. K. Carroll.
Independent, vol. 51 (Nov. 2, 1899): 2935–2937.

1899. How shall Puerto Rico be governed?
Independent, vol. 51 (Nov. 23, 1899): 3180.

1899. What has been done for Porto Rico under military rule.
H. K. Carroll.
American review of reviews, vol. 20 (Dec., 1899): 705–709.

1899. Status of Porto Rico.   H. G. Curtis.
Forum, vol. 28 (Dec., 1899): 403–411.

1899. Economic condition of Porto Rico.   L. Amadeo.
Independent, vol. 51 (Dec. 28, 1899): 3478–3480.

1899. Puerto-Rican insular police.   T. M. Alexander.
Harper's weekly, vol. 43 (Dec. 30, 1899): 1327.

1899. Puerto Rico's needs: a practical suggestion.   Roy Stone.
Outlook, vol. 63 (Dec. 30, 1899): 1023–1025.

1900. Report of Dr. Carroll on Porto Rico.
Independent, vol. 52 (Jan. 4, 1900): 75–77.

1900. Colonial government for Porto Rico.   G. G. Groff.
Independent, vol. 52 (Jan. 11, 1900): 102–105.

1900. Our policy towards Porto Rico.
Independent, vol. 52 (Jan. 18, 1900): 161.

1900. Trade and industry in Porto Rico.
Scientific American supplement, vol. 49 (Jan. 20, 1900):20120.

1900. Free trade with Porto Rico.
Independent, vol. 52 (Jan. 25, 1900): 221.

1900. Porto Rico.   Territory or a province?
Independent, vol. 52 (Jan. 25, 1900): 265.

1900. Agricultural outlook in Porto Rico.
Scientific American, n. s., vol. 82 (Jan. 27, 1900): 50.

1900. The Porto Rican tariff.
*Independent, vol. 52 (Feb. 1, 1900): 285; (Feb. 8, 1900): 345;
(Feb. 15, 1900): 446; (Mar. 1, 1900): 517, 559; (Mar. 8,
1900): 605, 613; (Mar. 15, 1900): 640, 665; (Mar. 22,
1900): 727.*

1900. Shall simple justice be done to Porto Rico?
Independent, vol. 52 (Feb. 1, 1900): 325–327.

1900. Suffrage in Cuba and Puerto Rico.
Public opinion, vol. 28 (Feb. 1, 1900): 136.

1900. Protectionists' victory.
Public opinion, vol. 28 (Feb. 8, 1900): 165.

1900. The Porto Rican inhumanity.
Nation, vol. 70 (Feb. 15, 1900): 122.

1900. Is Porto Rico a part of the United States? J. D. Richardson.
Independent, vol. 52 (Feb. 22, 1900): 467–469.

1900. Morals of the Porto Rican question.
Nation, vol. 70 (Feb. 22, 1900): 140.

1900. The Porto Rican tariff bill.
Outlook, vol. 64 (Feb. 24, 1900): 569; (Apr. 14, 1900): 841–843.

1900. Christian missions in Porto Rico.
Missionary review, vol. 23 (Mar., 1900): 205.

1900. The President and Porto Rico.
Nation, vol. 70 (Mar. 1, 1900): 158.

1900. The debate on the Porto Rican tariff bill.
Public opinion, vol. 28 (Mar. 1, 1900): 259–260.

1900. Deeds, not words.
Nation, vol. 70 (Mar. 8, 1900): 178.

1900. The act of the House on the Porto Rican tariff bill.
Public opinion, vol. 28 (Mar. 8, 1900): 292.

1900. Bishop Blenk in Porto Rico; the carnival. S. S. McKee.
Harper's weekly, vol. 44 (Mar. 10, 1900): 220.

1900. Congress and the Porto Ricans.
Outlook, vol. 64 (Mar. 10, 1900): 574–576.

1900. Duty of the Senate in tariff issue.
Independent, vol. 52 (Mar. 15, 1900): 671–672.

1900. Effects of the proposed Porto Rican tariff.   A. Ames.
Independent, vol. 52 (Mar. 15, 1900): 637–640.

1900. Taxing Porto Rico.
Outlook, vol. 64 (Mar. 17, 1900): 616.

1900. Our treaty relations to Porto Rico and the Philippines.   J.
Ross.
Independent, vol. 52 (Mar. 22, 1900): 693.

1900. Secretary Long's speech [about the tariff].
Nation, vol. 70 (Mar. 29, 1900): 236.

1900. Status of Porto Rico and Hawaii.
American review of reviews, vol. 21 (Apr., 1900): 387–389.

1900. Porto Rican relief bill.   A. J. Hopkins.
Forum, vol. 29 (Apr., 1900): 139–146.

1900. Porto Rico under the United States.   J. M. McElhinney.
Missionary review, vol. 23 (Apr., 1900): 270–275.

1900. United States and Porto Rico.   J. B. Foraker.
North American review, vol. 170 (Apr., 1900): 464–471.

1900. Citizenship for Porto Rico.
Independent, vol. 52 (Apr. 5, 1900): 845.

1900. Bishop Blenk in Porto Rico.
Independent, vol. 52 (Apr. 5, 1900): 852.

1900. What the press thinks about the Puerto Rico tariff.
Literary digest, vol. 20 (Apr. 7, 1900): 413.

1900. The President and the tariff bill.
Independent, vol. 52 (Apr. 12, 1900): 899.

1900. The government of Porto Rico.
Independent, vol. 52 (Apr. 19, 1900): 958.

1900. The Porto Rican bill.
Nation, vol. 70 (Apr. 19, 1900): 294.

1900. Home life in Puerto Rico.
Harper's Bazar, vol. 33 (April 21, 1900): 348.

1900. Franchises in Porto Rico.
Public opinion, vol. 28 (Apr. 26, 1900): 519.

1900. How Porto Rico will be governed.
American review of reviews, vol. 21 (May, 1900): 517.

1900. Charles H. Allen, the first governor of Porto Rico. H. Macfarland.
American review of reviews, vol. 21 (May, 1900): 563–565.

1900. The Porto Rican tariff bill.
Chautauquan, vol. 31 (May, 1900): 118–120.

1900. An humiliating situation.
Popular science monthly, vol. 57 (May, 1900): 100.

1900. The civil government of Porto Rico.
Protectionist, vol. 12 (May, 1900): 34.

1900. The Porto Rico tariffs of 1899 and 1900. E. B. Whitney.
Yale law journal, vol. 9 (May, 1900): 297.

1900. Porto Rican question. H. E. W.
Outlook, vol. 65 (May 5, 1900): 91.

1900. Governor Allen inaugurated.
Outlook, vol. 65 (May 12, 1900): 95.

1900. Government of Porto Rico.
American review of reviews, vol. 21 (June, 1900): 654.

1900. Porto Ricans and the Constitution. G. H. Smith.
Arena, vol. 23 (June, 1900): 626–634.

1900. In Porto Rican streets. A. Halliday-Antona.
Independent, vol. 52 (June 14, 1900): 1443–1445.

1900. The Porto Rican tariff upheld.
Outlook, vol. 65 (June 23, 1900): 424.

1900. The first Fourth. F. A. Ober.
St. Nicholas, vol. 27 (July, 1900): 795–796.

1900. Government of Porto Rico. Charles H. Allen.
Independent, vol. 52 (July 19, 1900): 1709.

1900. Porto Rico as a mission field. H. K. Carroll.
Missionary Review, vol. 23 (Aug., 1900): 588–593.

1900. Porto Rico and its future. Roy Stone.
Munsey, vol. 23 (Aug., 1900): 620–635.

1900. After two years' work in Porto Rico. G. G. Groff.
Independent, vol. 52 (Aug. 9, 1900): 1913–1915.

1900. Religion in Porto Rico.
Outlook, vol. 65 (Aug. 25, 1900): 950.

1900. The financial problem in Porto Rico.   J. D. Whelpley.
Independent, vol. 52 (Aug. 30, 1900): 2101–2103.

1900. Porto Rican discontent.
Public opinion, vol. 29 (Sept. 6, 1900): 296.

1900. United States commerce with Porto Rico
Scientific American supplement, vol. 50 (Sept. 8, 1900): 20645.

1900. The last Spanish budget in Porto Rico.   J. D. Whelpley.
Independent, vol. 52 (Sept. 13, 1900): 2206–2209.

1900. Education in Porto Rico.
Outlook, vol. 66 (Sept. 1, 1900): 6.
Forum, vol. 30 (Oct., 1900): 229–237.

1900. Ex-President Harrison on Porto Rico.
Nation, vol. 71 (Oct. 18, 1900): 302.

1900. Political beginnings in Porto Rico.   J. Finley.
American review of reviews, vol. 22 (Nov., 1900): 571–575.

1900. The needs of Porto Rico.   Ramon B. Lopez.
Independent, vol. 52 (Nov. 29, 1900): 2857.

1900. Some reasons for the high death rate of Porto Rico.   P. R.
Egan.
Sanitarian, N. Y., vol. 45 (Dec., 1900): 528.

1900. Porto Rico and our tariff.
Public opinion, vol. 27 (Dec. 21, 1900): 773.

1901. Porto Rico and a necessary military position in the West
Indies.   W. A. Glassford.
*Journal of the Military service institution, vol. 28 (Jan.
1901): 15.*

1901. The American impasse.   W. Clarke.
Speaker, n. s., vol. 3 (Jan. 26, 1901): 456.

1901. Status of Porto Ricans in our policy.   S. Pfeil.
Forum, vol. 30 (Feb., 1901): 717.

1901. The constitution in Porto Rico.   Le Roy Parker.
Yale law journal, vol. 10 (Feb. 1901): 136.

1901. Military training as a factor in the civic reorganization of Porto
Rico.
American review of reviews, vol. 23 (Mar., 1901): 334.

1901. The first Porto Rican legislature.   T. S. A.
Nation, vol. 72 (Mar. 7, 1901): 191.

PORTO RICAN ADMINISTRATIVE DOCUMENTS, REPORTS OF LOCAL ORGANIZATIONS, ETC.

Porto Rico. *Asociación de agricultores.* Estatutos y reglamento.
Puerto-Rico: Sucesión de J. J. Acosta, 1894. 26 pp. 16°.

—— —— Exposicion elevada por el consejo de dirección al excmo. sr. ministro de ultramar, solicitando la rebaja en este año y la supresión absoluta en adelante, de los derechos de exportación sobre el café . . .
Puerto Rico: Tip. del "Boletín Mercantil," 1893. 22 pp. 8°.

—— —— Memoria y liquidación de las cuentas del año último y proyecto de presupuestos para el año próximo, que se leerán en la junta general de 15 de Julio de 1895.
Puerto Rico: Sucesión de J. J. Acosta, 1895. 49 pp. 8°.

—— *Administracion general de comunicaciones.* Anuario oficial de comunicaciones de la provincia de Puerto-Rico . . . Año I.
Puerto-Rico: Imprenta de gobierno, 1890. vi, (2), 168 pp. 8°.

—— —— Anuario oficial de comunicaciones de la provincia de Puerto-Rico . . .
Puerto Rico: Tip. del "Boletín Mercantil," 1894. 8°.

—— —— Escalafon general del cuerpo de comunicaciones, creado en Puerto Rico por decreto de 9 de febrero de 1870.
Puerto Rico: Tip. de J. G. Font, [1889]. 6 pp. 16°.

—— —— Reglamento orgánico del cuerpo de comunicaciones . . . Aprobado por real orden no. 233 de 17 de junio de 1891 que rige desde el 11 de julio del mismo año.
Puerto Rico: Imp. del "Boletín Mercantil," 1891. 16 pp. 8°.

——— Instrucción aprobada provisionalmente por decreto del gobierno general de 22 Enero de 1875, relativa al modo de proceder para hacer efectivos los débitos á favor de la hacienda pública. Edición oficial.
Puerto Rico: Imp. de Sancerrit, 1875. 37, (1), (2) pp. 8°.

Porto Rico. *Banco español.* El canje de la moneda en Puerto-Rico. La opinion del Banco español de esta isla.
Puerto-Rico: Tip. al vapor "La Correspondencia," 1898. 14 pp. 12°.

—— —— Estatutos del Banco español de Puerto-Rico aprobados por real decreto de 5 de mayo de 1888, que acordo su creación.
Puerto-Rico: "Boletín Mercantil," 1888. 48 pp. 12°.

—— —— Estatutos y reglamento.
Puerto-Rico: Sucesión de J. J. Acosta, 1894. 31 pp. 12°.

—— —— Memoria[s]. 1891–1896, 1898.
Puerto-Rico: Sucesión de J. J. Acosta, 1891–1898. 7 pphs. 8°.

—— —— Reglamento, aprobado por real orden de 22 de Noviembre de 1893.
Puerto Rico: "La Cooperativa," 1893. 79 pp. 12°.

—— *Banco territorial y agricola.* Estatutos.
Puerto-Rico: Sucesión de J. J. Acosta, 1894. 33 pp. 8°.

—— —— Memoria[s]. 1894–1897.
Puerto-Rico: Sucesión de J. J. Acosta, 1895–1897. 4 pphs. 8°.

—— *Capitanía general.* Cartilla del voluntario de la isla de Puerto Rico.
Puerto-Rico: J. J. Acosta, 1893. 133 pp. 12°.

—— —— Reglamento para los cuerpos de voluntarios de la isla de Puerto-Rico. Aprobado por real orden de 10 de Julio de 1888.
Puerto-Rico: Imprenta del "Boletín Mercantil," 1888. 56 pp. 16°.

—— — *Carabineros de real hacienda.* Reglamento constitutivo del cuerpo de carabineros de real hacienda de la isla de Puerto-Rico, año de 1839.
Puerto-Rico: Imprenta de S. Dalmau, [1839]. 34 pp. 12°.

—— *Census.* Memoria referente á la estadistica de la isla de Puerto-Rico, espresiva de las operaciones practicadas para llevar á cabo el censo de poblacion que ha tenido lugar en la noche del 25 al 26 de diciembre de 1860. Adicionada con la descripcion geográfica, histórica, física y política de la enunciada isla y su dependiente la de Vieques.
Puerto-Rico: D. I. Guasp, 1861. 67 pp. 8 sheets (7 folded).

Porto Rico. *Colegio.* Lista de los abogados del ilustre coegio del
Puerto Rico . . .
Puerto-Rico: Gonzales, 1875. 1 vol. (1876). 12°.

———— *Compañía anónima de la luz eléctrica de Ponce.* Memoria leida
en la junta general ordinaria de accionistas de la compañía
anónima de la luz eléctrica de Ponce, el día 10 de Enero
de 1899.
Ponce: Tip. de "La Democracia," 1899. 13 pp. 4 tables. 8°.

———— *Compañía de los ferrocarriles de Puerto-Rico.* Indicador oficial
de los ferrocarriles de Puerto-Rico. 1ª ed. April, 1897.
*Puerto-Rico: Impr. del "Boletín Mercantil," 1897. 67 pp.
F°.*

———— *Compañía de ferrocarriles de vía estrecha de Mayagüez.* Memoria presentada á la junta general de accionistas por el consejo de la misma en 13 de Marzo de 1898.
Mayagüez: Imp. " El Progreso," 1898. 52 pp. 8°.
> Pp. 41–52, Línea de Añasco á Lares.

———— *Concursos agrícolas. Junta edificadora.* Programa para el
que ha de celebrarse el 25 de Mayo de 1876, en la ciudad de
Ponce.
*Puerto-Rico: Tip. al vapor de " La Correspondencia," 1896.
12 pp. 8°.*

———— ———— Memoria presentada á la Junta calificadora por . . .
J. G. del Valle . . .
Puerto-Rico: J. J. Acosta, 1894. 25 pp. 8°.

———— *Constitution. 1897.* Constitucion autonómica, política,
administrativa de las islas de Cuba y Puerto Rico.
[Puerto-Rico]: Sucesión de J. J. Acosta, 1897. 67 pp. 8°.

———— ———— Constitucion autonómica; decreto sobre igualdad de
derechos políticos y ley electoral de Puerto Rico.
Puerto Rico: Imp. " El País," 1898. 29 pp. 16°.

———— ———— New constitution establishing self-government in the
islands of Cuba and Porto Rico. (Authorised translation of
the preamble and royal decree of November 25, 1897 . . .)
With comments by Cuban autonomists on the scope of the
plan . . .
New York: At the office of " Cuba," 1898. 75 pp. 12°.

———— *Diputación provincial.* Memoria relativa á la escuela de artes
y oficios.
*Puerto Rico: Tip. de la Escuela de artes y oficios, 1898. 24–31
pp. 8°.*

Porto Rico. *Diputación provincial.* Memoria, 1897 a 1898.
　　Puerto-Rico: Tip. de la Escuela de artes y oficios, 1898. 31
　　pp. 8°.

———— ———— Memoria sobre la administración del asilo de benefi-
　　cencia, 1872–73.
　　Puerto-Rico: González, 1873. 14 pp. 6 tables. 12°.

———— *Dirección de administración local.* Reglamento general de
　　beneficencia.
　　Puerto-Rico: Gonzalez, 1868. (2), 12 pp. 12°.

———— *Director of public instruction.* The school laws of the island
　　of Porto Rico, enacted by order of General Guy V.
　　Henry . . . May 1, 1899.
　　San Juan, Porto Rico: The San Juan News Power Print,
　　[1899]. 48 pp. 24°.

———— *Dirección de instrucción pública.* Leyes escolares de la isla de
　　Puerto-Rico decretadas por orden del General Guy V.
　　Henry . . . Mayo 1°, 1899.
　　Puerto-Rico: Imprenta de "El País," 1899. 51 pp. 24°.

———— ———— Programas de inglés para oposiciones al grado supe-
　　rior y elemental.
　　Puerto Rico: "Boletín Mercantil," 1898. 10 pp. 16°.

———— ———— Reglamentos de escuelas publicados por el periódico
　　"la Instrucción Pública."
　　Puerto-Rico: Tipografía de González & co., 1882. 126, (1)
　　pp. 12°.

———— *Escuela de artes y oficios.* Memoria leida en el solemne acto
　　de la apertura inaugural de la escuela de artes y oficios de
　　Puerto-Rico.
　　[Puerto-Rico]: Imp. del "Boletín Mercantil," 1886. 12
　　pp. 8°.

———— ———— *Same.* 1886–87.

———— *Escuela profesional.* Memoria leida en el acto solemne de la
　　apertura del curso de 1884 á 1885 de la escuela profesional
　　de Puerto-Rico.
　　[Puerto-Rico]: Imp. de José González Font, 1884. 12, (2)
　　pp. 8°.

———— ———— *Same.* 1885–1888. 3 pphs.

———— *Gobierno general.* Bando de policia y buen gobierno.
　　[Puerto-Rico, 1841 ?] 40 pp. 24°.

Porto Rico. *Gobierno general.* Instruccion para la cobranza por la via de apremio de los débitos á favor de los ayuntamientos y para la gestion de las diputaciones provinciales.
Ponce: "Revista de Puerto Rico," 1891. 8 pp. 16°.

—— —— Ley de Puertos vigente en la isla de Puerto Rico
Puerto Rico: J. G. Font, 1886. 32 pp. 12°.

—— —— Ley para el ejercicio del derecho de asociacion.
Puerto-Rico: Imp. de gobierno, 1888. 6 pp. 8°.

—— —— Lotería real para satisfaccion de atrasados que debe establecerse en la isla de Puerto-Rico con arreglo á lo dispuesto por s. m. en real orden de 31 de Enero de 1818. Reglamento que ha de gobernar: formalidades que han de observarse en los sorteos; y finalmente método que ha de seguirse en el pago de créditos, contra la real hacienda. Dispuesta por la intendencia de la misma isla.
Año de 1829. Impreso en Puerto-Rico. 24 pp. 12°.

—— —— Reglamento económico-administrativo del ramo de caminos vecinales.
Puerto-Rico: Tip. del Boletín Mercantil, 1879. 43, 12 pp. 8°.

—— —— Reglamento interior de la secretaria del gobierno general de Puerto-Rico.
Puerto Rico: Imp. de Larroca, 1875. 12 pp. 12°.

—— *Intendencia general de hacienda.* Disposiciones oficiales de Puerto Rico. Año que comprende desde 1° de Julio de 1870 á 30 de Junio de 1871.
Imprenta de González. Puerto-Rico: [1871]. 2 parts in 1 vol. 12°.

—— *Intendente de ejército y superintendente delegado de hacienda.* Balanza mercantil de la isla de Puerto Rico. 1851–52.
Puerto-Rico: Imp. de Márquez, 1852–53. 2 vols. F°.

—— *Junta central del partido oportunista.* Manifiesto-programa.
Puerto-Rico: Tip. al vapor de "La Correspondencia," 1898. 25 pp. 8°.

—— *Junta provincial de registros y amillaramientos.* Ganadería. [Resumen de la ganadería existente en esta isla.]
Puerto-Rico: Imp. de gobierno, 1896. 5 pp. Obl. 16°.

—— *Junta superior directiva de hacienda.* Reglamento para la administración y rejimen de la renta de penas de camara y gastos de justicia de la isla de Puerto-Rico.
Puerto-Rico: Imprenta de D. Francisco Márquez, 1850. 15, (1) pp. 12°.

Porto Rico. *Marina de la provincia.* Junta economica de subastas. Número trescientos cuarenta y siete. Contrata para el suministro del pan fresco, buques de guerra de este puerto. [*Puerto Rico*]. *1887. 14 pp. 8°.*

—— *Obras públicas.* Reglamento general para ʜa nueva organizacion y servicio de las obras públicas. *Puerto-Rico: Gonzalez, 1874. 92 pp. 24°.*

—— —— Relacion circunstanciada de todas las obras públicas que se han emprendido y continuado en la isla de Puerto-Rico, en el año de 1829, por disposicion del excmo. d. Miguel de la Torre . . . *Puerto-Rico: Imprenta del gobierno, 1830. 34 pp. 8°.*

—— *El partido autonomista.* Constitución orgánica del partido autonomista puertorriqueño reformada en la asamblea de Mayagüez. *Puerto-Rico: Tipografía de A. Córdova, [1887]. 28, (1) pp. 24°.*

—— Programa de nociones de agricultura, industria y comercio. *Puerto-Rico: Imp. del "Boletín Mercantil," 1898. 8 pp. 12°.*

—— *Secretaría de hacienda.* Aranceles de aduanas para la provincia de Puerto Rico, aprobados por real orden 28 de Julio de 1882. *Puerto-Rico: Impr. y libr. de Acosta, 1882. 67, (4) pp. F°.*

—— —— El cabotaje con la península y el tratado de comercio con los Estados-Unidos de la América del Norte . . . *Puerto-Rico: Imp. de gobierno, 1891. 1, (2), 247, (2) pp. 8°.*

—— —— Cartilla-guía para los comisiones, sub-comisiones y ayuntamientos de la isla de Puerto-Rico para la contribucion territorial. *Puerto-Rico: J. J. Acosta, 1899. 46 pp. Tables. 8°.*

—— —— Estadística general del comercio exterior de la provincia de Puerto-Rico correspondiente al año de 1887. *Puerto-Rico: Imprenta de hacienda, 1888. 4°.*

—— —— Estadística general del comercio exterior de la provincia de Puerto-Rico . . . *Puerto-Rico: Imp. de hacienda, 1897–1898. 2 vols. F°.*

—— —— Instruccion provisional para el régimen del tesoro publico de esta isla, aprobada por el . . . gobernador superior civil á propuesta de la intendencia general de hacienda pública en 25 de Julio de 1867. *Puerto-Rico: Imp. del gobierno, 1867. 32 pp. 8°.*

Porto Rico. *Secretaría de hacienda.* Reglamento para los colectores de rentas internas.
Puerto Rico: A. Lymé hijos de Pérez Morís, 1899. 14 pp. 8°.

——— ——— Reglamento provisional para la imposicion, administracion y cobranza de la contribucion territorial en la isla de Puerto Rico.
Puerto-Rico: Imp. de hacienda, 1880. 28 pp. 9 tables. 8°.

——— ——— Reglamento que ha de servir de guía á las comisiones municipales y ayuntamientos, para el impuesto de la contribucion á la riqueza urbana.
Puerto Rico: J. J. Acosta, 1899. 15 pp. 2 tables. 8°.

——— ——— Reglamento sobre pesas y medidas del sistema métrico decimal para la isla de Puerto Rico.
Puerto Rico: J. J. Acosta, 1899. 50, xlii pp. 2 tables. 8°.

——— ——— Tabla de valores para la estadística comercial y el arancel de aduanas . . . ed. oficial.
Puerto-Rico: Imprenta y librería de Acosta, 1881. 21 pp. 8°.

——— Tarifas de los haberes, sueldos y gratificaciones que deben abonarse á los diferentes cuerpos que existen en la isla de Puerto-Rico, con las notas y explicaciones que en cada uno debe tenerse presente, segun sus particulares reglamentos y reales órdenes vigentes que en ellas se citan; con otras noticias que se ponen para facilitar las operaciones de la contaduría de esta provincia en ajustamientos.
[Puerto-Rico: 18—.] (2) pp. 13 tables. 8°.

San Juan de Puerto-Rico. *Ateneo puertorriqueño biblioteca.*
Catálogo por orden alfabético de autores y de materias de las obras existentes en la biblioteca del Ateneo puertorriqueño.
Puerto-Rico: Tip. de "El País," 1897. 63 pp. 8°.

——— *Ayuntamiento.* Informe . . . sobre el balance del presupuesto de gastos é ingresos correspondiente al año de 1884–85.
[San Juan]: J. G. Font, 1885. 27 pp 8°.

——— ——— Memoria de la administracion municipal de la ciudad.
Puerto-Rico: Tip. de González, [1873]. 82 pp. 12°.

——— ——— Reglamento del personal de servicio . . .
[Puerto-Rico]: Imp. del "Boletín Mercantil," 1887. 15 pp. 24°.

San Juan de Puerto-Rico. *Cámara de comercio.* Exposición que
acerca de la cuestión monetaria . . .
*Puerto-Rico: Tip. del "Boletín Mercantil," 1894. (2), 10
pp. 8°.*

———— ———— Memorias . . .
*Puerto-Rico: Tip. del "Boletín Mercantil," 1888–98. 10 nos.
8°.*

———— ———— Reglamento . . .
*Puerto-Rico: Imp. del "Boletín Mercantil," 1887. 51, (1)
pp. 24°.*

———— *Exposición, 1893.* Cuarto centenario del descubrimiento de
Puerto-Rico. Exposición para 1893. Reglamento.
*Puerto-Rico: Tip. del "Boletín Mercantil," 1893. 16 pp.
8°.*

———— *Junta de obras del puerto de San Juan de Puerto Rico.*
Memoria relativa á . . . las obras de este puerto
. . . 1894 á 1895.
*Puerto-Rico: Tip. del "Boletín Mercantil," 1896. 134 pp.
Table. 4°.*

———— *Policía.* Instrucciones para la guardia de orden público
. . . 1889.

> (*In* San Juan de Puerto Rico. Policía. Reglamento . . . pp.
> 17–28. Puerto Rico: 1895. 8°.)

———— ———— Reglamento para la reorganisación . . .
*Puerto-Rico: Imp. del "Boletín Mercantil," 1895. 28 pp.
8°.*

Sociedad abolicionista española. La abolicion de la esclavitud en
Puerto-Rico. Reunion celebrada, 25 de Enero de 1873.
Madrid, 1873. 8°.

Sociedad anónima de crédito mercantil. Memoria sobre las operaciones. 1878 (Mayo–Dic.); 1879–84.
Puerto Rico: González, 1878–84. 2 vols. 8°.
1878 and 1883 lack some numbers.

Sociedad cooperativa el Ahorro colectivo. Estatutos.
Puerto-Rico: A. Córdova, 1893. 12, (4) pp. 16°.

Sociedad de crédito agrícola é industrial. Liga defensiva de los
agricultores. Proyecto.
Puerto-Rico: Sucesión de J. J. Acosta, 1897. 20 pp. 8°.

Sociedad de instrucción y recreo "la Nueva Aurora," Puerto-Príncipe. Reglamento.
Puerto-Príncipe: 1886. 14 pp. 16°.

———— ———— *Same.* 1888.

Sociedad de socorros mutuos "Los amigos del bien público." Reglamento, 1873.
Puerto Rico: "La cooperativa," 1893. 41, (4) pp. 8°.

———— Reglamento para las operaciones de préstamos de la sociedad, 1893.
[*Puerto-Rico, 1893.*] (7) pp. 8°.

Sociedad de socorros mutuos "La Esperanza," Puerto-Príncipe. Reglamento.
Puerto Príncipe: "El Progreso," 1887. (2), 12 pp. 16°.

Sociedad do socorros mutuos "El Porvenir." Reglamento.
Puerto Príncipe: "El Progreso," 1887. (2), 21 pp. 16°.

———— ———— *Same.* 1888.

Sociedad de socorros mutuos "San Eugenio de la Palma." Reglamento.
Puerto-Príncipe: "El Progreso," 1888. 26 pp. 16°.

Sociedad Montepío médico-farmacéutico. Estatutos y reglamento general.
Puerto-Rico: Sucesión de A. Córdova, 1894. 8°.

Sociedad popular de Santa Cecilia. Reglamento.
Puerto-Príncipe: "El Progreso," 1885. 20, (4) pp. 16°.

Sociedad protectora de la inteligencia. Memoria leída por el presidente, 31 diciembre 1883 [29 de diciembre, 1884].
Puerto-Rico: Imp. de "El Agente," 1884, 85. 2 vols. 24°.

O

THE PUERTO RICAN EXPERIENCE

An Arno Press Collection

Berle, Beatrice Bishop. **Eighty Puerto Rican Families in New York City:** Health and Disease Studied in Context. New Foreword by the author. 1958

Blanco, Tomas. **El Prejuicio Racial en Puerto Rico.** (Racial Prejudice in Puerto Rico). 1948

Carroll, Henry K. **Report on the Island of Porto Rico;** Its Population, Civil Government, Commerce, Industries, Productions, Roads, Tariff, and Currency, With Recommendations. 1899

Cebollero, Pedro A. **A School Language Policy for Puerto Rico.** 1945

Chiles, Paul Nelson. **The Puerto Rican Press Reaction to the United States, 1888-1898.** 1944

Clark, Victor S., et al. **Porto Rico and Its Problems.** 1930

Coll Cuchí, José. **Un Problema en América.** (The American Problem). 1944

Colon, Jesus. **A Puerto Rican in New York and Other Sketches.** 1961

Enamorado Cuesta, J[ose]. **Porto Rico, Past and Present:** The Island After Thirty Years of American Rule. A Book of Information, Written for the American Reading Public, in the Interest and for the Benefit of the People of Porto Rico. [1929]

Fernández Vanga, Epifanio. **El Idioma de Puerto Rico y El Idioma Escolar de Puerto Rico.** (Language and Language Policy in Puerto Rico). 1931

Fleagle, Fred K. **Social Problems in Porto Rico.** 1917

Friedrich, Carl J. **Puerto Rico: Middle Road to Freedom.** 1959

Gallardo, José M., editor. **Proceedings of [the] Conference on Education of Puerto Rican Children on the Mainland (October 18 to 21, 1970).** 1972

Geigel Polanco, Vicente. **Valores de Puerto Rico.** (Puerto Rican Leaders). 1943

Institute of Field Studies, Teachers College, Columbia University. **Public Education and the Future of Puerto Rico: A Curriculum Survey, 1948-1949.** 1950

Jaffe, A[bram] J., editor. **Puerto Rican Population of New York City.** 1954

New York [City]. Welfare Council. **Puerto Ricans in New York City:** The Report of the Committee on Puerto Ricans in New York City of the Welfare Council of New York City. 1948

Osuna, Juan José. **A History of Education in Puerto Rico.** 1949

Perloff, Harvey S. **Puerto Rico's Economic Future:** A Study in Planned Development. 1950

Puerto Rican Forum. **The Puerto Rican Community Development Project:** Un Proyecto Puertorriqueño de Ayuda Mutua Para El Desarrollo de la Comunidad. A Proposal For a Self-Help Project to Develop the Community by Strengthening the Family, Opening Opportunities for Youth and Making Full Use of Education. 1964

Puerto Ricans and Educational Opportunity. 1975

The Puerto Ricans: Migration and General Bibliography. 1975

Roberts, Lydia J. and Rosa Luisa Stefani. **Patterns of Living in Puerto Rican Families.** 1949

Rosario, José C[olombán]. **The Development of the Puerto Rican Jíbaro and His Present Attitude Towards Society.** 1935

Rowe, L[eo] S. **The United States and Porto Rico:** With Special Reference to the Problems Arising Out of Our Contact with the Spanish-American Civilization. 1904

Siegel, Arthur, Harold Orlans and Loyal Greer. **Puerto Ricans in Philadelphia:** A Study of Their Demographic Characteristics, Problems and Attitudes. 1954

[Tugwell, Rexford G.] **Puerto Rican Public Papers of R. G. Tugwell, Governor.** 1945

United States-Puerto Rico Commission on the Status of Puerto Rico. **Status of Puerto Rico:** Report of the United States-Puerto Rico Commission on the Status of Puerto Rico, August 1966. 1966

United States-Puerto Rico Commission on the Status of Puerto Rico. **Status of Puerto Rico:** Selected Background Studies Prepared for the United States-Puerto Rico Commission on the Status of Puerto Rico, 1966. 1966

United States Senate. Select Committee on Equal Educational Opportunity. **Equal Educational Opportunity for Puerto Rican Children (Part 8):** Hearings Before the Select Committee on Equal Educational Opportunity of the United States Senate. 91st Congress, 2nd Session, Washington, D. C., November 23, 24 and 25, 1970. 1970

Van Middeldyk, R. A. **The History of Puerto Rico:** From the Spanish Discovery to the American Occupation. 1903

Wakefield, Dan. **Island in the City:** The World of Spanish Harlem. 1959

White, Trumbull. **Puerto Rico and Its People.** 1938